D0839566

FRENCH FAIRY TALES

SUNY series in Psychoanalysis and Culture
—Henry Sussman, editor

FRENCH FAIRY TALES

A Jungian Approach

BETTINA L. KNAPP

STATE UNIVERSITY OF NEW YORK PRESS

Published by
State University of New York Press, Albany

For information, address State University of New York Press,
90 State Street, Suite 700, Albany, NY 12207

Production by Kelli Williams
Marketing by Michael Campochiaro

Library of Congress Cataloging-in-Publication Data
Knapp, Bettina Liebowitz, 1926–
    French fairy tales : a Jungian approach / Bettina L. Knapp.
        p. cm. — (SUNY series in psychoanalysis and culture)
    Includes bibliographical references and index.
    ISBN 0-7914-5469-X (alk. paper)—ISBN 0-7914-5470-3 (pbk. : alk. paper)
        1. Fairy tales—France.   2. Psychoanalysis and fairy tales—France.
    3. Symbolism in fairy tales—France.   4. Jung, C. G. (Carl Gustav), 1875–1961.
    I. Title.   II. Series.

GR161 .K57 2002
398.2'0944'09—dc21   2002020901

10 9 8 7 6 5 4 3 2 1

To my beloved Mother
Emily Gresser Liebowitz

CONTENTS

I WOULD LIKE TO EXPRESS MY GRATITUDE TO NORMAN CLARIUS, librarian at Hunter College, for his unstinting help in making certain important and rare texts available to me.

INTRODUCTION

THE WORLD OF FAIRY TALES opened its fantasies to me when I was four years old—in 1930. My parents, my brother, Daniel, and I were living in Paris at the time. It was spring and we were scheduled to leave for the south of France. Prior to taking the train, we had planned to greet Yvette Guilbert, the French *diseuse,* who would be returning from a concert tour at the same station from which we were scheduled to depart. During the 1880s and 1890s she had won international fame singing her naughty songs at cabarets such as the Divan Japonais and the Chat Noir. And indeed it was she who had been immortalized by Toulouse-Lautrec in his lithographs. At the outset of the twentieth century, however, Yvette Guilbert had changed her style—researching, setting to music, and singing poems and songs from medieval to contemporary times that were pithy, moving, acerbic, tragic, and frequently ribald; she performed these unique works to packed houses. It was in Berlin in 1914, at a gathering of royalty, diplomats, artists, and intellectuals, that my mother, Emily Gresser, a student of the violin, first met the *diseuse.* Two years later, on tour in New York, Yvette Guilbert, in need of an artist to perform classical works on stage for half the concert time, called upon my mother. For the next four years, they toured together throughout the United States and Canada, after which the singer returned to Paris. My mother married, and did not go back to France until 1930, where she again performed with Yvette Guilbert on special occasions.

While my memories of Yvette Guilbert stepping from the train to the platform in the Paris station, bending over and kissing me, then giving me a copy of *Perrault's Fairy Tales,* are relatively dim, the occasion remains engraved in my mind. As for the beautifully illustrated volume of Perrault's tales, I have treasured it all these years. I pleasured in the fantasies and the imaginary trajectories of the supernatural beings Perrault evokes. I was, I must admit, stunned and even terrified by some of his stories. Nonetheless, they constellated my waking and sleeping dreams.

After our return to New York in 1932, I was sent to the progressive Lincoln School, the brainchild of the philosopher John Dewey, which emphasized the imaginary and the creative factor in children. Studies in French, comparative literatures, and history led me to Barnard College and to Columbia University, where I earned a doctorate. In time, my interests expanded to include world religions and the myths upon which they are based. Little did I realize that I was embarking on yet another adventure. A friend, Estelle Weinrib, suggested I read C. G. Jung's *Symbols of Transformation*, predicting correctly that they would fascinate me. Jung's psychological analyses of eternal and universal motifs and beliefs shed light for me on so many unanswered questions concerning human behavioral patterns. My unassuaged appetite for answers to all kinds of questions not only catalyzed my readings of Jung's writings, but encouraged me to turn to the works of those who had studied with him: Erich Neumann, Esther Harding, Marie-Louise von Franz, Jolande Jacobi, and others. Each volume contained a treasure of information; each provided me with new insights and a variety of perspectives that allowed me better to understand the meanings embedded in literature in general, and those secreted in myths, folktales, and fairy tales in particular. Cumulatively speaking, they yielded clues to the complexities impacting so weightily—deleteriously and/or positively—on today's individuals and societies.

Most arresting for me in my researchings and probings of hidden meanings locked in fairy tales were the innovative writings of Marie-Louise von Franz: her *Interpretation of Fairy Tales, The Feminine in Fairy Tales, Individuation in Fairy Tales, Shadow and Evil in Fairy Tales, The Golden Ass of Apuleius*, and so forth. A remarkable cryptographer of hidden messages and feeling tones, Franz was a scholar—conversant with Greek, Latin, alchemy, gnosticism, philosophy, and the mystical writings of ancient, medieval, and Renaissance creative spirits—and a psychoanalyst as well.

The uniqueness of C. G. Jung's approach to psychology is due in part to his involvement of the *whole being*—not solely the intellectual or sexual—in the psychological process. To this end, he studied myths, legends, and fairy tales—cultural manifestations of all kinds in both their personal and universal frames of reference. Explorations of this nature gave him insights into primordial images: *archetypes of the collective unconscious*. Drawing parallels between the workings of the individual unconscious revealed in images produced in the dreams of his patients, and the universal recurrent eternal motifs found in religions, works of art and literature, Jung enlarged the scope of psychotherapy. It became not only a curative agent that related to "the whole history and evolution of the human psyche," but a technique that could help develop the potential of well-adjusted normal and superior human beings as well (Edinger, "An Outline of Analytical Psychology" 1).

Jung's archetypal analysis lifts the literary work—in our case the fairy tale—out of its individual and conventional context and relates it to humankind in general. In so doing, it takes readers out of their specific and perhaps isolated worlds, allows them to expand their vision, relate more easily to issues that may confront them daily, and understand their reality as part of an ongoing and cyclical reality. Awareness of the fact that people in past eras suffered from alienation and identity crises—to mention but two problems—and went through harrowing ordeals before they knew some semblance of fulfillment, may help certain readers to face and understand their own gnawing feelings of distress and aloneness.

The archetypal analyses in *French Fairy Tales: A Jungian Approach* are designed to enlarge the views of readers, to develop their potential, and, perhaps, to encourage personal confrontations. Such encounters may be painful or joyous, terrifying or serene. Hopefully, they will prove enlightening. The very process of probing, deciphering, amplifying, and ferreting out coded or mysterious messages may help us to find new directions in life, thereby increasing our understanding of some of the eternal factors implicit in human behavior, and perhaps permitting us better to deal with the problematics of both our personal and collective situations.

While specialists in the field of folklore and fairy tale—V. Propp, A.-J. Greimas, and C. Brémond, J. Bédier, S. Thompson, and L. C. Seifert, to mention but a few—have served us brilliantly in the theoretics and evolution of this genre, I have chosen a different path in *French Fairy Tales: A Jungian Approach*. By basing my explorations on the peregrinations, inclinations, ideologies, feeling-tones, physical makeup, and interconnectedness or disconnectedness of the protagonists in the fairy tales probed in this volume, I necessarily included analyses of imagery, associations, and philosophical/spiritual intent. I felt that the probing of fairy tales, like an anamnesis, could open readers to new and pertinent information applicable to their own lives. Catalyzed in this manner, the fairy tale could become a free-flowing "mouthpiece" that neither imprisons readers in a single voice nor confines them to a specific linear time frame. Like an artifact of some past age, such as the waking or sleeping dream imaged by an individual, the intricacy of fairy tales may be experienced and responded to by contemporary readers with the intensity and power of a living imprint of the soul!

To set the fairy tales in a historical context permits increased understanding of the times in which they were written, underlying the problems as well as the spiritual and philosophical yearnings adumbrated in the works. With this in mind, I have included a brief and a very general "highlighting" of the historical and cultural events occurring in the five centuries from which I have drawn and analyzed the fairy tales in this volume. For further delineation, I have incorporated an *ectypal analysis*—a lean biographical sketch of the authors and of the settings of the works—followed by an *archetypal analysis* of the individual fairy tale. The latter, making up the largest segment of each chapter, explores psychological, spiritual, artistic, cultural, actional, and empirical information, which, hopefully, will involve the reader closely in the fairy tale's dramatic unfoldings.

WHAT IS A FAIRY TALE?

Marie-Louise von Franz defines the fairy tale genre as follows:

> Fairy tales are the purest and simplest expression of [the] collective unconscious psychic process. Therefore their value for the scientific investigation of the unconscious exceeds that of all other material. They represent the archetypes in their simplest, barest and most concise form. In this pure form, the archetypal images afford us the best clues to the understanding of the processes going on in the collective psyche. In myths or legends, or any other more elaborate mythological material, we get at the basic patterns of the human psyche through an overlay of cultural material. But in fairy tales there is much less specific conscious cultural material and therefore they mirror the basic patterns of the psyche more clearly. (Franz, *Interpretation of Fairy Tales* I, 1)

Focusing more directly on C. G. Jung's concepts, she adds:

> Every archetype is in its essence an *unknown* psychic factor and therefore there is no possibility of translating its content into intellectual terms. The best we can do is to circumscribe it on the basis of our own psychological experience and from comparative studies, bringing up into light, as it were, the whole net of associations in which the archetypal images are enmeshed. The fairy tale itself is its own best explanation; that is, its meaning is contained in the totality of its motifs connected by the thread of the story. The unconscious is, metaphorically speaking, in the same position as one who has had an original vision or experience and wishes to share it. Since it is an event that has never been conceptually formulated he is at a loss for means of expression. When a person is in that position he makes several attempts to convey the thing and tries to evoke, by intuitive appeal and analogy to familiar material, some response in his listeners; and never tires of expounding his vision until he feels they have some sense of the content. In the same way we can put forward the hypothesis that every fairy tale is a relatively closed system compounding one essential psychological meaning which is expressed in a series of symbolical pictures and events and is discoverable in these.
>
> After working for many years in this field, I have come to the conclusion that all fairy tales endeavour to describe one and the same psychic fact,

but a fact so complex and far-reaching and so difficult for us to realize in all its different aspects that hundreds of tales and thousands of repetitions with a musician's variations are needed until this unknown fact is delivered into consciousness; and even then the theme is not exhausted. This unknown fact is what Jung calls the Self, which is the psychic totality of an individual and also, paradoxically, the regulating center of the collective unconscious. Every individual and every nation has its own modes of experiencing this psychic reality. (Franz I,1ff.)

HUMANKIND'S NEED FOR THE SUPERNATURAL AND THE PARANORMAL

The *fée* or *faerie* (Prov. *fada*; Sp. *hada*; It. *fata*; med. Lat. *fatare*, to enchant, from the Lat. *fatum*, fate, destiny) has existed in one form or another since prehistoric times. Many theories have been expounded to explain the origin of the supernatural creatures we identify as fairies, appearing at times as ancestral spirits, elemental beings, incarnations of the Greek and Roman Fates, or otherwise (Krappe, *The Science of Folklore* 87). Known in a variety of forms—human, reptile, animal, bird, snake, ogre, giant, witch, Nereid, jinn, pixie, lamia, dwarf, Norn, gnome, fairies entered into the consciousness of individuals and of societies according to the psychological needs of the collective and the individual narration of the oral folktale or setting down of the written fairy tale: a rendering that also depended upon the locality, family, and class of the transcriber.

Fairies in whatever form have been associated with water, mountains, chthonic or heavenly worlds, deserts, forests, pastoral realms, and other topographies. Many fairies live away from humans, in their own kingdoms: in secret underground domains, in the sea, in enchanted forests, distant lands, mountainous regions, and as rulers in mysterious domains. To gain access to them has proven difficult at times, and, in other instances, surprisingly simple, depending on the unfolding of fortuitous happenings or, in Jungian terms, the *synchronistic event* (the meaningful coincidence) that triggers them into existence. A case in point is Mélusine, the beautiful protagonist in Jean d'Arras's fifteenth-century fairy tale by the same name, who appeared to her future husband standing in a forest beside a fountain, as if from nowhere. The fairy Viviane, well known in Breton tradition, lived under a hawthorn bush in the depths of the Bréchéliant forest, where she held Merlin bewitched (Maury, *Croyances et légendes* 18). Beautiful or hideous fairies were said to have inhabited Auvergne, Oise, Creuse, and other areas in France, in close proximity not only to fountains but to Druid monuments as well: grottos, mounds, menhirs, cairns, dolmens (Maury 30).

With the onset of Christianity, fairies, along with other supernormal figures, were said to have descended from ancient Gods and Goddesses, or in other cases from nymphs, fallen angels, unbaptized souls. Visualized as tall and beautiful, or as small and/or wizened female or male (like the leprechaun), or as terrifying anthropophagous giants (the ogre), they could easily transform themselves into animals, birds, or other living creatures. Each in his or her own way could be kind, gentle, tender, loving, nurturing, helpful, or its opposite—mean, destructive, death-dealing enchantresses, castrators, or man killers (the Lorelei, Morgan Le Fay). In the old days—and today as well, in certain remote areas of our globe—some supernatural creatures were believed to have become manifest as succubi and/or incubi, entering into love affairs with mortals. Saint Augustine reported that

> trustworthy Scripture testifies that angels have appeared to men in such bodies as could not only be seen, but also touched. There is, too, a very general rumor, which many have verified by their own experience, or which trustworthy persons who have heard the experience of others corroborate, that sylvans and fauns, who are commonly called "incubi," had often made wicked assaults upon women, and satisfied their lust upon them; and that certain devils, called Duses by the Gauls, are constantly attempting and effecting this impurity is so generally affirmed, that it were impudent to deny it. (Saint Augustine, *Basic Writings. The City of God* XV,xxiii, 307)

Ancestor worship was also considered a factor explaining the origin and the calling forth of fairies and other supernatural beings into the empirical sphere. Thus, a link may be established between them and human beings. In this context, we may associate fairies with certain religious beliefs—animism (Lat. *anima*, soul), fetishism (Lat. *facticius*, artificial), totemism (of Native American, Algonquin origin), transformationism (Lat. *transformare*, to change in shape), and cannibalism—as forms of assuagement of humanity's eternal need to confront what transcends human comprehension. Nor must we omit mentioning the importance of *hierophanies* (Gr. *hieros*, sacred; *phainein*, to show, reveal), the manifestation of living and active transpersonal powers in objects. For example, a human or supernatural spirit may be venerated in an inanimate plant, stone, metal, stick, or other object which becomes endowed with sacrality. Sometimes carved into special shapes, these objects have been transformed by tribes, individuals, and even highly sophisticated religious groups from meaningless entities into holy talismans. By extension, it may be suggested that anything that is believed to be provided with magic and/or sacred powers—trees, flowers, sun, moon, stars, lakes, mountains—is endowed as well with a conscious life and/or with human qualities capable of working in favor or to the detriment of individuals and collectives, depending upon how humans honor, respect, or worship it (Eliade, *Patterns in Comparative Religion* 7). Well-known hierophanies, such as Pygmalion's humanized statue of Galatea; the doll in *The Tales of Hoffmann*; the sword, Durandal, in *The Song of Roland*; and less-known charms, idols, and wands, associated with Christian saints, blessed by popes or other religious figures, or allegedly dipped in sacred waters by supernatural powers, have attained sacrality (Yearsley, *The Folklore of Fairy-Tale* 51). In like manner, mirrors may be bewitched, as in *Snow White*, and horror chambers may work their evils, as in *Bluebeard*. So, too, in Mme d'Aulnoy's *The Bluebird*, incidents of homeopathic and contagious sorcery involving medicine men and shamans feed the fancy of readers.

In one of the most engaging of religious narratives, *The Tale of Two Brothers*, discovered on Egyptian papyri and stelae dating from c. 2000 B.C.E., magical powers are put to the inevitably successful test. Spells and enchantments are factors in *The Golden Ass* by the Latin writer Lucius Apuleius (155 C.E.). Included in this work is the famous *Amor and Psyche* tale, reminiscent in so many ways of our relatively modern and ever-popular *Beauty and the Beast*. In a Chinese version of *Cinderella* that existed in the ninth century, her golden slippers were awarded her by a marvelous fish rather than by a fairy (Delarue, *Le Conte populaire français* 7). Supernatural and/or paranormal beings able to transform themselves into humans or into animals, and comport themselves like normal men and women, were vastly popular fare for folktale tellers and fairy tale transcriptors. (The word *transcriptor*, rather than *author* or *transcriber*, will be used to identify writers who availed themselves of one or more versions of a fairy tale handed down from a single or multiple lands.) Some fairy tale figures became guides, assisting, protecting, and even saving those in peril. We may note that in the Bible, Balaam's ass talked at just the right moment (Numbers 22: 21–38); Solomon, and later St. Francis of Assisi, among many others, were believed to have understood the language of trees, beasts, fowls, creeping things, and fishes (Kings IV: 29–34). Nor should the animals in Aesop's Fables (c. sixth cent. B.C.E.) be omitted from the variety of creatures endowed with human traits or vice versa. The Gallic priestess Sena claimed to be able to change herself into any animal. Gods, saints, fairies, gnomes, pixies, banshees, elves, trolls, jinns, no matter their gender or name, populated not only revealed religions, but myths, folktales, and fairy tales as well. Swan maiden cycles featured birds transformed into beautiful maidens; humans magically assumed the shapes of werewolves; destructive or helpful dragons and other supernatural powers either devoured their victims to assuage their voracious appetites or disgorged and immobilized them, thereby saving them from annihilation. Witchlike creatures, such as the Medusa in the Greek myth of Perseus and Andromeda, were able to transform humans into hideous forms, or into stone, or condemn their victim to sleep for a hundred years, as in *Sleeping Beauty*.

Among other supernatural beings, godly creatures were also called upon via prayers, litanies, sacraments, and meditational or magical devices to help individuals or groups through calamitous situations and/or transitional life experiences. Visitations, annunciations, apparitions, hallucinations, or evocations of supreme beings and Creator Gods and Goddesses were basic to many organized religions. The Gods and Goddesses were also recipients of appreciation and/or gratitude for happiness bestowed upon individuals and societies. Thanks to divine intervention—or what was and is believed to be just that—supernormal beings have always functioned, for better or for worse, in the imaginations, beliefs, and/or realities of people since liminal time. In keeping with the notions of the Cyrenaic philosopher Euhemerus (fourth century B.C.E.), who suggested that Gods and Goddesses *were* deified beings, we may, by extension, suggest that fairy tales were and are largely based on real people and actual events as well.

Let us take one of Charles Perrault's fairy tales—*Tom Thumb*—as a case in point. A devastating famine having brought starvation to the land inhabited by Tom Thumb's parents, they were unable to feed their children. Rather than see their young ones starve, they set them astray in a great forest, hoping they would be able to feed themselves on berries, herbs, wild vegetables, and the like. Tom Thumb, so named because of his tiny size, had the genial idea of dropping white pebbles along the way into the heart of the forest. Forethought on his part enabled him and his siblings to find their return route home. When, however, his parents again purposely lost their children in the forest, Tom Thumb, perhaps unthinkingly this time, chose to drop along the way crumbs of bread, which birds unfortuntely gobbled up in no time. The hopelessly lost children wandered about, eventually happening upon the house of an ogre . . . And the story goes on!

While Marie-Louise von Franz scattered her white pebbles during the course of her psychological probings into fairy tales, she failed to spread bread crumbs as well, at times leaving her readers in a quandary. They, like Tom Thumb, may have attempted to return home—or at least sought to tread directly on familiar ground—but indirect and circuitous routes forced them to alter their course. So, too, with the analytical trajectories offered in *French Fairy Tales: A Jungian Approach*. Although frustrating, such roundabout and even oblique directions may prove to be beneficial to readers, compelling them to probe in order to grasp the broader perspectives. Regardless of the individual's assessment of the symbols and images implicit in a specific fairy tale, whatever the terrains and personalities involved, the events depicted, or the associations or family dynamics evoked, we may be sure of one central truth: the enormous complexity of everything relating to fairy tales. While some may seem utterly naive and infantile to the casual observer, they are all but that. Indeed, it may be suggested that no single answer or interpretation of any supernatural tale is conclusive. In fact, no single answer to anything is conclusive! What we may aver, however, is that Tom Thumb's second and most dangerous circuitous return route, taking him and his family to the house of the ogre, eventually led to the saving of his siblings and of his parents. Such a positive ending, however, resulted in large measure from a powerful drive for survival on Tom's part, accounting as well for the development of his innate ingenuity, sensitivity, devotion, sense of responsibility, love for family and for life. That he survived the ordeals to which he and his siblings had been forced to submit eventually led to expanded consciousness on his part.

In like manner, may readers of the fairy tales presented in *French Fairy Tales: A Jungian Approach* find their own circuitous return routes according to their temperaments, personal values, assessments, and reactions to their own pressing problems. May their inner watercourses, like those in the ancient Cambodian myth imaging churning waters, be agitated to the point of turning the psyche and its contents upside-down. The waters may be turbid at first, but as they calm they will reveal new clarities, different junctures and perspectives, and recognition of the individual's formerly repressed, depressed, suppressed conflicts. Once the wall of silence and of stasis is dissolved, new adaptations may be ventured, encouraging individuals to peer into the conflicts facing them, or to see through nonexistent ones.

No panaceas are offered the reader. The psyche, no sooner divested of one problem, burgeons with new ones, like nature's growth factor. How many of us, for example, are "in denial" as we go our merry way? How many of us reject the so-called shadow factors within our personalities, aspects of ourselves that we cannot seem to accept but see very clearly in others? The reviewing of an individual's inner climate via projection onto one or several protagonists in *French Fairy Tales: A Jungian Approach* may serve, hopefully, to create unconscious connections between the reader and the character(s) involved, which may increase that person's awareness of him- or herself. Nor will human beings be spared an encounter with the Ogre or the Witch factor—that devouring blind force existing in both one's inner and outer worlds during the person's life process. To recognize the monstrously alienating powers of the uncultivated, so-called savage (Lat. *silvaticus*, wild, or belonging to a wood) nature existing in each one of us is to take the first step toward the enlightenment and refinement that transform the unworkable into the workable, the discordant into the harmonious, and the noncreative into the creative within the psyche. To help us on our way are the ever-present compensatory powers in fairy tales: the Fairy Godmother and Fairy Godfather. Nor may the intrusion of the *marvelous* and/or the *sublime* lived out by the believer be discounted in effecting a change in her or his outlook.

ARCHETYPAL IMAGES IN FAIRY TALES

As previously noted, *archetypal* or *primordial* images, emerging as they do from the deepest layers of the unconscious, are a key to an understanding of fairy tales and to the exploration of the *feeling values* aroused by the concomitant emotional reading experience. Dr. Edward Edinger has compared the archetype to the instinct:

> An instinct is a pattern of behavior which is inborn and characteristic for a certain species. Instincts are discovered by observing the behavioral patterns of individual organisms and, from this data, reaching the generalization that certain patterns of behavior are the common instinctual equipment of a given species. The instincts are the unknown motivating dynamisms that determine an animal's behavior on the biological level.
>
> An archetype is to the psyche what an instinct is to the body. The existence of archetypes is inferred by the same process as that by which we infer the existence of instincts. Just as instincts common to a species are postulated by observing the uniformities in biological behavior, so archetypes are inferred by observing the uniformities in psychic phenomena. Just as instincts are unknown motivating dynamisms of biological behavior, archetypes are unknown motivating dynamisms of the psyche. Archetypes are the psychic instincts of the human species. Although biological instincts and psychic archetypes have a very close connection, exactly what this connection is we do not know any more than we understand just how the mind and body are connected. (Edinger, "An Outline of Analytical Psychology" 6)

Franz adds:

> An archetypal image is not to be thought of as merely a static image, for it is always at the same time a complete typical process including other images in a specific way. An archetype is a specific psychic impulse, producing its effect like a single ray of radiation, and at the same time a whole magnetic field expanding in all directions. Thus the stream of psychic energy of a "system," an archetype, usually runs through all the archetypes as well. Therefore, although we have to recognize the indefinable vastness of an archetypal image, we must discipline ourselves to chisel sharp outlines which throw the different aspects into bold relief. We must get as close as possible to the specific, determinate, "just so" character of each image and to try to express the very specific character of the psychic situation which is contained in it (Franz, *Interpretation of Fairy Tales* I,2).

Because fairy tale archetypal images focus on collective, universal, and eternal motifs, to omit studying the "human basis from which such motifs grow," Jung and Franz maintained, would be to ignore their vital essence and fail to understand the specific variations presented in each individual tale (Franz, I,9). Just as farmers before they plant have to know the lay of the land and the type of soil with which they are working, similar groundwork must be laid by investigators of fairy tales. While many tales of enchantment have been structured in the same manner *grosso modo*, variations are forever being spawned from the so-called original versions. Why the differences? As the *Tao Te Ching* tells us, everything is as of necessity in a state of flux. Cultural factors, therefore, effect societal changes, certain values increasing or decreasing in importance with fluctuating times, some even dropping out completely from the collective eye. It follows, then, that styles, yearnings, hatreds, loves, goals, all alter as well. How and why, for example, did medieval fairy tales emphasize certain factors, while others, written in the nineteenth century, assign different ideations? One might even ask whether or not a real dichotomy exists between ancient and modern thematics. Might we, in our analyses of archetypal images, symbols, and associations, be fortunate enough to discover certain significant missing links?

FRENCH FAIRY TALES

Folktales (oral) and fairy tales (written), delving as they do into the supernatural, have been alluded to as "the fossil remains of the thoughts and customs of the past" (Yearsley, *The Folklore of Fairy Tale* 16).

Troubadours, minstrels, jongleurs, bards, poets, scholars, clerics, novices, or simply storytellers from different areas of France, as well as transcriptors of written tales, entertained audiences throughout the thousand-year period marking the Middle Ages. Not only were they adept at conjuring preternatural forces; they seemed to be in touch with nature's mysteries, susceptible to a whole world of unknowns provoked by dense fogs, harsh seas, tenebrous forests, dunes, lush green pastures, star-lit heavens, dawns, and dusks. Some questioning individuals looked beyond the evident bark of a tree, aroma of a flower, sheen of a river, or enormity of a geological formation. What supernatural power, they may have asked themselves, had been responsible for creating these natural forces? What unseen benevolent or malevolent power lay hidden within them? No matter, they may have concluded, these now *sacred* entities and spaces must be approached with care and awe. Transcriptor-entertainers regaled their audiences with clusters of fabulous happenings and supernal or chthonic presences: fairies, elves, pixies, witches, Gods, Goddesses, ogres, animals who could speak.

In time, the veneer of sophistication added notable elegance to the raw material emerging from the imaginations of transcriptors and *raconteurs*.

Fairies appeared beside an ancient Druid fountain, namely, that of Baranton, near the Bréchéliant forest. As the twelfth-century Norman poet Wace wrote: "Là solt l'en les fées veeir" (Maury, *Croyances et légendes du Moyen Age* 18). These happenings were believed to be as true as the Gospels. Hadn't Mélusine, standing near a fountain in the Colombiers forest in Poitou, appeared to Raimondin? Hadn't Marie de France's *Lais of Graelent* indicated that her eponymous hero had caught sight of his fairy standing near a fountain, that the two had fallen in love, then disappeared from sight, never to return? Hadn't Joan of Arc experienced her first vision near one of these "fairy fountains"? Hadn't a fairy appeared the night Ogier the Dane was born to bestow a special gift on him? Hadn't it been recounted that three fairies built the famous Castle of the Fairies, only three leagues from Tours? (Maury 23). That certain fairies had been identified as witches sent shivers up the spines of awestruck listeners. No sooner had these evildoers been identified with megalithic monuments than townspeople were warned to maintain their distance from the sites. How did it happen that the community of Bouloire (Sarthe), for example, boasted of a fairy's visible footprint on top of a rock formation? (Maury 38). Nordic, Anglo-Breton, Anglo-Norman, and Celtic beliefs, among others, endowed imaginative transcriptors with seemingly soaring poetic licence. "Mother-goddesses, nymphs, fairies, druidesses, sorceresses" lived their charmed follies and realities everywhere (Maury 40).

Religious, ethnic, and historical traditions blended to become nourishing food for transcriptors, who, driven by their own creative impulses, rarely failed to bring their supernatural creatures into sharp relief. Fashioning their tales with a plethora of miracles, phantasmagorias, and transformations, they heightened the sense of eeriness inherent in the marvelous. Frequent were encounters with the dead, with mysterious fraternal groups (some of whom had the power to transform themselves into animals), with heroes seemingly predestined to perform marvelous feats, and with others, who, having lost their way, reaped the glories of their misadventures. Courageous or suffering young ladies, rescued by such famous heroes as Arthur, Tristan, and Merlin, elicited tales of love and grief before eager listeners.

French society was increasingly fascinated by the marvelous, the miraculous, and the world of magic, sometimes identified with satanic practices and witchcraft. Haunted forests, lakes, mountains, and caves, both above and beneath ground, instilled fear into the noblest knights. But belief in the good acts of fairies of folklore, vestiges of polytheistic deities, was so strong that it was not uncommon for meals to be prepared especially for these supernatural beings to celebrate a birth, a christening, or other Christian religious events. After all, the folk may have reasoned, wasn't it the fairy who decided an infant's destiny? (Maury 27).

Fairy tales, emanating from "popular" or "folklore" motifs, were re-worked during the Middle Ages, particularly in the twelfth and thirteenth centuries. While considered oppositional to the official vernacular writings produced by the learned classes and the Latin writings of clerics, folklore nonetheless permeated these milieus. Such infiltration furnished the élite with profane material, luring them toward other than clerical imperatives, and in so doing, enriched France's cultural heritage.

The paradoxical relationship between the disparate social classes—for our purposes, the folk and oral traditions, and the aristocrats in their written literatures—became evident in the development of what is called courtly liter-ature. The "evolution of the Church's attitude toward popular culture and pagan beliefs" was instrumental in creating a period of "relative tolerance" during the early Middle Ages, to be superseded by one of repression in the High Middle Ages (Harf-Lancner, *Les Fées au Moyen Age* 7).

A plethora of fairies appeared in a variety of literary cycles in the twelfth century: the *Roman de Thèbes*, based on the writings of antiquity; the Breton cycle, depicting the marvels of enchantment, as in *Tristan and Iseut*; Chrétien de Troyes's *Erec and Yvain*; and the *Lais* of Marie de France: *Lanval*, a knight loved by a fairy, and *Guingamor*, who, while hunting in a forest, wounded a white hind, a genuine fairy in disguise. Tales of erotically moti-vated fairies featured these supernatural creatures falling in love with mortal men; imposition of fairies' interdicts on the relationships also became stylish. Other fairies identified with witches concocted unholy brews; still others en-tered both oral or written domains thanks to transcriptors motivated by a desire to spread Christianity.

Ambiguities and contradictions revolving around the origin of fairies have been, as previously mentioned, hotly debated. Were fairies remnants of supernatural figures preoccupying priest/philosophers in the Egyptian mystery schools? Or descendants of Greek and Roman Fates? Could they, like their pos-sible ancestors, predict destinies in general, and those of children in particular? Had they the power to enchant? Had they been sent by God to intervene in earthly affairs? By nymphs? sorceresses? giants? or other types of fantastic be-ings? Had they been protectors of knights in armor, as in *Erec and Enide*? Had humans sacrificed to them? Had their mysterious presences been the object of tree or stone cults, or of cults centered around other venerated objects?

For the opening chapter of this book, I have chosen, I believe, one of the most fascinating and deeply moving French fairy tales—Jean d'Arras's *The Romance of Mélusine* (1392) (3). Not only does the text contain a plethora of fairy tale elements—love pacts, metamorphoses, fountains, forests, hunts, murders, births, and miraculous architectural wonders—but it narrates the fulfillment, albeit temporary, of the experience of love.

Oral and written folklore and tales of wonder of the sixteenth century differed in emphasis from those of the Middle Ages: extremes of fantasy, imagination, spirituality, symbology, and beauty were played down. With few exceptions, the modus operandi of Renaissance tale tellers, although preoccupied with spiritual matters, increasingly involved earth matters, empirical factors, the here and now. For these reasons, I have—perhaps unfortunately—omitted analysis of a fairy tale from the sixteenth century.

Mention, however, must be made of the great François Rabelais (1490–1533), humorist and satirist, physician, monk, lawyer, scientist, and philologist, whose legendary boisterous and licentious giant Gargantua, and his son Pantagruel, were movers of mountains, scoopers of rivers, displacers of megaliths. Levity, satire, irony, and a unique feel for humor interspersed with profoundly philosophical, political, religious, and scientific asides, transformed his work into something much more than a compendium of the legendary aspects of the world of giants.

A Norman, Noël du Faïl, purveyor of popular culture for adults and author of *Rustic Tales* (1548), was less smitten with the glimmer of magically oriented deeds than with the domain of reality. As Counselor to Parliament in Brittany, Faïl enjoyed regaling his listeners at evening gatherings with strange occurrences attributed to extraterrestrials, but he was more impressive in his presentations of daily happenings. Bonaventure des Périers, humanist and poet, and protégé of Marguerite de Navarre, was believed to have authored tales and short stories (1588), among which was a "very altered" version of the Cinderella cycle (Delarue, *Le Conte populaire français* 17).

By the seventeenth century, the more educated higher classes having made their needs manifest, literary genres such as the inordinately lengthy novel *The Great Cyrus* and tales of wonder flourished. Mme de Sévigné, quoting her daughter in a letter (6 Aug. 1677), recounted the enjoyment of the ladies of Versailles at their get-togethers as they listened to tales revolving around the peregrinations of fairies, among other supernatural beings. Even "the austere Colbert" took pleasure in the relating of fairy tales and the miraculous events associated with them during social gatherings (Storer, *La Mode des contes de fées* 13).

While fairy tales were fare for adults in the seventeenth century, the "association of folk- and fairy tales with an archetypal story-telling for children was an integral part of the salon game" (Seifert, *Fairy Tales, Sexuality, and Gender in France* 45). Written mostly by and for the *mondain*, fairy tales evolved within the framework of the parlor game. Witty and polished, these narratives were intended to charm and entertain guests at receptions. Their publication was effected in "waves": the first, from 1690 to 1715; the second, from 1722 until 1758. The more than 250 fairy tales published in seventeenth- and eighteenth-century France included such well-known works as *Beauty and the Beast, Little Red Riding Hood,* and *Sleeping Beauty.* Because these works were designed to suit the needs of sophisticated adults, it may come as no surprise to learn of the publication of a forty-volume collection of tales, *Le Cabinet des fées* (1785–1789) (Barchilon, *Le Conte merveilleux français de 1690 à 1790* 9).

Outside of the illustrious Charles Perrault—whose *Donkey-Skin, Sleeping Beauty,* and *Bluebeard* have been chosen for analysis in this book—mention may be made of François de la Mothe-Fénelon and Claude-Prosper Crébillon, two writers less known for their fairy tales than for their other works. The seventeenth century, however, may boast of a plethora of highly sophisticated female writers of this genre: Charlotte-Rose Caumont de La Force, Marie-Jeanne Lhéritier de Villandon, and Henriette-Julie Murat, to mention but a few. I have chosen Marie-Catherine d'Aulnoy's *Bluebird* for scrutiny. While dramatizing and analyzing their fabulations in delicate and precise classical prose, their intent in many cases was to entertain and to educate their listeners and/or their readers and encourage them to draw moral lessons from the tales. The interweaving of ethical contents into their narratives, however, in no way detracted from the wit, spiciness, and enchantment of their captivating writings (Robert, *Le Conte fées littéraire en France* 8).

Since women in the seventeenth century were sequestered for the most part in their homes—the better to fulfill household obligations including those of breeding—feminists have commented on the fact that their importance as authors of fairy tales did not, strangely enough, diminish their reputations as writers, even though the fairy tale genre was considered inferior to the novel, poetry, and essay. Because of this perceived low status, fairy tales posed little threat to male writers, so the men did not bother to criticize the female writers severely enough to damage their reputations.

Women such as Mme d'Aulnoy found themselves in the position of being obliged to earn a living via their pen. Being forced to face the vagaries of life encouraged her and some of the other ladies mentioned above to firm up their yearnings, to draw on their principles and philosophical credos as they took pen in hand. Their serious use of the fairy tale genre was definitely intended for adults. Until the latter part of the seventeenth century, fairy tales as we know them today were not geared to the entertainment of children. Indeed, it was Mme Le Prince de Beaumont, the author of *Beauty and the Beast,* who was considered responsible for inaugurating children's literature in France (Seifert, "Fairy Tales," in Sartori, ed., *The Feminist Encyclopedia of Literature* 199).

By the eighteenth century, the social climate had so altered in France that women could no longer boast of having authored the preponderance of fairy tales. While the tales of Denis Diderot, Jean-Jacques Rousseau, Jacques Cazotte, Claude-Prosper Crébillon, and Voltaire had trappings of the super-natural, these authors aimed their humor and satire at adults, their intent for the most part being to destabilize their readers by debunking religious and political institutions. Cerebrality, satire, irony, and sexually explicit scenes characterize Diderot's *The White Bird*, which has been chosen for analysis in this volume. His images and cataloguing of distinctive truths would have been highly offensive to the "pure in heart" if he had published the work dur-ing his lifetime; he wisely secreted this tale among his other private unpub-lished papers. Not to the same degree but still shockingly licentious was Rousseau's fairy tale, *The Fantastic Queen*, which likewise will be discussed in this book.

Generalizing, it might be fitting to suggest that nineteenth-century France returned to a spiritual/mystico/romantico fairy tale genre, reminis-cent to some extent of the deft and imaginative fantasies of the Middle Ages. Identified frequently with what was known as the "poetic principle," fairies in postrevolutionary France were conjured up to fullfill the dreams and yearnings of writers. That these supernatural beings reflected the author's own *état d'ame* is a given, as shown by the following two works, which were chosen for scrutiny in this volume. To heal or to destroy a young lad who was fighting insanity was the thrust of Charles Nodier's *The Crumb Fairy*. The resurrection of a Muse to inspire a protagonist whose creative principle was on the wane was the focus of Théophile Gautier's *Arria Marcella*.

Women writers, such as Marceline Desbordes-Valmore, turned their at-tention to children in *Contes en prose* and *Le livre des mères et des enfants*, among others. Similarly, the Russian-born emigrée to France, Sophie Rostop-chine, countess of Ségur, wrote nearly exclusively for children. Her *New Fairy Tales*, although riddled with extreme moral and spiritual conservatism—and with scenes of brutality, as evidenced in *Rosette*, a work I have elected to ex-plicate in this volume—enjoyed great appeal in her day, and still does for some contemporary readers. Nonetheless, her writings, paradoxically, also under-score a need for female independence, even pointing to ways of avoiding pre-arranged marriages and of retaining doweries.

While George Sand may be considered the very antithesis of the conser-vative Ségur, she had deeply maternal, artistic, and socially oriented interests, and she lauded family values, love marriages, and harmonious relationships between parents and children. *The Castle of Crooked Peak*, chosen for discus-sion because of its gem-like quality and healthful cast, was written for and told to her daughter and grandchildren.

An analysis of Maurice Maeterlinck's metaphysically oriented *Pelléas and Mélisande* is included in our volume for its dramatic rendering of the birth and burgeoning of love and of the destruction of its protagonists by this same passion.

Although fairy tales are still in vogue in the twentieth century, lovers of the genre rely to a great extent on the reprinting of traditional titles, such as *Blue Beard, Cinderella,* and *Tom Thumb.* Nonetheless, some well-known writers, namely, Guillaume Apollinaire, Paul Valéry, Jean Cocteau, Antoine de Saint-Exupéry, Jean Giraudoux, Romain Weingarten, Michel Tournier, and Andrée Chedid have used this genre as well. Cocteau's reworked film version of Mme Le Prince de Beaumont's *Beauty and the Beast,* and Andrée Chedid's *The Suspended Heart,* dating back to ancient Egyptian times, have been singled out for probing for their striking relevance to today's readers—young and old.

What of the future? Has the reality of interplanetary travel—formerly Sci Fi—usurped the dominion of fairy tales? Or have they commingled? May beautiful or handsome, kind, and gentle fairies—or their opposites—live someplace in outer space? After all, haven't they always been implicit in our psyches? Like astronauts, readers may enter space, their own inner cosmos, and enjoy the luxury—or terror—of meandering about amid their own incredible fabulations!

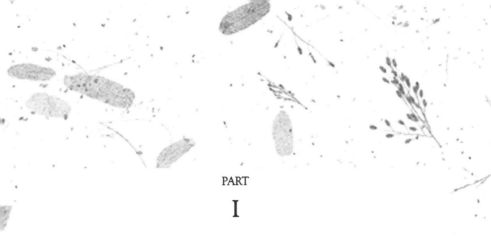

THE MIDDLE AGES
FEUDALISM AND "LA SOCIÉTÉ COURTOISE"

THE MIDDLE AGES, A PERIOD WHICH EXTENDED from about 400 to 1500, was breathtaking in its intellectual, scientific, political, social, commercial, and artistic achievements. Feudal leaders, having actively extended and consolidated their power in surrounding domains, brought fiefdoms into existence. They contracted with farmers to render them service in exchange for protection from marauders and invaders. As fiefs became hereditary and great landlords sought to increase their rights, political balance altered, leading ever so relentlessly to the diminution of the king's authority. Meanwhile, fortified stone castles and monasteries, abbeys, and houses of worship dotted the landscape.

Monastic life injected not only a note of stability in the politically uncertain climate of Europe, but was instrumental in preserving learning. Religious orders, namely, the Benedictines of Cluny (tenth century), the Cistercians (twelfth century), and Dominicans (thirteenth century), were known for their classical and patristic learning, for their asceticism, and for their high moral standards. Theologians and philosophers, such as Abélard and Hugh of Saint-Victor, taught at cathedral schools in Paris, which, thanks to the efforts of Robert de Sorbon, grew into the University of Paris. The resulting climate of intense intellectual, architectural, musical, and artistic fervor attracted other European teachers of note—Alexander of Hales, Bonaventura, Albertus Magnus, and Thomas Aquinas. Paris became not only the capital of France, but the mercantile center of northern Europe as well.

Religious fervor, in consort with the great building boom, led to the erection of memorable Gothic structures such as the spectacular cathedrals of Chartres, Rheims, Amiens, and Beauvais, and the choir of Saint-Denis (1140) in the royal abbey near Paris. Christianity became the chief unifying force following the disarray created by invading Saracens, Norsemen, Magyars, Germans, and Anglo-Saxons. As a result, popes such as Gregory VII and Innocent III acquired inordinate secular authority.

The notion of chivalry, having allied itself with military, political, and religious institutions, paved the way for what has been alluded to as "divinely inspired violence," or the Crusades. Pope Urban II, motivated to a great extent by St. Augustine's writings, preached the first Crusade in 1095 at the Council of Clermont. Ostensibly aimed at reconquering the Holy Land, the Crusades, lasting even until the latter part of the sixteenth century, turned into bloody massacres of Muslims and Jews, and pillagings of lands for material gain. The Black Plague, thought to have been brought to Europe by returning Crusaders, introduced the deadliest of dismal times to France. The Hundred Years' War, the name appended to military battles waged between England and France from 1337 to 1453, resulted in the latter's devastation.

The emergence of a new feminine mystique was in the process of altering psychological and societal dividing lines between the sexes. The patriarchal nature of medieval chivalry, with its emphasis on military feats and male friendships as attested to in such epics as The Song of Roland (eleventh century), was in the process of yielding its hegemony to a new zeitgeist. The increasingly popular courtly romances and love songs delivered by celebrated troubadours, such as Bernard de Ventadorn (twelfth century) answered an underlying need for increased equity in love relationships. Although hailing from the Limousin, Bernard spent much time at the court of Eleanor of Aquitaine (1122–1204). An intelligent, strong-minded woman, Eleanor married Louis VII only to have her sacramental bonds annulled, after which she wed Henry, duke of Normandy, later Henry II of England. Due to his infidelities, their relationship grew strained, and Eleanor established her own court at Poitiers in 1170. Known as the center of artistic creativity, it drew under Eleanor's aegis such great figures as Wace, Benoit de Sainte-Maure, and Chrétien de Troyes. The emphasis placed on courtly manners encouraged the burgeoning and later preeminence of courtly love, with its special ritualized code. True love, or the fin d'amors doctrine, identified mainly with Christianity, motivated lovers to emulate godlike morality, aspire toward virtue, and devote themselves to the service of Lady Mary. The celebration of the oneness of woman's *celestial* and *earthly* qualities increased the popularity of an already growing cult of the Virgin. Fals'amors, or false love, on the other hand, the lot of the majority, was said to be plagued by jealousy, hypocrisy, and vacillation (Fierz-David, *The Dream of Poliphilo* 14).

Just as a lover submitted to his lady, a knight to his lord, so the Christianized and sublimized female was bound by convention as well. While such behavioral patterns underscored the nobility of love, the at times unattainable lady in question was expected nonetheless to yield some favor(s) to her lover. Nonetheless, so strict had the codes become that Andreas Capellanus's *De Arte Honeste Amandi* (twelfth century) became the standard treatise on courtly love. In cases of infraction or blatant disregard of etiquette, the courts based their arguments and verdicts on this volume. It comes as no surprise that the verdicts of these special love courts led to the glorification of women by heroes such as Tristan, Arthur, Launcelot, Yvain, and Perceval. No longer simply a source of sexual gratification, nor merely a means of fulfilling their childbearing functions, the woman's new image included a fresh understanding of esthetic, moral, and social principles—behooving the lover to devote himself to her as a "perfect lady" (Harding, 1973, *Psychic Energy* 104 ff.).

The growing yearning for feelings of relatedness and understanding between male and female led to a revision of moral principles: the male was required to exercise great control in sexual and family matters. No longer were instinctuality or immediate gratification compatible with the new code of ethics. Instead, a sense of equality in love relationships had taken root by the fourteenth century. While courtly etiquette required the banishing of brute force except in battle, automatic and unthinking behavioral patterns were equally unacceptable. A valiant nobleman and/or husband had to make certain he had gained dominion—or was capable of doing so—over himself by moderating rather than by being enslaved to his sexual impulses. An increasing demand for commitment and responsibility in relationships was anticipated by both partners as well. Even as a husband was expected to serve a wife, she was assigned similar authority over her own and her beloved's physical and spiritual well-being.

In many instances, Jean d' Arras's *Romance of Mélusine* points to moral, religious, social, and esthetic questions dating back to a period extending roughly from the ninth to the thirteenth centuries, when faith and a sense of chivalry reigned in France, but an undercurrent of melancholy—of life's transience—may be noted as well. Although living hundreds of years before Jean d'Arras, the sixth-century Roman philosopher, Boethius, prophetically conveyed the dominant mood implicit in Jean d'Arras's romance: "The beauty of things is fleet and swift, more fugitive than the passing of flowers in the spring" (Eco, *Art and Beauty* 9; from Boethius, *The Consolation of Philosophy* III.).

1

MELUSINE
"THE BEAUTY OF THINGS IS FLEET AND SWIFT"

Variations of the story line and theme of Jean d'Arras's deeply moving *The Romance of Mélusine* (1392 or 1393) date back to ancient times. Associations have been made between the French protagonist, Mélusine, and the Vedic heroine Urvasi, a beautiful and voluptuous Apsara, or heavenly nymph; the Japanese Shinto Toyo-tama, daughter of the sea god, married to Hoori, deity of the hunt; to Psyche, Eros's wife, as depicted in Apuleius's *Golden Ass*, and others. Be it in Jean d'Arras's version of the Mélusine legend, or others appearing during the course of the twelfth and thirteenth centuries and even prior to that time, couples who respected the pact into which they entered prior to their wedding were awarded joy, love, fulfillment, and prosperity. Violation of the contract cast misfortune and suffering on both.

ECTYPAL ANALYSIS

Duke Jean de Berry, count of Poitou and brother of Charles VI of France, ostensibly to amuse his sister, Marie, duchess of Bar, had commissioned Jean d'Arras to write *The Romance of Mélusine* (Nodot, *Histoire de Mélusine* vff.). In his prologue, the author cited a similar tale written in prose two centuries earlier by the monk Gervais of Tilbury (c. 1152–1234), first, a protégé of Henry II of England, then entering into the service of Otto IV of Brunswick. Mention must also be made of the rhymed octosyllabic version of *The Romance of Mélusine* composed by Coudrette in c. 1401 for Jean Larchevêque, lord of Parthenay.

Poitiers, the ancient capital of the province of Poitou, was the seat of much of the action in *Mélusine*. A stronghold of orthodoxy under its first bishop, the fourth-century St. Hilary of Poitiers, the area was also known for its monasteries, Roman amphitheaters and baths, the baptistery of St. John (fourth to twelfth centuries), the Cathedral of St. Pierre (twelfth to fourteenth centuries), and the royal residence (twelfth to fifteenth centuries). Plundered by the Normans (ninth century), and twice by the English (1152–1204, 1360–1372), Poitiers was nonetheless as previously noted, the location of Eleanor of Aquitaine's brilliant court. Indeed, certain critics maintain that Eleanor of Aquitaine had been the inspiration for Jean d'Arras's protagonist, Mélusine.

Some scholars whose names appear in the vast literature on Mélusine theorize that the tale was strictly of Poitevin origin; others, that it was of Scythian provenance, having been brought to the West by returning Crusaders. These maintain that Mélusine (or Mélisende) is to be identified with one of the daughters of Baudoin II, king of Jerusalem (Marchant, *La Légende de Mélusine. Jean d'Arras* vii).

Jean d'Arras is divided into two parts: the first, focusing on Présine, and the second, on her daughter, Mélusine, the ancestress of the famed Lusignan family of Poitou. The stirring lives of these two hauntingly mysterious women veer from dream scheme to actuality, their earthly trajectories taking them from deeply forested areas to cleared terrains, from shadowy caves to mountainous heights and flat lands. Nor are the psyches or physical makeups of these two extraordinarily beautiful feminine figures clear cut. Présine, endowed with prescience, is blind to the realities of human nature. Like her mother, Mélusine is intuitive and provided with inner sight which, when subjectively motivated, dims her thinking principle, blinding her to otherwise evident truths. Unlike her mother—and most surprisingly—she takes on the form of a snake from her waist down, but only on Saturdays!

Due to the changing status in love relationships, as has been mentioned, women were acquiring greater equality vis-à-vis their husbands. Both Présine and Mélusine in Arras's *The Romance of Mélusine* (referred to henceforth as *Mélusine)* imposed ethical and social adjustments on their partners. Might their comportment be labeled intransigeant? Just as knights of old had to learn to curb their ardor for fighting, hunting, and for sexual matters in general, so increasing restrictions were foisted on husbands in *Mélusine*, heightening tension in these changing times. On occasion, both partners gained physical and spiritual support from each other, each cognizant of the love, feeling, and respect due them as individuals and as an ideal/real couple. At other moments, mercurial changeableness prevailed, with dire results!

Présine and Mélusine, as well as the members of their families, were firm believers in Christianity and adherents of church ritual, yet were bogged down in superstition and taboos. Animism, a strikingly important factor in *Mélusine*, opens readers up to a universe in which natural phenomena are not only considered living entities, but are endowed with souls that, under certain circumstances, exist apart from their material bodies. The mélange of attributes of earth people and supernatural beings was acceptable not only to the masses in the Middle Ages, but also to certain highly placed individuals and, frequently, to the clergy. Hadn't Godefroy de Bouillon (1061–1100), leader of the first Crusade, prided himself on descent from a fairy on his maternal side? And hadn't Henry II Plantagenet claimed ancestry from King Arthur? Richard the Lion Heart asserted proudly that "the sons of demons" had been responsible for the birth of his dynasty (*Jean d'Arras, Le Roman de Mélusine*. Mis en français moderne par Michèle Perret 9).

Occult yet vitreous, audible although silent, static despite their motility, Présine and Mélusine were, like many archetypal figures, a complex of opposites who, although living in the Middle Ages, survive in our contemporary city-jungles and dwindling forests.

ARCHETYPAL ANALYSIS

Part I: Présine

Our tale opens as the valiant King Elinas of Albania (the ancient name for Scotland), recent widower and father of several children—the eldest of which is Nathas (Mataquas)—has gone out hunting. Seeking distraction after the death of his beloved wife, he makes his way on horseback ever more deeply into a thickly forested area near the sea, loses all sense of direction and of time, realizes he is thirsty, and stops to drink at a fountain. No sooner does he approach the fountain than he hears a voice "more melodious than any siren" (*Mélusine* 18). The virtually hypnotized Elinas first believes he is listening to the music of angels on high. Deeply touched by its tender quality, he follows it to their source. Dismounting from his horse, which he secures to a tree, he walks closer to the fountain and notices the most beautiful woman he has ever seen standing next to it. He observes her from behind a cluster of trees. So mesmerized is he by the vision that he does not know whether he is awake or dreaming. Having forgotten his thirst and his hunt, he sinks ever more deeply into a state of seeming somnolence—or a hypnotic trance state—and awakens with a start to find his two dogs frolicking about him. Moments later, both his memory and his thirst return. He walks toward the fountain, drinks its waters, is greeted by the lady, and is told her name—Présine. Soon her valet arrives to spirit her away. She mounts her horse and leaves.

So overwhelmed is Elinas by the aura of "The Lady of the Fountain," that, after her departure, he follows her almost mechanically to her forest retreat. The two meet again. Much to his surprise, she knows his name, and asks him what brings him to the forest. He responds by requesting her love and good will. Not easily persuaded by amorous intent, she replies forcefully, that his intentions must be honest, for "no man will make her his mistress" (*Mélusine* 22). Aware that he is deeply smitten, she considers it appropriate to impose her conditions. If he seeks to marry her, she tells him, he must promise never to visit nor to look at her during her lying-in period. He swears to abide by her interdict. They marry and live out a profound love relationship. Not only is she a perfect wife, but she even surprises and delights Elinas's "people" by her wise and ethical rule of her household domain (*Mélusine* 9). Only Mataquas, Elinas's son by his first wife, despises her. In time, she gives birth to three daughters, Mélusine, Mélior and Palatine.

THE HUNT. Hunting, one of the most popular sports of medieval times, held special allure for knights, and the bereaved Elinas was no exception. Not only had the art of the hunt become a test of physical dexterity and endurance, it was of spiritual and psychological value as well; hunting was understood as the symbolic trapping and killing of the animal within each being. Only after expelling the beast within, or, paradigmatically, the aggressive instincts buried inside an individual, could one experience feelings of redemption. If the hunter Elinas was successful in catching his prey—the animal within—he would become master of his "mount" and would be able to encourage the rule of the rational and/or conscious. A new and more fruitful orientation of his life might very well lead him to his center, bringing balance and harmony to his now empty and one-sided world. As on a journey or pilgrimage, a knight such as Elinas, having entered the forest on horseback, was being put to the test: that is, to the search, or the quest (Lat. *quaestus,* and "question," *quaestio,* the two being associated in this connection). Like Druid priests, poets, and knights of old, Elinas, the hunter entered his shadowy forest world on horseback, happened upon a fountain, and suddenly grew thirsty for want of its spiritually/psychologically nutritive regenerative power.

FOREST. Since time immemorial forests have been considered the habitat of an ever-nourishing, ever-thriving, ever-relational, and at times ever-voracious lunar force, that of the Great Mother. Fertility, in all of its colorations and manifestations—verdant green grasses, red, mauve, or yellow flowering or non-flowering plants, along with molds, mildew, and rot—luxuriate chaotically in her darkened domain. Identified at times with the nonregulated and hidden womb-like *unconscious*, the forest stands antipodally to the consciously cultivated solar-fed garden with its ordered, planned, and restricted vegetation. As the great dispenser of rain and water, the forest—or "green world"— and the animals thriving within its parameters, exists and flourishes thanks to the sustaining power of the Great Mother, as lunar force. Associated with the most primitive levels of the feminine psyche, this protective, relatively obscure maternal shelter holds many a lonely wanderer in its thrall.

Even as the forest's uncultivated growth has become a paradigm for the regressive spheres of the psyche, its nonlinear time schemes and rhythmical behavioral patterns follow their own quixotic motifs as well. Understandably, then, did oracles, sybils, mediums, and other supernatural figures—including fairies—choose this relatively obscure and uninhabited realm to murmur their ambiguous prognostications. In this darkened liminal, no-time sphere, prophets, seers, and world creators were known to have lost their direction or rational outlook, thereby allowing them the luxury of tapping into their transpersonal spheres—or collective unconscious.

VISION. Visionaries, poets, philosophers, theologians, scientists, seers, and artists have for centuries chosen remote and sparsely inhabited realms to allow their resplendent inner materializations to take on concretion. Elinas's visionary experience, having given him access to his collective unconscious, thrust a much-yearned for archetypal image into his mind's eye. Overwhelmed by the sight of the beautiful woman standing next to the fountain, he felt himself inexplicably imbued with a sense of lightness and well-being. So powerfully had these sensations encapsulated his psyche, that he seemed to have fallen into a remarkably deep slumber, losing contact with reality. Was this the path chosen by the Great Mother to assuage his sorrow? By severing his ties with the empirical domain, was she ushering him into deeper subliminal dimensions, inviting him to cohabit with eternal and universal spheres? Having blocked out Elinas's reason and concomitant feelings of loneliness, sorrow, and abandonment, the Great Mother had created a fertile field for his trance state, which served to release him from the troubling dichotomies in the differentiated world and the weight of his obsessive feelings of bereavement. Now capable of communicating with natural forces, he was attuned to his own matrix: that womblike, containing, and "dynamic aspect of the unconscious" which has the capacity to move and to "act on its own accord," and is even responsible for the composition of dreams (Franz, *On Divination and Synchronicity* 20). As long as the "no-man's land" of the collective unconscious prevailed, Elinas's diminished intensities and reduced agitations, virtually cut him off from the domain of discord.

Explaining the "dynamic" aspects of the unconscious and its active participation in the composition of dreams, Franz writes:

> One could say that composing dreams while one sleeps is an aspect of the spirit; some master spirit or mind composes a most ingenious series of pictures which, if one can decipher them, seem to convey a highly intelligent message. That is a dynamic manifestation of the unconscious, where the unconscious energetically does something on its own, it moves and creates on its own, and that is what Jung defines as spirit. (Franz 20)

When finally Elinas did awaken, or emerged from his inner-forest world, he was so disoriented that he was hard pressed to decide whether he had seen an actual woman before him, or whether, as previously mentioned, his vision of her was the outcome of a waking or sleeping dream. Either way, while giving birth to his vision, he also internalized a much-yearned-for *anima* or soul image which would serve to inject a new life principle into his depleted affective psyche.

Both his entry into the forest and his emerging vision of Présine may be looked upon as the outset of an initiation (Lat, *initiatus*, "gone within") ceremony, a descent into the Self, defined psychologically as a submersion into the total psyche, or in religious parlance, into God. Elinas's rite of passage had, therefore, taken him from one level of consciousness to another. His new sense of connectedness, experienced as a *katabasis*, or inner descent, would encourage him to link up with both his own personal past and with the primordial existence of humanity. His participation in the forest's mysteries concretized his vision and invested it with broader perspectives: new qualities garnished his formerly limited understanding of truth and beauty.

The altering of one's concepts following a traumatic visionary experience is in keeping with the propensity of medieval theologians and philosophers to link ethics with form. Indeed, as experienced by Elinas, the two had become virtually interchangeable. According to the thirteenth-century English Franciscan scholar, Alexander of Hales, "[T]ruth was the disposition of form in relation to the internal character of a thing; beauty was the disposition of form in relation to its external character" (Eco, *Art and Beauty in the Middle Ages* 23. From Hales, *Summa Theologica* I, no.3).

The greater were the feelings of love Elinas projected onto *form*, or onto his anima figure standing at the fountain, the more powerful was the hold this image would have on his psyche. Indeed, Présine's power, even at the onset of his visionary experience, had succeeded in routing him from his hunt. Not that his life force had been depleted by his foray into his unconscious—rather, the reverse had taken place. Her image, as associated with the fountain, may be said to have flowed into him, thereby renewing, nourishing, and sustaining his entire being.

The Greeks might have defined Elinas's sudden feelings for the feminine power standing before him as a case of overwhelming lovesickness, an example of Eros's powerful arrows having pierced his flesh. But his was an endopsychic experience, one "belonging to the subject," whose effect on the spirit became "transsubjective," that is, appearing as if from some spiritual or spirit world (Franz, *Projection and Recollection in Jungian Psychology* 34).

MUSIC. The melodious voice of Elinas's vision-lady produced in him nearly endless varieties of resonating pulsations, which increased his awareness of the myriad foreign elements in his mind's eye. The combination of the visual image and the oral sonorities altered the components of his psyche, reaching deeply into his inner void—that area of his subliminal sphere which had remained vacant following the death of his first wife. As the stirrings of the tonalities filled his inner vacuum, they catalyzed in him a need to involve himself with the apparently gentle woman appearing to him in his vision.

The mood-altering effect of the pitches, amplitudes, and rhythms flowing into him, moreover, aroused his body/psyche/mind complex to what we would today call a "high," actuating unknown contents within the folds of the psyche. Elinas's vulnerability and need of healing had virtually transformed him into a kind of receptacle, attracting him to the musical strains issuing forth from "The Lady of the Fountain." A parallel may be drawn between Elinas's reaction to music and the effect of the tones emanating from Orpheus's lyre—an instrument that was deemed to have the power of mesmerizing animals and moving stones.

The more Elinas was exposed to what he considered to be celestial harmonies, the greater was his devotion to his soul figure. Like hallowed tonal phrases of medieval music, so Présine's verbal sonorities drew Elinas's feelings toward supernal spheres, encouraging him to identify the strains he heard with angelic voices. His associations reflect St. Hildegarde of Bingen's "'symphonic' organization of nature, and how the experience of the Absolute unfolded in the manner of music" (Eco, *Art and Beauty in the Middle Ages* 36), as well as Boethius's notations on the connection between musical modes and their rhythms, which affects people in various ways. Boethius cited the Spartans who claimed that certain sonorities modified their souls, an effect which we may identify as changes in their moods! We may add that Pythagoreans "made use of certain lullabies to help them get to sleep, and when they awoke they shook the sleep from their eyes with the help of music" (Eco 31). As an advocate of "the music of the spheres," had not Pythagoras connected micro and macrocosm, soul and body, love and hate, thus uniting the disparate in transcendence? (Eco 32).

The greater the reality of Elinas's fantasy figure, the greater the increase of her saintly attributes. Having previously allied ethics and form, he now assigned to tone and cadence moral and esthetic characteristics. How such a transformation constellated in him and how it may be explained, is moot. Jung compared "the musical movement of the unconscious" to "a sort of symphony" whose dynamics still remain unfathomable (Jung, *Seminar on Dream Analysis* 440).

MUSIC AND SIRENS. Elinas associated Présine's singing not only with the spiritual images of angels, but with the song of sirens, adding destructive sexual inuendoes to the heretofore godly ones.

As airborne and water-borne creatures, sirens allegedly were endowed at times with the heads of women, and at other instances, with their breasts. The rest of their bodies bore the shape of birds. Aristotle, Pliny, and Ovid, on the other hand, had depicted sirens as women endowed with fish or serpent tails. Of several types, many of these semi-human females were known for their mesmerizingly seductive powers. Although tantalizing the male, sirens were in all cases unable to fulfill their own or their partners' sexual desires. While Orpheus and Odysseus were said to have survived the hypnotic chants of bird-women, other navigators, less well centered did not.

The image of the siren throughout history—whether or not associated with aspects of the Great Mother Demeter/Ceres, Aphrodite/Venus/Cybele, to mention but a few—has come to indicate a handicapped physical and/or emotional condition. Because the charge for sexual failure always fell on the female, the siren image was created as a symbol of female deformity. Instead of assuming accountability for his acts, the male was forever pictured as devoured and enslaved by the female, victimized by a formidably evil temptress. Such a notion is fantasized in the biblical Book of Revelation with its depiction of the city of Babylon as woman:

> Come hither; I will shew unto thee that judgment of the great whore that sitteth upon many waters:
> With whom the kings of the earth have committed fornication, and the inhabitants of the earth have been made drunk with the wine of her fornication . . .
> . . . and I saw a woman sit upon a scarlet coloured beast, full of names of blasphemy, having seven heads and ten horns.
> And the woman was arrayed in purple and scarlet colour, and decked with gold and precious stones and pearls, having a golden cup in her hand full of abominations and filthiness of her fornication:

And upon her forehead was a name written, MYSTERY, BABYLON
THE GREAT, THE MOTHER OF HARLOTS AND ABOMINATIONS
OF THE EARTH. (Rev. 17:5)

The identification of woman with Evil/Eve, the greatest of temptresses
for believers in ancient times and even today, was a reality for medieval man.
In depictions of bird- or snake women in the bestiaries of the times, they were
"deadly creatures" whose melodies served to "entice the hearing of . . . poor
chaps by a wonderful sweetness of rhythm, and put them to sleep. At last,
when they see that the sailors are deeply slumbering, they pounce upon them
and tear them to bits" (A Book of Beasts, trans. T. H. White 134). Nor are images of these semi-human females lacking in chapel and church sculptures in
France and elsewhere, as, for example, the carvings of two-tailed sirens on the
tympanum of the chapel of St. Michel d'Aiguilhe at Le Puy; and siren-birds at
Saint-Benoît-sur-Loire. Sirens, loreleis, ondines, and snake women are part of
humanity's archetypal heritage.

The connection in Elinas's mind between Présine and the siren figure—
or her semi-human nature—suggests not an inability on his part to experience
sexual fulfillment, but rather indicates his complete submission to the dictates
of this outerworldly lady. Not surprisingly does the onus of a woman-domi-
nated relationship in patriarchal societies—such as those existing in medieval
Europe—fall on the female. To assuage any sense of possible humiliation, the
male, who by yielding to the madness of his love had already succumbed to
temptation and to all of its concomitant evils, conjured these semi-divine or
malformed female powers, thereby creating the ideal excuse to avoid responsibility for psychological and/or physiological sexual malfunctioning.

Although Présine's physical appearance was not deformed, like that of
the sirens perched on rocky crags jutting up from ancient Greek seas, she
knew that music, an intermediary zone between the material, physical, and
spiritual domains, had the capacity to generate an anima figure in a grieving
widower. Her powerful intent at a time when women sought to elevate men
from their formerly brutish, one-sided patriarchal comportment, was the acculturation of the male. To introduce Elinas to courtly standards, to feeling
attitudes, and to seemly comportment toward women, may have been in part
Présine's motivation in establishing a love relationship. She sought to teach
him—medieval man—respect and consideration for a woman in a marriage relationship. No longer would she, as was the case of so many other women of
the time, be used simply as an object created to satisfy a husband's sensual
needs and/or provide him with children.

Aware of her attributes, Présine knew she could give Elinas compan-
ionship, understanding, and love, but she would remain unyielding in her

requirements. Sensing the effect her tonal gradations had on Elinas, Mother Nature or Mother Protectress activated the acculturation process by having sound strike deeply into the heart of Elinas's being, transforming the once valorous king and hunter into a courteous, thoughtful, but increasingly dependent man.

FOUNTAIN. Like the waters of the fountain where Présine stood when Elinas first glimpsed her, she came to symbolize the source, the center, the *fons et origo* of his life. Reminiscent of the Kabbalistic image of the fountain in the Zohar *(Book of Splendor)*, indicating the mystery of the Infinite, the supernal point, or the center of Centers from which "the fount of all bliss and all blessings flow," so Présine was identified by Elinas with lustral waters.

From his newly found mystical Eden within the forest would be born his new reality. The fountain whose waters he imbibed would nourish his lonely and vacant heart. Its spiritual waters would redirect him into the great sea of life, comparable to the alchemist's first operation: that of *solutio*, involving the cleansing of the metals, or, psychologically, the purification of Elinas's unredeemed traits. The waters of the fountain revivified him, injected him with sufficient energy to follow "The Lady of the Fountain" to her domain, thus allowing him to experience the precontaminated condition of the newborn through baptism: the sprinkling of water that, symbolically, washed away sin. Not surprisingly, alchemists often quoted Jesus' recommendation to purify oneself through waters: "Verily, verily, I say unto them, Except a man be born of water and of the Spirit, he cannot enter into the kingdom of God" (John 3:5).

The fountain's spray, arising from uncontaminated Mother Earth, quenched Elinas's thirst, and in so doing, ritualized the very mystery of baptism. Reminiscent of the alchemist's elixir of life, the waters of the fountain revivified what had grown atrophied following Elinas's divestiture and his ensuing condition of morbidity.

THE LYING-IN TABOO. Taboos have existed since earliest times. Although conversant with those of Pandora and Cupid and Psyche, Westerners may be intrigued by a lesser-known Hindu myth related in the Catapatha-brahmana, about the peregrinations of a Puruvaras, or king, who fell in love with Urvasi. As an Apsara, this beautiful and voluptuous fairylike being who rose from the waters, was looked upon, as were her sisters, as both "a daughter of pleasure" and as a celestial musician (Wilkins, *Hindu Mythology* 483). Prior to her marriage, she was forbidden to look upon her husband in his nakedness. Tragedy likewise struck in the Kojiki, a Shinto text in which Toyo-tama ("Rich-jewel"), the daughter of the God of the Sea, married the hunter, Hoori.

After giving birth to a child, she turned into a dragon, slipped back into the sea in shame leaving her child behind (Davis, *Myths and Legends of Japan* 37).

The notion of taboo with regard to an object (tree, amulet, charm, particularly if it has been blessed by an awesome figure), or to an individual (Présine), inspires sacred dread. Touching or injuring the person(s) involved in this kind of prohibition would, it was believed, severely damage the object and/or persons.

Why a lying-in taboo in Présine's case? A mysterious connection has existed since ancient times between a woman and the moon (Gr. *mene*, moon) because of the rhythms of her monthly cycle (Lat. *menstruus*, from *mensis*, month), as in menstruation.[1] Because women in most Western and Eastern societies were considered unclean during their menstrual periods, they were placed under certain restrictions—or taboos. Compelled to live in a room apart from others, or in special houses located at the outskirts of villages, they remained frequently without care and were obliged to fend for themselves. Similar exclusionary conditions awaited birthing women, who were forced to withdraw to another house or town. To even look upon their shadows, it was believed, might infect an onlooker. Although food could be brought to them, it had to be left at a distance from the pregnant woman to avoid contamination of the bringer. Infractions of these governing rules were severely punished. As late as the early twentieth century, in certain areas in England, a mother at the conclusion of her birthing period, which lasted one month, had to participate in a special Anglican and/or Roman Catholic ritual that would disinfect her, "not surgically, but religiously," from her contaminated condition (Harding, *Woman's Mysteries* 55ff.).

The vacuum in the household by physical separation during the birth of a child, working in tandem with psychological ostracism, created a void in both empirical and psychological realms. The ensuing emptiness catalyzed feelings of fear, awe, and envy in the male because of the power of creation that had been invested only in the female.

That Elinas had unthinkingly agreed to Présine's taboo which forbade him to look at her during and following her lying-in-period, suggests the valuation of an ideal, notably, the sacrality of an oath taken by a knight of the Round Table. One may wonder why the preservation of Elinas's oath represented a more difficult task for him than the risking of his life in the capture the Holy Sepulchre. The injunction to which he agreed to abide required dominion over his instinctual and affective world, a virtually impossible task to accomplish when under emotional stress.

During the birth of his three beautiful daughters—Mélusine, Mélior, and Palatine—Elinas, in keeping with the interdict, remained away from his palace. His immediate anxieties were alleviated when his son, Mataquas, informed him of the infants's perfections. Jealous of Présine's power over his father, Mataquas encouraged him to repair to Présine's rooms to see for himself the beauty of his three daughters. Forgetting his vow, Elinas entered the birthing room as Présine was bathing her daughters and blessed her. Présine's response was wrathful: "Felon you failed to keep your word," she shouted, blaming Mataquas alone, for the future of sorrows Elinas and his family were to know (*Mélusine* 23). That the lying-in taboo was extracted by Présine, and not by Elinas, indicated the empowerment of the woman not only over herself, but over the man as well, particularly with regard to matters of birthing. No longer willing to abdicate or subvert her destiny to a man's will, Présine demanded that her goals, her prerogatives, her attitudes and feelings be recognized. Intransigeant to the extreme, she may have unconsciously believed that a single infraction of the rule would be sufficient to destroy the world of amity and togetherness she and her husband had created. While Présine's love for Elinas had in no way diminished, she was unable to forgive his disregard of his oath. Ethics, more importantly than sexuality or marital status, remained uppermost in her mind. Breaking a sacred promise under emotional stress indicated a lack of self-control, an inability to live up to a commitment, the destruction of the high values placed on their marital relationship. A woman of her word, Présine demonstrated, despite the emotional cost, a highly tuned will-power and ability to discern right from wrong. Was she adhering to the dictum of the ninth-century Christian theologian, Duns Scotus, who wrote that "the will controls its act just as the intellect controls its act" (Eco 72. From *Opus oxoniense*). If so, Présine's intransigeance revealed an extremist's lack of malleability and understanding, particularly of a husband's natural instinct to see his newborns. Moreover, by punishing her husband, she was not only depriving herself of love, but her daughters of a father, thereby instilling in them by extension an inner rage to the male principle.

She immediately took her three daughters to Avalon, or "the Lost Isle," so called because one gained access to it only by chance. Mélusine, Mélior, and Palatine were brought up with the knowledge of their father's transgression and its ramifications for their lifestyle. Remaining in exile with their mother until the age of fifteen, they never again set eyes on their father. Mataquas was given the kingship and ruled well.

MOTHER/DAUGHTER IDENTIFICATION. As mother figure, Présine emphasized not a father's love for his wife, but rather his "felony," blaming Elinas for her isolation, suffering, and penury. She assured her daughters that at Judgment Day, God would punish evil doers, namely, their father, and recompense good people.

Bearing her mother's words in mind, the resonsable and protective young girl that Mélusine had become identified with her mother and rejected her father. She took her sisters aside, suggesting to them how best they might reveal their love for their mother while at the same time punish their father for having reduced them to virtual penury. The two sisters would act as one to assure the success of their planned vengeance. Their adroit schemings having come to fruition, their father was shut up for the rest of his life in the enchanted mountain of Brumborenlion in Northumberland.

Subsequently, the daughters returned to their mother and, expecting to be praised for their action, met with her wrath. Aghast at her daughters' cruelty, Présine told them that, by incarcerating their father, they had destroyed the only happiness she had ever experienced—his love for her. The punishments she meted out to her daughters were severe: Mélusine, who had initiated the horrendous act, would, like Cain who killed his brother, go through life with the knowledge of her transgression and pain of its consequences. Her father alone could absolve her from her "fairy destiny," a terrible punishment that would be hers throughout her existence: every Saturday the lower half of her body, from the umbilicus down, would assume the form of a serpent. If she found a man willing to marry her, he would have to promise not to look at her on Saturdays, nor ever reveal the taboo to anyone. As long as he adhered to the pact, Mélusine would be capable of extraordinary achievements: the building of great fortresses, multiple towns, the amassing of inordinate wealth. She would bear many children, thus creating the great Lusignan lineage. If, on the other hand, her husband violated the oath, she would not only return to and retain her serpent form until Judgment Day, but each time the Lusignan fortresses changed hands or a descendent died, she would appear in the environs in her serpentine form for three days of painful lamentation.

Her sister, Mélior, would be banished to the richly provided Sparrowhawk Castle in Armenia, and remain there as a virgin throughout her earthly days. Once a year (from June 23 to June 25), if a knight succeeded in remaining awake during the entire three-day interval, she would grant him a lavish earthly gift, provided he asked neither for her love nor for her hand in marriage. Failing this, malediction would be meted meted out to him and to nine generations thereafter. As for Palatine, she would be imprisoned in Guigo (Canigou), the mountain in which her father's treasure had been stored, until a knight of the same lineage used the treasure therein to conquer the Holy Land.

On Elinas's death, Présine returned to the enchanted mountain, buried him in a richly outfitted coffin, and garnished the mortuary chamber with golden candelabras destined to burn night and day for eternity. At the foot of his tomb, she had a statue erected of him, holding a golden tablet on which his life story had been engraved. A horribly fearsome giant was hired to guard both the tomb and the statue.

Part II: Mélusine

Following her mother's searing chastisement, Mélusine went her own way. That she had become emotionally divested of her personal mother, may have accounted for her choice in settling in the domain of the Great Mother—the Coulombiers forest near Poitiers. The uncontrolled and disorderly vegetation in her new habitat mirrored Mélusine's own psychological condition of disarray. Deprived of the sun, associated with consciousness and the rational sphere, the exile's inner moon-drenched topography cast an eerie glow on the surroundings. Nonetheless, the fundamentally strong and well-intentioned Mélusine was aware of the difficulties facing her, particularly those involving men.

At this point in the story a Breton nobleman, Raimondin, astride his horse, like the bereaved Elinas who had penetrated the forest's *temenos*, entered the Great Mother's shadowy or unconscious sylvan realm. The reader learns that the trauma Raimondin had experienced after accidentally killing his uncle and benefactor, Count Aimery of Poitiers, had incapacitated him psychologically. Dazed, unable to focus on anything, he allowed his horse to guide him through the thick forest. His destiny paralleled that of his father, the Count of Forez (Forest), who, after having guilelessly killed the nephew of a Breton king in a youthful skirmish, then sought refuge in a forest.

What were the circumstances that led Raimondin to murder his beloved uncle? Chance or destiny, he lamented, decreed his murderous act. The solid relationship that existed between the knight's father and his uncle dated back to the former's marriage to the sister of the Count of Poitiers. The handsome and gracious Raimondin, one of three children born to the couple, so favorably impressed the Count of Poitiers that when he had reached adolescence he took him under his wing. It was during a wild boar hunt that the trackers, most notably the count and Raimondin, grew so hostile to one boar in particular—excited by its huge size, its ferocious comportment, and what they considered to be its increasingly defiant ability to elude them—that they, and the other knights to a lesser degree, took the entire venture as a personal challenge.

A millennial object of fascination, the wild boar was regarded by the Hindus as an avatar of Vishnu. The Babylonians considered the animal sacred, the Romans and Gauls represented it as a military insignia, and the Druids used it as sacrificial food for their "intensely spiritual" feast of Samhain (Halloween today), a time when "the Other-world became visible" to humankind (Ellis, *A Dictionary of Irish Mythology* 205). The boars's range of attributes for medieval man was varied and contradictory: courageous, rash, debauched, and brutal, but also spiritual. The image of the boar as constellated in Raimondin's psyche had taken on such power as to make his knightly prowess dependent on his ability to hunt down this animal.

His sense of humiliation and defeat following his repeated ineffective lungings at the wild boar suggest the misplaced vanity of an adolescent—a frustration that turned into rage when he saw himself outmaneuvered by what he personified as his duplicitous foe. In blind pursuit of his prey, he made for the heart of the forest. Fearing for the lad's life, the altruistic count of Poitiers ordered him to return. Unheeding, Raimondin bolted further into the darkness of the forest. The uncle, mounting his steed, rode in pursuit of his beloved nephew. When finally he reached him the two stopped to rest.

During the pause, the count studied the contours and movements of the brilliantly incised moon set against a blackened sky filled with constellations. An artful astronomer/astrologer, he read and interpreted the mysteries revealed to him by God, basing his judgments on the configurations and placements of the stars. Raimondin, taken aback by the count's repeated sighs, begged him to share with him the arcana hidden within these distant bodies. Reluctantly, the uncle complied, revealing in deeply disturbing terms his future betrayal and murder by a young vassal, who, in turn, would be enriched and honored as founder of a noble lineage.

Aghast at the thought of anyone killing his beloved uncle, Raimondin refused to believe the prognostications. As the two continued on their way, noises from a thickly wooded area made the boar's presence known, both men thought, as they seized their swords. A dangerous tussle ensued. Although Raimondin urged his uncle to seek shelter in the branches of a high tree, he refused to do so. While pursuing his chase, Raimondin cast his spear at the boar with such violence that the weapon ricocheted, striking the count in the navel and killing him instantly.

Only after the boar's death, indicating symbolically the temporal world's invasion of the spiritual domain, did Raimondin realize what had occurred. Rather than accept his guilt, as behooves a knight, he blamed "treacherous Fortune" for having destroyed a man who "had done him so much good" (*Mélusine* 37). Anxious as always about his own reputation and fearing the punishment that would surely be meted out to him by the count's family and entourage, Raimondin mounted his horse and, increasingly oblivious to the outer world, rode away from the murder scene.

ASTROLOGY/ASTRONOMY. That the Count of Poitiers was knowledgeable in plotting the movements of celestial bodies in order to divine future events was neither unusual nor surprising for the times. On the contrary, astrology/astronomy was a relatively popular art/science among nobles and the intelligentsia in the Middle Ages. Not only were translations of Greek and Arabic scientific and philosophical texts available in twelfth- and thirteenth-century Europe, but chairs in astrology were being awarded increasingly in its universities. Famous astrologers included Guido Bonatti, advisor to the Holy Roman Emperor, Frederick II (b. 1194); Albertus Magnus (1190–1280), the much revered teacher of Thomas Aquinas, an astrologer and an alchemist as well as a theologian; and the Franciscan scientist and philosopher Roger Bacon (1214–1294), a believer in the influence of astral powers on earthly happenings, a practitioner of alchemy. Some contemporaries believed he had even performed successful wonder-working feats. Muslim philosophers such as Alkindi declared certain stars and planets to be endowed with the power to radiate negative influences on humans, thus serving to explain seemingly magical events. Even more significant was the determination that certain constellations could be identified with specific personality types, disclosing, thereby, "a complete projected theory of human character" (Franz, *Projection and Re-Collection* 74).

The science of astronomy or the pseudo-science of astrology, dating back to Chaldean, Assyrian, and Egyptian cultures, had been studied and explored for the most part by priests who made no attempt to separate the two. Practitioners in ancient as well as in medieval times were particularly drawn to detailed studies of planetary positions in the preparation of horoscopes. Numerative schemes used in prognosticating events were based on or inspired by biblical examples, such as the Three Wise Men who followed the Star of Bethlehem and announced the coming of The Divine Child; or the sign of the scorpion, which suggested death and resurrection.

Although no information is given the reader regarding the count's astrological calculations, the certainty of his forwarnings indicates that he was privy to the latest scientific learning on the subject. The nature of his astrological readings was to trigger what Jung referred to as a synchronistic (or acausal) happening: when "concrete events take place in the individual's outer environment that have a meaningful connection with the inner psychic contents that are constellated at about the same time" (Jung, C.W. 8, #855). While observing the constellations, the count was in effect projecting his psychic contents onto matter, that is, interpreting his own inner darkness and morbid fears according to the light of the astral movements and designs he had learned. His intuitive ability to project, to penetrate, and to experience the luminosities emerging from within the blackness of the heavens indicated his recognition of a nonlinear experience, which he recorded in a future time frame and to which he related.

Moreover, the count was dictated by his feeling tones, for why else would he have taken his nephew under his protection when he had children of his own? Why else would he have followed him into the heart of the forest if not to protect the imprudent young man from the wild boar? His emotions expanded in power and density on that fateful night, the resulting reactive charges flowing into his psyche opened him up to a whole numinous sphere— to his inner cosmos. The horoscopic findings and the explanations he offered his nephew reflected the weight of the disabling and disheartening moods flaring in his own unconscious (Franz, *Projection and Re-Collection* 73,91). His affects spoke first, and his thinking function acted only later, making his painful intuitions audible in the form of lamentations and sighs. As M. L. von Franz notes: "[A]ffects lift *one* content, which occupies the forefront of consciousness, into *super*-normal clarity, but at the same time darken the rest of the field of consciousness. This brings about a lowering of the orientation to the external world and therewith a relativization of time and space." (Franz 91).

FROM TRANCE TO EXTASIS. Raimondin's irremediable feelings of bereavement at his uncle's passing soon took on an understandable personal cast: he became what he considered a fugitive from justice and the trauma over his own future became a dominant in his psyche. Victimized by his increasingly corrosive feelings of guilt and loss, the dazed and crazed Raimondin erred into an ever-thickening no man's land, or forest. Lamenting his fate, begging to be imprisoned with the angel Lucifer, then yearning for death, he finally asked Mother Earth to swallow him up, take him back into her protective womb.

Although the brilliantly shining moon lighted Raimondin's outer world, he grew increasingly encased in the semiconsciousness of his trance state. Like Elinas, he arrived at about midnight at the "Fountain of Thirst" or "The Enchanted Fountain." Unlike his predecessor who had stopped at the sight of Présine, our sleeping knight, unaware of Mélusine's existence, breached the knightly code by not even seeing her or the two beautiful ladies flanking her. His lack of courtliness moved the exquisite Mélusine to approach the intruder and, when out of sight of her companions, rebuke him for his lack of civility and disregard of etiquette. Upon realizing that he had been in a deep sleep— that is, withdrawn into himself or deaf to the outer world—she took hold of his hand, thus awakening him to life in all senses of the word.

Startled, the guilt-ridden Raimondin, believing his uncle's men were after him, grabbed his sword. As for Mélusine, she could only laugh at the sight of this helplessly disoriented young man. Dazzled by her beauty, the knight dismounted and admitted that he had neither seen nor heard her, and excused himself for his "villainy." While attempting to justify his inappropriate behavior, he was interrupted by Mélusine, who addressed him by his name and, much to his embarrassment, told him that she was cognizant of his crime, adding boldly that second to God, she was the best person to advise him as to how to profit from his tragic experience. Nor must he, she added, think her a phantom, nor some diabolical creature. To the contrary, she was flesh-and-blood and a good Catholic.

Mélusine's gift of prescience, like the astrological prowess of the count of Poitiers, gave her access to transpersonal realms. Identified with "The Fountain of Thirst" or "The Enchanted Fountain," she was confident of her ever-flowing source of inner knowledge. With nearly contractual precision, she told Raimondin that if he took her advice and agreed to her conditions, he would not only become the richest and the most powerful man of his kingdom, but would be the progenitor of a great lineage. Entranced by Mélusine's beauty, the nonrational and grieving Raimondin could not help but remain spellbound by the archetypal anima figure standing before him. Deeply feeling, but unthinking as to the consequences of the pact into which he was about to enter, he agreed to wed this fascinating and all-comforting avatar of the Great Mother who promised in exchange for the marriage bond to care for him throughout his life. There were, however, ramifications to their agreement. While Mélusine promised to put his empirical travails to an end, Raimondin had to swear never to divulge her identity, nor her heritage, nor attempt to see her on Saturdays. Curiously, no mention is made of her attraction, if any, to Raimondin, or whether her offer to help him is motivated by altruism or her need for a husband. Let us recall that Présine's curse—placing the onus of finding a mate on Mélusine—was the only means at her daughter's disposal of becoming completely humanized and ridding herself of her partially serpent form.

Was Mélusine the answer to Raimondin's previous unconscious death wish—to be embraced by Mother Earth and be taken back into her womb? Perhaps, since the trancelike state to which he had succumbed, in addition to his synchronistic meeting with Mélusine, so markedly diminished his responsiveness to environmental stimuli that it paradoxically brought on a prolonged condition of ecstasy. In keeping with the Greek meaning of the word *extasis*—to derange, to cause to stand out—Raimondin had allowed himself to come under the spell of a savior figure. While such instant dedication to Mélusine presaged a need on his part to blur his own unacceptable reality, it also suggested a complete divestiture of his identity and surrender of his field of consciousness.

MELUSINE AS PSYCHOPOMP AND ANIMA. So rich an archetypal figure was Mélusine, so powerfully did she answer Raimondin's need for healing and for guidance that her aura alone, paradoxically, took on reality for him (Jung, 91,

#102). As a dominant in his psyche, she, like "an immortal daemon that pierces the chaotic darkness of brute life with the light of meaning," became his psychopomp (Jung, 91, #77).

That Mélusine, like her mother, is associated with a fountain located in the heart of a forest, suggests a capacity in both of them to alter, cleanse, heal, and regenerate an ailing psyche. The ever-renewing waters from a fountain, emerging from the depths of the earth (the unconscious), rising into the air (consciousness), may indicate a timeless as well as a restless and continuously mobile quality in mother and daughter. Never would Raimondin know stasis with Mélusine. The fountain's gushing, upwardly thrusting waters were paradigmatic of her ability as anima figure to nourish and help the bereaved and deeply depressed Raimondin to participate in a new life she would create for him, her first task being to heal the malady that had brought on his cognitive dismemberment. As psychopomp, representing an outerworldly sphere, she revealed herself to him as a thrilling, perceptive, and loving presence, an animating power that both lived off itself and generated life as well. Had Mélusine not been endowed with strong, dogmatic, and authoritarian tendencies, she might never have succeeded in luring Raimondin into her world of snares from which, it would become clear, he would never disentangle himself. As Mélusine's relationship with the young knight endured, she, unlike the nixie, mermaid, siren, or wood-nymph, would be be able to acquire the characteristics of a lamia or succubus, those supernatural forces to whom young men—so myths and fairy tales inform us—become emotionally enslaved.

For the immediate present, however, Mélusine functioned for Raimondin as the embodiment of the ancient Moon Goddess, advising him how to proceed in the dark, that is, in deceit and secrecy. As a pledge of her love, she gave him two rings decorated with entwined staffs encrusted with stone. Upon them she had bestowed the power to protect him from death by combat and, should his cause be righteous, bring him victory over those who wished him evil. Her wise yet deceitful counsel to Raimondin was to return to Poitiers, meet with the hunters he had left behind, dissimulate the truth about his uncle's death, convincing them that he had lost sight of him while chasing the boar, and feign shock upon hearing of the count's disappearance. Once his uncle's body would be found, he must persuade his entourage that the boar, and not a human, had been the instrument of death. Everything went as Mélusine had predicted. The entire court mourned the count's passing. The barons, and rightly so, declared their allegiance to his son, Bertrand.

In keeping with Mélusine's commandment, Raimondin returned to her abode, startled to note that during his absence an entire stone chapel had been erected where there had heretofore been an empty prairie; that luxurious surroundings, as well as beautifully clothed damsels, knights, and squires, also appeared on the scene as if by miracle. Before he could assess the marvels that greeted him, he was taken to Mélusine's quarters, where he found her seated in a richly furbished pavilion. She welcomed him and the two dined together. Speaking to him in strong but loving terms, she urged him to first return to Poitiers for Bertrand's installation, then to ask his cousin to grant him a gift of land with no strings attached in return for everything he had done for the count. Raimondin, she added, would have to emphasize the fact that the piece of property, located on the rock above "The Fountain of Thirst," should be only as large as a deer's hide could encircle, and should cost him nothing. On his way home to her, he would meet a man carrying a deer's hide. He must buy it, then have it cut lengthwise into as thin a leather strip as possible, enabling it to encompass a large tract of land. Within its circumference there would be space enough for a river, streams, mountains, valleys, fortresses, castles, windmills, and, indeed, a whole city complex. Wealth and pleasure for concerned citizens would be generated thanks to the future burgeoning of industries and fertile farmlands.

After fulfilling Mélusine's directives, Raimondin was to return to Poitiers and invite the newly installed count, his mother, and friends to their wedding on Monday (moon day) next. Like a refrain, the terms of his pledge and its consequences were reiterated: if his acts and speech remained veiled in secrecy, and he did not view her or come near her on Saturdays, everything he asked for would be granted. If he broke his pact, poverty, failure, sorrow, and dispossession would ensue.

Mélusine's predictions again came to pass. The couple's wedding took place in breathtaking surroundings: pavilions draped in gold and decorated with pearls and precious stones; exquisitely arranged foods served on gold and silver platters to the accompaniment of multiple instrumentalists; jousting bouts for entertainment. During the two weeks of memorable celebrations, the awestruck guests attempted to discover the secrets of Mélusine's illustrious ancestry and how she had amassed such wealth. Their questions were greeted with silence.

As an active living power in Raimondin's psyche, Mélusine was mystery. Her presence not only accentuated the supernatural or fairy tale nature of his depressed and dependent psyche, but nourished it as well. On the other hand, it also suggested that buried within the complexities of Raimondin's hidden tropological (moral) and analogic (mystical) realms, lay an inner and all-important wisdom, which encouraged him to follow Mélusine's dictates as psychopomp and anima figure. For these, he sensed, would allow him to participate in an otherwise unattainable life experience.

THE GNOSTIC SOPHIA/WISDOM AND MELUSINE—AS RATIONAL AND AS ORDERING PRINCIPLE. A psychopomp and anima, Mélusine may also be looked upon as a *daemon* of paradoxical traits including certain qualities attributed to Sophia/Wisdom, as noted in the Valentinian Gnostic myth.

Gnosticism (Gr. *gnostikos,* knowledge), as practiced in France by the Cathars at Orleans in 1022, the Albigensians at Albi in 1208, and the Waldensians at Lyon in 1170, permeated religious thought throughout the Middle Ages. The breach between Christian Gnostic cults—distinguished by the conviction of the never-ending struggle between the dual forces of Good and Evil—and the Roman Catholic Church grew increasingly wider. After declaring Gnostic sects heretical, Pope Innocent III launched a crusade against Albigensians and other Gnostic sympathizers, the issue concluding in the bloodiest of massacres at Montségur. Some Gnostics, the Waldensians in particular, survived the killings either by converting to Catholicism or by emigrating to Lombardy, Spain, Germany, Austria, Poland, Hungary, and Bohemia.[2]

Although the overt practice of Gnosticism was forbidden, the doctrines of this religious group lived on in France clandestinely, even ironically, infiltrating Roman Catholicism. A case in point is the paradigm of the ancient Gnostic image of Sophia/Wisdom, identified in many ways with the healing figure of nursing mother in general, and specifically in the miracles of the Virgin recounted by Cistercian and Dominican monks (Warner, *Alone of her Sex* 198).[3]

Incorporated within Mélusine's personality are certain characteristics of the Gnostic figure of Sophia/Wisdom: the capacity for love, bonding, and relatedness, as evident in her identification with her mother, Présine, and with God; and her ordering and rational activities as spiritual and empirical guide to Raimondin. Mélusine had lived according to her mother's dictates during her formative years, helping her in every way, and meeting her obligations. Similarly Sophia/ Wisdom, lived according to God's rule, "in harmony with what [the Father] ha[d] willed," to the point of being looked upon as God's helper (Pagels, *Adam, Eve, and the Serpent* 75).

Although mother and daughter were saintly in many ways, problems and punishments befell them in the world of contingencies, of conflict, hardship, love, and hate. Disregarding the ruling hierarchical system, Mélusine consequently was chastised for having taken it upon herself to punish her father, while Sophia/Wisdom was penalized for having disregarded the role her father had authorized her to play. Mélusine's dehumanization deriving from her mother's curse would endure, as predicted, for the rest of her days. As for Sophia/Wisdom, to her anguish imposed by supernatural powers was added a diminished status which altered her relationship with deity. No longer would she be known as God's helper, but rather, as the fallible "Thought of God"[4] (Jonas, *The Gnostic Religion* 176). Her lamentations earned her partial "recovery"—she was awarded the supplemental name of Pistis Sophia (Faith Wisdom)—but her suffering continued during her existence as a "soul forlorn in the world" (Jonas 65).

Also important were the semiotic similarities in the punishments awarded to both Mélusine and to Sophia/Wisdom. The former was to live with the fearful reality of transformation of the lower part of her body into a snake every Saturday. While the divine Sophia/Wisdom, according to the Gnostic teachings of St. Irenaeus, was also fated to turn into a snake for having remained "hostile to the creator of Adam," her import was heightened when she was, paradoxically, referred to as being "more prudent than all (others)" (*The Gnostic Scriptures*, trans. and annotated by Bentley Layton 181).

TRACING THE TRAJECTORY OF THE FEMININE PRINCIPLE IN GNOSTICISM. Better to understand Mélusine's impact on Raimondin's psyche, let us briefly trace the trajectory of the feminine principle in her counterpart, the divine Sophia/Wisdom, during the early centuries of Christianity. According to the credo of the Valentinian Gnostics, generally speaking women were "considered equal to men; some were revered as prophets; others, as teachers, traveling evangelists, healers" (Pagels, *The Gnostic Gospels* 60). With the solidification of the feminine principle in Christianity, however, Sophia/Wisdom as incorporated in the image of the Virgin Mary, melded with "Christ as Logos, the Word of God," and thus ceased to be identified with the feminine archetype. In fact, in The Gospel of Thomas, she was rejected in toto: "Simon Peter said to them [the disciples]: 'Let Mary leave us, for women are not worthy of Life.' Jesus said, 'I myself shall lead her, in order to make her male, so that she too may become a living spirit, resembling you males. For every woman who will make herself male will enter the Kingdom of Heaven'" (51:19–26, Pagels 49).

After the Virgin Mary had been "deleted" from the Godhead, "the Christian image of deity as a trinity of Father, Son and Holy Spirit" became identified exclusively with the archetype of the male, nature (female) being looked upon as lower in the hierarchy than spirit (male) (Baring and Cashford, *The Myth of the Goddess* 611). That the male in Roman Catholicism had assumed Sophia/Wisdom's wisdom unto himself suggests that a condition of psychological and sexual confusion permeated the very notion of the godhead. Such usurpation by the male of formerly female characteristics may serve to explain in part why some contemporary critics erroneously identify Mélusine's wisdom, energy, and authoritarianism as exclusively masculine characteristics.

While Mother Nature, unlike some of the Great Mother Deities of antiquity—Isis, Demeter, Cybèle—was downgraded in Christianity and looked upon as subordinate to the male logos and word, the feminine principle was not diminished in Christian Gnostic thought. Indeed, the image of Sophia/Wisdom, as previously noted, was maintained as "the Great Mother, the consort and counterpart of the male aspect of the godhead" (Baring and Caseford 611). Following the suppression of the Gnostic sects by Constantine (326–333), and the affirmation of the doctrines of the Incarnation and the Trinity at the Councils of Nicaea (325 C.E.) and of Chalcedon (451 C.E.), Sophia/Wisdom remained very much alive in altered form throughout the Middle Ages among such groups as the Knights Templar, Hebrew Kabbalists, Islamic philosophers, and troubadours, not to mention her inspiratory role in such creative works as *The Divine Comedy*, *The Romance of the Rose*, the Grail legends, and, of course, the story of our Mélusine.

MELUSINE: BUILDER OF CITIES AND FORTRESSES. Mélusine may be identified not only with Sophia/Wisdom, but with the biblical Cain, who was the first who "builded a city" (Gen. 4:17). Like Cain, Mélusine was a generative power seeking to order, stabilize, and build a future for herself and her successors. That a woman should be identified with this function points to her uniqueness, as builders were usually men (e.g., Daedalus or the Hindu Vishvakarma). Unlike Cain, who had killed his brother, Abel, Mélusine had not murdered, but she had imprisoned her father within a mountain, which was tantamount to a living burial. Both Cain and Mélusine would have to bear the "mark" of shame throughout eternity (Gen. 4:15). The years of travail expiating the sin against the father may have inspired her to enter the esoteric order of the Masons, who had formed strong guilds in France during the Middle Ages. Upon initiation, each member of the society was obliged to take a vow of secrecy. Similarly, Mélusine imposed a vow on Raimondin, as Présine had on Elinas prior to their wedding—or initiation into matrimony.

The mystical order of the Masons not only built monuments, but were looked upon as builders of souls—or inner worlds. Since their construction of Solomon's Temple (1000 B.C.E.) in Jerusalem, they knew, according to the mystic Hermes Trismegistus (or the Thrice Great), that what existed beneath the ground also pointed toward heavenly spheres. Like the heavenly Jerusalem of the New Testament, referred to as "the mother of us all: (Gal. 4:26). Mélusine's fortified cities were built to contain the protecting and nurturing aspects of the archetypal Mother within them. Her secret knowledge enabled her to lay the foundation of future fiefdoms for her husband and progeny. Her earth- and celestial-oriented understanding, endowed her with the potential of transmuting human energy into higher, purer, and more spiritually directed works. Because of her capacity to maintain the castles, towers, monasteries, and other fortifications she had constructed, peasants and animals alike could take refuge in her fiefdoms. Indeed, she was in all senses of the word a head of state.[5] As noted by the historian Georges Duby: "Each chief who was responsible for the fortified castle, within a canton composed of forests and clearings, pieced together around that fortress a small independent state" (Duby, *The Age of the Cathedrals* 33). While not the "lord," dominus, she was the lady, domina, of her domain and of its inhabitants. Her constructs symbolized her personal power and the sovereignty and ascendancy of her future lineage.

At the outset of the building process, Mélusine, encouraging her workers to burrow within the earth, was adhering symbolically to the ancient Masonic credo—*Visita interiora terrae, rectifi-candoque, invenies occultum.* Just as the secret society of Masons—using the plumb, square, level, and compass—was said to have been instrumental in building great monuments in ancient times, such as the Temple of Solomon, so the special privileges its members enjoyed in the medieval era encouraged them to participate in the construction of many of the great cathedrals of Europe. Their work was earth-oriented as they laid the foundations, and ascensionally inspired as they built upward. Not only were they cognizant of the polarities involved in bringing their engineering feats to fruition but, as members of their fraternal order, they were preoccupied with the spiritual values involved: *physis* and *gnosis*.

Like the Masons, Mélusine proceeded in an ordered and methodical manner, using symbols to gather around her and to direct sufficiently large numbers of trained construction workers. Her rigorous method, directed by her thinking function, proceeded as follows: the felling of the thickly forested areas; the digging of ditches; the leveling of mountainous regions within the boundaries that had been awarded her; the hauling of megalithic stones into the city complex in order to lay the foundations of future buildings, their hoisting into place to be sized and fitted in the construction of the walls and roofs of the future fortresses, chapels, and castles. Her many constructs with their architectural and architectonic complexities, the elegance of their high-roofed dungeons, their imposing towers with machicolations and crenelated walls, began dotting the landscape with impressive speed. In virtually *no time*, that is, in the timelessness of fairy tale moments, thickly walled enclaves, posterns, abbeys, boroughs, castles, fortresses, chapels, and churches came into being.

According to some of the uninitiated, Mélusine's accomplishments verged on the miraculous! But aren't similar opinions verbalized by our contemporaries when looking at the great European cathedrals, the Egyptian and South American pyramids, and the sculptured monuments of Angkor Wat?

Melusine's constructs, systems of defense, and houses of worship were graceful, beautiful, comfortable, and safe—the thought of protecting the city dwellers against enemies and intruders being of utmost concern to her. May it be said as well that to penetrate her city's portals was tantamount to entering the inner sanctuary of a living mystery—its arcana being known to Mélusine alone.

MELUSINE: THE POWER BEHIND THE MILITARY. Although details are glossed over in Jean d'Arras's tale, history informs us that Mélusine's constructional achievements were identified with some of the most famous castles and fortresses of the time: Mervent, Vouvant, St. Maixent, Parthenay, Châtelaillon, Talmont—some of these surrounded by moats and protective walls sixteen to twenty feet thick. Nor had she neglected the restoration of ancient monuments, including the great tower, known as the English tower, erected by Julius Caesar.[6]

Not only was Mélusine a builder of cities, but, like the biblical Deborah, she was the programmer of Raimondin's military junkets. He must, she told him, retake the lands that had been so treacherously wrenched from his father by usurpers. By ridding the area of such infringers, he would not only be avenging his father's stalwart reputation, but would be retaking his rightful heritage. The valiant Raimondin, in spite of the plots and counterplots hatched against him by the felons and their families, fulfilled his dangerous mission dexterously. He retrieved for his cousins the lands that were rightfully destined to them. In response to Mélusine's compliments for his valor, he replied modestly that he had succeeded in his encounters "thanks to God and to you" (*Mélusine* 139). Having succumbed to Mélusine's erotic charms, Raimondin not only accepted, but predictably grew dependent on her wise counsel in political, social, economic, religious, and military matters.

THE PUER AETERNUS. The couple's marriage was love-filled but one may wonder whether Mélusine's wisdom and libido (psychic energy) stultified Raimondin to the point of impeding his emotional development? Was he destined to remain forever a puer aeternus because of Mélusine's formidable powers? It may be averred that he was psychologically stillborn from the very outset of their relationship, and he had never attempted to deal rationally with problems at hand. He certainly had never faced nor struggled through the implications of his accidental murder of his uncle. Nor had he ever demonstrated an urge to seek an outlet for his own creative energies—other than what was suggested by his dynamic wife.

As an authority figure and a paragon of wisdom, Mélusine was self-contained, reasoned, measured, and loving. Rarely if ever, did she inspire in her husband anything save admiration and love. A mother figure par excellence, Raimondin obeyed her every wish/command, behaving like a child, forever gratified by a mother's incredible gifts. As a passive recipient, never did he attempt to amplify, question, or absorb her intellectual or psychological riches with the goal of furthering his own inner development. Had he, who adored but must have also feared Mélusine, abdicated all notions of independence? Would she continue to function simply as a conduit leading to his further emotional crippling, to the point of rendering him incapable of thinking through the minutest of problems himself? (Jung, 9, #53 ff).

The archetypal figure of Mélusine was a power principle who evidently answered a need in Raimondin. Had not such strong women of the past fit the conscious or unconscious ideal of many men who had lost their way in life; or who had lived with the corrosive onus of sin? Mélusine, the pragmatist, despite her mother's curse, strove to achieve greater humanity, greater activity, and greater knowledge—building cities, distributing funds to the poor, and activating human relationships. She was continuously catalyzed into action—perhaps her way of expelling her sense of humiliation for the half-snake physicality that had been imposed on her.

To avoid castigation by his peers, Raimondin had escaped into the forest after his uncle's murder, thereby repressing his act. His reputation would remain intact in the outer world. Nor did he ever grapple with his sin; the impulsive, irrational shadowy side of his personality remained closeted. By rejecting his act, he eluded any haunting repercussions. Nonetheless, he lived with the reality of fear: fear of reprisals, fear of humiliation by family, courtiers, or other knights, fear of discovery of his inadvertent, yet evil deed. He snakily slithered away from any and all responsibility. Mélusine brought him temporary happiness, but her dominance served to both devaluate his sense of self-worth and to diminish his already severely marred thinking function.

A one-sided approach to life and its problematics may block further understanding of one's intentions, reflections, and ability to adapt to situations. Without a relatively objective exploration and dissection of an event, deed, statement, or relationship, one of two extremes is likely to come to the fore: the shadow or the sublime side of the individual, who thus will never know balance.

Mélusine being the sole object of Raimondin's wonderment and fascination, her image traced a powerful trajectory in his psyche, even while stunting his independence and threatening an abdication on his part of all possible potential. Not surprisingly, then, would Raimondin play the puppet/adolescent role in his marital relationship.

THE TEN CHILDREN. Reminiscent of the fertility goddess Cybèle, whose Roman icon featured her upholding small towers representing the cities she protected, so Mélusine, the builder, the provider, became during the course of her married life the mother of ten healthy children for whom she cared with love and devotion. Much to the sorrow of the parents, only the last two offspring were completely normal, the others having been born with a series of congenital defects: one red and one blue eye, a single eye, one eye higher than the other, one small and one large ear, a cheek bearing the imprint of a lion's claw, a monstrously large tooth that jutted out of the child's mouth, and another child with a propensity for cruelties, and so forth. Could these congenital flaws be understood as paradigmatic of some outstanding psychological problems existing in the parents and/or their marital relationship?

As Raimondin's life unfolds, his psychological impotence becomes increasingly obvious to readers. His incipient unconscious frustration and his lack of initiative in empirical matters were reflected in his inability to deal with the stress caused by his children's abnormalities. Inasmuch as birth defects in the Middle Ages were ascribed to a mother's adulterous affairs, doubts may have been activated in Raimondin's mind as to his wife's purity, thereby adding irritants to his already exacerbated querulousness.

THE FIRST TRANSGRESSION: BATH AND/REVELATION. Commendably, Raimondin observed for long years the oath he had taken not to look at Mélusine on Saturdays, when she withdrew into her the well-bolted secret chamber, nor to question her reasons for secluding herself. But on one particular Saturday, Raimondin's half-brother, the Count of Forez, paid him a visit during which they attended mass and dined together, both delighting in each other's company. To the count's query about Mélusine's whereabouts, the naive *puer*, never suspecting his guest's ulterior motive, answered graciously that he would see her the following day. Leaning toward him, and speaking in confidential but artful terms, the count made reference to the medieval superstition associated with birth defects, suggesting to Raimondin that rumor circulated to the effect that every Friday Mélusine yielded to debaucheries, making penance on Saturdays.

Stunned by his half-brother's insinuations and "drunk with rage," Raimondin stirred up in his mind the doubts he had nurtured all these years about his wife's fidelity. Rising abruptly from the table, Raimondin went to his room, seized his sword, and rushed to Mélusine's bolted secret chamber. After boring a hole in the iron door with his sword, he peered into the room, where he saw Mélusine bathing in a marble tub around fifteen feet in circumference. Upon closer scrutiny, he noticed she was combing her hair, and, although her upper torso was that of a woman, from her umbilicus downward her body had taken the shape of a snake's huge tail, which splashed about in the tub, flooding the chamber. His rage now dissipated, he not only realized the baseness of his act and its implications, but cursed himself for having doubted Mélusine's fidelity. Running to his room, he took some wax from one of his letters, returned to the scene of the crime, and filled in the hole he had made in the iron door. Moments later, he returned to his brother in the great hall. "Flee from here, ignoble traitor!" Raimondin shrieked. "Your infamous lies forced me to perjure myself," to castigate "the most loyal and the best of ladies, second only to the one who bore our creator" (*Mélusine* 231).

Several factors are involved in the bath ritual. Let us first note that in ancient times bathing was considered by some to be a means of purification and regeneration (for example, in myths about Athena, Hera, and Artemis). Christians linked it to baptismal rituals (John was the Baptizer of Christ). Nonetheless, it may be noted that an erotic element was also associated with bathing: David, for example, "saw a woman [Bathesheba] washing herself; and the woman was very beautiful to look upon [inciting him to lie] with her; for she was purified from her uncleanliness" (II Sam.1:2:4). The Church fathers considered the act of exposing the body lascivious and sinful—an indication of an over-preoccupation with *physis*. Particularly notorious in arousing the male were communal and hot baths, which understandably were forbidden by the fathers of the Church. In contrast, St. Augustine agreed that women should be allowed to bathe once a month.

That Mélusine was combing her hair while bathing introduced an erotic note to the picture, bringing to mind Mary Magdalen, frequently represented iconographically in the Middle Ages with long and loosely hanging hair symbolizing her abandon to God. Her body, so it was claimed, having been discovered in the crypt of St. Maxin's church in Aix-en-Provence in 1279, gave birth to a flourishing cult revolving around Mary Magdalene. Even more stunning is the tale in the *Golden Legends*, by Jacobus de Voragine, revolving around Mary Magdalene preaching Christianity in the forest of Sainte-Beaume (Warner, *Alone of her Sex* 228*)*.

Like other supernatural creatures, namely, the amphibious sirens and water sprites, or the half-woman, half-bird harpies, or doglike Erinyes, Mélusine may be identified with cold, enigmatic, and unfeeling chthonian primordial powers. Understandably so, since she relied on her creative energy, her perceptions, and her sense of commitment to fight against her predicted destiny. Female powers, as builders, thinkers, or procreators of worlds, have frequently been associated with snakes, vipers, and dragons: the dragon Tiamat in the Sumerian *Enuma Elish*; the Greek Medusa, whose strands of hair were characterized as snakes by Hesiod and Pausanius; Eve, convinced by the serpent that she would expand her understanding if she ate from the *Tree of Knowledge*. Had not St. George and St. Michael been known as heroic dragon/snake slayers, thus, symbolically, as killers of female energy? Because the snake motif in Judaism and in Christianity was linked to Eve/Evil, and to the legendary Lilith, Adam's first wife in post-biblical legends, both women were blamed for the Fall and for menstruation. One may suggest that Mélusine's bath may also be considered a paradigm of the ancient Hebraic monthly cleansing ritual, the *mikveh*, which served to cleanse women of all impurities (Lev. 15:28).

The snake, a crawling animal, was alluded to in some twelfth-century bestiaries as "the slippery one." Those who feared its venom went so far as to liken it to the dragon.

> Adam was deceived by Eve, not Eve by Adam. Consequently it is only good sense that the man, who was first got into trouble by the woman, should now take the leadership, for fear that he should once again be ruined by feminine whims.
>
> Well, is a man always to be choosing new wives? Even a horse loves truly and an ox seeks one single mate. And if one ox is changed in a yoke of oxen, the other one cannot drag the yoke but feels uncomfortable. Yet you women put away your husbands and think that you ought to be changing frequently. . . . Adultery is unpleasant, it is an injury to nature. (White, *The Bestiary* 171ff.)

How may these harpings be interpreted except to say that they simply reiterate age-old deprecation of the female sex?

WHY SATURDAYS? The Jewish sabbath may have played a greater role than at first suspected in Mélusine's weekly bathing ritual. Ironically, despite the massacres of Jews in France during the Crusades in 1096, 1147, 1189, and other years, the blame heaped on them for the outbreak of the Plague in 1348, and the burning of their books (notably the Talmud in Paris in 1240), the influence of Jews, albeit limited, was present in French intellectual circles.[7] Hebrew scholars doggedly pursued their writings on Kabbala, grammar, philosophy, poetry, as well as biblical exegeses. Nathan ben Isaac's arrival in Narbonne, for example, was followed by the establishment of a Talmudic academy. The works of Rashi (b. 1040), a native of Troyes, and one of the greatest Talmudic and biblical commentators of all time, were translated into Latin in the thirteenth century. Some of his followers—Samson of Sens, Moses of Evreu, Joseph ben Isaac of Orléans, Jehiel ben Joseph of Paris, Jacob of Chinon (1100-1300)—became known for their commentaries on scriptural law (Kravitz, *3,000 Years of Hebrew Literature* 319ff. ; Sholem, *Major Trends in Jewish Mysticism* 85).

The seventh day of the week was chosen as the Jewish sabbath, in keeping with biblical injunctions (Gen. 2: 1–3; Ex. 20: 8–11). Saturday (Fr. *samedi*; L. *sabbati dies*; Heb. "shabbath" <shabbath, to rest) was set aside for prayer, study, and relaxation. Such spiritual activities were intended to abolish anguishing and oppressive thoughts in the worshipper, thus liberating the soul for the contemplation of God.

Let us also note that, according to Masonic credo Mélusine paid her workers very generously and on Saturday, the very same day she withdrew from the human world as penance for having sinned against the father. Was it to make amends for her transgression that she increased her charitable deeds toward the poor and gave extra meat and wine to them on that day?

Some, but not all scholars maintain that the word *shabbath* was etymologically linked to the Babylonians *sabattu*—"the day of rest which the moon takes when full"—and therefore may be identified with Ishtar, their Moon Goddess. Her menstrual cycle, however, symbolized evil, sickness, and pollution, so that in this case, its meaning would be antithetical to the very notion of the Hebrew sabbath (Harding, *Woman's Mysteries* 62ff.). Prohibitions aimed at menstruating women appear in religious laws the world over, whether written or endorsed by Manu, Zoroaster, Moses, Christ, or the Christian fathers. It comes as no surprise that this natural function associated with women was believed to be noxious. In ancient and medieval times, as previously mentioned, the moon, whose shapes altered during the course of the month, was not only identified with menstrual cycles, but with factors influencing women's personalities and moods. During the "upper-world phase, corresponding to the bright moon, she is good, kind, and beneficent. In the other phase, corresponding to the time when the moon is dark, she is cruel, destructive, and evil" (Harding 111). Not surprisingly, then, the full moon at times, was associated with the woman's shadowy, secret, arcane, chthonian side, and the witch's *sabbat*, with its nocturnal revels, orgies, and practices in celebration of devil worship. "From the Christian point of view it is well-nigh impossible to conceive of a God who is at once kind and cruel, who creates and destroys. For God is conceived of as good; evil is always the work of the devil" (Harding 111). But then, who created the Devil—or Prince of Darkness—if not God?[8]

MELUSINE'S SERPENTINE FORM. Mélusine, considering her cold-blooded serpentine personality a humiliation and a disfigurement, kept it hidden from all would-be eyes, unlike Isis, who wore the royal cobra on her forehead *(uraeus)* in full view of the world at large; nor like Hecate, who revealed herself as partly snake; nor like Ishtar, depicted sometimes as covered with snake scales (Harding 53).

That Raimondin did not react negatively to Mélusine's serpentine form upon his first sight of her in her bath may have been due to his extreme relief that any thought of adultery could be annulled. He may also have associated the waters splashing out of her tub with the ablutionary, sacramental, and baptismal waters of Christian ritual. In either case, in his self-centeredness, he gave no thought at all to Mélusine's torment or victimization due to her physical malformation. Obsessed exclusively with his own pain, what he feared most with regard to the violation of his oath would be its terrifying re-purcussions on his life.

Rushing to his room, out of Mélusine's hearing, the emotionally dis-abled Raimondin cried out his sorrow in secret. "Ah! Mélusine, about whom everyone has said such wonderful things. I have just lost you forever. I have just lost beauty, goodness, ternderness, affection, wisdom, delicacy, charity, humility, all my joy, all my comfort, all my hope, all my happiness, my pros-perity, my glory, my valor . . . " (*Mélusine* 232). Just as he had done after the murder of his uncle, Raimondin castigated "blind, hard, bitter Fortune" for having caused him to break his oath. Instead of assuming the guilt, he attrib-uted his nefarious act to an abstract principle—Fortune—resorting once again to repression and dissimulation of his crime. Was he to blame for such deceit? Not entirely. Hadn't his mentor, Mélusine, a politician and pragmatist at heart, taught him to use deception to gain his end? The count, Raimondin's half-brother, had worked in tandem with Fortune, thus becoming a flesh-and-blood scapegoat for Raimondin's latest sin. It had not been he who lacked confidence in his wife's integrity, but the count who had insinuated her adul-terous comportment, which alleviated somewhat his psychological impotence.

When Mélusine entered their bedroom at dawn, the distraught Rai-mondin pretended to be asleep. He observed her undressing and slipping into bed next to him. His feigned sighs and moans caused her to bend over and kiss him and to ask him whether he was ill, even though she was aware of his breach of faith. Replying in the affirmative, he complained of a fever. As if comforting a child, her soothing words promised him full recovery, "God willing." Since secrecy had been maintained concerning his transgres-sion, their relationship continued as before, at least on the surface. Both rose the following morning, went to mass, ate, and the day afterward Mélusine left for Niort, where she saw to the construction of another fortress, this time with twin towers.

WHY SECRECY? WHY TABOOS? Secrecy and taboos, be they in Masonry, Gnosticism, or other religious cults, in the sciences, or in the arts, produce a yearning in individuals to experience the awesomeness of the unknown, or a need to relieve the terror and/or mysteries of the infinite: the *mysterium tremendum*. While some feel compelled to disclose their innermost secrets or unburden themselves of painful thoughts or behavior, as in confession, oth-ers conceal or repress their feelings of humiliation, thus protecting them-selves and their acts against vilification. According to Jung, secrets may

> act like psychic poison that alienates their possessor from the community.
> In small doses, this poison may be an invaluable medicament, even an

essential precondition of individual differentiation, so much so that even on the primitive level man feels an irresistible need actually to invent secrets: their possession safeguards him from dissolving in the featureless flow of unconscious community life and thus from deadly peril to his soul. (Jung, 16, # 124)

Mélusine's fear of disclosing her deformity—the punishment for her sin— created a virtually insoluble schism within her psyche. Her determination to hide her serpentine form obliged her to always keep her *affects* under control. Restrained and self-disciplined to the extreme, she possessed an "ascetic continence," "stoical endurance," and "self-restraint" that allowed her to separate her inner guilt-laden shame from the external world and encouraged her rational sphere to take over. In her isolation from others, her loneliness served to magnify what her ego considered her imperfect, inferior aspect. To compensate for her prevailing inner void, she doubled her building and humanitarian projects, shutting herself off increasingly from her own vital feeling world.

May Mélusine's behavioral patterns be metaphorized by her snake-like acts—the imprisoning of her father without her mother's knowledge, the duplicity of her directives to Raimondin, disculpating him in the eyes of others? The ruse of the deer's pelt to acquire a large tract of land for the city-state she would build to afford her citizens a higher standard of living might certainly have been inspired by Dido's equally ingenious act in Virgil's *Aeneid*.

Was altruism, we might ask, at the root of Mélusine's projects? The answer remains moot. Whatever the conclusion, her inability to face the "the cave of the unconscious" prevented her from achieving self-enlightenment. Had she explored the reasons behind each of her projects, she might have been able to partially distinguish the conflictual polarities that had been tearing her apart. Like an automaton, she continued in her behavioral patterns, reinforcing her built-in rationalizations and her lack of perception in her emotional involvements. The monstrous snake so deeply hidden within her for these long years had diverted her libido (psychic energies) from focusing on her ego-development. To correct her one-sidedness would have required renunciation of her comfortable dual existence—by the opening up of her closeted, vulnerable, sensitive, affective, and undifferentiated side. Instead this one-sidedness had served to blind her vision into herself (Jung, *Visions Seminars* II, 310).

THE SERPENT AS HEALER. For Aesculapius, the semidivine healer and God of doctors whose clinic was at Epidaurus, the serpent was daimon. It symbolized both healing and poisonous properties, as it did for alchemists and other hermeticists in the Middle Ages. Lest it be forgotten, Christ as well had been identified with the serpent in Gnostic and Christian iconography:

His blood is the essence of his life, and the healing poison for the world. Only when Christ puts that magic drop of his essence into the chalice does the wine become blood, only then does it become magic, the medicine of immortality . . . . [For although the church persecuted the Gnostics as heretics] it absorbed as much, if not more, from the heresies as from antiquity. (Jung, Visions Seminars I, 199)

Within Mélusine's soul/psyche there existed a serpent factor, represented by a "good-evil" spirit, referred to as a daimon, and an "evil one," labeled demon (Franz, *Projection* 138). Had the chemical contents of one or the other been blended and measured according to formulaic proportions, the mixture of poisons could have decanted their healing powers on either one of our protagonists. Had Mélusine and Raimondin understood the necessity of balancing undeveloped antithetical contents—the shadow, anima, animus—in their personalities, they would have experienced a new connectedness, which would have enabled them to function wholeheartedly, that is, in keeping with their individual psychic systems.

The symbol of the *uroborus* (the Gnostic symbol of the snake biting its tail, thus forming a circle), imaged frequently by psychologists, came to represent undifferentiated wholeness. This animal that crawls on the ground has been associated with primordial waters surrounding the earth and/or the womb. That Mélusine and Mary were identified with both water and the serpent linked them as well with fertility—reservoirs of potential life, and/or as yet unaccessed energy—and with the capacity for fidelity, love, and joy in the human sphere (Warner, *Alone of All her Sex* 259, 274).

THE SECOND TRANSGRESSION. Raimondin's violation of the taboo broke the condition of stasis between husband and wife and revealed Mélusine's inability to succor her partner by her miraculous feats. Would Raimondin's extreme emotional stress lead to the eventual destruction of their marriage?

A traumatic incident triggered the climax of our fairy tale. Their son, Geoffroy the Big Tooth, having become morbidly distressed to learn that his brother, Froidmond, had become a monk, gave vent to his titanic instincts by burning down the abbey in which his brother lived. Not only his brother, but all the monks inside died in the flames. Raimondin's sorrow at the loss of Froidmond exploded into uncontrollable outrage against his wife who, as previously mentioned, had gone to Niort to attend to her latest building projects, for having given birth to congenitally deformed children.

By the faith I owe to my God, I believe this woman to be an evil spirit. I don't believe that the fruit of her womb could possibly be completely good, for the children she brought into the world bear some kind of strange sign. . . . Didn't I see their mother on Saturday in the form of a serpent from her umbilicus down? She is a type of malignant spirit, or an apparition, an illusion who has deceived me. Didn't she, the very first time we met, know everything about me? (Mélusine 247)

Raimondin's barons, failing to appease his pain, called Mélusine back from Niort. She attempted to explain to her husband that God absolves those who repent, and that Geoffroy would certainly do so, but to no avail. Nor did she succeed in healing his sorrow by underscoring the mystery behind God's acts: since the monks of the abbey were dissolute, she told him they had betrayed their monastic vows and, therefore, had to die. Having transformed Geoffroy into an instrument of God, she concluded that since Raimondin had the means, he could now build an even greater abbey for God's followers. By way of concluding her argumernt, she admonished him to cease his lamentions over an action already committed and for which there was no remedy. Rather than assuaging his sorrow, however, her justification of Geoffroy's act—as earlier she had supported Raimondin's own crime—succeeded only in firing his wrath.

Overwhelmed and enraged by Mélusine's words which only heightened his sense of bereavement, he shouted out the *unspeakable* to his wife and to their entourage. "Ah! Infamous serpent, in the name of God, you and your actions are but illusion. Never will any of the children you carried come to a good end" (*Mélusine* 250).

Was Raimondin unconsciously attempting to extricate himself from Mélusine/snake?—which he looked upon as the female principle? Was he rejecting everything she had done for him? Or had this incident served in part to disclose his own inadequacies as well as those of his wife? Or was he, like St. George, St. Patrick, St. Michael, Marduk, Indra, attempting to annihilate the serpent/dragon—that formidable personification of *woman*—that had taken hold of his life?

Stripped of its veneer, Raimondin's undifferentiated thinking function reigned anew, this time in conformity with medieval thought: *woman*, as Mélusine/Sophia/Wisdom, must be chastised for her ignominies. Having regressed to his preconscious forest level, Raimondin slithered into a world of extremes, where woman was either saintly like the Virgin Mary, or evil like Eve/Serpent. No middle course was possible.

Such an approach to the feminine principle brings to mind the experience of the martyr, Perpetua of Carthage. A product of the "patriarchal one-sidedness of the early Christian God-image," she was transformed into a man in order to fight the "giant Egyptian, [that is] the spirit of heathendom." She accomplished her goal by denying her "feminine consciousness and her physical reality" (Franz, *Projection* 138). So Raimondin, in a moment of truth, looked at Mélusine, his Savior and Protectress, his "feminine consciousness," as an evil, rejecting her as woman, wife, and mother.[9]

Upon hearing Raimondin's words, the emotionally flayed Mélusine lost consciousness. By the time the barons revived her, his temper had cooled, having been replaced by feelings of grief and loss. Bemoaning the day she had met Raimondin and allowed herself to fall in love with his handsome face, body, and courteous ways, Mélusine knew that his betrayal had sealed their fates.

> Although you failed to keep your promise, I had pardoned you in my heart for having tried to see me, for you had revealed the secret to no one, and God would have pardoned you after having done penance in this world. Alas, my friend, our love has now been transformed into hatred, our tenderness into cruelty, our pleasures and our joys, into tears and sobs, our happinesss into terrible misfortune and harsh calamity. Alas, my friend, had you not betrayed me, I would have been saved from pain and torment, I would have lived out the natural course of my life as a normal woman, and would have died normally, receiving the sacraments of the church and buried at Notre-Dame de Lusignan. . . . But because of you, I shall have to suffer penance [for her sin against her father] until Judgment Day, because you betrayed me. May God absolve you! (Mélusine 252)

Prior to her departure from his world, Mélusine asked Raimondin to fulfill several requests to which he agreed. The first was to put to death their three-eyed son for the evil deeds he was predestined to commit; then to protect their other children from the malignancy of those who would call her a fairy or an evil woman. Handing her husband two golden rings that would protect him in battle, she revealed her identity to him and to the court: she was the daughter of King Elinas of Albania and of Queen Présine.

As if miraculously provided with wings, Mélusine uttered a deep sigh, and like the living soul that she was, flew out of the window. During her flight she was transformed into a sixteen-foot serpent. Three times she encircled the fortress, uttering such a piercing cry of sorrow, each time she passed the window where her husband and courtiers had gathered, that everyone "wept with compassion" (*Mélusine* 259). Suddenly, she hurled herself against one of the towers she had herself built, creating such a deafening noise that everyone mistakenly thought the fortress had collapsed. Then, flying in the direction of Lusignan, she vanished from sight.

Although Raimondin was never to see his wife again in the form of a woman, it was said that she returned each night to Lusignan, where seen but unrecogized by the nurses, who kept secret the miraculous event, she breast fed her two youngest infants until they were weaned. Wise in the ways of the world and in those of the heart, the archetypal eternal mother figure that was Mélusine remained available in time of need to her progeny, and to her beloved Raimondin—her secret companion through eternity. In the years to come, as Mélusine revealed herself in serpent form three days prior to the demise of each of her descendents until the last member of her lineage had died, her presence became manifest by her screams of despair. (Still today in France a sudden scream is known as *un cri de Mélusine*.)

The last lap of Raimondin's earthly sojourn was spent in profound devotion, including a penitential pilgrimage to Rome, after which he withdrew as a hermit to a high mountain retreat in the monastery of Monserrat in Aragon, where "the moon and the serpent as divine attributes" survive, having been awarded to Mary, who "is venerated [there] as a source of fertility and delight" (Warner 274). Following his demise, Raimondin's body was brought back to Lusignan and was interred after the celebration of a funeral mass at the church of Notre-Dame.

As dream images, Présine and Mélusine represented highly rational women who not only thought out their every act, but knew how to deal pragmatically with each situation in a down-to-earth manner. Their husbands saw them, depending on the circumstances, as their beloveds, their desirable and empirical spouses, and their exalted and idealized soul figures. Because neither husband developed a sense of himself, nor a personality of his own, his instinctual fears led him to break a taboo—thus to self-destruct.

By victimizing and anathematizing Mélusine, Raimondin—the more interesting of the two men—revealed how solidly he identified with society's archetypal view of women, thereby serving as his wife's executioner. The joys she brought him, the architectural wonders she erected, the children she bore him, the wealth she secured for the Lusignan family, no longer mattered. Like the penitents of the Middle Ages, Mélusine and Raimondin would both pay for their transgressions through mortification of the body/soul complex.

Like the Gnostics who had assigned to women the right to heal, teach, prophesy, even hold the rank of bishop, Mélusine had taken it upon herself to heal Raimondin's being. She did not, however, indoctrinate him into the process of *metanoia* in order to awaken his psyche to the necessity of "turning [itself] around" so that it could "face the inner world of the soul." Instead, as an indulgent mother, she gave him every possible material gift, believing that these alone would contribute to his happiness (Franz, *Projection* 158; from *Poimandres*).

As builder of towers and fortresses, ruler of kingdoms, regulator of her husband's, her family's, and her community's life, Mélusine's had formidable preternatural powers, which had, paradoxically, blinded her to the one ungraspable power she had undertaken to control and to dominate—human nature—allotted to divinity to direct.

Mélusine cried out her sorrows, as did Wisdom, that eternal force within each individual which seeks to be heard:

> Wisdom crieth without; she uttereth her voice in the streets:
>> She crieth in the chief place of concourse, in the openings of the gates: in the city she uttereth her words, saying,
>> How long, ye simple ones, will ye love simplicity? and the scorners delight in their scorning, and fools hate knowledge? (Proverbs 1:20–22)

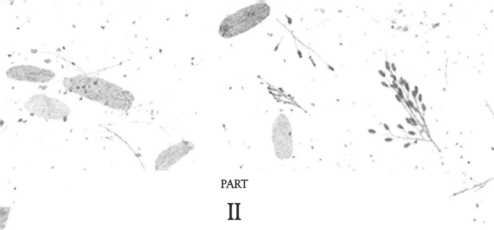

THE SEVENTEENTH CENTURY
"LE GRAND SIÈCLE"

THE SEVENTEENTH CENTURY—"le grand siècle"—began quite inauspiciously. The period was rife with political instability and religious wars—Catholics killing Protestants. Wisdom prevailed somewhat only after the the peace-loving Henry IV (1553-1610) was named king. A Protestant by birth and by conviction, he converted to Catholicism to placate the majority of the French, uttering his famous affirmation, "Paris is worth a mass." In1598, he issued the ground-breaking "Edict of Nantes," granting Protestants freedom of worship. To alleviate the economic hardships plaguing his country, he appointed the duke of Sully to restore its finances, a task he accomplished successfully. Although he enjoyed enormous popularity with his people, Henry IV was assassinated by François Ravaillac, plunging the French into sorrow.

Henry IV's son, Louis XIII (1601-1643), only nine years old at the death of his father, became king, and his mother, Marie de Medicis, an unintelligent and highly superstitious woman, regent. Fighting again raged between Catholics and Protestants, the most violent episode being the siege of the latter's stronghold of Montauban in 1621. By 1624, the political situation had become so unsettled that the king appointed cardinal Richelieu (1585-1642) to direct the affairs of state. This militant man of the cloth who had his own war agenda impressed the nation when, armed conflict against Austria having broken out (1524-1525), he personally directed on horseback the operations leading to the siege of La Rochelle (1628). The cardinal's astute manipulations led to the disabling of Protestants at Montauban

(1629), and among other military conflagrations, war with Spain in 1635. Richelieu wielded such power that anyone conspiring against him or the throne was summarily executed. Plots and counterplots hatched by Richelieu gave rise to cloak-and-dagger politics based on intrigue and deception, concluding with the "Thirty Years War" (1618–1648) which established France's hegemony in Europe. Not only the creator of *absolutism* in France, Richelieu, a would-be playwright, was deeply involved as well in theater and the regulation of social behavior (he outlawed dueling). Much to his credit, he founded the still-extant French Academy.

Cardinal Mazarin (1602–1661), appointed after Richelieu's demise, was also a fine diplomat, and in this capacity an unscrupulous hypocrite who amassed a fortune for himself. Anne of Austria, the mother of Louis XIV (1638–1715), who served as regent during his minority, appointed Mazarin to govern. Under his direction, during the king's minority, wars pursued their course, with the triumphs of heroes such as Turenne and Condé, which led to the signing of the advantageous Peace of Westphalia (1648). But Mazarin's extreme unpopularity was instrumental in fomenting riots in Paris (1648–1652), known as the Fronde ("a child's game"). These disturbances not only warranted the erection of barricades in the city, but provoked two unforgettably romanesque events. "The Great Condé," France's military hero, was ordered to besiege Paris to quell the riots. He carried out his mission successfully, but judging his reward insufficient, he allied himself with Spain and marched on Paris, to find the gates of the city locked. High drama followed: the cannons of the Bastille thundered; the great doors of the city opened, and Mlle de Montpensier, the famous Grande Demoiselle, daughter of Gaston d'Orléans and a self-appointed general, mounted the platform of the Bastille and so as to protect Condé, ordered the great cannons to fire on the royal troops.

Louis XIV, "The Sun King," as he was called, despite his inglorious act of repealing the Edict of Nantes in 1685, ushered in one of the most glorious reigns, artistically speaking, that France had ever known. Mazarin, who had attempted to restore France's financial and economic stability, recommended to the monarch the appointment of Colbert as minister of finance. While favoring protectionist tariffs on industry and commerce, Colbert also encouraged arts and letters. His attempts to diminish Louis XIV's wild spending and all-too-frequent military interventions, however, remained unsuccessful. The War with Holland (1676–1678) and the War of the Spanish Succession (1713), to mention only two conflagrations, led to the severe depletion of the treasury. Nonetheless, he fulfilled his mission with strength, punishing such well-known men as Fouquet, the superintendent of finances, who had amassed great personal wealth by confusing "private with public finances."

Although a swindler, Fouquet, to his credit, protected poets, such as Jean de La Fontaine (1621–1695), author of the famed *Fables*.

Louis XIV's early years glowed with jubilance and romantic interludes. His liaisons with Mlle de La Vallière, Mme de Montespan, and Mme de Maintenon, among others, remain famous. But following the death of his wife, the Spanish Infanta Marie-Thérèse, in 1668, he secretly married the ultra devout Mme de Maintenon, paving the way for the somber and depressive atmosphere that permeated Versailles until his death.

Creatively speaking, France flourished during the seventeenth century. In the domain of the theater, Pierre Corneille (1606–1684), inspired by Roman and Middle Eastern history, as well as by the heroics, passionate loves, and dangerous adventures spawned by the Thirty Years War, regaled his audiences with such plays as *The Cid, Horace,* and *Rodogune.* Jean Racine (1639–1699), orphaned early in life, was taken to live at Port-Royal, a Jansenist religious retreat. There he witnessed first hand the persecution of his community by the Jesuits, explaining in part the conspiratorial element in many of his plays—*Andromaque, Britannicus, Phèdre*—in which calamitous moments are followed by periods of calm and silence. In sharp contrast were Molière's (1622–1673) inimitable comedies and farces: *The Would-be Gentlemen, Tartuffe, The Misanthrope, Don Juan, The Doctor In Spite of Himself.* No one since Molière has ever struck such high notes of humor, irony, satire, and profundity in the mockery of humanity.

Nor was there a dearth of philosophers wanting in seventeenth-century France. René Descartes (1596–1650), the originator of analytical geometry, the proponent of methodical doubt, of rational ontology, and of deductive physics, held reason to be the only valid God-given instrument capable of leading humankind to truth and enlightenment. Blaise Pascal (1623–1662), a renowned mathematician and the inventor of a portable "arithmetic machine," is best remembered for his *Provincial Letters* and his *Thoughts.* As a Jansenist, he not only verbally parried Jesuit attacks against his religious group, but devised a most incredible gambling paradigm in his *wager* in favor of the existence of God and the immortality of the soul.

Women in society and in literature during *le grand siècle* played an increasingly important role. To the social gatherings known as *salons,* hosted at the homes of Madeleine de Scudéry and the Marquise de Rambouillet among others, were invited celebrated philosophers, dramatists, poets, novelists, and musicians to discuss what they considered to be pertinent subjects of the day. Emphasized by many of the *salonnières* was the refinement and purification of language and of comportment, which reached such an extreme that not only a *precious* and *mannered* vocabulary was adopted but also an equally excessive code of etiquette. Romanesque writing was also in vogue, as attested to by the overly lengthy pastoral novels of Mlle de Scudéry and Honoré d'Urfé. Even as Mme de Sévigné was perfecting the art of epistolary writing, La Fontaine was creating his unforgettable fables.

In the field of architecture, decorative arts, and landscaping, the names of Le Vau, Le Brun, and Le Nôtre, among others, were credited with the marvels of Versailles and of other noteworthy architectural wonders. The pictorial arts also reached new heights with Nicolas Poussin, Georges de La Tour, Claude Lorrain, Philippe de Champaigne, the Le Nain family, Nicolas Mignard, Jacques Callot, and others. In great demand were the creations of the cabinet maker André-Charles Boulle and the works of composers such as Jean-Baptiste Lully and Philippe Quinault, the latter writing the former's opera librettos.

Understandably was the seventeenth century known as France's *Classical Age!*

2

CHARLES PERRAULT'S MULTI-VEINED DONKEY-SKIN, SLEEPING BEAUTY, AND BLUEBEARD

B ORN INTO MOMENTOUS TIMES, little did the Parisian-born Charles Perrault (1628–1703) know that the publication of his *Tales of Mother Goose* (1695) would bring him fame both during his lifetime and for centuries to come.

ECTYPAL ANALYSIS

That Charles Perrault had a mind of his own was made evident when, at the age of fifteen, following an altercation with one of his teachers, he left school, greatly disappointing his father, an attorney at the Parlement of Paris. Henceforth, the largely self-taught Perrault studied not only the required curriculum, but the Bible, La Serre's *History of France*, and Latin authors, such as Tertullian, Vergil, and Cornelius Nepos. Although he earned a law degree in 1651, he gave up his career five years later to become "secretary" to his brother, Pierre, Paris's tax receiver. Having also taken to writing *vers galants*—"Iris's Portrait" and "Portrait of Iris's Voice"—by 1661 he had become a "public poet," his mission being to proclaim the achievements of Louis XIV. Appointed to Colbert's "little council" in 1663, then advisor to this renowned statesman, he was made a member of the French Academy in 1671. At the age of forty-four

Perrault married the nineteen-year-old Marie Guichon, who died after the birth of their third child.

Perrault's vociferous support of contemporary arts in the famous "Quarrel between the Ancients and the Moderns" is evident in his poem, "The Century of Louis the Great" (1687), written in praise of such creative spirits as Corneille, Molière, Racine, La Fontaine, and La Tour. His four dialogic volumes include commentaries on a broad spectrum of topics: *Parallels of the Ancients and the Moderns . . . On the Subject of the Arts and the Sciences, Dialogues* (1688), *Eloquence* (1690), and so forth.

At the age of sixty-three Perrault branched out to the new and relatively popular field of narration of moralistic legends in verse. Unlike the poet and critic Boileau, a misogynist who attacked the female sex, Perrault defended women in his creative writings as well as in such tracts as *Vindication of Wives* (1694). He urged men to marry early and to care for and be caring to their wives.

ARCHETYPAL ANALYSIS

Donkey-Skin: An Adolescent's Struggle Against Incest and for Independence

The sources for Perrault's *Donkey-Skin* may be traced back to the *The Golden Ass* by the Latin writer, Apuleius (second century C.E.); to the Nerones episodes in the anonymous fourteenth-century French novel *Perceforest*, and to "The She-Bear" by the seventeenth-century Italian Giambattista Basile (included in his *Pentameron (The Tale of Tales)* (Barchilon and Flinders, *Charles Perrault* 92).

Characteristic of many a fairy tale, *Donkey-Skin* opens in an Edenic world. The king and queen of a powerful kingdom share a deep love and harmony in their marriage, and are blessed with a beautiful, delightful, and gentle daughter. Unique among the royal couple's possessions is a donkey who, rather than excreting manure, discharges gold coins, thereby assuring the economic wealth of the nation.

A state of bliss being incompatible with the vagaries of life, the royal family's perfect existence screeches to a halt. The still-young queen becomes mortally ill. Whether out of bitterness or an unwillingness to allow another woman to replace her upon her demise, she extracts the following promise from her husband. If he marries again—and she is certain he will—he must promise that his future wife be more beautiful, better formed, and wiser than she. Although he agrees to her request, the king tells her outright that he has no intention of ever remarrying.

Following his beloved's passing and the king's period of mourning, the perceptive courtiers predict he will soon be looking for a new bride. Indeed, the king's messengers are sent far and wide to scour the land in search of a match that would fulfill his bond. All efforts are in vain, until he suddenly realizes that his daughter not only fits his wife's requirements, but surpasses them in every way. Fully aware of the interdict placed on father/daughter marriages, the king, now burning "with extreme love" for the princess, decides to rid himself of all possible judicial impediments to such a union. He consults a casuist, who, by basing his reasoning on devious argumentations, justifies the monarch's intent. Traumatized by her father's injunction, the princess begs him to reconsider. Her efforts are fruitless. His mind is set.

INCEST. That the theme of incest should rear its ugly head in a fairy tale was not unusual, given its importance in ancient myths, such as the marriage of the Egyptian brother and sister duo, Isis and Osiris; the Greek Oedipus, who unwittingly wed his mother, Jocasta; the Irish hero, Cuchulain, the son of Conchobar and his sister Dechtire; and Adam and Eve. The Rig Veda's concept of primeval incest ("the One who creates a Second with whom he unites") is in accordance with Hindu stories of Creation (O'Flaherty, *Hindu Myths* 23).

Since ancient times, consanguinitiy was practised for political, economic, and religious reasons. Blood marriages were not considered immoral, as attested to by the Egyptian/Greek Ptolemies (third cent. B.C.E.) who married their sisters; the Persian monarch, Artaxerxes (fifth cent. B.C.E.), who wed his two daughters, and so forth.

Psychologically speaking, incest indicates an inability on the part of one or both partners to reach outward, that is, to go beyond the family enclave. To remain bonded within a household or a ménage is to stunt individual or familial evolution. It signals a failure to pass from an endogamous to an exogamous condition. The imprisoning of oneself in the closeted quarters of a family cell encourages insalubrity and regression, conditions that frequently foster perversion, retardation, and/or physical malformation.

The sexual anomalies Perrault had either witnessed or heard about among the courtiers and the nobility of his day may have also been a source of inspiration for *Donkey-Skin*'s theme of incest. Related to this motif, and common among wealthier classes the world over, was the marriage of young girls to older men, for money, status, or because of a powerful father complex. To stand up to a parent in Perrault's day, particularly if he was the ruler of a mighty land, as was the case of the princess in our tale, was not only difficult, but quite unusual. Her intense struggle to free herself from her father's grip revealed a will of iron, an inordinate sense of purpose, and a desire to direct her own future.

So repelled was the princess by the king's plan that the psychic energy (libido) directing and motivating her drive to liberate herself soon reached flood-tide proportions. The more powerful her inner surges, the more difficult they were to contain, as in any affective or spontaneous state. The functioning adolescent began to reason as to how best to deal with her problem. Her inner chaos slowly seemed to simmer down, her outrage and disgust yielded to the working out of a *modus vivendi* that would be determined by personal and reasoned choices.

Of strong moral orientation, the princess was deeply aware of religious and social interdicts. These, rather than scientific reasonings—such as the notion that hybridization or inbreeding would result in an increase of recessive traits in offspring, about which she was certainly unaware—prevailed in her *modus operandi*. Participation in a morally unacceptable relationship frequently not only serves to accentuate an already underlying disparity between right and wrong, but provokes increasing consciousness of a predicament and of the crucial choices that must be made. Rather than harboring the blind love and admiration a child normally bears a parent, she saw him—without admitting it—as emotionally blind, weak, and worse, deceitful. His unwillingness or psychological inability to seek exogamous ties by creating new contacts, thus encouraging his feelings and inclinations to flow out of the family cell, had stunted his mind, suggesting a deteriorating regressive psychological state. Indeed, his fixation on his daughter was paradigmatic of a man stuck in an infantile, or adolescent stage of development. Metaphorically speaking, the king's emotional stasis could even herald the breakdown of his kingdom.

Another important factor implicit in the psychological makeup of the father figure in Perrault's tale was his surrender to his emotions. As head of state (Lat. *caput*, head), he should have thought of the welfare of his vast domain. Given the high post he occupied, his *head* should have first been consulted. Only afterward, could he allow his emotions to be called into play. Rulers of kingdoms, states, and nations owe their primary loyalty to their governments and to their people, and not to their personal concerns. A king's actions should be based on a collective abstract ideal, permitting no obstacle to stand in the way of fulfilling his empirical commitments, but the opposite was true in the case of our king. As the archetype of supreme consciousness, a king—ideally, to be sure—must be endowed with high moral standards and with the vision and wisdom to rule. The king in Perrault's tale had had recourse to a casuist to legalize his devious proclivities and lascivious urges, indicating an inborn penchant for corruption. By failing to take dominion over his own sexual drives, he paved the way for his future unwise acts. Did the demand of the king's wife on her deathbed precipitate a deep-seated fear of having to face his own mortality? Was he rejecting the aging process and the terrors of loneliness? What better way was there, he may have sensed, of staving off the ravages of time than to marry one's own progeny? By transferring his sexual passions onto her, he may have unconsciously believed that he would not only replicate the paradisiac condition he had once enjoyed with his wife, but would also prolong her essence in the birth of the child his daughter would give him.

The futile attempts to find a perfect bride for the king seemed to validate, at least in his mind, his choice of the princess for his wife. Hadn't Mother Nature herself intervened in his favor? On the other hand, given his powerful attraction for his daughter, one might question his ability to be objective in evaluating another woman's physical and spiritual assets. The answer is moot.

As the days passed, the delay tactics the princess was arranging compelled the monarch to put off his possession of his nubile daughter. Postponement of the event proved to be sexually intolerable to the king, increasing his fixation on his daughter to such a degree that he was unable to cope with the daily matters of governing his kingdom. Indeed, his obsessive condition, which may be alluded to as *psychological autism*, encouraged him further to transgress convention by allowing a condition of collective stasis to prevail in his land.

The princess's intransigence, which may be associative with self-protective aggressivity on one level, proved instrumental in expanding her horizons, spurring her efforts, and strengthening her ego (center of consciousness). Her outward psychological movement disclosed a fundamental need in her to develop beyond the adolescent stage. Aware that she had reached a nadir, she understood that the time had come to save *her own skin!*

THE SURROGATE MOTHER AS FAIRY GODMOTHER. Divestiture of a personal mother in fairy tales, myths, and in real situations frequently encourages an adolescent to seek a surrogate maternal and/or paternal principle to comfort and to direct her or his life course. The dual parent motif is also evident in the custom of awarding a godfather and a godmother to a newborn (Jung, 91, #93). Accountable for the child's welfare, godparents, in keeping with custom, are endowed with a kind of "magic authority . . . a wisdom and spiritual exaltation that transcend[s] reason" (Jung, 91 #158).

Anguished, bereaved, and victim of a destructive paternal power, the princess in *Donkey-Skin*, having reached a crossroad in her life, and despite the delay tactics she was developing, reached the point of not knowing how to proceed. In the throes of desperation and profound solitude, she had recourse to a surrogate godmother—a paradoxically *real* fantasy figure in whom she placed her trust and to whom she looked for guidance. The princess, like many worshippers, also consulted a cult figure for enlightenment.[1]

In olden days, and even today, fairies, saints, Gods, godparents, or friends seem to come forth miraculously in moments of great need. As messengers from subliminal spheres—or that Other World—these presences serve to expand the consciousness of injured parties, thereby broadening the choices they can make as they see them through their ordeal.

Because the princess still lived in close contact with ancient animistic powers like the Banshees, Morgans, Ondines, Mélusines, and Ladies of the Lake, her world was redolent with the spirit of magic and enchantment. Other religious figures evoked by humanity in times of stress in legend, literature, or life have included Sophia (Divine Wisdom), the Virgin Mary (Mother of Christ), Innana (Sumerian Queen of Heaven), Demeter (Persephone's mother), Kali (Hindu fertility Goddess), or Kuan Yin (Chinese deity of compassion). Whether in monotheistic or in polytheistic religions, these mother figures have been looked upon psychologically as soul *(anima)*: forces or powers that could be called upon for help when and if the need arose.

So powerfully and with such immediacy did the princess experience the numinosity of her substitute or surrogate mother that she felt herself being wafted away into another sphere by this transpersonal power. Her fairy godmother's natural habitat, a hidden grotto decorated with glittering mother-of-pearl and coral, gave feelings of comfort to the distressed young girl.

Since prehistoric times grottoes and caves, archetypes of a maternal matrix or womb, have been considered protecting and nourishing. Greek Eleusinian fertility rituals—those honoring Demeter, for example—were frequently carried out in contained spaces, as were those identified with the mysteries of the Japanese Shinto sun goddess, Amaterasu, who periodically withdrew into darkness. To penetrate a grotto or cavern enables one to experience a *regressus ad uterum:* or, psychologically, to inhabit one's unconscious, where latent energies may be stirred up. Images (at times, archetypal), may emerge into consciousness, thereby serving to point up a new way of dealing with the problem(s) at stake.

Mysterious inner spaces are conducive to parapsychological events. When the princess repaired to her fairy godmother's grotto—or, psychologically, to her own subliminal spheres—she saw a glowing vision of "an admirable fairy"—a parapsychological figure that she experienced as flesh and blood. She listened carefully to every word the fairy godmother uttered. Because the confidence she inspired in the princess filled a deep-seated void in the adolescent, her suggestions had catalytic effect. However, the princess did not passively accept the proposals of her anima figure like a robot. The relationship between the two rendered the service of triggering the princess's own thought processes. By opening her up to the possibility of several options and their consequences, the fairy godmother aroused a spirit of self-help in the young girl, encouraging her to draw on her own resources to solve her problems.

The reader may wonder how the mentoring relationship between the princess and her fantasy figure proceeded. As an extension of the adolescent's own surprisingly rational and commonsense approach to the king's "mad" intent, her anima figure may be looked upon as a projection of an inborn compensatory factor within herself. The fairy, representing certain factors in the princess's collective unconscious—or, metaphorically, her inner cave—stirred into consciousness images that could aid her in time of crisis. As a mentoring entity, the fairy godmother was working symbiotically with the adolescent, teaching her how to cope with her father's hyperemotional nature.

The mutually dependent princess and her surrogate mother looked upon each other with love and respect. The fairy offered suggestions as to how to destabilize the king's plans, advising the princess to adopt a balanced and conciliatory attitude toward her father, in order to dispel suspicion on the king's part of her true feelings and calm his irascible outbursts. A confrontational approach, by contrast, would lead to an impasse between father and daughter. The diplomatic approach, the fairy godmother insisted, would be "to refuse [his demands] without contradicting him," lest she diminish the king's sense of worth and drive him to extremes (*Donkey Skin* 225). The princess should ask her father to fulfill certain demands prior to the betrothal. The very challenges provoked in the tasks she would propose would engage him in contest, thus gaining time for the princess and enhancing her self-confidence as well.

The fairy's delay tactics would incite the princess to reason, assess, and better understand the ramifications of the direction she would take to gain release from her nefarious fate. She suggested that the princess ask her father to give her what she considered an impossibility: a dress made of empyrean blue.

Much to the princess's dismay, the king acquiesced, calling upon the greatest couturiers of his kingdom to create and to deliver the spectacular garment. Upon consultation with the fairy godmother, a second dress was ordered, this time replicating subdued moon rays. Upon receipt of the second gown, a third, in brilliant sun tones, was ordered and given to the increasingly despairing princess. Had her mentor made a judgmental error? Had she failed to take into account the amount of time, effort, and money the king was willing to expend to fulfill his incestuous urges?

DRESSES AS PERSONAE. Dresses and garments of all types may be looked upon as *personae*, concrete objects able to hide an individual's identity, as well as the real motives of his or her acts. Like an actor's mask, the three gowns requested covered, adorned, and formalized, thereby dissimulated for the unseeing the real issues at stake. What, then, did the dresses in our fairy tale imply? A cutting to size, a shaping, a symbolic coloring, and thus a transformation of the attitude of the wearer-to-be. Each dress may be viewed as a metaphor, or artificial means of disclosing the princess's need to assume or to develop other identities or personality traits that would help her solve her dilemma.

The first dress replicated the empyrean, or azure blue spheres, which in medieaval cosmology symbolized the highest heavenly domains. Could such an unparalleled color tone be paradigmatic of the princess's transcendental values? Her yearning for possible dematerialization or sublimation? Would such an air-born condition pave the way for her liberation and allow her to escape into some limitless domain? Or could it also have symbolized an unconscious need to bedazzle a possible onlooker, including her father? Was she—though unadmittedly—captivated by his charms and his love for her? Did she unknowingly harbor a shameful attraction for the king and attempt, in some hidden way, to trigger his libidinous desires? By contrast, the fairy godmother's intent in ordering the creation of an empyrean-toned dress could have been to spiritualize the princess's values, with the hope of further developing her thinking faculties. If so, the path ahead would be arduous: the adolescent would have to learn to differentiate and to particularize her thoughts, and in so doing, develop her judgmental faculties. In this connection, let us note that in keeping with numerical symbolism, the first, (or number 1) dress, that of empyrean blue, indicated an undifferentiated condition of psychological wholeness, as evident in Adam and Eve's comportment prior to their Fall. Once earth-born, having been separated from primordial oneness, they began—and possibly the princess could have as well—to live differentiated existences, that is, as 2.

The silvery moon-hues of raiment number 2, those of Earth's ever-transforming satellite, having since ancient times represented feminine biological cycles, would indicate the princess's urgent need to become initiated into the feminine world or, psychologically, into the maturation process. While the moon's darker, or chthonian, sides usher in negative, funereal, and indirect insights into the princess's subliminal world, they allow her to glimpse her own perhaps fearsome and unacceptable traits as well. Once extremes are recognized, the healing of an anguished soul may begin. Indeed, the narrative tells us that the Princess was so taken by the exquisiteness of the lunar dress that, had her inner voice not spoken to her—in the commanding tones of her fairy godmother—she might have succumbed to her father's desires. Let us also note in this connection that because God had omitted saying "it was good" on the second day of Creation (Gen. 1:6–7), the number 2 since medieval times has been identified with divisiveness and conflict, the lot of many a woman facing her dark as well as her luminous aspects.

The dazzling golden hues of dress number 3, replicating the sun, or the blinding light of consciousness, refer not merely to rational processes, but to cosmic intelligence—the sun being a metaphor for the Eye of God. The enlightenment brought on by reason, in tandem with the conflictual colors associated with the second dress, and the spirituality evoked in the empyrean tones of the first dress, although difficult for an adolescent to assess, are to be taken into consideration in the restoration and growth of the princess's identity. The conjunction of 1 (sky), 2 (moon), and 3 (sun), representatives of celestial spheres only, lacks completion, as does the concept of the trinity—Father, Son, and Holy Ghost—in Christian dogma. Earth matters—number 4—had to be added, particularly with regard to the feminine principle, for a quaternity spells completion and harmony. Unfulfilled, the princess would have to leap over a fourth hurdle: that of an active earth experience—or life experience—that would teach her how to deal with the vagaries of human existence.

In that the first three requirements had been met, much to the king's delight and to the daughter's trepidation, the fairy godmother urged the levying of a fourth labor that would, perhaps, enable the princess to set forth on the path of her inner transformation. Surely, the fairy godmother reasoned, the king would never agree to sacrificing his gold-laying donkey, a paradigm of the mysterious, but a continuous source of his kingdom's economic wealth. If he refused, the princess would be free to follow her own inclinations.

An enigmatic animal since earliest times, the donkey has been ascribed contrary characteristics: ignorance and wisdom, enlightenment and obscurity—even satanic powers. Sacred to Apollo, to whom it was sacrificed at Delphi, as well as to Dionysus, whose cradle/chest it carried, and to Jesus, present in his manger and his mount upon entering Jerusalem, the donkey in Apuleius's *The Golden Ass* was also instrumental in the author's transformation from instinctive to spiritual levels.

That the miracle donkey of Perrault's tale excreted gold is not as absurd as it might first appear. Dung, on an empirical level, may be identified with fertilizer, and thus with healthy crops, accounting for a nation's well-being and prosperity. The act of defecating, preceded by eating and digesting, may also suggest, psychologically, the metabolization of certain problematics.

Since the donkey excreted gold—in alchemical parlance, the only incorruptible metal, which neither decays nor corrodes—to order its killing would divest the king of all that had been pure, healthful, and productive in the land he ruled, and maybe such an order would also be viewed as a kind of cutting off of what he had heretofore held to be sacred. In a grand, but misguided gesture, the king had his animal slaughtered to win his daughter's affection. He was willing to sacrifice both his daughter's welfare and the economic status of his nation to satisfy his lust, thereby attesting to his increasing "headlessness" and virtually manic nature.[2]

Overwhelmed with terror upon learning of the sacrifice, the princess again had recourse to her fairy godmother who now advised her to flee the kingdom. All means—duplicity, or diplomacy—were encouraged by her mentor to achieve her goal. Prior to her departure, therefore, the princess would have to give her father the impression that she was agreeable to the marriage. Unsuspecting of her real intent, the father would not have her closely watched and would give her free rein.

THE FLIGHT. To assure her incognito during her flight from her father's kingdom, the princess discarded her royal apparel and donned the stench-filled donkey skin that she had acquired following the animal's death. Her new persona, a psychological replica of her unconscious attitude toward herself, indicated a willed displacement of her identity, and a prefiguration of the route she would now travel.

Her disguise not only repulsed everyone she encountered on her way, but it indicated a deep-seated need on her part to descend to the lowliest of social echelons by wearing such an offensive garb. A yearning to suffer, to experience the lot of the downtrodden in a kind of *imitatio Christi* was not uncommon in Christian communities. Medieval penitents and flagellants believed that self-punishment would serve to heal and purify what they considered to be their tainted, diseased, and guilty souls (Cowan, *Masochism* 19). Could the princess have been punishing herself for having, perhaps unconsciously, inspired her father's lust?

Yearning for redemption, the princess walked from one farming community to another begging for work. Her pleas fell on deaf ears. Adding to the fetidness emanating from her cloak, the grime of the road encrusted itself on the exposed areas of her body—arms, legs, and face. In past centuries, some saintly outcasts, St. Margaret Alacocque and St. Jean Labre, in their masochism took satisfaction in encouraging the rejection of others. Even as people drew away from the pariah princess, she remained firm in her self-debasement in order to experience her punishment—her Fall from Paradise. By defining her *sin*, by facing the traumas and burdens she had to bear in order to expiate the "evil" lust she may have inadvertently aroused, the princess began to live out a period of penance, or of victimization. Never once seeking the easy course, she followed a self-imposed agenda designed to give purpose to her life.

SERVITUDE. Upon reaching an unnamed distant kingdom, the princess was finally given the lowly job of scullery maid and swineherd. Reacting with equanimity to the farm laborers' continuous jeers, insults, and mockery, and to the new name they awarded her—Donkey-Skin—she became mentally stronger. Steadfastness and contentment marked her period of servitude (L. *servitudo*, slavery), suggesting a turning point in her psychological outlook. Having grown accustomed to the onerous tasks foisted upon her, she began to benefit from the relative security of her routine life. After the turmoil of the past, she could now take advantage of moments of repose—time enough for unconscious contents to set to work in the healing process (Franz, *Shadow and Evil in Fairy Tales* 35).

RITUALS AND VOYEURISM. The princess's disguise and flight from her father's kingdom indicated not an abdication of her former social status, but an understanding of the steps necessary to further her maturation process. Isolation from those she had known and depended upon in the past in a paradisiac environment, as well as deprivation of all physical comforts, forced her to learn to subsist in an unsheltered collective environment. She now felt a sense of her own responsibility and took pride in the long hours of dedication to her work. Strangely enough, the contrast between her former and her present lifestyle, having given her the opportunity to work for others, developed in her a sense of gratitude. Her solitude also served her well. During her rest periods, she conjured up a whole fantasy world—not an escape mechanism, but an unconscious means of coping with adversity.

On Sundays and fast days, when she was at liberty to enjoy a few hours of leisure, Donkey-Skin retreated to her room—her *temenos*—and created a whole theatrical universe for herself. Ritually, she first removed her donkey skin, washed herself, then opened the trunk her fairy godmother had sent to her via certain "secret underground passageways" or, psychologically via her own faculty for creating daydreams to enrich her existence. The contents of the trunk—her magnificent gowns, gems of all types, and other royal accouterments—enabled her to live out a variety of psychodramas of her own manufacture.

Secondly, each time Donkey-Skin donned one of her three magnficent gowns, she supplemented its intrinsic beauty with suitable gems. Once satisfied with her appearance, she gazed with joy at her radiant image in the full-length mirror before her. The sparkle of the gems (Fr. *joyau*, from medieval L. *jocus*, game) created a joyful, amusing, and dazzlingly motile atmosphere.

Such interludes with their mystifying interplay of wondrous lighting effects opened her up to new insights into her own being, which she was in the process of discovering.

Precious stones, extracted from Mother Earth's belly, have always been associated with primordial energy, and thus with active electric charges. The variety of jewels the princess chose to complement each gown in the mirror, enabled her to contemplate in the mirror, not the ugly penitent, draped in a mephitic donkey skin, but that remote, beautiful, ebullient, and loving being inside of her. During her ritualized play periods, her *other* nature projected itself onto the mirror's surface, thus dichotomizing what had once been whole. She was able to see into and *recognize* (L. *cognoscere*, to re-know, or to re-acknowledge) both sides of herself through reflection. The ensuing interplay of thought processeses and associations might provide her with feasible solutions to her heretofore insoluble problems.

Although metal mirrors had existed since antiquity, glass mirrors were invented in Germany only in the fourteenth century. As an object of reflection, the mirror (originally Lat. *speculum*) has always invited speculation. It is associated with the act of meditating, pondering, reviewing. Unlike Narcissus, who fell in love with his image reflected in a pool of water in which he later drowned, Donkey-Skin was not enamored of her own image. To the contrary, it helped her to objectify and to question herself. As she observed the masked, but nonetheless strong and feisty aspects of her other, hitherto rejected personality, she began to enjoy the variety of dazzling images, poses, and even distortions cast back at her by the mirror. The give-and-take of such activity gave her pause to evaluate her future course. Although nonverbalized, her pantomimic ritual seemed to afford her increasing enlightenment regarding herself.

THE PRINCE. One day while laboring on the farm, Donkey-Skin noticed in the distance the son of the king of the domain—a tall and handsome young man. She was captivated by his seemingly "martial" air and, paradoxically, gentle manner, and her affective reactions were, as usual, followed by rationalizations. She judged him to be "amiable." The feelings of tenderness he aroused in her also proved to her that, despite her hardships, her "heart," that is, her feeling world and her identity, had remained intact.

During one of her unspoken dialogic interludes, as fate would have it, the prince found himself walking in an obscure alleyway in the barnyard area of his father's domain. For no apparent reason, he stopped in front of Donkey-Skin's lodgings and looked through the keyhole. What he beheld overwhelmed him: a vision of Divinity in the form of a beautiful maiden clothed in a shimmering golden light. The interplay of the maiden/virgin contemplating herself in her image, as reflected in the mirror, and the prince's perception of this glittering figure, as cast back in the mirror image and also viewed by his direct observation of her, adds up to the sacred number 4. This number, referred to previously as one of completion, was now to impact powerfully on his soul/psyche.

Why he had unwittingly looked through a keyhole remains a mystery, unless, of course, he was a voyeur, in which case it may be suggested that he suffered from scopophilia (Gr. *skopein*, to look at; Gr. *philia*, friendship, affinity): an abnormal liking for viewing or observing to obtain sexual stimulation. So enflamed did the prince become by the vision of this sublime girl that he could scarcely control his urge to break down the door. Nontheless, he succeeded in containing his erotic instincts, thanks, perhaps, to the numinosity of the number 4.

Once back in his castle, the prince grew increasingly pensive and despondent, to the point of refusing all entertainment and, more dangerously, all food. Who was this "admirable nymph" he had seen? he wondered (*Donkey Skin* 230). She is neither a nymph nor is she beautiful, the courtiers replied. She is ugliness and filth incarnate. Paying them no heed,the prince dwelt in a world, no longer his own, haunted by the exquisite traits of his apparition.

As the days passed, the queen mother observed her son's rejection of food, and his tears of despair. She listened to his groans and sighs, and noticed his diminished powers of concentration and attention. In some cases, such an *abaissement du niveau mental* paves the way to a condition of collective, preconsciousness, as in "early childhood" (Jung, 91, # 264–265). A primitive mythical world began to guide the prince's behavior. To his mother's queries concerning nourishment, he replied—perhaps mindlessly for others—he would eat nothing but a cake baked by Donkey-Skin. Although the Queen Mother did not fathom the ramifications of her son's request, she, like many a loving mother who lives archetypally, counter to the judgment of her advisors, granted her son's wish.

THE CAKE AND THE RING. Donkey-Skin, agreeing to bake the cake requested by the prince, declined the use of the great kitchens of the castle. She retreated into her *temenos* to blend the sacred elements—salt, butter, fresh eggs—for her batter, into which, either inadvertently or purposely, she dropped one of her precious gold and emerald rings.

Batter, dough, bread, and pastry mixtures, as symbols of earth and water, are paradigms of unformed matter—passive substances that were once identified with the feminine or *yin* principle. On the other hand, the kneading of the dough—an aggressive act—was associated with male *yang* power. The person who physically works, and mentally wills the shape of a malleable substance into existence, engages in a creative process. Donkey-Skin had taken it upon herself to blend the components needed for the cake. In keeping with alchemical symbolism, as male principle, she *coagulated* the *fluid*; as feminine principle, she organized cosmic energy in such a way as to create new matter, forms, and shapes. Like the Judeo-Christian God who created Adam out of *adahma* or earth; the Egyptian God, Khnemu, a potter, who fashioned people and gods; or the Chinese Goddess, Nu Kwa, who, by grasping a handful of yellow earth and kneading it had brought a human likeness into existence, Donkey-Skin prepared her sacramental cake (Yingshao, *Feng-sut'ung-yi*, quoted in Bodde, *Essay on Chinese Civilization*, 64.). For Christian alchemists, Donkey-Skin as baker would be analogous to Jesus who "took bread, and blessed it, and brake it, and gave it to the disciples, and said, Take, eat; this is my body" (Matt. 26: 26). Working with *tellus matter*, Donkey-Skin became a fashioner of matter and, in a broader sense, the director of her destiny.

The fact that she dropped her gold ring encrusted with an emerald stone intentionally or not, into the batter indicated an inner need on her part for love and for conventionality in wedlock. The ring's circular configuration, like that of a marriage band, may be considered a symbol of eternity, of continuous rebirth in wholeness. In the latter sense, the circularity of the ring suggests an image of the *Self* ("the totality of the psyche as organized around a dynamic center") (Edinger, *Melville's Moby-Dick* 149). Overt or not, the act of placing the ring in the batter revealed an inner need to both regulate and connect in marriage an until-now detached, masochistically oriented existence. It also disclosed a new and impressive step toward inner balance and harmony, suggesting an understanding or acceptance of what could be consciously perceived, as well as what transcends rational awareness and is not connected with the ego (Franz, *Interpretation of Fairy Tales* V, 7).

The gold of the ring in her sacramental batter suggested a new source of divine and empirical nourishment, which would help her assume her rightful place in society and wed the man she loved. Although rings are usually given by the man to the woman as a token of love, in the princess's case, she was the aggressor in the relationship. By hiding the ring in the cake, she was passing her female energy into the languishing male. The emerald figuring in the ring's design, like many precious stones in fairy tales, indicated cohesion, durability, and oneness, as well as a reconciliation of oppositional worlds—sexuality, and a revulsion for it due to her father's deviant urges. Like the emerald that fell from Lucifer's head when he was cast out of heaven, the precious stone in the princess's case represented her inborn power to stave off her father's incestuous desires, her courage in taking flight from what had become her inferno, and her perseverance in overcoming her traumas. Like

Lucifer (Lat. *lux*, light + *fe*, bear, carry), she, too, lived out her ordeal and, and in so doing, worked toward her own enlightenment.

Similarly the prince, reminiscent of von Eschenbach's hero Parzival, who was prevented from beholding the emerald of the Holy Grail, upon sight of his divine figure, so our prince, although still unprepared for the fruition of his love, asked that a cake be baked, indicating, nonetheless, his coming to maturity.

THE SACRAMENT. No sooner had the sacramental cake been brought to the prince than he tasted it and found it so much to his liking that he ate it all, stopping short of ingesting the ring with its "admirable emerald" (*Donkey-Skin* 232). He placed it under his pillow, inviting further nourishment by its numinosity. Since no change in his life had occurred, he continued lingering through periods of distress and food rejection. His loss of weight, diagnosed by the doctors as lovesickness, could be remedied, they maintained, through marriage. Willingly the prince accepted the suggestion, on the condition that the bride-to-be's finger (an obvious phallic symbol) fit the emerald ring found in the cake. The obstacle posed by the prince brings to mind the princess's own demands of her father, to thwart his incestuous plans. In the younger man's case, throngs of young ladies from the highest to the lowliest classes vied for the honor of marrying him. As anticipated, all failed the test, except Donkey-Skin, whose finger alone proved sufficiently delicate to pass through the eye of "the fatal Ring" (*Donkey-Skin* 234).[3]

DONKEY-SKIN'S CHANGE OF PERSONA. During her ordeal as a farm laborer, the princess had become surprisingly courageous and necessarily aggressive as well. Prior to her presentation at court to meet the prince, "her [future] Lord and Master," she asked to be permitted to change her clothes. Although scoffing at the idea, the king gave his consent. Having donned one of her magnificent gowns, Donkey-Skin made her grand entrance into the royal apartments, revealing the beauty of her face and body. Her blond hair, intertwined for the occasion with glittering diamonds, gave her a special ethereality. The condition of inner wholeness—the *conjunctio* of her previously divided personality—was disclosed in her "proud majesty" and in the color tones of her empyrean-blue eyes (*Donkey-Skin* 234).

Donkey-Skin's wedding, with its magnificent display of wealth—elephants brought from Moorish lands, bountiful feasts—included among its guest list of rulers, her own father, whose once "odious flame" for his daughter had long since died. Needless to add, the prince was more than delighted to learn that his father-in-law was a powerful king. That the princess's fairy godmother was present at the wedding ceremony answered the bride's most profound desires, for it was in her countenance that the princess resurrected the spirit of her deceased mother. It was she, as well, who narrated Donkey-Skin's peregrinations for those present to hear, heaping upon the new bride her well-deserved "glory" (*Donkey-Skin* 236).

The incest taboo imposed by societies the world over and throughout time, as experienced by the princess in *Donkey-Skin*, motivated her healthy psyche to stand firm and alone. Intransigence, steadfastness, and personal determination paved the way for her eventual psychological growth. Donkey-Skin's ability to blend inner or dream world with outer reality indicated a rare and profound trust in her own capacity to gain release from the bonds that would have obliged her to live out a perversion—as a reflection of her father's shadow.

As a guiding principle, the fairy godmother, emerging at a crucial time in the young woman's life, set her on the right path by developing her innate sense of ingenuity and penchant for speculation. Had she not mustered the strength to take on the ugliness and foul smell of a pariah—she might not have been forced to call upon her inner reserves to save herself from extinction.

Unlike the pampered suicidal prince, who languished, wept, and starved himself, working on his mother's love/weakness to achieve his goal, the princess faced her ordeals with rigor, fortitude—and alone. Nonetheless, the prince's infantile behavior disclosed in its own way his determination to find a mate who would not only respond to his feeling function, but to his sexual and emotional needs.

Most remarkable, perhaps, was the balanced attitude Donkey-Skin maintained throughout the extremes she experienced: wealth/poverty, spirituality/earthliness, pleasure/pain, abstraction/concreteness. A Job-like figure, she may be considered a paradigm of one who, despite tragedies, goes to any lengths to maintain his *way*.

> Wherefore do I take my flesh in my teeth, and put my life in mine hand?
> *Though he slay me, yet will I trust in him: but I will maintain mine own ways before him. (Job 13:14)*

Sleeping Beauty: Passivity, Introspection, and Silence

Unlike the strong and down-to-earth Donkey-Skin, the female protagonist in *Sleeping Beauty* is passive and introspective. Nonetheless, in some strange way she is sufficiently wise to know that by maintaining her reserve, and most importantly her silence, her fondest hopes will be realized.

The sources for *Sleeping Beauty* are many and varied. The oldest dates back to Epimenides (c.sixth and fifth cent. B.C.E.), the Cretan philosopher and legislator, who supposedly slept for fifty-seven years in a cave, after which he awakened and prophesied. In the tale of *The Seven Sleepers*, referred to in the Muslim world as the "Two-Horned One," the protagonists remain dormant for two hundred years (*Koran*, Sura 18). Other sources include, the sixteenth-century prose romance, *Perceforest*; the *Volsung Saga*, in which the Walkyrie Brunhilde is awakened from her slumber by Sigurd (Siegfried); and *Sun Moon and Talia* in Basile's *Pentameron* (Barchilon and Flinders, *Charles Perrault* 93).

Perrault's tale begins on a religious note, with the enumeration of many pilgrimages, prayers, and pieties undertaken by a royal couple in an unsuccessful attempt to conceive a child. In due course, their wishes are granted and the queen is delivered of a baby girl. Seven fairy godmothers are invited to the baptism. Following the ceremony, they repair to the palace for a feast during the course of which they bestow, as is customary, perfections on the newborn. Magnificent place settings, including a solid gold case containing a spoon, fork, and knife decorated with diamonds and rubies, have been placed before each fairy. As the banquet commences, an old fairy angrily enters the great hall, protesting her exclusion from the ceremony and feast. Greatly embarrassed, the king explains that, since she had not stepped out of her tower lodgings for fifty years, he thought her dead or bewitched. To rectify a wrong, however, the host has a place setting put before her on the table. Since only seven solid gold cases had been ordered for the occasion, and these had already been distributed among the young fairies, an eighth could not be produced at a moment's notice. The old fairy considered such an omission an unpardonable slight.

Muttering veiled threats under her breath, she is overheard by one of the young fairies who decides to hide behind a tapestry to wait for the old fairy to utter her imprecation, after which she will step forward to mitigate the evil. Predictably, the old fairy places a curse on the newborn: the princess's hand will be pricked by a spindle and she will die. Above the din of the weeping guests, the disarmingly gentle voice of the young fairy is heard speaking her reassuring words: the spindle will prick the princess's hand, but rather than die, she will fall into a deep sleep that will last a hundred years, after which a king's son will come and awaken her.

SPINNER-FAIRIES:FATES. Just as the Fates in ancient Greek, Roman, and Germanic lore played a role in carving out an infant's future, the fairy godmothers bestowed physical and spiritual qualities on the newborn, while the old fairy called down a curse. Etymologically, the words "fairy" and "fate" are connected: "fairy," from M.E. *fais*; M.F. *fei*, *fée*; Lat. *Fata*; and the English *Fate* (Harf-Lancner, *Les Fées au Moyen Age* 9). The mythological Fates included the Greek Moerae, the Roman Parcae, and the German Norns. The Greek Clotho, for example, spun the thread of life; Lachesis determined its length; and Atropos cut it. In that the gifts the seven fairy godmothers were to bestow on the newborn were designed to protect the infant from harm, these suprapersonal women may be compared to Clotho and Lachesis. Endowed with both negative and positive maternal qualities, the Fates, as karmic powers, had the capacity to cherish, sustain, devour, or terrify all living beings. Thus, everyone may be said to be connected in some way with these spinning women—or with predestination. Hesiod, understandably, referred to them as "Daughters of the Night," and sisters of the Goddesses of death (*Theogony* 211–217).

The identification of wisdom and understanding with old age was not applicable in the case of the uninvited fairy in our tale. As a negative aspect of the Great Mother, she bore the royal family a grudge, revealing her feelings of spite and mean-spiritedness, which are characteristic of those who have never known or dispensed love. Unfulfilled, introverted, unable to relate to others, she had chosen to live a reclusive existence, erroneously assuming that isolation would protect her from further hurt. Deep in her collective unconscious were factors that she either ignored or repressed. Instead of attempting to dislodge them, she suffered the fate of those who try to relieve their pain without attempting to resolve the reasons for its existence. In her resentment, her unredeemed, dark, unlived shadow forces took on dimension, flooded her ego, and transformed it into an ever-festering instrument of destruction. Like the archetypal witch, the old fairy released her life-threatening haplessness on the helpless (Franz, *Shadow and Evil in Fairy Tales* 104, 5). As a prisoner of her own deadly powers, she may be identified with the third Greek Fate—Atropos—whose spectral form stands behind every individual as she cuts the thread of life.

Like the old fairy of Perrault's tale, so the quarreling and fighting Eris, a Greek Goddess, later assimilated to the Roman allegorical figure Discord, had not been invited to the marriage of Peleus, (king of the Myrmidons)[4] to Thetis, the Nereid. Eris avenged herself for the affront by offering a golden apple to Paris who was to award it to the most beautiful of three deities—Hera, Athena, or Aphrodite. That he chose Aphrodite set off the Trojan War. As in life, so agents of violence and hurt are perpetually evident in religions, history, fairy tales, and fables.

NUMEROLOGY AND ALCHEMICAL SYMBOLISM. In numerology and alchemical symbolism, widespread during Europe's Middle Ages and in Perrault's time as well, the number 7 (cf. the seven fairy godmothers in our tale) was considered to have mystical significance. According to Jung, numbers are archetypal. As such, they were not invented by the conscious mind, but emerged from the unconscious spontaneously, when the need arose, in the form of archetypal images. Like archetypes, numbers are psychic energy *(libido)*, thus fomentors of dynamic processes or virtualities in the psyches. They may lie latent in the unconscious as events or shapes until consciousness experiences them in the form of "images, thoughts, and typical emotional modes of behavior" (Franz, *Number and Time* 18; Jung, 92 31).

The number 7 brings to mind the paradoxical worlds of abstractions and of concretions: the days of the week, the seven petals of the rose, the seven heavens, the seven spheres of angels, the seven alchemical operations, the seven planets, and so forth. The ability of the fairy godmothers to circulate from one world to another enabled these supernatural beings to transcend the workaday domain. As inhabitants of both physical (earthly) and spiritual (heavenly) spheres, they would bestow qualities on the infant girl that would incorporate tangible and intangible values. Not only would she be beautiful, but she would also possess artistic accomplishments, such as dancing, singing, and musicianship. The child would bear the grace and spirit of an angel, thereby likening her to themselves. *Earth,* as previously mentioned, was associated by numerologists and alchemists with 4, and heaven with 3, the two adding up to 7, suggesting a harmony of opposites that would ultimately prevail in the child's psyche (Jung, 9_1, #425).

THE KING'S ATTEMPT TO ALTER FATE.

So destabilized was the king upon hearing of his daughter's fate that his psychic functioning became impaired to the point that he sought to dominate what has and would always elude mortals, the chance factor. Unlike Abraham who, in total humility, was willing to sacrifice his son Isaac (psychologically speaking, his ego or center of consciousness) to God (the Self, i.e., the whole psyche), and thus was spared the loss of his son (Gen.22: 7–18), the king in our fairy tale refused to submit, and thus failed in altering his child's fate. Unwilling to surrender his ego-power to the Self—perceived psychologically as a "matrix out of which the conscious individual develops"—the king attempted to play God, the "creator and preserver," and would suffer the consequences for his hubris (Cox, *Modern Psychology* 162).

Believing himself authorized to circumvent the infinite—God's world of imponderables—he tried to sidestep the old fairy's prognostication by concentrating his energies on ways of protecting his daughter. To this end, he issued an edict banning, under pain of death, all spinning and spindles from the palace.

TO LIVE UNDER A SPELL. A *spell*—in our case, the one cast by the old fairy—may be likened, psychologically speaking, to a *poisoning* (an autonomous content introduced into an individual's subliminal world). The implantation of a terrible fear in someone's mind may take on the aspects of a malediction, and if the malediction comes from several sources it acquires a cumulative power that may suck up the life force of the person involved. Thus, the imprecations of sorcerers, witches, astrologers, soothsayers, handwriting experts, enemies, and even friends, may vitiate the life of the vulnerable as well as the strong person.

In the case of the royal couple—emotionally fragile parents who had suffered a difficult conception and were concerned about the newborn's good health—the old fairy's spell exacerbated an already built-in sense of panic. However, the careful planning and vigilant supervision on the part of the royal parents succeeded in protecting their beautiful daughter from harm's way until she became of marriageable age. As fate would have it, an accident occurred on the day chosen by the royal couple to oversee repairs to one of their country homes. The unsupervised princess, imbued with a sense of excitement, and perhaps taking advantage of her parents' absence, yielded to her yearning to discover something on her own. Although she was wobbly emotionally, infantile in her expectations, and unsteady in her direction, curiosity had become her psychopomp. Having been imprisoned by understandably excessive restrictions imposed upon her by her parents, she took advantage of her day of freedom to investigate the, until-now, unseen upper floors of the palace. Gleefully, she climbed the stairs and peered into what must have been a thrilling but forbidden realm, where she happened upon a dungeon. There, she came upon a nice old lady spinning.

THE DUNGEON: ASCENSIONAL IMAGERY. Not a dark underground prison cell usually associated with medieval castles, the dungeon in Perrault's tale is a *donjon*, a massive inner tower located on the castle's top floor. The inner stairs, leading to what the adolescent considered a wondrously mysterious area, served to enhance the thrill of her ascension.

Ascensional symbols, such as stairs, ladders, and pyramids, are designed to encourage earthbound creatures to shed their mundane cares and opt for divine preoccupations. Although the tower-dungeon in Perrault's tale suggests a remote, repressed, virtually forgotten, and certainly neglected area of the palace, it may also be looked upon as a paradigm for the head or the human rational sphere (as cellars or underground areas are frequently identified with the body, instinct, and/or unconscious). The princess's climb up the stairs corresponded to a directional alteration, filling her with an increasing sense of freedom and release from a highly structured and imprisoning life style. But it served as well to cast all judgmental faculties to the wind.

Might her rapid and unheeding ascent have been motivated by an unconscious rejection of her fearful parents' apprehension? The headiness she felt in the tower's rarefied atmosphere, while serving to dispel the pall of fear that had weighted her down since infancy, triggered in her an oppositional mode of behavior as well: *enantiodromia.* This condition, now dominating her actions, is defined as "a one-sided conscious attitude [which] constellates its opposite in the unconscious" (Edinger, "An Outline of Analytical Psychology" 2). So exaggerated were the feelings of release and self-confidence in her adolescent ego that her imaginary world became her reality Never before having seen anyone practicing the art of spinning or weaving, it is no wonder that the princess stood in awe before the "nice" old lady.

THE "NICE" OLD LADY AND HER SPINDLE. Who was this seemingly endearing old lady living in a dungeon? Like the Fates, she spun, wove, and sewed, thus performing activities identified with creating, shaping, and structuring, but also with cutting the fabric of a person's earthly existence. As an aspect of the Great Mother or matrix, she stood for the transitory nature of the life process. As a personification of a disguised appeal for acceptance, love and recognition, she would entrap the princess, but on a positive note, she would offer her new possibilities of developing her consciousness within, of course, the preestablished or fated design of her future (Jung, 91, #187). Although seemingly destructive in Perrault's tale, the "nice" old lady may be considered a positive force in fulfilling the adolescent's life: for it is she who will bring her to the next stage of her emotional development. Like Lachesis, in charge of measuring time, the old lady, as spinner and weaver of the young girl's web of earthly activities, redraws and retwists the fibers into thread, thus altering the previous focus of her existence. No sooner, therefore, does the old lady allow the princess to take hold of the spindle than the young girl pierces her finger and falls into a dead faint. Predictably, all attempts to revive her are in vain.

Although needles, spindles, pins, darts, and other pointed intruments inserted into someone's skin or body may be considered phallic symbols, in the princess's case, they are to be looked upon as protective devices as well. She is psychologically unprepared for marriage (symbolized by her syncopal reaction to the phallic image—the piercing of her finger), and the hundred-year sleep would serve to impede any matrimonial union, cut her off from mundane pursuits, and, most importantly, shield her from the effects of puberty. The time allotted to her during her long slumber—not a death—will permit her to indwell, that is, to evolve subliminally, thereby preparing her for her future love and parenting experience.

THE GREAT SLEEP. Upon being alerted that the princess had fainted, the king had her carried into the most beautiful room in the palace and placed on a bed whose spread was embroidered in silver and gold. Although her eyes remained closed, the princess's cheeks retained their rosy hue and her lips their coral flush. Her audible breathing indicated that she was alive.

The good fairy, who had altered the curse placed on the princess, although a thousand leagues away, was instantaneously apprised of the catastrophe by a dwarf. Dwarfs or elves, often appear in fairy tales focusing on children for, like them, they may be devilish, roguish, and impulsive. Known for their skills and their diligent work habits, they frequently figure as helpers to the young. Their small size was not considered a deformity, but rather identified them with "tiny" or remote possibilities of finding alternative means of handling dangerous situations (Jung, 91, #268).

No sooner was she informed of the princess's condition than the good fairy hopped into her flaming chariot drawn by dragons (Gr. *drakon, derkomai*; see, sharp-sighted), which took her by air to the castle. Positive attributes are here ascribed to the fairy's dragons, in sharp contrast to the symbolism of the principle of evil in Christian lore. St. George, St. Michael, St. Patrick, and a host of other men proved their heroism as slayers of dragons and thus destroyers of evil. By contrast, dragons in ancient times were often considered guardians of treasures, as in the Greek legend of the Golden Fleece. In China, to these same fabulous monsters were ascribed dynamic intelligence, strength, and wisdom, so that they became identified with imperial power. Because many Christians thought that subhuman psychological characteristics were lodged in dragons, the animals became associated, psychologically, with a seemingly equally fearsome beast—the feminine. Throughout the Middle Ages and thereafter, the dragon as a female force was featured as spewing flames—thus as a monstrous destroyer of everything in her wake. What was not taken into consideration in the rigid patriarchy of the times was the meaning of fire in general, and of its issuance from the dragon's gullet in particular. Fire as energy, if properly directed, could produce positive results: it could cook and thereby transform what formerly was raw. As ably demonstrated by Claude Lévi-Strauss in his *The Raw and the Cooked*, fire transforms and acculturates what was formerly crude and unrefined. The fairy's choice of dragons to guide her chariot to the tower indicated not only a need to take her to her destination as rapidly as possible, but demonstrates as well that fire/energy, if directed toward positive purposes, may turn what originally was a curse into a carefully nurtured, fruitful life experience.

Upon arrival at the palace, the deeply sensitive fairy, foreseeing how lonely the princess would be when she awoke one hundred years later to find herself surrounded by strangers took it upon herself once again to protect her from sorrow. By touching with her magic wand everyone (except the king and queen) and everything (even the fires used for cooking) in the castle, she put them all to sleep. Psychologically fascinating is the fairy's intent to allow the parents to die at their allotted hour, thereby permitting the princess upon awakening to make her own decisions and take responsibility for her own wellfare. Indeed, she was endowing her with the prerogative of grown-ups. Moments after sleep had engulfed the palace, a protective wall of trees, shrubs, and thorny bushes was set in place to safeguard the area from intruders. Only the castle's towers remained visible from a distance.

THE MEANING OF SLEEP. Sleep, throughout ancient times, was recognized as crucial to the healing process, whether physical or psychological. Had not the Greeks in one of their most famous healing centers—Epidaurus, devoted to the physician God, Aesculapius—effected cures of the physically ill by analyzing their incubation dreams? Using procedures very different from today's psychiatric hours, the priests at healing centers in Greece first gave their patient a drink from the the spring of forgetfulness (Lethe) and then from that of remembrance (Mnemosyne), permitting the forgetting of the past and the recall of dreams. Interestingly, instances of Aesculapius's miraculous cures were identified during the early centuries of the Common Era with those of Jesus. Fearing the power this Greek physician exercised over the people, the early Church regarded Aesculapius as one of its greatest foes. Because some of Jesus' miracles had been confused with those of Aesculapius, it was claimed that the former's name derived from Jaso (Aesculapius's daughter), and from *Iashtai* (to heal) (Pongracz and Santner, *Les rêves à travers les ages* 55).

When the princess fell asleep, her adolescent ego was still weak and unprepared for marriage and motherhood. That the fairy had the genial idea of putting everyone in the castle to sleep, while also endowing the princess "with the pleasure of pleasant dreams," indicated her understanding of sleep as a working period, instrumental in the adolescent's maturation process. Although the princess's ego was submerged in repose, that is, in timelessness, dream activity continued, encouraging her, paradoxically, to grow in understanding. In a process like that of association in filmic sequences, the princess's unconscious took charge of linking together the separate images that were being formed in her subliminal sphere. The capacity to transform the disparate feelings, sensations, and/or ideations cohabiting within her unconscious into what might be called a scenario, encouraged her to "spin her yarn," so to speak, or fantasize freely in her sleep. Upon the princess's awakening, she might perhaps be able to articulate her inner drama coherently, by bringing subliminal sequences or happenings onto conscious levels.

Like the spinning, weaving, and cutting processes that are interwoven throughout *Sleeping Beauty,* dream images are also to be understood as threads connecting an ambiguous or visionless past with a still-undeciphered future. Wasn't it thanks to the thread Ariadne gave Theseus before he entered the labyrinth that he was able to find his way out of the dark and confusing maze—into enlightenment in the outside world?

So the princess's magical sleep, unlike death when the body decomposes, is to be regarded as a transitional and beneficial period in her life. This kind of *regressus ad uterum,* as in Orphic ritualistic descents, invited the princess's psyche to penetrate preexistent spheres of being: those matriarchal folds linking feelings of love, wholeness, and the sexual experience into one. The princess's passive acceptance of the dream sphere enabled her to descend into the chthonic domain of the nourishing Great Mother. That her body experienced a condition of physical stasis in no way, as previously mentioned, deterred her activity in subliminal spheres. The period of indwelling, which sleep had forced upon the princess, encouraged her to develop a broader approach to life that would, upon her awakening, endow her with a greater understanding of human nature. As written in the Mandukya Upanishad: "The life of man is divided between waking, dreaming, and dreamless sleep. But transcending these three states is superconscious vision—called The Fourth" (*The Upanishads* 49).

THE PRINCE'S ARRIVAL AND SEXUAL INTERCOURSE. After a hundred years had elapsed, the son of a neighboring king who had been hunting in the vicinity caught site of towers in the distance. Upon questioning several people, he was told that they were inhabited by spirits and sorcerers, as well as ogres who fed on little children. An old peasant, having heard a different story, reported that the towers housed a beautiful sleeping princess. Inflamed by the very thought of this exquisite creature, the prince, like any hero of old, braved the fearsome stillness and deathly immobility of the premises. Making his way through the thickly forested area, he noticed that the trees, thorns, and brambles parted before him, as though helping him walk with ease directly toward the castle. Guided, seemingly, by some unknown inner power, he proceeded through the great marble courtyard, ascended a stairway, continued through some rooms, and then beheld the most "divinely luminous" young maiden he had ever seen. Consumed with excitement, he knelt atremble before this resplendent creature.

As an *anima* image, defined as an "autonomous psychic content in the male personality," the princess took on the most exalted of qualities for the prince: not merely the incarnation of beauty and love, but of connectedness as well (Edinger, *Melville's Moby Dick* 5). Sensing, then recognizing her beloved from the many dreams she had had during her hundred-year sleep, the princess looked at him most tenderly, then asked: "Is it you, my prince? I have long awaited your arrival" (*Sleeping Beauty* 252). Charmed and moved by her words, the prince, traumatized by the sight of such exquisiteness, was unable to convey his joy and gratitude coherently. Finally mustering sufficient self-control, he told her he loved her more than himself. Warmed and comforted by each other's presence, the two spoke for four hours, at the end of which they realized they had still not told each other half the things they wanted to say. A note of levity is injected into the narrative when the prince, loath to hurt her feelings, refrains from mentioning her outmoded clothes.

What would be the role the princess would play in the prince's life? Would she be his *femme inspiratrice*, the idealized mate for whom he had evidently been waiting? Or would her love serve as a catalyst to arouse him sexually? Certainly, their meeting redirected the lives of both—giving them a new awareness of their great love for one another, and a mutual sense of commitment. The princess's awakening brought joy and a mood of ebullience to the palace. The entire court had begun to stir with activity. The hall of mirrors served as the lovers' dining hall, a metaphor perhaps for certain ancient sacred spaces. The continuous motility and interplay of glimmering reflections may be considered an externalization of their impassioned mutual love. Their marriage was celebrated that very evening in the palace's chapel, and was consummated in the princess's bedroom. A note of frivolity was interjected by the author after the princess's lady-in-waiting drew the curtain around the bed, and commented "they slept very little for the princess was not in need of it" (*Sleeping Beauty* 253).

Upon returning to his own castle the following morning, the prince did not inform his parents of his marriage. Seeking to allay his father's anxiety, he accounted for his absence by telling both parents that he had lost his way in the forest. His trusting father believed him. His mother, inured to the ways of the world, concluded that he had fallen in love.

Although time sequences are muddled in fairy tales, and those in *Sleeping Beauty* are no exception, readers learn that for the next two years the prince settled into a routine: by night he lived with his wife, by day, with his parents. Two beautiful children—a girl, Aurora, and a boy, Day—were born to the couple.

THE VAGINA DENTATA—OGRESS/MOTHER. Knowing that his mother was descended from a race of ogres, the prince took every precaution to protect his wife and children from her aggressive, vicious, and devouring proclivities. Although the queen was a veritable *vagina dentata* type, the prince nonetheless loved his piranha-like mother. In keeping with similar mother/son relationships, his was fraught with ambiguity.

The Terrible Mother archetype in myths is not in short supply: Kali, Hecate, Empusa, Gorgon, Lamia, Lilith, female demons, witches, and countless destructive spirits whirl about individuals who realize their helplessness against, and dependency upon, these devastating and overpowering mothers/maws (Neumann, *The Origins and History of Consciousness* 40). The benumbing dynamism of the ogress in *Sleeping Beauty* emphasizes the lengths to which the Terrible Mother would go to assuage her appetite.

Inhabitants of dark, hidden, and forbidding areas within the psyche, ogress mothers usually draw on vulnerable, malleable, and still-unformed beings for food. Although the prince in our narrative would have liked to be loved and cared for by his mother, her flesh-eating instinct had not gone unnoticed by him. While she inspired dread in those about her, the prince must have learned during his formative years how best to protect himself from this castrating predator. Rather than adopting a confrontational attitude toward her, which would have undoubtedly led to a dismemberment of his ego, he sidestepped, obfuscated, or clearly lied in order to ward off her maniacal outbursts. Such tactics caused neither a diminution of his ego's directive powers, nor a weakening of the masculine side of consciousness.

Imprisoned in her blind anthropophagous need to consume whatever might deter her from realizing her inborn phobic hunger to dominate, rule, stunt, and arrest the development of individuals who seek to evolve and mature, she, like the Terrible Father Kronos/Saturn, also sought to subvert time—or the life/death factor—by devouring his progeny. It comes as no surprise, then, that Kronos/Saturn was later called the God of time. Having rejected her role as genetrix, the ogress in *Sleeping Beauty* sought to destroy her genitors. Amoral rather than immoral in her flesh-driven appetite, she was oblivious of the suffering she brought to her entourage.

The prince had noticed on repeated occasions that in the presence of children, his mother was barely able to control her ravenous need to devour them. Indeed, her unappeasable appetite was nearly always focused on children—a metaphor for futurity—indicating an inborn terror of having her power usurped by younger, and eventually stronger, elements. Anxiety for those he loved dictated his unwillingness to confide in her the secret of his marriage and the birth of his children. Although he had succeeded to a great extent in becoming emotionally separated from his mother, the threat of matriarchal castration must have nonetheless loomed large on his horizon, urging him forever to take precautions. Nor did he trust his father. Not because of any malice on the part of his parent, but for his naiveté and his weakly structured ego which, under pressure, the prince feared, might easily be urged to reveal his closely guarded secret. Important as well was the fact that his father, having married his mother for her wealth, had never known the meaning of love. How could he possibly understand his son's feelings for his wife and children? Or his fears for their well-being? Although the ties of a mitigated love for the prince's mother and father remained, the young man was no Attis. The prince's psychological hiatus between him and his parents had already been effected; therefore, he suffered no guilt with regard to them. On the contrary, his ability to reason and his understanding of their positive and negative attributes, had set him well on the way toward independence (Neumann, *Origins* 117).

THE CHILDREN. The prince's daughter having been named Dawn, and his son, Day, suggests that their birth may have symbolized their mother's rebirth, her awakening to the light of consciousness, and her fulfillment in marriage and motherhood.

Dawn (Aurora), meaning to begin, to appear, to develop, suggests the birth of a series of days and the possibilities of realizing one's dreams and hopes. Such a time frame allows for a maturation process ands a birth of light, or God's victory over darkness:

> Hast thou commanded the morning since thy days; and caused the day
>   spring to know his place;
> That it might take hold of the ends, of the earth, that the wicked might
>   be shaken out of it;
> It is turned as clay to the seal; and they stand as a garment.
> And from the wicked their light is witholden, and the high arm shall be
>   broken. (Job 38:12–15)

While day represents both sunrise and sunset, as well as a succession of definite time periods, it contains not only each day's residue, but that of a lifetime as well. Whenever short or long expanses of time are activated, and past memories recalled, lessons may be drawn from the variety of each individual's experience. The birth of Dawn and Day, therefore, suggests a turning point in the lives of their parents. Just as every individual must live out her or his own rite of passage, so the protagonists in *Sleeping Beauty*, must confront theirs.

Only after the prince's father had died, and the kingship had passed to him, did he publicly announce his marriage and the birth of his children. With pomp and circumstance, he then went to his wife's castle and bought his family to live with him. Aware of his mother's anthropophagous inclinations, the reader may wonder why the prince, upon being called to war shortly after assuming the kingship, left his mother in charge not only of his domain but of his greatest treasures—his wife and children.

A NONINTERFERENCE COURSE. Instances arise when noninterference may be the most appropriate means of resolving life-threatening situations. With her son gone, free from his judgmental eye, the ogress mother—experiencing perhaps the same kind of freedom the princess had felt with the departure of her parents on that fateful day—allowed her instincts free rein. Repairing to the family's country home with her daughter-in-law and her grandchildren, she ordered her steward to *cook* the four-year-old Dawn and serve her in a sauce of spices and vinegar, symbolically masking her flesh-eating needs. The steward, sickened at the thought of committing such a heinous act and catching sight of the delightful little girl running happily toward him, dropped his knife and began to cry. Reversing his steps, he went to the barnyard, severed the neck of a little lamb, cooked it, and served it to the queen mother, who complimented him on the succulence of the dish. Unseen by the queen mother, he took Dawn for safekeeping to his wife's lodgings in the far corner of the barnyard. A week later, the ogress asked that Day, her three-year-old grandson, be served to her with the same sauce. This time, the steward substituted a baby doe for the boy, who was also sent into hiding with his sister. And again the queen mother consumed the morsels of flesh with intense gusto. Shortly afterward, she requested that the steward kill and cook her daughter-in-law. Again the steward refused to comply. Failing, however, to find an appropriate animal to serve to the ogress, he went to the young queen and apprised her of his dilemma. Since the demise of her children, she confided in him, life held no more meaning for her. It was, therefore, his duty to kill her. Moved to the extreme by the gentle woman's loving manner, the steward took her to her children, after which he slaughtered a young hind, which he served to the satisfied ogress.

One evening, however, while the ogress was prowling around the farmyard in search of fresh meat, she heard voices, which she recognized as those of Dawn, Day, and their mother. So outraged was she at the deception that she ordered a fire to be lit under a huge vat filled with toads, vipers, snakes, and a variety of serpents. After the queen, her children, the steward, his wife, and her servant had been bound, and just as the executioner was about to cast them all into the vat, the king entered the courtyard on horseback and demanded to know the meaning of this "horrible spectacle" (*Sleeping Beauty* 257). Foiled, the ogress threw herself headlong into the vat and was instantaneously devoured.

The very human king who had always loved his mother despite her anthropophagous instincts, was saddened by her death. Soon, however, he found consolation, joy, and enrichment in his wife, children, and kingship.

Fate, the supernatural, wish fulfillment, verisimilitude, and fabulous events such as a hundred-year sleep, were instrumental in paving the way for the maturation process of both the princess and her prince in *Sleeping Beauty*.

Generally passive, neutral, and apathetic, the adolescent princess acted overtly only once—on the day her parents had gone away. Aggressively and spunkily, she demonstrated a need to enter into the life experience. Her mother and father had so feared for their child's well-being that they had prevented her from stepping out into the world to carve out a life for herself. Like an infant taking her first steps, she, not surprisingly stumbled at the outset. In time, however, she ceased falling and developed a relatively strong self-image. With glee, abandon, and a tinge of rebellion, she found a sense of excitement and fortitude in her newly achieved independence.

The healing sleep from which the princess awakened brought her understanding and the capacity to love without fear or guilt. Prepared for the responsibilities of marriage and motherhood, she not only accepted the prince's difficult familial situation, but understood the importance of biding her time. The prince's ability to protect his wife and children against the continuous threat of his ogress mother indicated his strength of character and augured well for the rulership of his kingdom and for his role as husband and father. That he neither feared nor despised, nor took overt action against his mother, revealed his ability to cope with a panoply of vastly different personality types—necessary for any ruler. The ogress, "unable to satisfy her own inner rage," took her life, thereby ending the possibility of malevolence—at least temporarily—in the royal couple's world.

Bluebeard: Children's Fare On The Internet?

The terrifying and enthralling plot of Charles Perrault's *Bluebeard*, although it included typical fairy tale motifs (temptation and a magic key), was, seemingly, of his own manufacture (Barchilon and Flinders, *Charles Perrault* 93). Nonetheless, it has been suggested that his protagonist, Bluebeard, may have been modeled on the fifteenth-century historical Marshal of France, Gilles de Retz. As a young man this Breton nobleman had distinguished himself in battle at the side of Joan of Arc in the Hundred Years' War. After the conclusion of hostilities and his retirement to his castle of Tiffauges, his life changed so drastically that this once great hero became known for his villainy and murderous deeds. Not only beautiful young women, but children as well, were kidnapped, tortured, and killed at his demand. Indeed, he used the latter unmercifully in his alchemical experiments and satanic blood orgies. He was tried and executed for his crimes at thirty-six years of age (Wilson, *Bluebeard* 61 ff.).

Perrault's fairy tale, unfolding in detached filmic sequences, gives an impression of *pavores nocturni* (night terror) directed by some unknown preternatural power. The buildup of Bluebeard's strangely distorted behavioral patterns increases the intensity of the unfolding events, leaving readers spellbound under the weight of the character's sadomasochistic acts. Significant as well in Perrault's narrative is the treatment accorded to wives and, indeed, all females participating in the gruesome tale. Not only are they victimized within the trappings of the story, but they are minimized to the extreme.

Perrault's tale begins as the wealthy but ugly Bluebeard searches for a wife. Despite his attempts to curry favor with the eligible young girls in his hometown, his monstrously thick blue beard is repulsive and frightens them away. In addition, Bluebeard's past plagues him: it is rumored that he has been previously married, not once, but several times. The fate of these wives, however, remains a mystery. Bluebeard persists in pursuing the beautiful and socially acceptable young girls in the district, eventually narrowing his sights to his neighbor's two daughters. The older, and more sophisticated sister, Anne, sensing perhaps some violent, amoral, recidivist streak buried in Bluebeard's psyche, rejects him outright. Unwilling to compromise her well-being, her truth, and her integrity for money and rank, she stands firm in her decision. Gallant in his maneuverings, yet impatient in his attempt to finalize his situation, Bluebeard cleverly invites mother, daughters, and some of their friends to one of his country estates. The lavish feasts, dances, hunting, fishing parties, and all-night revelries last for eight days. At their conclusion, the naive younger sister, taken by Bluebeard's wealth and status and perhaps by some unfathomable erotic aura about him, grows more amenable. No longer considering his blue beard an unattractive element, she sees him more positively: as an honorable, well-meaning man, and, therefore, quite a catch. The two are wedded.

THE BLUE BEARD. Although beards have long been identified in religious paintings, statues, and texts with virility and wisdom (Hindu/Vedic, Indra; Greek, Zeus; Judeo-Christian, Samson; the Christian God, Father and Son), in Perrault's tale the beard's strange color caused the protagonist to be ostracized. The thick growth of blue hair on his face, unlike the beards of other men, was considered as a sign of eccentricity, perhaps even beastliness, and uncontrollable instinctuality. In that people sensed about him something odd, different—perhaps aberrant, even dangerous—young girls shied away. Attachment to an anomaly, they may have reasoned, might cause a wife to suffer the mockery of her peers, or even exclusion from society. How much easier it would it to choose a mate who fitted the stereotype—the pattern established by the collective—instead of trying to cope with nonuniformity.

Blue, the most transparent of colors (*trans,* through + *parens,* from *parere,* to appear), usually represents the ethereality of the nonmaterial, as in sky and air. There is also an important psychological association with this color: the antithesis of the red of fire or flame, which spelled life for Heraclitus, blue is usually identified with cold, remoteness, and purity, and for some even preludes death (Brun, *Héraclite* 138).

The composite nature of transparent blue tones and a thick, opaque beard, while perhaps signaling virility and power, also suggests obfuscation and hidden visual tones of ambiguity. The insightful Anne sensed a blockage: Bluebeard's thick growth of hair was like a wall separating the two. Anne's tenuous feelings of repugnance for Bluebeard may be contrasted with the younger sister's materialistic, unintuititve, and worldly outlook in her choice of economic status.

PERSONA: MASK. As a manifestation of the protagonist's ugliness, the blue beard may also be looked upon as a persona or mask, defined in ancient times as a covering worn by Greek and Roman actors to dissimulate, diffuse, disclose, or layer an inner emotional climate. From a psychological point of view, and as previously mentioned, the function of the *persona,* which "stands between the ego [center of consciousness] and the outer world," is multiple (Edinger, "An Outline of Analytical Psychology" 4). Having the power to conceal as well as to reveal profoundly troubling inner components, the persona serves as a mediating factor enabling the individual to adapt to his outer world.

Bluebeard's deeply rooted identification with his persona could signal a condition of alienation from both individuals and the collective. Could it conceal a hidden degenerative psychosis, or elements of a disturbed and/or depraved psyche? Particularly troubling was the ease with which Bluebeard donned the mask which conformed to his conscious purpose. Needless to say, he played his role to perfection. Not only had he learned to impress those around him with his charm and savoir-faire, thereby mastering his ego's requirements, but he also knew how to conceal and, thereby repress those contents it found unacceptable.

Despite his finesse and acumen, the protagonist's blue beard, like an indelible stain or blemish, remained visible on his face as a constant reminder of what he sought to hide from the world. What lay beneath the *persona?* Perplexing to the perceptive was the possibly explosive, unconditional violence and brutality contained therein. For the casual or superficial observer, however, such as his wife-without-identity—who judged only his self-imposed outward demeanor, his acts of seeming benevolence, hospitality, gallantry, and givingness—Bluebeard seemed to be an ideal husband.

A MINOTAURIAN INNER WORLD. Bluebeard comports himself in a more than socially acceptable manner, but readers are soon made privy to his dark, hidden, or *minotaurian* side. The Cretan myth tells us that because the Minotaur, endowed with the head of a bull and the body of a man, lived out his homophagic instincts by eating his victims, he was incarcerated in the labyrinth, a building constructed especially for his containment. Similarly, but in modified terms, Bluebeard, acting under his own volition, built himself an inner chamber that hid his bloody rituals. Like the minotaurian man—a paradigm of the empowerment of instinct (body) over the rational (head)—Bluebeard possessed closeted behavioral patterns that may be considered a reversal of Plato's ideal human combination, which has dominated Western thought since ancient times.

BLUEBEARD'S GUARDED SECRET. So firmly implanted was Blubeard's defensive persona that unless emotionally threatened, he was capable of maintaining his intrapsychic calm with relative ease. By contrast, anyone's attempt to intrude into his private world would have upset, if not destroyed, the delicate balance between his persona and his ego. Should his equilibrium have been shattered, the *shadow* factor might have taken over full force. As a psychic entity, the shadow, which stands between the ego and the inner world of the unconscious, is defined as a "composite of personal characteristics and potentialities of which the individual is unaware" (Edinger 4). Not only does the shadow contain characteristics the ego does not recognize; it considers them negative or inferior and thus rejects them.

Just as Bluebeard was cut off from verbal or actional communication with his wife, except on the most superficial of levels, the same disjointedness occurred on a collective level, further excluding him from any semblance of relatedness with another human being. Let us note in this connection that a husband's inability or unwillingness to confide in his wife may to a great extent be considered the norm for married couples in Perrault's time. The great common denominator between husband and wife in the seventeenth century—and even among some contemporary couples—revolved around household and family concerns, such as money and children.

For couples to enjoy meaningful connectedness required and still requires an inborn confidence on the part of partners. Bluebeard's unrelatedness, stemming from a condition of morbid inflexibility, manifested itself, to a great extent, in his inability to relate to women except very superficially. Such distanciation was also symptomatic of his fundamental blindness with regard to his own motivations and inner (unconscious) processes (Jung, 6, #593ff.).

Trust in anyone, certainly in his wife, was for the deeply introverted misogynist Bluebeard an unknown quantity. Like the mythological dragon who functioned for the most part as guardian of areas within which treasures had been concealed (the Golden Fleece, the Golden Apple in the Garden of the Hesperides, the Ring in *Siegfried*), our protagonist was forever vigilant, even on the defensive, when it came to protecting his *mystery*—that is, his secret inner domain.

Bluebeard's cold, judgmental, arbitrary persona so controlled his emotional problems that seemingly he could will his anxieties to cease. While giving the impression of friendliness and amiability to the object-woman, namely, his wife, he kept his inner uneasiness in abeyance, thanks to his minotaurian instinct of self-preservation. Always on guard, forever ready to depotentiate any would-be aggressive female, he became isolated by his show of overt manliness, affability, and wealth, and unconsciously embittered still further. Unbeknown to Bluebeard, such extremes of comportment encouraged his minotaurian side to further poison, destroy, and cripple whatever semblance of happiness he might have known in marriage.

The overall pattern of Bluebeard's life may be described as *serial* in nature: the greater his outward bravura and gallantry, the more evident his ingrained pathological fear of women became. His compulsive need to prove his dominion over them disclosed not only a heightening secret discomfort in their presence, but a necessity on his part to perpetually reconfirm their integrity—a quality that he was convinced they did not possess and of which he perhaps sought confirmation. A continuous round validated his distrust of the female sex. Putting women to the test, rather than helping him deal with his misogyny, seclusion, aloneness, and an out-of-hand fear of castration, had served until now to contain his subliminal contents. At this juncture in his life, however, the unredeemed powers haunting his inner world began to spill into consciousness with increasing violence.

The etiology of his fear of womankind may have dated back to his earliest childhood, undoubtedly to a wound inflicted upon him by his mother or another important female presence at the time. He erroneously believed that only by subjecting her—paradigmatically, any woman—to the most rigorous test of fidelity could he eventually gain *real* confidence (*con+ fidere*, trust) in womankind in general, and in his wife in particular.

Despite his belief that the testing of his wife's integrity was the only valid method of proving her worth, his sense of well-being, paradoxically, depended on her failure to pass the test. Any violation of the truth as he saw it was in his view an act of transgression against him. Under such circumstances, the violator would merit the fullest of punishments. No second chance was admissible.

TEST/TEMPTATION.   During the first several weeks of his marriage, Blubeard's outer magnanimity reigned. With the passing of each succeeding day, however, his ability to mask his psychosis, or those dark unredeemed factors haunting his unconscious, grew increasingly unmanageable. After a month, rage and chaotic pulsations became too difficult to contain. His addictive personality felt impelled to resort to his trusted standby: the ultimate, unforgiving test. Only by proving his initial negative contention concerning women could Bluebeard find release from his increasingly desperate and gnawing doubt.

With his predictable bravado and largesse, he informed his wife of his imminent departure on an important business trip. After giving her the keys to all the storerooms of his palatial home, he empowered her as well to enjoy his money and every material object in his residence as she saw fit. To dispel any loneliness that might arise from his absence, he suggested she invite her family and friends to feast and party with her. He did, however, add one caveat: he forbad her to use the key that opened the door to a secret chamber in the the home's lower levels.

Why such excessive generosity on the one hand, and such a grim taboo on the other? The answer may lie in the scenarios of his sadomasochistic rounds. The implantation of a prohibition in his wife's mind, he may have reasoned, would on the one hand excite her curiosity, and on the other trigger her conflict between the moral or the immoral path to follow. Should she—and he unconsciously hoped she would—decide to disobey a husband's interdict, he would be proving her vice-laden, thus deserving of the most egregious of punishments. The *test* motif triggered his fantasies. Her weakness would be a means of reinforcing his own strength. Such a devious—deviant—subterfuge ruffled his erotic sensations.

The power struggle between male and female, operative for millennia, allowed the male to keep strict control over his woman: wife, mistress, or concubine. In some ancient cultures, it was the standard way of life. But even in certain contemporary societies repressive measures, even institutionalized barbarity, are implicit. Plural marriages, female infanticide, wife beating and even killing, clitoridectomy (excision of the clitoris), infibulation ("the stitching together of the vulva . . . leaving a small opening for the passage of urine and menstruation" *(Webster's New Unabridged Dictionary)* are, in some societies enforced to this very day. According to Bluebeard's agenda, infidelity on any level, be it sexual or moral, as in the disobedience of an interdict, was punishable by death.

THE KEY TO THE CHAMBER/NECROPOLIS. The key, the only object that places *Bluebeard* in the fairy tale genre, will become the all-important, actively charged, supernatural force that paves the way for the narrative's conclusion. As expected, following the verbalization of the interdict, Bluebeard's wife was assailed by conflict. The thought of the enormous wealth and power her husband had put at her disposal was appositioned to a sense of growing torment associated with feelings of diminution. (Let us note that the word *torment* Lat. *toquere*, to twist as by rack or wheel, is applicable to both psyche and body.) That the fate of her husband's former wives still remained a mystery gave her cause for distrusting him, certainly not overtly, but in some closeted area of her psyche. Her motivation for opening the door to the secret chamber may, therefore, have rested on her desire to clear up the mystery—based perhaps on her own repressed fear—revolving around the fate of the other women in his past. Did the rapture aroused by the very thought of prying into a mystery excite some unacknowledged erotic delight in her?

Despite the arrival of family and friends, the wife's growing anxiety/curiosity mounted to obsessive proportions. Unlike her husband's rigid and protective persona, hers was flimsy. Affective and unthinking, as previously noted, her behavioral mode resembles that of her Greek sisters, Pandora and Psyche. Nonetheless, it is antithetical to that of the biblical Eve, who had higher purposes in mind when yielding to the temptation of eating the fruit of the tree of knowledge—"the day ye eat thereof, then your eyes shall be opened, and ye shall be as gods, knowing good and evil" (Gen. 3:5).

Deftly, quietly, and anticipatorily, Bluebeard's wife put the key into the lock and opened the door to the forbidden chamber. Since the window blinds were shut, closeting the *temenos* to the outside world, darkness prevailed. Closure imagery frequently reveals not only blindness or lack of insight on the part of the viewer, but also serves to emphasize certain zones of obscurity, or regressive areas in the psyche of that individual. Let us recall in this regard that unlike her older sister, Bluebeard's wife had chosen to *overlook* her husband's ominous beard, her eyes having been rendered sightless, so to speak, so dazzled had they been by the glitter of his gold.

As her vision slowly became acclimatized to darkness and she looked down at the floor, she began to distinguish certain outlines, then forms, and, to her horror, lumps of clotted globules of blood. Having seemingly taken on consistency, they stood out like small gleaming gelatinous mounds. So intense was their mirroring effect that, they disclosed reflected outlines of slain female bodies hanging on the wall. (Perrault's text never mentions whether or not the wife looked at the bodies directly, or only as reflected in the blood on the floor.)

Caverns, subterranean chambers, holes, inner hiding places, and protected areas in pyramids, castles, dungeons, or other concealed spaces, have been used since ancient times for the enactment of rites of passage—sacrificial or of spiritual rebirth—or other types of esoteric ceremonies. Remote and dark interior areas, comparable to the sealed inner spaces of the lobes of the brain, contain mysteries associated with the mind and its unexplained functioning.

This type of secret chamber which severs individuals, even temporarily, from the ouside world or from the collective, has been depicted in the novels of J. K. Huysmans *(Against the Grain* and *Down There)*, in short stories, such as "William Wilson" by E. A. Poe, and by alchemists who, fearing arrest by church and/or governmental authorities, secreted themselves for days and years in concealed laboratories, converting base metals into gold.

That Perrault interwove the mirror image into this sealed-off chamber is significant in terms of decoding the psychological underpinnings of Bluebeard's psyche. It also indicates the popularity of the object itself in his era. Mirrors had not only become the sine qua non of refined parlor games, but, as illustrated in Perrault's *The Mirror of Oronte's Metamorphosis* (1661), an object for inner reflection (Soriano, *Contes* 336; Lewis, *Seeing Through the Mother Goose Tales* 9ff.). Let us note in this connection that for thousands of years mirrors had been used to bring on or encourage illumination in Shaman ceremonies and in Buddhist and Shinto rituals, and to hypnotize trance-seeking patients.

The mystery revealed by the hanging bodies, as they cast their reflections on the shiny shimmerings and reflective mirrorings on the floor's surface, not only aroused speculation on the wife's part, but gave her access to an unexpected demonic death drama. The mirroring of the hanging corpses on the wall and the gleaming clusters of blood on the floor increased her apprehension, triggering a preternatural happening: the terrifying vision of her own body hanging alongside the others on the wall. While inadvertently opening herself up to a blood ritual, she unleashed her knowledge of hetofore concealed affects inhabiting the remotest areas of her husband's mind. The impact on her of such an unexpected and excoriating sight, was accentuated by the unexpected release of a preternatural mental image: the enactment of a second dreaded scenario in which she would be the star victim!

Artistic renditions of deformations and distortions may be seen in the works of Jean-François Niceron (1613–1646), author of *Curious Perspective* (1638) and *Thaumaturgus Opticus* (1652, posthumous), who experimented with perspective by placing a reflecting cylinder near the center of a given painting, and discovering that the scene, like the effect of deforming mirrors in circuses, when projected on the mirror-like surface of a curved cylinder, was distorted. While studies in perspective had been carried out in the Renaissance by Lomazzo (1584), and Father Andrea Pozzo, Niceron's strangely distorted paintings of Louis XIII (1635), St. Francesco di Paola (1635), a marriage scene (1656), and Louis XIII in front of a crucifix, went much farther. His particular method of applying the rules of projection via a mirroring cylindric object lent an eerie, magical and illusional effect to the imaged deformations of the original canvas. Simon Vouet (1590–1649) also experimented in this vein. Indeed, regulating projected images via mathematical calculations became a fad in France, in some cases, used strictly for fun and entertainment, in others, to hide erotic private fantasies (Onori and Vodret, *Capolavori della Galleria Nazionale d'Arte Antica Palazzo Barberini* 143).

The physiological repercussions of Blubeard's wife's vision of the hanging bodies, and the psychological trauma it provoked, accounted for her haste in leaving the scene and dropping the key her husband had given her. Since it was magic (or fée), this supernatural and baffling object, working in tandem with the horrible images projected before her, had soaked up some of the clotted blood on the floor. Once back in her room, she tried but failed to rub or wash off the stains. Reminiscent of Lady Macbeth's bloodied hands and her cry—"Out, damn spot! out, I say!" (V, 1)—the evidence of the wife's betrayal remained indelible. How could it have been otherwise? To eradicate blood stains from a magic key, and images from the mind, would have been tantamount to obliterating her transgression—and its memory.

The removal of a spot or stain on a material object may be allied metaphorically to the notion of forgetting, repressing, or excluding painful contents from consciousness. The very thought of her inability to remove the stain—or to rid herself of the memory of her transgressive act—recalled the cryptlike surroundings in which her husband's violent derangement of the senses had occurred.

While past memories may be brought back into consciousness by association with an object such as a key, repressed images or situations are far more difficult to recall. In either case, to cast aside moral or other problems via repression/denial, as Bluebeard's wife had endeavored to do, was an escape mechanism. Had she succeeded, it would have prevented her from facing her husband's threats, and, to a certain degree, her own blindness. Repression and denial of what one sometimes looks upon as a threatening and/or shameful side of one's nature, is virtually analogous to a psychological dismemberment, a cutting out, or rejection of a part of oneself. Inability to come to grips with traits the ego considers noxious reveals a powerlessness to face responsibility for one's acts. Simply forgetting or repressing "things which would endanger our idea of ourselves," while serving the wife's purpose, would be impossible to accomplish, given her husband's psychological makeup (Cox, *Modern Psychology* 59).

Meanwhile, the intensification of the wife's nightmarish vision and the lurid colors on the key, intractable reminders of her disregard of her husband's order, accentuated her feelings of dread. Still, might not these very reminders point to an indirect means of extricating herself from her dilemma? Perrault's ambivalent mirrorings and key image, the former with its power to reflect, dissimulate, and/or discriminate, and the latter enabling the wife to open and/or to close her own subliminal spheres, calls into play the surreal and magical qualities of her unconscious.

Let us note, in connection with key and door imagery, the importance accorded by the Romans to the God Janus, as guardian of the door opening on to ever new beginnings (*Januaris mensis* means the month of January). Christians awarded St. Peter the honor of opening or shutting the doors to heaven. It was more than probable that Bluebeard's wife, seeking to increase her knowledge of her husband's mysterious proclivities, had also taken the initiative by unlocking the forbidden door, to open herself up to a blood sacrifice and, in so doing, to life itself.

BLOOD SACRIFICES. According to Mircea Eliade, blood sacrifices were practiced when society changed from agriculture to metallurgy, when a "spiritual universe," with its "heavenly God," was "ousted by the strong God, the fertilizing Male, spouse of the terrestrial Great Mother." At this juncture of human development, "the notion of *creation ex nihilo* was replaced by the idea of creation by hierogamy and blood sacrifice" (Eliade, *The Forge and the Crucible* 31). Life came into being in the latter case only after another life had been sacrificed: the Babylonian Marduk conquered Tiamat the sea monster; the Germanic Ymir, the Chinese P'anku, and the Hindu Pusrusha, all formed of primal matter, brought forth the world following the bloody sacrifice of their own selves. Parallel sacrificial rituals are to be found in totem meals, Mithraic bull sacrifices, and the Christian communion. A sacrament is a way of binding together the human and the transcendental, or expressing brotherhood and spiritual unity, and thereby strengthening ties with the divine and the collective.

Blood sacrifice, symbolically speaking, is also evident in the alchemical process as depicted in *Bluebeard*. The word *caillé*, or *coagulated*, used by Perrault to describe the consistency of the blood on the floor, replicates the alchemist's stage of *coagulatio*: the hardening, and solidifying of a previous liquid condition—or, by extension, the fixing of a fluid attitude. The once naive, impressionistic, and *fluid* positive notions Bluebeard's wife had held about her husband had now been arrested and concretized in the bloody lumps and reflected corpses she saw in the secret chamber. Thus, she could begin to adapt to a more realistic point of view, to apply a broader-based ruling principle to her own plight. In so doing, her source of wealth—her own unconscious fears, as disclosed in her preternatural vision of her own body hanging alongside those of Blubeard's former wives, would direct her to ways of saving herself from what she sensed would be her bloody massacre.

The *redness* or *rubedo* color of blood intrinsic to the alchemical process may be interpreted psychologically as an increase in libido, or the psychic energy factor necessary to further life's transformatory operations. The wife's identification with the mirror images of the corpses had so *inflamed* her psyche that she was finally able to see a very real *disjunctio*: the existence of a second personality alive in a contained climate of flamboyant alchemical images. Only at this juncture, when dismissal of the ugliness of her husband's blue beard was no longer possible, could she acknowledge her judgmental error and thereby allow the healing process of her psyche to begin.

Nonetheless, ambiguities insofar as Bluebeard is concerned still remain. That he cut the throats of his former wives in butcher fashion, allowing blood to flow freely, is, to be sure, characteristic of certain types of dementia. So, too, is the fact that he did not rid himself of the evidence. Such comportment, suggests that he—like certain sadomasochists—sought to be discovered and punished for his murders. Herostratos, a prime example of this kind of comportment, burned down the Temple of Artemis at Ephesus on the day Alexander the Great was born in order to earn both fame and punishment. Was Bluebeard also attempting to prove his strong and virile nature via his incredibly grand actions? Or was he simply a pawn of his own depravity? Would his unconscious feelings of inadequacy be overcome by his Herostratic act (considered as expiation through punishment)? Was Bluebeard asking to be brutally killed? Or was he simply enticing his wife to join him in his sadomasochistic erotic rounds until death did them part? Could he have also been a practitioner of necrophilia?

Psychologically fascinating as well is the fact that Bluebeard's wife, even after she saw the horribly reflected hanging bodies, neither fled the castle, nor confided her feelings to her sister or friends. Was she finally attempting to assume responsably for her transgression, thereby evolving from adolescence to maturity? Or would subterfuge and calculated risk, she might have reasoned, better help her fend off disaster?

LYSIS. Bluebeard's travel plans having been a ploy, he returned home the very night of his wife's transgression. Understandably, he did not want to draw attention to his need to confirm her lack of integrity, so he waited until the following day to ask her for the keys. Not only did her hand tremble as she returned them to him, but upon noticing that the magic key was not in the lot, he requested its return. He understood that what he had anticipated—her deception—was a reality. Accusing her of having defied his interdict, he announced: "Well, Madam, you will enter [the room] and take your place along side the other Ladies you saw" (*Bluebeard* 264).

Rather than reason with him, which she knew to be to no avail, she humbled herself and, kneeling before him, begged for his mercy and, strangely enough, for his pity. She requested that he allow her to pray, thus opening herself up to a transcendent power. Although frenzied to the extreme, he nonetheless agreed to her request, but set a time limit of fifteen minutes, after which she had to return and he would kill her.

Seemingly in full command of her mental faculties—one of the psyche's defense mechanisms activated, strangely enough, when terror is extreme—the wife withdrew from her husband's presence. Undaunted, she ran up the stairs, and in desperation, called to her sister Anne, asking her to rush to the uppermost part of the tower to see whether their brothers, who had promised to visit on that very day, were visible in the distance. Repeatedly, she called to her sister, asking her if she could make out their forms on the horizon? In the ever-mounting intensity of her melodramatic dialogue, which has proverbial importance in French lore, the reader hears her cries ring out: "Anne, my sister Anne, do you see something coming?" Ambiguously, the phrase may also be translated "Do you see nothing coming?"

Meanwhile Blubeard, waiting downstairs and holding his knife in readiness, called up to his wife to either come down or he would go up and fetch her. As his threats gained momentum and his wife's desperate requests were answered in the negative, time was running out. When, suddenly, the wife heard Anne's blessed words—she had seen two knights on the horizon, and had signaled them to hasten—the *deus ex machina* motif was introduced. Although the savior brothers appeared in *no time*, they were, paradoxically, *in time* to prevent Bluebeard from slaughtering his wife. So startled was Bluebeard by the unexpected thunderous poundings at the door that just as he was about to raise his arm to stab his wife, he suddenly stopped to open the door.

The image of closure having been removed, first by the wife as she penetrated the forbidden chamber, and now by the outer world intruding into inner happenings, a brief struggle between doers of evil and doers of good unfolded. It took *no time* for the savior-brothers to run their swords through Bluebeard's body.

Because Bluebeard had no heirs, his wife not only inherited his fortune but became the wiser from her ordeal. Her newfound wealth was used to secure the rank of captain for her brothers, to marry Anne to a suitable young gentleman, and to find so fine a husband for herself that "he made her forget" her own nearly fatal experience. Perrault's use of the verb *forget* is somewhat troubling in this regard. As previously mentioned, to divest oneself of memory is to encourage amnesia (Gr. *amnéstia*, oblivion). The obliteration of large segments of the past and, simultaneously, the benefits derived from experience and compararisons between past and present activities, depletes, even stunts, the individual's psychological growth. By contrast, an *anamnesis* (Gr. *anamnesis*, remembrance) is a means by which one recalls past events, with increased awareness of the personal lessons derived from some act in that time, which, if reflected upon, may pave the way for individuation (Eliade, *Aspects du mythe* 112). Whether Bluebeard's wife forgot what she had learned from experience, or whether she sought to repress what she had lived through, is moot!

Perrault's *Bluebeard*, like the concatenations of a sleep walker, is gripping for the melodramatic effects worked into the text. It is also frighteningly real and as timely today as it was in the seventeenth century. That an individual on one level may be charmingly disarming, and on another, prey to the deviant pulsations that have made inroads in the cavelike lobes of his mind, is only too apparent. While the serial nature of Bluebeard's acts and their anticipated punishments take on momentum, they also serve to further his morbid fear of the feminine, and in so doing, to titillate him sexually in his attempt to dominate/destroy the opposite sex. The repeat performances of Bluebeard's blood rituals, each enactment aggravating his already splintered paranoid schizophrenic world, could only conclude with his own death. In that life is a continous process, however, and Bluebeards are born at all times and in all societies, how is it that the arteries of readers and listeners have continued throughout the centuries to pulsate at the very thought of such tales? And that we are still left spellbound by Bluebeards on television and on the Internet?

MME D'AULNOY'S THE BLUEBIRD
METAMORPHOSIS,
AN UNCONSCIOUS READJUSTMENT

FAR FROM UNEVENTFUL, the daily existence of Mme d'Aulnoy (1650[1]–1705) was interwoven with drama and mystery. Her pulsating psyche led her to penetrate both the light and shadow sides of human nature. So sensitive was her understanding of a person's capacity for suffering, loving, and hating, and so perceptive was she of hidden jealousies, rancors, and unrealized cruelties, and their opposites, kindnesses and consideration for others, that her fairy tales, *The Bluebird* in particular, live on as human documents of the soul.

ECTYPAL ANALYSIS

Of noble birth, the beautiful, curly-haired, blonde Marie-Catherine Le Jumel de Barneville, was a native of Normandy. Following the death of her father, her mother, Judith-Angélique, remarried a Marquis Gudane, about whom no information has thus far become available. In 1666, in cahoots with her lover, Courboyer, Mme Gudane married off her fifteen- or sixteen year-old daughter to the ostensibly rich François de la Motte, baron d'Aulnoy. From the outset, this man had two strikes against him: forty-six years of age, he was three times older than his wife, and as for his character, he was unpleasant, debauched, and impetuous. Despite her dislike for her husband, Mme d'Aulnoy gave birth to six children; the first two of which died shortly after birth (the last two, it was presumed, had not been fathered by her husband). The ostensibly wealthy baron d'Aulnoy, who had either lost all of his money or had never had any to begin with, was faced with mounting debts. Cloak-and-dagger episodes soon followed. Accused of the crime of *lèse majesté* whether by his wife, his mother-in-law, and/or "two friends" remains un-known, he was imprisoned. Thanks to his connections, he easily worked his way out of what he and his lawyers proved to be trumped-up charges. Fol-lowing his release, the "two friends," were sent to the Bastille. Under tor-ture, they confessed that Mme Gudane, who had grown to despise the baron, had hatched the plot, and the two were executed in 1669 (Barchilon, *Le conte merveilleux français 1690–1790* 37–51).

Facts concerning Mme d'Aulnoy's implication in this scandalous affair are sparse, and whether she had participated in the conspiracy against him is unclear. We know only that she was separated from her husband in 1670. Whether she felt any guilt for the deaths of the two culprits who were exe-cuted is questionable. Nor are we certain as to whether she had been arrested for complicity in the *lèse majesté* accusation. If so, her important connections must have been used to effect her release without trial. By contrast, so great was Mme Gudane's fear of imprisonment that she, apparently left for Spain never to return. Did her daughter join her mother in Madrid? Did she then venture to England, as some critics have suggested? We know only that, upon Mme d'Aulnoy's return to Paris in 1690, she took up residence in a convent, her only possibility for obtaining permission to live in the capital. The re-maining years of her life were spent writing and enjoying the company of lit-erary friends. After 1692, she became a regular member of Mme de Lambert's literary salon which included Mlle de La Force, l'abbé de Choisy, and Fénelon. The many topics broached during their Wednesday meetings, encouraged oral presentations of fairy tales (Barchilon).

That Mme d'Aulnoy was drawn to the fairy tale genre is evident in her first work, *Hippolytus Earl of Douglas* (1690), well known for its provocative theme of incest. Her following literary ventures touched on Spain, a very fashionable country at the time: *Memoirs of the Court of Spain* (1690) and *Trav-els into Spain* (1691). In keeping with the heavily religious tenor and suppli-cant mood of the times—one of the consequences of Louis XIV's marriage to the ultra-"devout" Mme de Maintenon—our author also dipped into devo-tional literature, as attested to in *Sentiments of a Penitent Soul* (1691) and *A Soul's Return to God* (1692). Another vein was struck with the publication of her *Memoirs of the Court of England* (1695). But it was her *Tales of the Fairies in Three Parts* (1697–1698) and her *New Tales or Fairies in Fashion* (1698) that earned her lasting acclaim and admiration.

While imaginative and charming, Mme d'Aulnoy is best known for the finesse of her protagonists' observations about themselves and the world about them. Her forays into dreams and preternatural, or magical happenings add metaphysical dimension to her narratives. Not be overlooked are the metamorphoses of some of her characters within the paradoxically realistic/fantastic frame she conjures for her readers. In keeping with the fairy tale mode in seventeenth-century France, Mme d'Aulnoy's works were not written exclusively for children. On the contrary, they were written for adults and designed to educate as well as to entertain.

Like many of the romanesque novels of her day, Mme d'Aulnoy's writings broached significant subjects, such as torture, imprisonment, injustice, and rebellion, and invited readers to identify with events and characters. Unlike the many redundant writings of some of her contemporaries, Mme d'Aulnoy's succinct and tightly-knit style was enriched by details of the living conditions, traditions, etiquette, and refined social habits of her protagonists. Elaborate feasts, masked balls, magnificent clothes, luxurious fabrics, elegant interiors, unusual knick-knacks, and impressive jewels, embedded in a truly rococo atmosphere, heightened the paradoxically realistic nature of the supernatural beings she brought into focus.

Archetypal Analysis

The Mysteries of Metamorphoses. The mysteries of inter- and/or intra-human metamorphoses, whether involving the transformation of people into animals or vice versa, are infinite. Their inexplicability or, for some, their miraculous nature, may have encouraged some organized and nonorganized religions to include certain instances of physical permutations in their credos. Since the beginning of humankind, *Homo sapiens* has called upon visible and/or invisible powers—be they Gods, Goddesses, or demons—to help unravel the enigmas of the unknown and confront seemingly irremediable problems. In ages past, many believed that the superhuman divine or demonic power lodged in a fish, insect, animal, or two-, three-, or four-legged creature could alter a devastating or dazzling life experience. While some may still find comfort and help in age-old religious motifs, others may draw upon the sciences, psychology, crystallography, exercise, meditation, magic, and other healing processes for an answer to the unfathomable.

Prophetic disclosures in apocalyptic and scientific writings foretelling the advent of cosmic or climatic catastrophes have spurred humans both to accept the end of life as we know it, and to look toward the natural world for consolation and emotional therapy. To gain a sense of relatedness with surrounding nature and an expanded community of feeling toward one's environment and universe is, indeed, comforting. Because in past ages certain trees, bushes, and other fetishes were, and for some still are, endowed with indwelling spirits, they were invested with sacrality: the Djed Column for Osiris, the boddhi tree for Buddha, mistletoe for Druids, the Tree of Life for Jews, Christians, and Muslims. All lent and continue to lend worshippers feelings of support and connectedness. May it not also be suggested that, diversity in the animal and plant worlds, paradoxically, imparts a sense of unity to those plunged in adversity? Don't totemism, fetishism, zoomorphism, to mention but a few of these credos, invite people to project characteristics, impulses, instincts, thoughts, or feelings onto existing or fabulous animals, plants, or other entities they believe will care for them?

The recognition of earthly or celestial wonder-working forces, if regarded as projections of inner psychic contents, may provide individuals and societies with a sense of authenticity and purpose. The kinship felt between divinities, humans, and animals is nowhere better conveyed than in the Ramayana, with the transformation of one of the protagonists of this Hindu epic into a deer. Egyptians worshipped many of their deities in the form of animals: Sekhmet/lionness, Horus/hawk, Apis/bull, Hathor/cow, Bast/cat, Ra/snake, Ba/bird, and so forth. To them they turned for help in time of need. Hadn't the biblical Solomon conversed with the hoopo bird? In certain pre-Islamic legends, to this same king's famous visitor, the Queen of Sheba (Bilqis), were attributed ass's hooves and webbed feet. The Bible tells of Balaam's she-donkey speaking words of wisdom (Numbers 22: 1–14). Griffons, ostriches, geese, sirens, harpies, dragons, mermaids, amphibious creatures of all types were depicted in medieval bestiaries. Sibyls and oracles at Delphi, Dodona, Cumae, or elsewhere, were frequently featured with wings and webbed feet. Did not the heads of animals symbolize three of the four Evangelists?—the lion for Mark, a cow or ox for Luke, and an eagle for John. The Holy Spirit was revealed to Mary in the form of a white dove. Devils with horns, claws, talons, hooves, webbed fingers, or goatlike cloven hoofs have paraded in frantic and frenetic disarray in cult worship throughout the centuries.

Humanized animals endowed with intellectual and emotional characteristics representing human vices, follies, and virtues have been featured in folk narratives and literary works—the *Fables* of the Greek Aesop (560–520 B.C.E.) and those of the Latin fabulist, Phaedrus (15 B.C.E.–50 C.E.), and such writings as Apuleius's *Golden Ass* (125 C.E.), the *Metamorphoses* of Ovid (43 B.C.E.–17 C.E.), the *Decameron* of Boccaccio (1313–1375), the *Canterbury Tales* ("The Man of Lawe's Tale") by Chaucer (1330–1400), A *Midsummer Night's Dream* by Shakespeare (1564–1616), and the *Fables* of La Fontaine (1621–1695). Nor was it uncommon for authors to portray nonhumans as more clever than *Homo sapiens,* even rendering them at times as their teachers.

The medieval Christian-oriented *mystery* play may be analogized to humankind's need to adjust and readjust to ever-altering empirical situations and relationships. Real and imagined worlds cohabited on the stage platform in these religious spectacles, in which a higher power manifested himself as an earthly being, or as an animal, plant, or other kind of creature. Spectators, projecting onto the metamorphoses were, psychologically speaking, transformed as well. Their broadening of outlooks toward certain situations that resulted from the alteration of their feeling and thinking functions, may have opened them up to new alternatives vis-à-vis the obstacles confronting them. Similar modifications occurred in Mme d'Aulnoy's *The Bluebird.* The hero, Prince Charming, was transformed into a bird; the heroine, adapting to this situation, set out on her rite of passage. Readers of the fairy tale may be encouraged by her strength and integrity to do likewise on a psychological level—transforming their limited approach to empirical situations into a broader and all-encompassing one.

Instrumental as well in triggering unconscious compensatory sensations in the reader may be the occult practices described in Mme d'Aulnoy's text. Lingering memory images in *The Bluebird,* reminiscent in some ways of Proust's technique in *Remembrance of Things Past,* may, for some resurrect bygone happenings in the psyche. The multiple sensations triggered by Mme d'Aulnoy's images—the bird, forest, castle, good and evil creatures—and the expanded consciousness to which they give rise, may help readers deal with their own difficulties (Jung, *Visions Seminars* I, 43; II, 489).

WAS IT BEREAVEMENT? OR BEWITCHMENT? Mme d'Aulnoy had more than likely found inspiration for *The Bluebird* in a short narrative in verse, *The Lai of the Nightingale,* by the twelfth century French writer, Marie de France. The latter's tale revolves around an unhappily married woman whose lover visits her in her tower home in the form of a nightingale. During these interludes, he reveals his passion for her in his warblings, which she interprets in keeping with her feeling world. Similarly, Mme d'Aulnoy's fictionalized Bluebird talks, feels, senses, and probes his own heart and psyche, and that of his beloved as well.

The tale opens on a memorable scene: a wealthy and powerful king is so distressed by the death of his wife that he locks himself in his room and spends his time knocking his head against its walls. His courtiers, fearing he might kill himself, hang mattresses about the room and in vain try to cheer him with sympathetic, sad, or merry tales. One day, a lady bedecked in a black mantle, veils, and robes comes to visit the king. So excessive is her sorrow for her deceased husband, that she wails and shrieks uncontrollably. They mutually lament the death of their spouses, but as the king's sympathy for the lady in black mounts, thoughts of his wife diminish proportionately, to the point of disappearing. When the lady in mourning reveals to the king that she wants to spend the rest of her life weeping for her deceased husband, the king asks her "not to immortalize her chagrin" (*The Bluebird* 74). That he marries his visitor comes as no surprise to the reader. In summing up the incident with her usual deftness, Mme d'Aulnoy notes: "To be aware of the weaknesses of people is frequently sufficient to gain entry into their heart and to manipulate it as one sees fit" (*Bluebird* 74).

The emotionally vulnerable (Lat. *vulnerare*, to wound), king, it may be said, having been wounded by his bereavement, was subject to infection and disease. His knocking of the head against the wall indicates not only the seat of his problem, but his morbid intent to further damage and fragment his thinking function. Indeed, so cut up was he, so to speak, that the lady in mourning, like an expert therapist, knew just how to further break down his virtually nonexistent defenses. While her lamentations gave the impression of sorrow for herself and sympathy for him, she was, in fact, beginning to voice an imperative agenda of her own. Manipulative and clever, this highly functional woman was an expert in the art of conditioning the king to accepting whatever situation she had in mind. It was she who set the stage for the growth of a new dominant in his psyche: the dependent, regressive, somatization of his ego-consciousness.

Could the king's complete subservience and blindness to the lady in mourning be alluded to as a *bewitchment*? Certainly, since falling under the influence or spell of a malignant power, or enslavement by a human being, indicates the ego's submission to an outside force. Indeed, the monarch's emotional divestiture due to his wife's death had been so complete that his meeting with this powerful woman whose sorrow seemed to replicate his own endowed him with a sense of communality. Knowing that others could suffer as deeply as he provided him with a sense of togetherness and thus comfort. The interplay of what he took to be their mutual pain, elicited in him a need to be magnanimous—to play the grand role of king—which might enhance his self-image. His complete misunderstanding of her intent, and of his ability to guide her to more positive activities, served only to increase his emotional dependency on her. The pragmatic lady in mourning, by contrast, uninterested in love, feeling, or relatedness, had but one goal in mind: to play the role of a controlling power in her victim's life.

THE CONTROLLING FEMININE. Immediately after having assumed the queenship, she moved toward achieving her primary goal—that of marrying her ugly daughter, Truitone, to a wealthy noble. Daily, she jealously eyed the king's beautiful daughter, Florine, as her despair over the ugliness of her own mounted. She suggested to the king that since both their daughters were fifteen years old, they should be wed—her daughter first, then his. Unwilling to "dispute" her wishes, the monarch accepted her proposal (*Bluebird* 75).

Florine (Lat. *flos, floris*), named after the Goddess of flowers and of springtime, who is imaged so beautifully on Pompeiian frescos, was not only externally exquisite, but was adorned internally with lovely attributes or character traits. Usually a symbol of Edenic purity and nature's ephemerality, the floral world has also been identified with inner attitudes of tenderness, gentility, and consideration. Loving to her father, and to all those around her, it may be said that like the flower, Florine related to both earthly and celestial spheres, the former because her feet were firmly implanted in reality, the latter since she yearned for spiritual transcendence.

Implicit in the name Truitone is its onomastic identification with the triton or with the French *truite*, or speckled trout (from the Greek *troktes* < *trogein*, to gnaw). Like the fish, Truitone was oily (her hair) and blotched (her face). Ugly externally, her personality was equally unsightly: jealous and vindictive, she was a mirror image of her mother. Unlike the queen, however, she was neither cunning nor clever. That Truitone bore the name of a fish identifies her with the water element, which, according to the sages of antiquity, enabled her to see her shadow, doppelgänger, or soul image whenever she peered into this transparent medium. Would she, working in tandem with her mother, be empowered to evoke demons by burning candles around a circular vessel filled with water, as was believed possible in the Middle Ages (Franz, *Projection* 184)?

THE QUEEN'S WITCHLIKE ADUMBRATIO. Let us note that when the queen first met the enfeebled king, knowing exactly how to attack his vulnerability/woundedness, she pretended to bond with him in their mutual sorrow. His ailing mental state combined with his self-destructive acts had transformed him into a passive recipient of whatever the queen suggested. Taking full advantage of his diminished will to live, she was empowered to cast over him her adumbratio (Lat. *ad, umbra*, shadow), or distorted, venomous, rancorous, and unlived aspects of her personality.

The master/slave dynamic that the witchlike queen (M.E. *wicche*, sorcerer; L. *vincere*, to conquer, victor, wicked) had set in place allowed her to play out her scenario. Reminiscent of the Egyptian demon, Set, who, driven by jealousy, cut up his brother Osiris into fourteen pieces, the queen would focus on the psychological dismemberment of her daughter's rival—Florine. Having made a pact with evil spirits, that is, her own psychologically nefarious unconscious propensities, this all-too-human witchlike woman proceeded to spread her malignant authority in all domains.

Shortly following the royal couple's decision to marry off Truitone and Florine, a stereotypically handsome, radiant, delightful, but not overly bright Prince Charming arrived at the palace. The queen's tactic of denigrating Florine rather than enhancing her own daughter's image served to diminish Truitone. Instead of being taken in by the queen's self-serving manner, the prince was shocked by her comportment. Moreover, her unctuous attempts to dismember Florine psychologically by emphasizing what she considered to be the young girl's undesirable traits—her coquettishness, stinginess, and bad temperedness—simply backfired. The greater the queen's castigations, the more irate Prince Charming became. Aware of her momentary defeat, the queen turned her manipulative arsenal of weapons on the forever-acquiescing king, extracting his promise to buy no more new gowns or jewels for his daughter. Her belief that to bedeck Truitone and to force paltry attire on Florine would magnify her daughter's chances with Prince Charming, was again misplaced. Florine's humiliation in the unseemly and dirty dress she was forced to wear during her meetings with Prince Charming explains why she remained huddled in a corner of the reception hall during his visits. Rather than reflecting the personality of the two girls, the vestments or personae worn by the overdressed Truitone and the raggedly garbed Florine, fell short of hiding the former's ugliness and the latter's beauty.

Rather than equating outer and inner beauty, the increasingly perceptive Prince Charming saw beyond Florine's ragged clothes/*persona* and was dazzled by the resplendence of her inner self. Refusing to believe that nature "could put such a badly made soul [Florine's] on such a Masterpiece," he understood her innate purity of heart and the feelings of humiliation foisted on her by the bleakness of her world (*Bluebird* 78).

Overprotective of her daughter, whose independence was totally stifled by the maternal pursuit of a single goal, the queen, "like a dog sniffing at garbage pails," as Jung put it so well, destroyed any possibility of her progeny's enlightenment (Sharp, *Personality Types* 57). She lavished magnificent gifts of clothing and of jewels—diamonds, pearls, and rubies as large as ostrich eggs—on Prince Charming, in tandem with her flagrant denigration of Florine. Predictably, Prince Charming was increasingly repelled by the queen's tactics, and taken by Florine's modest and gentle character.

The queen's failure to achieve her goal having brought on a condition of stasis in her marriage plans for her daughter, she was encouraged to take even rasher steps. To this end, she asked the king—who passively agreed—to have Florine secreted in one of the castle's towers. With free rein to take matters in hand, she ordered three masked men to kidnap the beautiful girl and lock her in the dungeon tower. Florine's sudden disappearance from court neither altered the prince's unwillingness to marry Truitone, nor deterred the queen from intensifying her witchlike plans.

Ruthlessly exploiting Florine's powerlessness, the queen sent double agents to query Prince Charming about his feelings toward the two girls. Psychologically sensitive to his mood changes, the queen's envoys reported that whenever they praised Florine, his exhilaration and ebullience mounted, but the pronunciation of Truitone's name had the opposite effect. It was not long before the exasperated prince began questioning the queen and her courtiers about Florine's whereabouts. Angered by his unflagging fascination with her daughter's rival, the queen told him that only after he and Truitone were married would the king allow his daughter to reappear at court.

Pressed into action by his distress, Prince Charming inquired of some ladies in waiting—in reality other double agents of the queen—whether he might be granted an interview with Florine at her tower window. His request having been accepted, he waited patiently for darkness to fall, in the hope that his rendezvous with Florine would remain secret. With joyful heart, he went to the meeting place. Once within hearing range of his "beloved," he declared in passionate but controlled terms his eternal love to his lady. When she appeared at the door, he placed a gorgeous ring on her finger and took leave of her, promising to return the following night. Unable to distinguish the features of the girl in question, the prince never realized that he was speaking to Truitone and not to Florine. Reappearing the following night, he asked his future wife to seat herself next to him on a flying chair drawn by winged frogs, which a magician friend had made for him. At the propitious moment, the thickly veiled Truitone emerged from a mysterious door in the tower and was embraced by her future husband. After swearing his eternal fidelity, he asked her where she would like the wedding to take place. In Fairy Soussio's castle, she replied. An understandable choice, since this supernatural being had not only been her mother's close friend, but had also played the role of surrogate mother to Truitone, whom she loved as her own. Mme d'Aulnoy's proclivity for irony is again evident in the onomastic derivation of Soussio's name: a combination of the Spanish word, *sucio* (dirty) and the French, *sous* (beneath; inferior).

THE MAGIC FROG-BORNE CHARIOT. That Prince Charming's marriage proposal had taken place in darkness—under the aegis of the queen's adumbratio or shadow—encouraging the fishlike Truitone, and those identified with her, to live out a hoax.

The frog figure played an important role in medieval times in France, appearing, for example, in all of its glory on the standard of the politically astute—or conniving—Clovis (481–511), king of the Franks. Winged frogs as conveyers of the couple's chariot are psychologically intriguing: familiar with "the general map of the universe," they were able to find their direction in any type of maze, or, psychologically, any specious or perfidious situation (*Bluebird* 82). Mme d'Aulnoy endowed the aquatic amphibians in her story with wings, giving them the capacity to fly to their destination during night hours. Thus, they may be identified with both lunar and solar forces. Like other fabulous beings, such as the winged lions worshipped by the Assyrians, Babylonians, and Persians, these frogs had an inner eye and an ability to ascend into the air that allowed them, as mediating powers, to transcend their chthonic and watery habitats and gravitate toward celestial spheres. In touch with the highs and lows of both cosmic and human environments, they functioned on earth, in water, in the air, and in fire.

The future couple's flight through the air to their new destination ideally might have provided them with a broad view of the earth, that is, the problems associated with their empirical situation, but the duplicity of the queen and her daughter, and Prince Charming's blind naiveté served to cloud their vision. His inborn impulsiveness was revealed by the fact that he rushed, unthinkingly, into a clandestine, sexually motivated marital arrangement. Unlike Florine who was physically incarcerated in a tower, our near-sighted prince of the night was imprisoned in his own limited universe.

Chariots—those of Mithra, Attis, Cybele, Cuchulan, Zeus, Santa Claus, and countless other deities and heroes, were associated with the Sun principle. Prince Charming's, however, was identified with moonless blackness. That the magician who designed the flying apparatus was an alchemist, a practitioner of this so-called "black art," is more than likely, the two being virtually synonymous in the fairy tales of the time. In this regard, the entire night time sequence may be associated with the first, or *nigredo,* stage of the alchemical process. Bathed in a type of primal darkness, the unconscious or unaware travelers slumbered in a state of paradisaic ignorance, thus becoming fertile field for future inner turmoil.

THE FAIRY GODMOTHER SOUSSIO. In sharp contrast to the blinding darkness during the couple's flight, Soussio's castle stood brilliantly illuminated. Soussio, unlike evil fairies or evil sorceresses, offered love, kindliness, and understanding, particularly with regard to Truitone, whom she treated as her own daughter. She was the antithesis of the queen, motivated not by an irascible jealousy and hatred, but by truth. While Antoine Furetière defines, in his *Universal Dictionary* (1694), sorceresses and fairies as fictions of the mind, Victor Delaporte maintains, in *The Marvelous in French Literature under the Reign of Louis XIV* (1891), that "the word fairy could be synonymous with sorceress," thus either good or evil (Marin, "Féeries ou Sorcellerie?" 45).

The open and sincere Soussio may be identified with sorceresses. (Lat. *sors, sortis,* to throw or cast a lot). Having cast her lot with the would-be bride, she hoped to enlighten her to the reality of her situation. When Truitone took Soussio aside, begging her to use her powers to make Prince Charming love her, the fairy reluctantly explained that in the face of his all-consuming love for Florine, her supernatural powers would fail. Despite her pessimism, however, Soussio would strive for Truitone's welfare.

The beaming intensity of the lighting in her castle reflected Soussio's truthfulness and sincerity. Light suggests both clarity of vision and insight into one's own shadowy acts or those of others, as well as the ability to take stock of realities. Perhaps Soussio thought that if Truitone could shed light on the bleakness of her self-image, she might succeed in coming to terms with her own ugliness, and learn to accept what she feared most—rejection by Prince Charming. So, too, would the prince have to learn to see clearly into others as well as into his own emotionality and sexually driven needs. Neither would be spared the difficulties of developing a *clear* understanding of their motivations, behavioral patterns, and values.

Soussio and Truitone, secluded in one of the brilliantly lit rooms in the castle, in order to converse, were overseen by the prince through the transparent diamond walls of the adjoining room. Peering at them, he saw to his horror that the now unveiled lady was Truitone and not his beloved Florine. Instead of taking part of the blame for the betrayal, however, he resorted to the usual facile scapegoat psychology, heaping the onus for his plight exclusively on Truitone's deceit. To his declaration of intent to leave the castle, the fairy-sorceress calmly retorted that he had promised marriage to Truitone, and the ring he had given, which she was now wearing, was positive proof of their agreement. The two would, therefore, be betrothed shortly. Unable to deal with his sense of shame resulting from his own lack of insight, Prince Charming cried out: "Do you think I would marry this little monster!" (*Bluebird* 83). Calling for his chariot to take him home, as he was about to leave the premises, he suddenly felt himself immobilized—as if his feet had been glued to the floor. Soussio had resorted to her magical art. While his condition of stasis indicated an inability on his part to function in the empirical world—due to his adolescent petulance—he swore that though Sussio attempt to "lapidate or flay" him, he would stand firm in his determination to marry Florine and not Truitone (*Bluebird* 83).

His enslavement to his subliminal pulsations had led Prince Charming to arrange the nighttime rendezvous and depart with Truitone. Now subject to Soussio's sorcery, he was forced to take responsibility for his actions, no matter how unpleasant the consequences. As mentioned before, he felt as if his feet had been glued to the floor. In that feet are in touch with earth, they have come to represent power over one's direction in life and the ability to move toward a sought-for goal. They are, however, also emblematic of the phallus. The prince had allowed his sexual urges and instinctual nature to guide him thus far; the time had come for him to indwell: to reflect, meditate, and question, thereby activating psychological development. The prince's condition of stasis brought his physical activity to a halt but, as we shall see, his mental and psychological powers pursued their permutations.

After twenty days of stasis, Soussio rendered her ultimatum. The future groom was to marry Truitone, or, as punishment for his breach of contract, be metamorphosized into a bluebird, a form he would have to bear for seven long years. Having chosen the latter alternative, he was summarily transformed into a bluebird.

THE TOWER SYNDROME. Prince Charming, as a bluebird, directed himself toward aerated or spiritual spheres, even as the earth-oriented Florine remained, ironically, locked in a high tower. Not only did her imprisonment cut her off from life; but like a corpse buried underground, she was hidden from view as well—left to linger and die. The height of her tower afforded her increased perspective into her earthly problems, releasing her from an over-preoccupation with details, and thereby giving her greater objectivity in considering her plight. The broader framework awarded her a new vantage point; while not alleviating her sorrow, aloneness, or sense of rejection, it did invite her nonetheless to bide her time, and in so doing, allow the chance factor to work in her favor. Undoubtedly she spent long hours mulling over how best to cope with a virtually nonexistent, certainly nonfunctional father, and a queen determined to destroy her at all cost. Her bitter weeping, rather than dissipate her psychic energy, worked as an Aristotelian *catharsis*, encouraging her to delve into the positive and negative effects of imprisonment. It taught her the necessity and the healing power of non-action or waiting (Jung, 6, #390).

During Florine's imprisonment, her harmonious and well-adjusted personality having had time to unfold, she was motivated to take hold of her life rather than rely on others, particularly, on her "unconscious" father, to free her from turmoil. Since release, in psychological terms, may be prepared inwardly and secretly, Florine, whose activities had been forcibly circumscribed, was ironically to expand her effectiveness in depth and in breadth.

Sufficiently wise to realize that any aggressive act on her part against the queen might not only jeopardize her life, but victimize her further, Florine developed the strength to accept her plight. Even though she was invisible to the outer world, the time she spent probing her past, present, and possible future afforded her increased knowledgeability of her own patterns of behavior. Consciously assessing the damage perpetrated by the witch-queen, she understood that only when she would be emotionally prepared to confront this virago could she achieve her ends. In that timing was crucial, the wise yet deeply distressed young girl realized that her years of imprisonment not only did not preclude indwelling, but gave her the opportunity to develop her own means of depotentiating harmful demonic powers. Because each stage of life had significance for Florine, she looked upon her incarceration in the tower as a learning experience designed to trigger greater awareness into the meaning of freedom. As written in Ecclesiastes: "To everything there is a season, and a time to every purpose under the heaven" (3:1)

METAMORPHOSIS FROM HUMAN TO BLUEBIRD. Prince Charming and those others who fall victim to the powers of fairies/witches/sorceresses and are transformed into animals or monsters, frequently regain their original forms through acts of heroic love or altruism. Ordeals, sufferings of all types, if regarded as rites of passage, help to expand understanding, and transform relationships with others. Prince Charming's self-awareness and ardor for his love object would teach him to encompass the woman as a whole and not focus exclusively, as he had initially, on lower (erotic) physical sensations. Desire for sexual gratification, uppermost for him until this time, would yield to integrity, fortitude, honesty of spirit and feeling. The prince's spiritual and angelic values, considered by Mme d'Aulnoy to be of higher caliber than singleminded preoccupations, had the potential to encapsulate spirit and earth, to meld opposites—spirit/love and matter/sex—and thus pave the way for increased balance and bonding in the love experience. (The question remains as to whether Prince Charming had the emotional capacity to fulfill such goals.) The deprivation and suffering that Prince Charming and Florine would undergo during their rites of passage would give them ample opportunity to probe and test the truth of their passions for one another.

Why, one may ask, had Prince Charming been metamorphosized into a bluebird? A spiritual, nonmaterial hue, identified with the sky and with the color of the Virgin Mary's "starry mantle," blue implies the need for sublimation of the love experience, and the diminution of its carnal side (Warner, *Alone of All her Sex* 266). The bluebird may be identified, in Platonic terms, with the soul/anima. The bird's ability to fly liberates it, symbolically speaking, from the weight of the world of contingencies. It may be suggested that birds, like Gods and angels, are able to transcend gravitation as well and thus are looked upon frequently as connecting forces between heaven and earth. The nexus is reflected in the Greeks' consideration of birds as the incarnation of Gods (eagle, Zeus; white dove, Aphrodite; peacock, Juno); and the Koran endows Solomon with the ability to speak the language of birds (Sura 27:16). In a twelfth-century Sufi allegory, "The Conference of the Birds" by the Persian poet Attar, human characteristics are conferred on winged creatures.

Prince Charming's metamorphosis from human to bird may be considered, psychologically speaking, a replication of the individuation process, signaling a change from adolescence—or an exclusively ego-centered condition—to maturity, and its reintegration in expanded form, into the Self (or total psyche). As an agent of transformation, the avian image may be envisaged as a kind of bridge, the crossing of which requires the extreme measure of dehumanization. Prince Charming's life as a bluebird would serve, if he survived, to teach him not only to accept his failures, but to learn from them. Nor would Florine be disculpated from an equally severe rite of passage. If she properly assessed her errors, stemming from her passivity, an attitude that had prevented her from confronting her self-involved and unthinking father and the irascible queen, she would be able to manage her emotional needs.

Numbers—for example the seven-year period of Prince Charming's incarnation as a bluebird—in general are relevant for psychologists, as previously mentioned, not only because of the mathematical structure or order they impose, but because they may be seen as archetypal "mirrorings" of psyche and matter. As an "archetypal preconscious basic structure," numbers not only reflect certain mental processes, but are endowed with a personality, or energy span of their own. Thus, they are able to foment emotions, thoughts, and sensations.

For mystics, alchemists, and magicians, whose visions take them into divine and/or infernal realms, numbers possess reflective and analogical powers. Seven, for example, symbolizes completion and, paradoxically, renewal in an ongoing process: God created the earth in six days, and rested on the seventh (Gen. 2:2). In Proverbs, numbers were given moral attributes: "For a just man falleth seven times, and riseth up again" (24:16). In Ezekiel, seven created a link between human and divine realms, and in so doing, healed the schism that had come into being with the Creation and the Fall (I:1,8). In Matthew, numbers enabled humans to learn the meaning of sin and forgiveness: "Then came Peter unto him, and said, Lord how oft shall my brother sin against me, and I forgive him till seven times?" (18:21). In Luke, seven was attached to the believer of evil: "Then goeth he, and taketh to him seven other spirits more wicked than himself; and they enter in, and dwell there; and the last state of that man is worse than the first" (11:2). Seven also symbolized a complete cycle: the marriage of four (the square), associated with the earthly realm and the world of matter; and three, identified with supernal spheres (the pyramid, the triangle). Added together, the seven may represent a unification of disparate entities: the welding of the incomplete with the complete, consciousness with the unconscious—and, for the alchemist, gold with lead.

THE CYPRESS TREE. Following his metamorphosis, Prince Charming, visibly overcome with melancholia, instead of flying back to his kingdom, returned to the area surrounding Florine's tower, hoping to locate the room in which she was imprisoned. Rather than attempt to shed his grief by flying haphazardly here and there, which would simply serve as an escape mechanism, he perhaps reasoned, he must aim his flight to discover his beloved's exact whereabouts. After nightfall, Bluebird, who had serendipitously alighted on a high cypress tree adjacent to the tower, suddenly heard sighs and moans issuing from one of its open windows. The thought of Florine's sorrow had become a continuous source of torment for him, and the feeling that she might be imprisoned in this section of the tower raised his hopes that she would at least be able to gaze at him from a distance. In Bluebird's pitifully mournful song was conveyed his anxiety that she might be unwilling to wait seven long years for him, and that she would surely find a suitor in the interim.

The slender elongated cypress tree on which Bluebird had alighted, to be viewed perhaps as a kind of Tree of Knowledge, would help him to broaden his unidimensional and self-indulgent attitude toward womankind: that is, his *anima*: the *eros* principle, which determined his attitude toward the female sex (Woodman, *Addiction to Perfection* 195). Until a conscious assessment of the trials that are implicit in most relationships is undertaken, advancement toward a so-called "higher" understanding of the female as Wisdom—or Mother Sophia—is well nigh impossible (Woodman 172).

After Prince Charming heard what he believed to be the lamentations of his beloved, he instinctively sought to alight on her windowsill. But reason, now intervening, pointed to his previously ill-considered nighttime venture, when he mistook Truitone for Florine. Having been fooled once before during the night, or *nigredo* hours, he reluctantly decided to wait until morning, thus avoiding another possible entrapment. By opting for daylight, he was identifying with rationality, lucidity, and consciousness, thus placing him in a better position to distinguish reality from illusion. He may have also hoped that, as day follows night—each dawn being a *revelation*—the daylight would afford him a new beginning. Alas, what may be the right path in countless fairy tales, turned out to be the wrong one for Bluebird. No sooner had the sun risen than his beloved Florine—or the unknown person at the window—closed the shutters and withdrew into the darkness of her chamber. Waiting would be his only alternative!

THE OPEN WINDOW. Having endured vicious treatment at the hands of her stepmother and stepsister, Florine had taken to standing at her open window at night when, in privacy, she allowed herself the privilege of sobbing until dawn. Unwilling to expose her pained face to the outer world during daylight hours, she then chose to withdraw into the darkest corner of her lonely prison cell.

Imprisonment and the deprivation of external influences and relationships, thrusts certain personality types into themselves. The Spanish mystic, St. John of the Cross (1542–1591), imaged his suffering during his period of withdrawal in terms of the "dark night of the soul." Florine's extreme exclusion forced her to rely on her own devices for emotional release. Reviewing the circumstances leading to her imprisonment and sifting out options that surfaced from amid her churning inner pulsations, she learned ways of *mobilizing* her time (Jung, *The Visions Seminars* I, 239). Indeed, for some, suffering has creative value. As the theologian, Meister Eckhart (1260–1328) suggested: "Suffering is the fastest horse that carries you to perfection" (Jung, *Visions Seminars* 126).

FROM TREE TO OPEN WINDOW. The following night the moon shone brightly, and Bluebird, perched on the cypress tree, saw Florine again appear at her window. As she spoke softly, yet audibly, Bluebird listened carefully to her words, making certain that they really emanated from his beloved. Hearing her convey her intense yearning for him, and learning that during his absence she was toying with the idea of terminating "her fateful destiny," he flew toward her and alighted on the window. Frightened at first by the sudden appearance of so "extraordinary" a feathered creature, she quickly became enraptured by the beauty of his feathers and the intelligence of his communication. While he imparted his love for her in high-pitched sounds, Florine sensed their meaning in human terms. Thrilling in each other's company, they confided their love and pathos as they lived their idyll. Confession served to ease their pain, and the knowledge that their mutual love transcended earthly wounds encouraged them to remain together until the sun rose. Fearing discovery, they wisely parted at dawn, promising each other to pursue their nightly rendezvous.

To the the tree/phallus/tower image, may be opposed the open window icon, suggestive of an orifice, which may be associated with the vagina symbol as the point of contact, or exposure, between male and female. In a broader context, such an image might represent a newly discovered connection between outer/conscious, and inner/ unconscious worlds. In association with Solomon's mystical/sexual allegorical poem, "The Song of Songs," we read:

My beloved is like a roe or a young hart: behold he standeth behind our wall, he looketh forth at the windows, shewing himself through the lattice. . . .

The flowers appear on the earth; the time of the singing of birds is come, and the voice of the turle is heard in our land. (2:9, 12)

It was is via the open window (vagina) and the cypress tree (phallus) that interchanges of ideas and intuitions were to occur, sublimating to a certain extent what had initially been only the erotic side of Prince Charming's nature. The *sublimatio* process, alchemically speaking, concentrates on the distillation of all preceding feelings, ideations, and actions in a relationship, and the ventilation and/or reassessment of previous operational attitudes. Abstract mediating powers, namely, the open window, the tree, and Bluebird's ability to ascend to his beloved, paved the way for vocal, verbal, and limited tactile communication between the two. His upward, outward, and downward flights, from the windowsill to the cypress branch below—that is, from airborne or abstract indeterminate spheres, to earthly domains—enabled him not only to renew a heretofore formal and distant acquaintanceship, but to enjoy one on a completely different level, via close contact. No longer did a humiliated Florine sing her lonely and haunting chants during the nightly hours. As Bluebird's beloved, she met him halfway.

In keeping with the sexual symbology previously noted, the branches of the cypress tree point heavenward and its trunk downward; taken as a whole, it indicates the participation of celestial and earthly spheres in the dramatic unfolding of a love motif. Embedded in the immobility of the tree image, is its motility in the form of sap (Lat. *sapere*, to taste, perceive), which circulates in order to bear water and food to the tree's tissues. Thus, it is vital to the life of the organism, and crucial to its energetic development. Just as sap rises and descends between lower and upper branches, nourishing the tree's activity, so the desire of the young lovers to live out a sexual relationship mounted.

Lying in the hollow of the cypress tree, which he now called his home, Bluebird felt so energized by his love that he flew to his own kingdom, entered a private chamber of his castle through a broken window, removed an exquisite pair of diamond earrings, flew back to the tower, and gave them to Florine that very night. The following evening he brought her an exquisite multifaceted emerald bracelet and, on succeeding visits, a watch embedded in a pearl, diamonds, bouquets of multicolored precious stones cut in a variety of floral designs, and other treasures. Although she accepted these with grace and pleasure, Florine questioned Bluebird as to whether he believed her love was dependent upon his presents. Gallantly, he replied that the intensity of his joy in her company had motivated the bestowal of these gifts, and nothing more. In keeping with the couple's custom, no sooner did daylight appear than Bluebird flew to his tree, availing himself of nourishing fruits, after which he burst into rapturous song, thereby expanding and prolonging the sensory experience the lovers had enjoyed in their togetherness. Bluebird's melodies not only entertained his beloved, but were heard by passers-by as well, who, fearing spirits were in converse, dared no longer enter the fabulous forest. Mme d'Aulnoy's proclivity for irony, encouraged her to add that "general terror made for Bluebird's individual safety" (*Bluebird* 91).

After two years had elapsed, without the queen receiving any complaints from her captive, she and Truitone began to suspect secret machinations on Florine's part. Bursting into the tower room at midnight, and overhearing a two-part love song, these two "devouring furies" sensed betrayal (*Bluebird* 93). Time permitted neither Bluebird to fly away—he hid instead in the room's open chimney—nor Florine to remove and sequester the exquisite jewels she wore nightly to receive her lover. Faced with the evidence, the two harpies accused Florine of intrigue and deceit and of having accepted the jewels as payment for the sale of her father's kingdom. When the queen attempted to hide some false accusatory documents in the chimney, which would have led to Florine's undoing were they to be found, Bluebird, invisible to all, saw through her devious plans and cried out: "Take care, Florine! Your enemy is here to betray you" (*Bluebird* 94). So terrified was the queen by this mysterious voice emerging as if from nowhere that she desisted from all action. Cleverly playing on her enemy's fears, Florine reminded her that "the spirits hovering about her were favorable to her," and not to the queen. Whereupon mother and daughter left post-haste. Far from having given up their battle, however, the queen sent a maid to spy on Florine, with strict orders that she simulate sleep, but remain awake so as to be able to report the goings-on in the room.

Utterly distressed by the turn of events, Florine lamented her fate but did not face her latest setback passively: she adopted a methodical and rational attitude to block any progress on the spy's part. By counting the days the spy remained awake, she was able to determine the exact night she would be overcome with sleep. Her judgment was so sound that after a certain number of days, as soon as the maid fell into deep slumber, she called to her Bluebird to return to her and he reappearied as if instantly. The two pursued their love duets until the fourth night when, unbeknown to Florine, the spy, having heard unusual sounds emanating from the direction of the window, feigned sleep. The light of the moon enabled her to see the most beautiful bird in the universe speaking with the princess, who caressed his foot, as he pecked at her gently. Able to grasp certain parts of their conversation, the maid was astounded by the bird's ability to speak to the beautiful Florine as a lover and by her tender response to his feelings.

As dawn broke, the lovers, still entranced by their idyll, wisely separated. Upon parting, however, both seemed to be overcome by some premonitory fear, and with cause, since the spy had slipped out of the room and informed the queen of their interludes. Astute as always, the witch-queen, vowing that such insolence would not go unpunished, ordered the spy to return to the tower to continue her dissimulations and reportages.

THE BIRD BLEEDS: SWORDS, KNIVES, AND RAZORS. Florine's apprehension of the perverse and intrusive queen mounted. Aware of her enemy's destructive bent, she feared deeply for Bluebird's safety. Would he succeed in escaping from this harpy's maiming claws? What of the hunters in the forest? They too could kill her beloved. Or a vulture? So negative were Florine's thoughts that sleep eluded her—a condition caused by feelings that Mme d'Aulnoy had assessed so perceptively: "[W]hen one loves, illusions appear to be truths" (*Bluebird* 89).

Concomitantly, and despite Florine's frantic calls, Bluebird abruptly broke off his appearances at her windowsill. Why? The sadistic queen had ordered that swords, knives, and razors be attached to the branches of the cypress tree in order to lacerate Bluebird each time he attempted to alight on a branch. These murderous weapons made deep gashes in Bluebird's feet, causing him to fall and to cut his wings. Although he finally, and with great courage and difficulty, escaped from his tree, bloodstains left a trail behind him.

Unaware that the queen was the instigator of this dastardly deed, Bluebird, through some unknown lucubrations believed that it was Florine, who no longer loved him. "Oh! barbarian! Is this how you repay me for the purest and tenderest of passions ever?" (*Bluebird* 97) How could she, he lamented, sacrifice him to their "common enemy"? Physically and emotionally destitute, Bluebird, like Florine prior to their first meeting on the tower window, sought death as his only alternative.

THE MAGICIAN. Weakened by his loss of blood, Bluebird, lying listlessly in the hollow of the cypress tree, attempted to fathom Florine's reasons for, such a murderous act. Suddenly, as if from nowhere, his friend the magician, the very one who had created the frog-drawn carriage for him, appeared on the scene. He had spent months looking for and shouting out his friend's name wherever he went, but all in vain. Still unaware of Prince Charming's metamorphosis, he had not heeded Bluebird's dirgelike songs. Injecting a humorous note in the nonrecognition scene, Mme d'Aulnoy features Bluebird, who responds to the magician's frantic calls and approaches him, but the latter, oblivious to his presence, keeps on searching. Finally,

Bluebird's persistent efforts at identifying himself are rewarded: the magician, aghast at the magnitude of his friend's bleeding gashes, immediately effects wonderworking formulae and balms to heal them.

When religious leaders—priests, ministers, rabbis, fakirs, shamans, magisters—pray, gesture, and even posture in their attempts to persuade divinities to fulfill their wishes, they are in effect externalizing their spiritual needs. Magicians who seek similar goals proceed via equally mechanical incantations, adding scientific processes to conjure and thus constrain invisible, but active powers to conform to their will. Appropriately has the art of magic been called the "mother of science." Indeed, in the late Middle Ages and Renaissance, science in the hands of an Albertus Magnus, a Paracelsus, or a Rabbi Judah Loew, was linked to magic (Jung 8, #90). By the seventeenth century, scientific thought had advanced to such a point that Descartes had undermined Ptolemaic astronomy; Galileo, Aristotelian physics; Vesalius and Harvey, Galen's medicine. Magic nonetheless was still very effective in the minds of many either to help heal the souls/psyches of those in need, or to take advantage of the gullibility of the weak and needy (Kearney, *Science and Change 1500–1700* 2).

Reciting his formulaic incantations, Mme d'Aulnoy's magician succeeded in healing the ailing Bluebird and in convincing him of Florine's innocence with regard to the murderous attempts on his life. He also enlightened the prince regarding the plight of his rulerless kingdom. It was incumbent upon Bluebird/Prince Charming, he told him, to return to his people, adding that he would personally see to his protection. There was only one caveat: he would be obliged to remain encaged until Soussio's spell had run its course. Upon further reflection, however, the magician realized that for a monarch to rule his kingdom in the form of a bird would divest the monarch of all credibility. Unable to counter Soussio's spell, he hopped on his frog-drawn chariot to go to ask her to withdraw it.

Having remained on good terms with her these many years, he encountered no objection from Soussio to his proposal—providing Bluebird agree to marry Truitone. In view of what was at stake, reluctantly the offer was accepted. Bluebird's humanization was immediate; the future couple repaired to Prince Charming's kingdom.

FLORINE'S QUEST. Meanwhile, not only did Florine's increasingly tormented nightly calls to her lover remain unacknowledged, but momentous events of another nature impinged on her life as well. Her father had died, the kingdom's inhabitants had lapidated his wife, and Florine had been proclaimed queen. Deeply moved by her people's love, she nonetheless was determined to quest for her beloved. To be regarded as a rite of pasage, this quest would, if successful, transform her psychologically from a self-preoccupied starry-eyed adolescent, to a realistic young woman able to cope with life's vagaries. Florine's quest would be physically and psychologically taxing.

Let us note the connection existing between the words *quest* (from the Latin *quaestus*, seek, search for) and *question*. Each in its own way implies the need to flesh out, to doubt, to puzzle, to query, in difficult or untenable situations. Answers may not be immediately forthcoming, but the very act of digging into specific obstacles usually endows the searcher with a sense of inner plenitude and fulfillment—indicating the ego's new and broader connection with the transcendental function of the Self (total psyche).

Florine's ordeal would require her to surmount many hurdles, which, on a psychological level, would demonstrate her ability to synthesize her conflictual unconscious and conscious contents. The psychic energy, or libido, dispensed in the struggle, might increase the scope and breadth of her understanding of the complexities of life in general, and of human nature in particular. The increase in *gnosis* and/or *sapiens* gained during her struggle, would excite, rather than deplete her ardor and will to confront difficult life situations. No miracles, however, are to be expected, learning being garnered via the intensity of the experience itself.

That Florine's rite of passage might possibly engender a *multiplicatio*, to use the alchemist's word, or an augmentation of inner understanding, would empower her to redirect or reevaluate certain relationships and events she had previously taken for granted or simply discarded. No longer the passive, subservient, unsure princess of yesteryear, she would be called into action. Her new orientation, like a journey or pilgrimage, might serve to center her, thereby bringing balance and harmony to a psyche torn by extremes.

Just as Prince Charming had been dehumanized during his ordeal, Florine also chose to wear a disguise—a persona—as she launched on her own path. Her decision to wear a poor peasant's garb, an equally unseemly hat, and to comb her hair in such a way as to virtually hide her face, revealed innate wisdom on her part. Aware of the dangers involved in her quest, particularly those a beautiful young queen might encounter while traversing the countryside alone on foot, she understood the importance of remaining hidden from view. Moreover, to disclose her identity, after having been cloistered in a tower for two years, would have been psychologically deleterious. Imprisonment had taught her to secrete her feelings for survival purposes, and thus to live inwardly. To suddenly reveal to strangers what she had held most sacred—her love—might invite their ridicule and mockery. The outcome of the emotionally charged experience she was to undergo would be as flesh-piercing as the knives and swords had been for Bluebird.

The excessively simple garb Florine chose for her journey, while in conformity with her humble and unobtrusive nature, was antithetical to her social role. The protection her persona would grant her, however, would help her build and test her aptitudes in secret, enabling her in the process to make the transition from extreme introversion and low self-esteem, to relative extroversion and greater self-trust. Her cautionary approach vis-à-vis strangers underscored a growing maturity in her wait-and-see attitude. On another, but related level, Florine's ordeal was designed to test her physical stamina as well. Outside of short rides on horseback and a few water crossings on small boats, she would be required to walk great distances to reach Prince Charming's kingdom.

THE FOUR EGGS. Despite her fatigue, the single-minded Florine walked on and on. Coming one day upon sight of a glistening fountain—"its silvery waters bouncing on to adjacent small pebbles"—she felt a yearning to soothe her feet in the healing spring (*Bluebird* 103). No sooner had she seated herself on the surrounding grass and begun to pleasure in her new sensations than an old and bent woman, leaning heavily on a cane, appeared before her. Warmed by the gentleness of the beautiful young girl, the stranger inquired about her presence there and also remarked on the impression of aloneness she gave. Was it prescience that encouraged Florine to open up to this old woman who showed tenderness and understanding of her plight? What other reason might have compelled her tearfully to confide her sorrows to a stranger? Florine's tears served once again as a catharsis, just as during her tower years, to release her from a condition of extreme despair.

The crippled hag, perhaps a mirror image of what Florine might have become had she followed a psychologically destructive path, was suddenly and miraculously transformed before her eyes into a beautiful, gracious, and superbly garmented fairy. Might her metamorphosis have been a premonitory image of Florine's future as well? After all, the young queen's naturally loving and endearing disposition had already helped her to overcome hurdles in the early stages of her emotional turmoil.

To further nurture and strengthen Florine's soul/psyche, the fairy gave her four eggs, admonishing her to crack them only in time of great stress, after which she vanished. An egg, whether produced by an animal or a human, may contain not only the germ of a new entity capable of independent existence, but food for its development. Such a gift in Florine's case was in no way coincidental, as we shall see. In keeping with egg symbolism, let us note that in some religions, an egg was believed to have been at the origin of cosmogonic and theogonic processes. In Brahma's golden egg, he himself was born again, and he divided it into two to fashion the heavens and the earth; the Egyptians of Hermopolis considered the egg, together with the lotus, to be a single cosmogonic symbol; for the Japanese, heaven and earth—Izanagi and Izanami—were born from a cosmic egg; the Dioroscuri, Castor and Pollux, emerged into the world within Leda's egg, which had been fertilized by Zeus; the Easter egg implies a new birth in Christ.

Since eggs contain the germ of the future, they have come to represent birth and rebirth, be it cosmic, seasonal, cyclical, spiritual, ideational, or psychological. Appropriately, therefore, did Mme d'Aulnoy introduce this symbol as a prelude to the birth of Florine's new personality.

That the good fairy had given her four eggs—that is, a quaternity—brings to mind the four cardinal points, the four seasons, the four psychological functions (intuition, feeling, sensation, and thinking), and the notion of completion as well. As spiritual and physical corollaries, they invite a reshaping of a constantly changing space/time continuum, including the ever-watery and churning subliminal spheres of the digit 4, the notion of renewal. Four also suggests the four-eyed child imaged in certain mandalas. Jung writes:

> The child in the center . . . looks in every direction—to both sides, and forward and backward. Seeing on all sides would mean an all-round consciousness, a complete consciousness. You see the field of consciousness coincides with the field of vision, so the kingdom of the unconscious is thought of as behind us. But with four eyes, two could see everything in front, and the other two whatever is behind. (Jung, *Visions Seminars* II 338)

Like the four-eyed child looking "in every direction," Florine availed herself of increased insight into how best to deal with the problems confronting her. After putting the four eggs carefully into her sack, she spent the next eight—twice four—days and nights walking. Upon reaching a huge mountain, which she would be compelled to cross to arrive at Prince Charming's kingdom, she noticed, much to her dismay, that its polished ivorylike surface made it impossible to climb. Concerned as to how to proceed, she suddenly thought of the eggs and decided to crack one of them. To her delight, and as if by some sleight of hand, golden clamps suddenly appeared before her. She took them, attached them to her hands and feet, and ascended the mountain with relative ease. Upon peering down at the other side of the mountain, she realized that to descend such a smooth surface would be treacherous. After she cracked a second egg, a pigeon-drawn chariot appeared before her. Once seated inside this incredible machine, she felt herself being drawn down the mountain to safety. Out of gratitude, she kissed the two pigeons, then went on her way.

THE CHAMBER OF ECHOES. After another long trek, Florine finally reached Prince Charming's kingdom. Much to her consternation, whenever she inquired of passers-by the location of the palace in which the king held his audiences, she was greeted with scorn and laughter at the idea that a lowly, dirty, and ragged creature should seek to converse with their high and mighty king. Most devastating to her, however, was the discovery that Prince Charming had agreed to marry Truitone. Unable to take another step, she stood still, bemoaning her fate, aghast at the thought that her monstrous rival had triumphed over her and, even worse, that her beloved had proven to be unfaithful and treacherous.

Sleep evaded the exhausted Florine and her appetite vanished. As the days passed, something within her—a sixth sense, perhaps—kept prodding her on, forcing her to find the means of wangling her way into Prince Charming's throne room. Having by dint of effort succeeded, she immediately walked toward her rival, Truitone, and listened to her words of indignation: "Who are you to dare approach me and my golden throne?" Introducing herself as a scullery maid, she unctuously layered irony upon irony, and finally told her that she had brought her some beautiful emerald bracelets. At the sight of these magnificent gems, Truitone asked Prince Charming to assess their worth, so that she might quote a fair price to the dirty little stranger. The bracelets stirred the prince's memory, reminding him of the one's he had given to Florine. Sighing with sadness, he responded: "Those bracelets are worth as much as my kingdom" (Bluebird 107). Aware of Truitone's shock at their enormous value and of her inability to acquire such a sum, Florine suggested another mode of payment: to be allowed to sleep one night in "The Chamber of Echoes," located beneath the king's bedroom. Truitone agreed.

What motivated Florine to choose "The Chamber of Echoes"? During one of Bluebird's visits to her tower, he confided that he had had a special room constructed directly beneath his own, which permitted him to hear the inaudible words or sounds emanating from below. Spending a night in this room would allow Florine to speak to the king in secret without diminishing his reputation. She would remind him of his heartless infidelity and the intensity of her sorrow, and she hoped to instill in him a strong sense of guilt and shame.

The word echo, as in the special chamber, indicates by definition a condition of psychological passivity, and of duality. An ancient Greek myth tells us how the nymph Echo was punished by Hera for having distracted her from spying on Zeus's sexual adventure with Echo's sister. The punishment for the nymph's infraction was severe: she could never initiate a conversation, only repeat what she had heard. A later legend narrates that Echo's inability to convey her love for Narcissus left her so pained that she fled to forests and grottoes, communicating with the external world only via reverberating sequences. Like Echo, Florine was unable to talk directly to her Prince Charming. Unlike the nymph, however, she would persist in furthering her cause indirectly.

During Florine's first night in "The Chamber of Echoes," she not only whispered her sorrows to her beloved, but berated him for having forgotten her and for loving her rival. That no response was forthcoming from the room above brought her to sobs. How to proceed? On the following night, she decided to break another egg. Miraculously, there emerged a little steel carriage garnished with tiny gold fixings, drawn by six green mice, driven by a small rose-colored rat, and provided with an equally minuscule linen-gray coachman, also of the rat family. Four charming and delightfully entertaining marionettes, two of whom were Egyptian dancers, were in place in the carriage. After showing this incredible feat of artistry to Truitone, who was again taken by this second marvel, visibly far exceeding her means, Florine informed her that if she allowed her to spend another night in "the Chamber of Echoes," it would be hers. Her wish was granted.

Faring no better on the second night than she had on the first, Florine decided to crack the remaining egg. Lo and behold, another incredible wonder appeared: six beautifully clad singing birds! So charmed was Truitone by this latest object, that when Florine again requested to spend another night in the special chamber, her rival quickly acquiesced.

Meanwhile, Florine had learned from one of the valets that since Prince Charming's separation from his beloved, he had developed insomnia, which he remedied with a nightly dose of opium. Strengthened by this knowledge, Florine readied herself to deal with the dark forces of the unconscious in a realistic manner. Seeking out the valet in charge of dispensing the drug to her beloved, she offered him her remaining pearls and diamonds if he would refrain from giving the king opium on this night. He agreed.

Prince Charming's usual dose of opium served to benumb his anxiety, but concomitantly allowed repressed or forgotten memories of happier times to emerge. Memory, instrumental in allowing an individual to travel through time and space, permits "voluntary" and/or "involuntary" mental displacements, to use Henri Bergson's words. Within memory's mysterious subliminal regions, rhythms alter, tonalities pulsate, concatenations multiply, and feelings and nuances, both organic and inorganic, come to possess their own evanescent beauty and meaning.

Florine's melodious words of love resonated in the tonal nuances of her complaints, while the brashly sonorous verbalizations of her resentment and sorrows, she hoped, would rouse the prince's sense of decency and commitment. Her words, indeed, became audible to Prince Charming; they struck a singular note in his heart. Could he have heard correctly? he wondered. Why did the harmonious flow of phrasings, interspersed by high-pitched cacophonies, recall Florine? How, he asked himself, could a peasant girl also be Florine? Was he hallucinating? So disturbed was he by the uncertainty of his recollection of things past, that he impulsively descended a secret staircase to the special chamber.

Meanwhile, Florine had removed her ugly, dirty clothes, had donned a white taffeta dress. When Prince Charming opened the door and saw her standing before him in her dazzling beauty, he realized that she was, indeed, his beloved Florine. In a burst of joy, he wept, then threw himself at her feet.

Although the two declared their love and intent to marry, one stumbling block remained. Soussio's spell, which exchanged humanization for marriage to Truitone, would return the prince to his Bluebird form. Sensing the couple's dilemma from a distance, the magician returned to the scene, along with his friend the good fairy who had given Florine the four eggs. Acting in consort, they used their powers to break Soussio's spell. Immediately thereafter, the couple married in the joy and felicity of love. As for Truitone, she was metamorphosized into a trout!

Mme d'Aulnoy's language, like that of other authors of fairy tales, is often stylized and elaborate, inviting readers to focus on certain recurring paradigms to make a point. A garden, a tree, a window, water, and other graphic symbols serve to mirror various stages in an increasing consciousness. Such mental activity encourages readers—in Mme d'Aulnoy's time or in ours—to transcend spatial and temporal spheres of sense perception, thereby merging with her illusory world that which is yet reality.

The spontaneity, fantasy artistry, even outlandish qualities injected into Mme d'Aulnoy's narration of events bring to mind André Breton's deployment of the incredible universe he brought to light in his novel *Nadja*. The sequences of stillness, stasis, and distortions of time in *The Bluebird* evoke Salvador Dali's "The Persistence of Time." And the fairy tale's exploration of musical sensations, its blendings of timbres, chords, and prosody, recreate Claude Debussy's *La mer*.

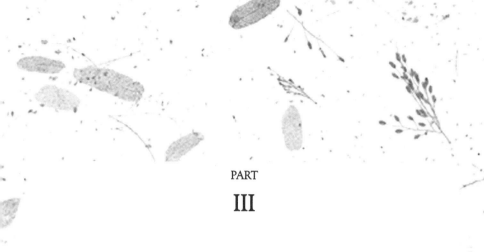

III

THE EIGHTEENTH CENTURY
"L'ESPRIT PHILOSOPHIQUE"

SINCE LOUIS XV WAS ONLY FIVE YEARS OLD at the death, in 1715, of his great-grandfather, Louis XIV, Philip d'Orléans was named regent of France. A fine historian, painter, and musician, he was also known for his dissolute amusements. When reprimanded by his mother for his debaucheries, he allegedly answered: "I work every day from six in the morning until night. If I didn't seek some distraction, I would die of boredom."

One of the most talked about events during the regency was the "Law Affair," revolving around a business enterprise that attempted to replenish French finances, which had reached a new low at the conclusion of Louis XIV's reign. When the Scottish financier John Law (1671–1729) suggested a plan that would succeed in bolstering the French economy, the regent granted him permission to found his new banking system. Special privileges were accorded to Law's so-called *General Bank,* including the power to issue banknotes or money intended, so the regent believed, to stimulate commerce and industry. Although great wealth in paper money and stock was amassed by poor and rich, Law, now heady with success, created the Occidental Company, designed to exploit the Louisiana and Mississippi valley areas, thereby linking France's fate with that of the French colonies. By 1719, the bubble had burst. The crash struck. Law escaped to Italy, where he died in poverty.

Louis XV (1723–1774) was neither intelligent nor a good monarch. Spoiled, arrogant, he was opinionated, bored with everything, until his mood changed overnight and for the better with his marriage, at the age of fifteen, to Marie Leszczynska, the daughter of the dispossessed Polish king

Stanislas. Soon, however, her company palled. The king returned to his former despondency, alleviated for short spans by hunting parties. He indulged in such secret pastimes as the opening and reading of his courtiers' private letters, relishing them in all of their scabrous details. His "favorites," one of whom was the duchesse de Châteauroux, encouraged him to play a significant role in the War of the Austrian Succession (1741–1748), while the marquise de Pompadour, about whom Voltaire had allegedly said, "she was one of ours," unfortunately and detrimentally involved herself in the Seven Years' War (1756–1763). At its conclusion France lost its posssessions in India and in Canada. As for the king's playmate, Mme du Barry, she was arrested in 1793, and died on the guillotine during the French Revolution (1789–1799).

Enlightenment, a term identified with the eighteenth century, refers to a movement brought about mainly by a group of *philosophes* who, though not philosophers in the strict sense of the word, nor founders of any specific school of thought, adopted certain views held by René Descartes (1596–1650). Although they rejected his physics and metaphysics, they admired his experimental method, his emphasis on clarity and order, and his belief in the development of reason—factors they hypothesized would eventually lead to humankind's perfectibility. Ironically, Descartes's method led to what he would have despised: a rejection of authority on a political, economic, and religious plane. What the philosophes considered illogical, nonfactual, or insufficiently backed by evidence, was generally deemed invalid. Tradition and the status quo yielded in the eighteenth century to an independence of spirit that helped fight dogmatism and superstition, thereby paving the way for toleration, deism, skepticism, and even atheism.

The philosophes not only became great disseminators of science, philosophy, and the humanities, but they helped popularize and simplify these disciplines through the use of reason. Geology, botany, chemistry, astronomy, law, education, and history, no longer regarded as inviolably scientific domains, fell within the purview of many. History was no longer a matter of Providence. Political, economic, and military events were not a question of God's will being carried out on earth, as theologians such as the seventeenth-century prelate Bossuet had categorically affirmed. History was strictly a human affair. Wars, treaties, victories, and defeats, therefore, should be recounted accurately, basing conclusions on source material and analyses of facts, and, insofar as Voltaire was concerned, a moral should be drawn from great historical events, in order to help humankind learn from previous mistakes. Warriors can only bring destruction upon their country, Voltaire declared in his *History of Charles XII* (1731), no matter how idealistic their intentions. Not only Voltaire but Montesquieu—who, before Gibbon's *Decline and Fall of the Roman Empire,* had published his *Consideration on the Greatness and Decadence of the Romans* (1734) focused on human ideas and actions rather than divine intervention. He believed that once a country has lost its need or desire for virtue, it disintegrates and decadent tyranny sets in.

A sentimental current also became evident in eighteenth-century France in the plays of Marivaux, the novels of Abbé Prévost, and in the multiple genres in which Rousseau conveyed his ideas. Foreign influences—from England, in the writings of Richardson, Fielding, Sterne, Gray, and McPherson; from Germany, in those of Goethe, Schiller, Lessing, to mention but a few—buoyed up the intellectualism of the day.

With the declining influence of the court and of the aristocracy, Versailles yielded its prerogatives to Paris. In this Age of Enlightenment as it came to be called, literary cafés, such as the Procope and the Régence, became stylish gathering places for intellectuals, namely, Diderot and Voltaire who were, among others, instrumental in bringing the art of conversation to its peak. *Salons,* begun in the sixteenth century and developed in the seventeenth, retained their popularity in the eighteenth. *Salonnières,* such as the duchess du Maine, the marquise de Lambert, Mme de Tencin, Mme du Deffand, Mme de Lespinasse, and many others, exerted great influence on taste and on new currents of thought. Nor were the pictorial arts to be minimized: the canvases of Watteau, Lancret, Fragonard, Boucher, Van Loo, Chardin, and Greuze added a tone of elegance and dreaminess, but also of reality, to both public and private interiors.

As Talleyrand (1754–1838), the famed prelate and diplomat, was purported to have said, "He who has not lived prior to 1789 never experienced the sweetness of life."

DENIS DIDEROT'S THE WHITE BIRD
AS HOLY GHOST/HOLY SPIRIT

AT FIRST GLANCE ONE WOULD NEVER ASSOCIATE Diderot, man of the Enlightenment, with the fairy tale genre. Nonetheless, *The White Bird* (1749), includes all of its earmarks: a fairy, miracles, transformations, evil geni, and supernatural events. Author of such ground-breaking works as *Philosophical Thoughts, Letter on the Blind, D'Alembert's Dream, Rameau's Nephew,* and *Paradox of the Comedian,* and general editor of, as well as contributor to one of the century's great achievements, *The Encyclopedia, Methodical Dictionary of the Sciences, Arts, and Trades*—Diderot chose the fairy tale to point up the absurdity of certain religious, political, and social ideas. Ultra reflective in its philosophical thrust, *The White Bird* may be considered a blend of Diderot's fundamental rebelliousness with high doses of satire, parody, and mystifying intent. Mixed with these are Diderot's usual provocative signs, sensations, and images whose purpose is to destabilize, if not eradicate, the repressive and regressive religious dogmas, mores, and political regimes flourishing in the France of his day. To his bent for humor, one of the most powerful weapons to gain the reader's attention, he added an arresting psychological technique which we today label "active imagination."

ECTYPAL ANALYSIS

Born at Langres, in eastern France, Diderot belonged to a family that had for several generations been involved in the cutlery trade and in the Church.

Taught by the Jesuits, as were many French children of the day, the precocious lad was then sent to the Collège d'Harcourt in Paris, where he completed his formal education. Acquiescing to his father's wishes, he enrolled at law school, but after two years of desultory study, he opted for what he enjoyed: classics, physics, and mathematics—resulting in his father's withdrawal of financial support. Although details are scarce concerning the hardships the young man subsequently suffered, certain scenes in some of his works, and particularly in *Rameau's Nephew,* reveal that he may have gone many a day without food. Sociable by nature, whenever time and funds permitted the young man spent many pleasant hours at the celebrated Café Procope, and later at the Régence which attracted not only chess players, but the intelligentsia of the day as well. His marriage in 1743 to Antoinette Champion, a simple girl whose mother kept a lace and linen shop, came as a surprise. The two had nothing in common intellectually. Their only surviving child—Diderot's beloved daughter, Angélique, the future Mme Vandeuil—wrote her father's memoirs.

Life for a person of ideas and ideals was not easy in eighteenth-century France. To write or speak openly on science, religion, and/or politics frequently invited imprisonment, exile, or, even death, yet Diderot, together with his "liberal" contemporaries, determined to infuse a spirit of inquiry into these fields. Deism, for example, an English import, emphasized the existence of an impersonal God who was neither manifest in history nor immanent in nature. Although Deists accepted the notion of immortality of the soul and the reality of good and evil, they considered organized religion superfluous and dangerous—a spreader of bigotry, hatred, and war. In *Philosophical Thoughts* (1746), Diderot increasingly freed his beliefs from constriction by adopting a virtually pantheistic view of divinity: "Enlarge God," he wrote, "see Him everywhere or nowhere at all." In *Promenade of a Skeptic* (1747), he pointed to his disbelief in religious mysteries and in the supernatural. Nor did he hide his antagonism toward Christianity and its powerful and exploiting clergy. Scientific in thrust, Diderot expressed his virtually atheistic views in his *Letter on the Blind* (1749). Following its publication, he was predictably condemned by the Parlement of Paris to imprisonment at Vincennes for several months. In the years to come, his literary career burgeoned with *D'Alembert's Dream, Jack the Fatalist, The Paradox of the Comedian, The Nun, Indiscreet Jewels, Salons,* and more.

Diderot's innovative thoughts and thirst for knowledge, his perceptions, humor, rambunctiousness, and licentiousness, his gracious, and extroverted temperament, drew friendly and illustrious minds to his side. Among these, were D'Alembert, Condillac, Grimm, and Baron d'Holbach. Meanwhile, Diderot's reputation, which had spread far and wide, elicited an invitation from Catherine II of Russia to visit her court in 1773. He did so. Not only did she buy his library, but made him its curator. Two years later, Diderot's meeting with Sophie Volland (1755), a woman he called "a trifle baroque," led to deep emotional ties, a lifelong friendship, and brilliant correspondence between them (Furbank, *Diderot* 187f.).

Throughout his life, Diderot worked tirelessly—and mainly covertly—to condemn and fight superstition, intolerance, persecution, and religious dogmatism. He reiterated his credo of a godless universe just prior to his death at the dinner table. "Life is merely a long workday, death a long sleep, the grave a bed of repose, and the earth a pillow where it is very pleasant, at last, to lay one's head in final sleep" (Fellows and Torrey, *The Age of Enlightenment* 210).

ARCHETYPAL ANALYSIS

The world of dream and sleep, and all that lies beyond the rational physical sphere, is metaphorized in *The White Bird*, essentially a parody of the Christian dogma of the Immaculate Conception. Understandably his fear of retribution governed his decision not to have the parody published during his lifetime. He probably composed *The White Bird* at about the same time he was writing his innovative risqué novel *Indiscreet Jewels* (1748). Both works are parodic, replete with ribald humor and wit, supernatural intercessions, allegorical digressions, and pungent ironies.

Diderot's reconstitution of exotic lands, his fluid transpositions of varied lifestyles, and his injection of somewhat fictitious mores in *The White Bird* were seemingly influenced by Antoine Galland's translation or version of *Thousand and One Nights* (1704–1717). The original work (1450), a selection of ancient Persian-Indian-Arabian tales featuring fanciful creatures, supernatural beings, outlandish happenings, and satiric innuendoes, had become popular fare in the France of Diderot's day. Similarly, Antoine (or Anthony) Hamilton's novel, *The Four Facardins* (1730), written ostensibly "for the beautiful sultan who slipped between two bed sheets for two thousand consecutive nights to listen to tales *à dormir debout*," earned popularity as well. Its semiotic perspective and its accompanying sensations aroused the reader's lustful desires. After all, "what woman would have slipped between two sheets to simply listen to old wives tales" (Barchilon, *Le Conte merveilleux français from 1690 to 1790* 81).

Diderot's proclivity for the risqué prompted him to well-modulated, yet overt sexual pronouncements and innuendoes in *The White Bird* (Barchilon 79–81). Nor was he alone in preparing rich brews of drollery. Equally humorous and searing was Montesquieu's *The Persian Letters* (1721), in which Persians visiting Paris ridiculed French mores and the country's dogmatic political and religious climate. Voltaire, likewise, attempting to rectify some of the France's governmental and religious injustices and fanaticism had recourse to miraculousness and licentiousness in some of his philosophical tales, particularly *Zadig* (1747); to giants and extraterrestrial travel in *Micromégas* (1752); and to unicorns, griffins, and talking birds in *The Princess of Babylon* (published posthumously in 1768). What better way was there in times past (and times present) to proclaim intellectual and religious freedom than to insert impossible happenings into a fairy tale—certainly a perfect device to avoid the greedy appetites of anthropophagous censors. Nor must we forget that the philosophes, "the libertines, and libertarians" added to their list of demands, not only "freedom to pleasure," but "freedom to investigate," ergo, to gain enlightenment (Starobinski, *L'invention de la liberté* 10).

The White Bird, written in the form of a dialogue, is set against an exotic backdrop: a harem. A sultana with difficulty sleeping hires to combat her insomnia a specialist to tickle the soles of her feet, and two women and two men to improvise a tale that would last for seven nights. The narrative's exoticism, locale, and most importantly, the unmoderated thirst for sensuality are, to a large extent, a simulacrum of humankind's miraculous capacity to fantasize. By playing on people's thirst for novelty, Diderot underscored in a titillating way the oddities and inequities involved in France's regressive political and religious systems.

The White Bird hones in on a single Japanese prince, Genistan, who, during the course of events, is transformed into a white pigeon. The variety of female types introduced into the narrative during the seven evenings, each ambiguous in her own way, ranges from the prude and the ascetic, to the hetaera and the coquette. Not without interest is the author's emphasis on women. Although *The White Bird* is not a diatribe in favor for or against women's rights, Diderot, like Montesquieu, D'Holbach, and Grimm, believed that the oppression of women was but one aspect of many injustices existing in eighteenth-century France. Neverthelesss, Diderot was far from kind in his characterization of women in his essay "On Women" (1772). Although he expresses pity of the fair sex for their physical sufferings, he depicts them as being obstinate, secretive, superstitious, curious, ignorant, arrogant, vain, violent, given to jealousy and hysteria. When prey to mood swings, their faces became grotesque and their bodies distorted (Diderot, *Oeuvres* 953). Believing women to be in general intellectually inferior to men, Diderot nevertheless courted (with the exception of his nonintellectual wife whom he married on impulse) intellectually oriented women, notably Mme de Puisieux—perhaps not without purpose in her case, since he was composing at the time his libertine novel, *Indiscreet Jewels* (1748).

His ideas concerning women's education were contradictory. Although he was in favor of the furtherance of women's education collectively speaking, his daughter Angélique's instruction revealed his own mysogyny. Her intellectual explorations were restricted to the home, to rearing children, and to caring for the household. Like many other thinkers of the Enlightenment, Diderot remained "a prisoner of the gynophobic mentality of the past" (Trouille, "Sexual/Textual Politics in the Enlightenment," *Romanic Review* 85: 197, 202).[1]

SLEEP: TICKLING AND ACTIVE IMAGINATION. Reminiscent of *Thousand and One Nights*, Diderot's tale deals inter alia with the problem of insomnia—not the sultan's, as in the original work, but rather the sultana's. Nor was the sultana's life at stake in Diderot's tale as it had been in the fifteenth-century collection of Arabian, Hindu, and Persian tales. Unlike its predecessor as well, Diderot's tale recounts that sleep was brought on not only by the narrator's expertise as a storyteller, but by a combination of this talent with mastery in the art of tickling the soles of the sultana's feet. To prevent "overworking" the imagination and vocal chords of the two emirs and two women called upon to participate in the tale-telling process, each took up the plot where the former had left off.

Although one might initially surmise that the act of tickling would excite rather than subdue a person, it had the contrary effect on the sultana, whom we encounter at the beginning of Diderot's tale resting comfortably on her divan. Indeed, so pleasing and so relaxing were the sensations elicited by the tickling process that they lulled her to sleep. The continuing droning and lilting of the narrators added the magical effect of language to the experience. By enticing his readers into far off realms, Diderot awakened them to the intangible, supernatural and abstract domains of "active imagination." A technique used by Diderot and referred to in *D'Alembert's Dream* as "associationism," active imagination, invites the protagonists in *The White Bird* to confront their psyches by encouraging their full participation in the "fantasy-drama" related (Hannah, *Active Imagination* 1).

The technique of "active imagination" is the heart of storytelling—and is to a great extent the basis of religions, myths, epics, fairy tales, and fiction in general. It is only in recent centuries that it has been used with positive effects in mental hospitals for healing purposes. As a process that encourages both listener and teller to gain possession of a nonfunctional libido (psychic energy), active imagination also allows associations and fantasies the greatest possible latitude in the structuring of the individual's scenarios. Diderot, by highlighting subliminal yearnings in painterly patternings and plot lines, had instinctively understood what Jung noted two centuries later: "We know that the mask of the unconscious is not rigid—it reflects the face we turn towards it. Hostility lends it a threatening aspect, friendliness softens its features" (Jung 12, 29; Hannah 7).

As conjurer of fantasy realms, each installment of Diderot's tale is a paradigm of the author's foray into active imagination. Heretofore dormant archetypal images, awakened in the sultana's unconscious, flood her mind with memories, intuitions, auditive, or tactile sensations. The hypnagogic or pre-sleep condition into which the four narrators lull the sultana divests her of her empirical concerns, ridding her, at least temporarily, of her responsiblities, aggravations, and controversies. Disturbing problematics having receded into the background, she is free to dwell on mysterious scenarios that offer the glitter and excitement of novelty. The resulting condition of affective interaction and dependency among the participants creates a psychological porous climate that leads each into heretofore uncharted territories.

Just as painters and sculptors give visible shapes to unmanifested essences, sensations, and abstractions that lie dormant in their subliminal spheres, so the dramatis personae in Diderot's tale spin out multiple events in concrete form. In so doing, they not only give expression to their moods and fantasies, but imbue the entire scene with idea, pitch, and rhythm. Unusual was Diderot's technique of unifying dualities: each pictorial representation contained its opposite, or its struggle against the very notion enunciated within the same context. The energy charges summoned by these moral and ideological dichotomies served either to liberate or further incarcerate the protagonists' inner demons, spirits, ghosts, or loving deities, affording them in the process the opportunity of undergoing new inner experiences.

THE MANIFESTATION OF THE HOLY GHOST AS A MIRACULOUS WHITE BIRD—MASS HYSTERIA! Diderot's tale opens in a convent in China delineated in salient and rapid brushstrokes. The first female narrator recounts the miraculous advent of a white bird to the young virgins in this house of worship. All express their overwhelming delight at the appearance of this splendid pigeon that has just alighted on the branches of a palm tree within the convent's precincts. With its beak, described in curt and semiotically significant terms as emerging from within its thickly clustered plumes, it begins to groom its wings and tail. A titter is heard among the young virgins, who are immensely attracted to this spectacularly plumed creature. They gather around it and most surprisingly speak to it in loving terms. "Bird of my heart," Agariste whispers, "bird, my little king, come to me, fear nothing; you are too beautiful for us to want to hurt you. Come, a charming cage awaits you. Or, if you prefer freedom, you may roam free" (Diderot, III, *The White Bird* 303). Compliantly, the bird flies toward the cluster of virgins, landing ever so lightly on Agariste's bosom. As a welcoming sign, she glides her fingers with seemingly lustful glee over this God-sent creature's thick, smooth, and shiny feathers (*White Bird* 304).

The excitement of the giggling convent girls attracts the attention of the old mother superior, referred to as "la grande guenon" (a hag-like "fire-colored female monkey"). She, in marked contrast to the convent girls, looks at the beautiful bird with pronounced "disdain" (*White Bird* 304). The young virgins rush toward Agariste, bombarding her with questions about the bird. With everyone's attention focused on him, the magnificent creature ascends into the air, hovers over the postulants, and "its *shadow* encloses them in its embrace." All the girls, Agariste and Mélissa in particular, are suddenly overcome by strange, utterly sublime, but heretofore unknown sensations. Their aroused bodies move about in erotically inspired poses. Filled with rapture, they give expression to their reaction to the White Bird's hovering presence through unimagineably indecent wigglings, gyrations, and frenzied tremblings. It was as if, Diderot wrote, "a divine fire, a sacred ardor [had] lighted in their heart " (*White Bird* 305). Suddenly, as if invaded by the subtle luminosities of this heavenly being, the intensity of their gyrations reached such a pitch as to become the first known miracle to have taken place in the Chinese convent to date. Diderot noted simply that the miraculous manifestation of the bird as the third person of the Trinity, unlike that in the biblical account, transformed "two idiots" into the most "spiritual and awakened" females in China (*White Bird* 305).

When the White Bird burst into song, no ordinary tonalities emanated from its throat. The "melodious" resonances reverberating throughout the convent impressed themselves so powerfully on the tittering virgins that they "[fell] into a state of ecstasy," or experienced their first orgasm (*White Bird* 305). Even the "grande guenon," who had until this moment scorned the bird, upon hearing its celestial sonorities throbbed with sexual desire. As if a pulsating vibrator had been placed on her, she felt ravished by the energy charges coursing through her body. Overwhelmed by the powerful sexual stimulation and the concomitant urges the sound waves had activated in her body, she screamed: "Oh! I can no longer bear it! I'm dying! Charming bird, divine bird, just one more little melody" (*White Bird* 305).

The confusion, the breathlessness, the pantings, frenzied climaxes, ravings, and "wild-eyed" gazes accompanying the protracted bodily gestures of the convent virgins, and carried to most shocking extremes by their mother superior, had divested them all of the ability to verbalize their sensations. The outbusts of erotico-spiritual frenzy visibly experienced by the "grande guenon" during the event had so hyped her that she fell to the ground, landing on her prayer cushion.

"Ecstasy," the word used by Diderot to narrate the occurrences in the convent during the White Bird's advent, is defined as a "state of being beyond reason and self-control," as "a mystic or prophetic trance," a psychological condition in which the individual undergoing the experience surrenders to it completely, allowing it to "occupy the entire field of consciousness" (*Webster's Ninth New Collegiate Dictionary,* 1983; Campbell, *Psychiatric Dictionary* 233).

The miraculous event followed by the ecstatic experience aroused the virgins' heretofore hermetically sealed sexual urges to the extent of opening them up to the joys of complete abandon. As former prisoners of their elemental powers (or energy centers), the postulants understood for the first time the meaning of the sexual experience. The sudden release of their pentup instinctual powers, having overcharged their inner electric counters (libido), led to bouts of intense mental confusion on their part—ergo, to a condition of mass hysteria. What had just become operational in young and old was a whole new source of life: sexuality, as conveyed in the image of the shadow cast by the white bird hovering over the virgins.

Defined by Jung, the *shadow* is "an unconscious part of the personality usually containing inferior cararacteritiscs . . . which the individual's self-esteem" will not "recognize as his [or its] own" and thus rejects (Edinger, *Melville's Moby Dick* 149). When the shadow remains unconscious or is experienced only affectively, that is, with little or no discernment, it divests the individual[s] involved of all capacity to differentiate or evaluate its meaning or impact. Accordingly, the individual cannot be expected to assume responsibility for his or her actions.

Having been educated to believe that sexual matters were evil and that lives were to be devoted to spiritual matters only, the convent girls understandably considered everything identified with sex—shadow—as anathema, degrading, and thus evil. Since shadow power had been, since their earliest years, securely locked in some subliminal alcove of their psyches, their ignorance in these matters had posed no problem to them. With the White Bird's manifestation in the convent, however, the undiscerning virgins, delighting in new sensations, could not know what magic force had been unleashed in their bodies. Moreover, the massive undifferentiated instinctual pulsations inhabiting their subliminal spheres had erupted with such vigor and so precipitously that they were suddenly enveloped in a paroxystic/ecstatic experience. The greater the psychological split between human austerity (good) and indulgence (evil), the more powerfully does the irrational prevail—and in the virgins' case, the dam had given way!

Hypnotists, magnetizers, exorcists, medical doctors, and charlatans have for centuries been treating people suffering from visions, visitations, hallucinations, somnambulism, ecstasy, and hysteria, frequently linking their ailments together in the process. Friedrich Nietzsche depicted his own shattering ecstatic experience in *Ecce Homo* (1888):

There is an ecstasy so great that the tremendous strain of it is at times eased by a storm of tears, when your steps now involuntarily rush ahead, now lag behind a feeling of being completely beside yourself, with the most distinct consciousness of innumerable delicate thrills tingling through you to your very toes; a depth of happiness, in which pain and gloom do not act as its antithesis, but as its condition, as a challenge, as necessary shades of colour in such an excess of light. (Jung I, #184)

The powerful affects that were unleashed by the White Bird in the convent may be associated not only with ecstasy, but with outbreaks of morbid in hysteria. A mental ailment identified by the ancient Egyptians, hysteria was considered strictly a woman's illness (and the word is derived from the Gr. *hysterikos*, womb). It was thought that hysteria was caused by a detachment of the womb, which proceeded to wander about the body, and the cure consisted in fastening and/or steadying this part of the female anatomy. Hippocrates (460 B.C.E.) treated cases of hysteria, but it was the physician Galen (2nd cent. C.E.) who first rid this disease of its theological etiology by focusing on its psychogenic aspects. With the passing of centuries, however, regression set in and doctors, rather than attempting to heal the illness, victimized the sufferers by burning them or imprisoning them, convinced that in so doing they would rid them of their sinful natures. Carlos Piso in the sixteenth century, and Thomas Sydenham a century later, made some headway in further defining this mental illness. Although the French physician Paul Briquet was one of the earliest to write a systematic "Treatise on Hysteria" (1859), the French neurologists Jean-Martin Charcot, Pierre Janet, and Hippolyte Bernheim were the first to approach hysteria from a clinical point of view (Elenberger, *The Discovery of the Unconscious* 141ff). Freud claimed that a trauma or "psychological wound in childhood" repressing sexuality was the etiology of hysteria. The resulting blockage and repression of the affect prevented psychic energy from being released, thus allowing it to be transformed into a differentiated physical system. According to Jung, hysterical symptoms are to be considered "symbolic representations of repressed unconscious events." In that these strong emotions cannot be discharged or consciously expressed because the contents of the fantasies are incompatatible with the conscious outlook, the energy is then diverted into the wrong channels (somatic), resulting in symptoms (conversion). "The patient constructs in his imagination little stories," writes Jung, "that are very coherent and very logical, but when he [she] has to deal with reality, he [she] is no longer capable of attention or comprehension (Jung 4. #36; Niel Micklem, "On Hysteria: The Mythical Syndrome," *Spring* 148–151).

Alhough Hippocrates, Galen, Avicenna, Paracelsus, Paré, Harvey, and countless others studied what they considered to be the disease of hysteria, in many cases they erred in their diagnoses. Because the feelings of women had been considered insignificant throughout history, the roles of the women being restricted mainly to procreation, medical men were unaware of their struggle against not a sickness, but against unfulfilled female sexual desire! Diderot mockingly emphasized this side of his scenario, the larger picture: that of the convent-bred and sex-starved female denied the nourishment of these most basic and natural instincts.

The "grande guenon" and the young virgins were unquestionably suffering from deep-seated psychological predispositions to fantasies and traumas nurtured by all sorts of religious myths, accreted in potency with the passage of years. Having been taught from early childhood that sex was a contaminant, that to be sexually aroused was tantamount to a bewitchment, or to the imbibing of some Devil's brew, understandably the young girls believed that everything that revolved around the body was out of bounds. It was, therefore, allowed to wither, *but not to die.* Overpowered by the sexual urge during the hovering of the bird's shadow, the virgins were aroused to what could be called a sacred furor, which filled them with delight and awe. Understanding that they had embarked on an unknown adventure—an odyssey of sorts—they were driven, literally, out of their minds.

THE BIRTH OF "SIMPLEMINDED SPIRITS". The first of the two emir storytellers called upon to recount the White Birds peregrinations announced the advent of a truly miraculous event: the birth to the convent virgins of a plethora of "simpleminded spirits, without," he added, "their virginity having been impaired in the slightest" (*White Bird* 306). While the sultana objected to the emir's "ridiculous" reference to unimpaired virginity, he announced to her the reality of the arrivals. Nor, he declared, categorically, could the fact that they were not flesh-and-blood beings, but only "spirits," and "simpleminded spirits" at that, be overlooked: their birth was the outcome of the union of human and divine powers (*White Bird* 306). The sultana, responding to what she considered an outlandish story, yawned.

Meanwhile, the mother superior, having been informed of the miraculous event, invited the priests to attend an important meeting at the convent, their task being to unravel the mystery revolving around the prodigious births of "simpleminded spirits." The "grande guenon" made her grand entry amid the august presences to the accompaniment of tambourines and bells, and the aroma of burning incense. She realized that "it would be difficult to convince the faithful that the bird had fathered little spirits," but after "an hour and a half" of "genuflexions, incensings, and other monkeyshinings," she "scratched her ear," then recited some second-rate prose which the assembled believed to be "heavenly poetry" (*White Bird* 306). Following a lengthy debate, it was decided that "the libertine bird should be locked [up in some back hall] for fear it would continue what it had so happily begun, the multiplying of its species *ad infinitum*" (*White Bird* 307).

THE WHITE BIRD: HOLY SPIRIT/HOLY GHOST. As evidenced by the drawings in the Lascaux caves, which date back to the Magdalenian culture in France's Dordogne region, certain types of birds, and especially doves, have been associated with soul forces, considered mainly as celestial messengers. In Neolithic times and, later, in the Bronze Age, birds were identified with the Great Mother, who produced the universal egg from which the earth emerged. In ancient Egyptian friezes, the dove hieroglyph symbolized the departed soul. In Greek times, birds were linked to both the divine feminine, as manifested in the dove associated with Aphrodite, and to the divine masculine, Zeus, (who transformed himself into a swan when seducing Leda, into a cuckoo upon becoming Hera's suitor, and into a pigeon when coupling with the Achaian nymph Phthia). In Christian iconography, the Holy Spirit or Holy Ghost, or Paraclete, was associated with the dove and the divine masculine. To signify their liberation from earthly matters, the Immortals of Taoism were frequently portrayed with bird faces. For the Hindus, the bird symbolized livingness as Atma or Universal Spirit. In Islam, the presence of birds had premonitory meaning, as attested to in Attar's poem, *Language of the Birds,* in which the Simourgh, as king of the birds, was looked upon as the incarnation of divinity.

Diderot's White Bird is of course, a paradigm of Christianity's Holy Spirit, or Holy Ghost, or Paraclete (Gr. *Parakletos,* advocate, intercessor). In keeping with the Apostles' Creed, developed in the fourth century, but not codified until the eighth, the Holy Spirit, although masculinized, retained nonetheless certain feminine functions: "[I]t carried the whole child into Mary's womb to be nourished there, rather than quickening it to life." Thus was Jesus Christ conceived "by the Holy Spirit, born of the Virgin Mary. . . . The Holy Ghost, like a mother, conceived the child and then took possession of Mary until the day of the child's birth" (Warner, *Alone of All Her Sex* 38). In the General Epistle of James, "the dove flies from Joseph's staff as a sign that he has been chosen as Mary's bridegroom" (Warner 38). Jesus is at once divine (with the Holy Spirit as father) and human (with Mary as mother), but the role played by the latter in Jesus' birth has been reduced to that of a simple vessel carrying the egg.

There is a plethora of complex and confusing interpretations concerning the gender of the Holy Spirit. The Neoplatonist Plotinus, alluded to the Holy Spirit as "the world-soul," and the "energy of the intellect." And, "what lies enclosed in the intellect comes to birth in the world-soul as Logos, fills it with meaning and makes it drunken as if with nectar." Nectar, like soma, is the drink of fertility and immortality. Since "the soul is fructified by the intellect; as the 'over-soul' it is called the heavenly Aphrodite, as the 'undersoul' the earthly Aphrodite. It knows the pangs of birth." Jung wrote, "[T]he dove of Aphrodite is the symbol of the Holy Ghost" (Jung 5, # 198). The tempera painting on wood in the Erfurt Cathedral (1620–1640) depicts the insemination of Mary in terms of "a sort of tube or hose-pipe [that] comes down from heaven and passes under the robe of the Virgin, and we can see the Holy Ghost flying down in the form of a dove to fecundate the Mother of God" (Jung 8, #319). The Eucharist prayer compounds the complexity of the Holy Spirit's feminine gender:

> That revealest the great things of all greatness . . .
> Come, holy dove,
> Which hast brought forth the twin nestlings;
> Come secret mother. (Jung 5, #561)

Diderot's obvious reference to the myth of the Holy Spirit represents both the psychic and sexual energy required for the insemination process. The bird's presence in the convent is to be understood as a parody of the miracle of the Pentecost (Acts 2: 4). So traumatic was the religious experience for the apostles that it brought on what is identified as the affliction of glossolalia. Glossolalia or psitacism, defined as "an unintelligible conglomeration of sounds," is most commonly heard when people experience "ecstatic and somnambulistic states (Campbell, *Psychiatric Dictionary* 307). Diderot was obviously aiming his slings and arrows at the very concept of the Holy Ghost, and the ceremonies, gestures, prayers, and progeny it had engendered in its wake. As Marina Warner has written:

> Ever since the Holy Spirit descended on the head of Christ at his baptism in the form of a dove, the Third Person of the Trinity had been commonly depicted as a bird. The Holy Ghost presents such a pitfall for theologians and has tumbled so many into heresy that the visual imagery has been remarkably static and uninventive, Christian artists preferring to play it safe with the traditional white bird poised in flight, like a hawk or a lark, but quite unlike a dove, which in reality does not hover. (Warner, *Alone of All her Sex* 37)

THE MUSICAL VOICE OF THE UNCONSCIOUS. Music was a source of rapture in Diderot's tale, especially for the "grande guenon." The ear, a hearing organ, functions additionally as a birth canal according to various religious beliefs. Hadn't the heretic Elien been condemned at the Council of Nicea

(325 C.E.) for claiming that the "The Verb had entered into Mary through her ear"? Because the Church preferred not to delve too deeply into this matter of dogma, it allowed Ennodius to take up Elien's thesis, and agreed to allow the Salzbourg missal to read as follows: "Gaude, Virgo mater Christi/ Qua per aurem concepsti" ("Glad us maiden, mother mild. Through thine ear thou were with child.") (Warner 37ff.)

Music was a discipline to which Diderot reacted overtly, particularly during the celebrated Quarrel of the Buffons (1752–1753), in which he expressed his preference for Italian over French tonal works. Because varieties of melodious modulations worked incisively on Diderot's senses, he was able to introduce the timbres and resonances in *The White Bird*, which acted as excitants on the convent virgins. Indeed, so penetrating had been the bird's warblings that they took on the power and solemnity of archetypal music, opening the naïve girls up to the sex experience, and resulting in the ensuing birthings. Unaware of the interaction between musical motifs, systems of intensity, patterns of tonality, rhythmic sequences, and the energy charges these can stir up, the convent sisters pleasured in their charismatic effect. Their ears had given entry to sound which then pulsated throughout their bodies, awarding them a paradoxically intense sense of abandon.

Just as archetypal music arises from the collective unconscious in song, so too do archetypal images emerge in Diderot's tale in the form of the White Bird, performing as messenger from celestial spheres. The gentleness, charm, and beauty of this suprapersonal power descending to earthly domains appealed to the eye and to the ear of the young virgins, the combination arousing them to untold heights of physical enjoyment. The stimulation of auditive and visual senses served to answer the needs of the congregants incarcerated in their ascetic community—and ironically such stimulation would also have been fulfilling to women who lived in harems, since these women, although saturated with sexuality, also lived in a highly constrained environment.

Once released from their physically and emotionally cramped and restrictive existence, the convent girls were initiated into Aphrodite's world of empirical love.

THE EXTREMES OF INTRAPSYCHIC CONFLICT. The convent's austere atmosphere prior to the advent of the White Bird and its mass insemination of the virgins, suddenly altered following the "grande guenon's" appearance on the scene when extremes of modal behavior reached unparalleled frenzy. Such intraspsychic veerings may be identified as *enantiodromia*: "If one side of a pair of opposites becomes excessively predominant in the personality, it is likely to turn into its contrary" (Edinger, *Quadrant* 1, 1968). It follows that "the energy-charge of the repressed contents adds itself, in some measure, to that of the repressing factor, whose effectiveness is increased accordingly. The higher its charge, the more the repressive attitude acquires a fanatical character and the nearer it comes to conversion into its opposite, i.e., an enantiodromia. And the more highly charged the collective consciousness, the more the ego forfeits its practical importance" (Jung 8, #425).

Since "every psychological extreme secretly contains its own opposite," we may suggest that the individual identities of the virgins, as frequently happens in collective religious and political experiences, were drowned in the mass movement. Indeed, so starved for sex was the convent community that it overreacted to the sexual experience. Equally significant is the sexually saturated sultana's response to the episode. After ridiculing the antics of the overly sheltered girls, she fell asleep. Was the time ripe, then, for the depraved to ridicule the deprived?

The newly enlightened virgins enjoyed to the fullest the beautiful bird's extraordinary talents. Hadn't this celestial pigeon, by dint of magic, afforded their unblemished and unused bodies unsuspected physical thrills? In time, their encounter with the White Bird was to prove miraculously creative—its fruit developing to term in so many blessed events.

THE WHITE BIRD'S EXPANDING SEXUAL/SPIRIT. Because the sultana is now bored by the "foolishness" of the convent virgins, the emir telling this part of the story reveals to her and the other listeners that the White Bird has departed from the convent and flown to a harem in India, where the incarcerated women are as hypocritical, egotistical, and sexually active as any male could be. Using the artifices of language and complex bodily and facial gestures, these women, as well as their eunuch male keeper, bask in carnal abandon and fulfillment. Eye movements, sighs, cries are but a few of the devices used by Diderot to keep the reader informed as to the pigeon's adventures (Starobinski 55).

The beautiful Princess Lively (a satire on the "lively" and "superficial" Mme de Pompadour), enraptured by the very sight of the White Bird, attracts him to her by wearing short skirts and dialoguing in exaggeratedly tender terms. He in turn is taken with her voluptuous ways and "beauty spots," and expresses his passion via a rhetoric of gesturally active language. By alighting on her breast, as he had on Agariste's and, later, Mélissa's, prior to the mass orgy, he achieves the same results.

Time wears thin, as the saying goes. The White Bird's continuous love acts with Lively so exhaust him that she takes pity on him and puts him in a basket where he will be able to sleep and recoup his strength. So dominated is the dove's sleep with premonitory nightmares—imagining his neck being wrung and his defeathering following—that his cries and sobs awaken Lively. To calm the bird, she takes him on her breast, and, with "the most tender caresses," reassures him of his safety even as he, perhaps to show his gratitude, returns her passion by "pecking her most ardently" in rhythm to her accompanying sighs. The bird's song so enraptures her that she faints, but she then recovers and asks for more and more until the poor White Bird becomes so exhausted that he loses his voice (*White Bird* 311). Even more traumatic for her is the "simpleminded spirit" she finds one morning lying next to her pillow. "Where did this newborn come from?" she wonders (*White Bird* 311).

No sooner does Lively's father, Sultan Kinkinka, learn of the event than he rushes to his daughter's room. Seizing the newborn and preparing to throw it out of the window, he is stopped by "a swirling light spread[ing]" throughout the room. So dazzled is he by this divine intervention that the "simpleminded spirit" succeeds in escaping (*White Bird* 312). And so traumatized is the White Bird by the experience that he loses his feathers. Lively, who has no real understanding of what has transpired, asks for the immediate removal of the ugly "good for nothing." Angered by her "ingratitude" and "perfidy," the White Bird nonetheless continues to sow his wild oats among adoring women on his way to his next port of call (*White Bird* 313).

TO FAIRY TRUTH. Flying high and on course, the White Bird takes full advantage of the freedom, silence, beauty, and greenery of the prairies below him. Suddenly he spies a remarkably constructed castle in the distance. Recognizing it as the abode of Fairy Truth, he descends and enters its portals. In one of the alcoves he sees his much-admired and beloved spiritual guide seated with compass in hand, studying a globe. To convey his delight, he caresses her, then entwines his large wings around her body. Her affectionate response is translated into action. She touches the White Bird with her magic wand, whereupon it—he—returns to his human form as Genistan, the son of the emperor of Japan.

The wand in fairy tales has come to symbolize the power of transpersonal beings over both humans and the elements. Originally carved from the wood of a tree, it brings to mind the tripartite image and symbolism of the tree: its branches linked to heavenly spheres, its trunk to earthly domains, and its roots to infernal regions. A simple touch of the wand afforded Celtic Druids, for example, the ability to transform humans into birds, and the nymph Circe was able to change her guests into swine. Let us recall that the God Aesculapius used his caduceus (wand-like instrument) to restore health to the sick. Similarly, Cinderella's good fairy touched a pumpkin with her magic wand and turned it into an opulent carriage. To be noted as well is that a wand in Diderot's tale, like a phallus, becomes a sexual symbol, and thus a generative power. As for the psychological attributes of the wand, not only does it protect against danger, it represents the will, intelligence, ability, and fertility of its bearer (Jung 18, #198).

Despite her great affection for Genistan, Fairy Truth lets him know that his lack of maturity and his inability to discern the machinations of others have made him vulnerable to the subtle maneuvers of one of his enemies, namely, the evil magician Rousch ("Liar" in their language), who seeks to destroy him (*White Bird* 317). Great perception and intellectual perspicuity on his part, and minimization of his mindless sexual acivities, will be necessary to activate Genistan's awareness, and to develop his inner sight and maturity. As future emperor of Japan, she indicates, he must learn to accept responsibility, to develop a code of values and ethics, and thereby become cognizant of the meaning of righteousness. To put an end, or at least a limit to his insensate wanderings, Fairy Truth insists he marry Polychresta ("All Good" or "Good for Anything," a subtle reference to Louis XV's wife, Marie Leszczynska), despite the fact that she is thirty-two and he only twenty-five. Not only is she a serious woman, but she has integrity—characteristics he will in time come to esteem (*White Bird* 318). Genistan, although willing to comply with her conditions, poses one proviso: that Lively remain his mistress. The lengthy humorous debate on this matter, although not resolved at this time, will be broached again later on. Nonetheless, to assure Genistan's safety, the motherly but adamant Fairy Truth informs him that for the present she will return him to his previous form. Once again she touches him with her magic wand and once again he is transformed into a White Bird (or pigeon, Diderot using one or the other term interchangeably), the form he will keep until he and Fairy Truth, who will accompany him, reach Japanese shores.

FROM BIRD TO PRINCE. The Japanese emperor greets Fairy Truth with warmth, but he has no inkling of the bird's identity. Exerting her miracle-working powers, Fairy Truth blows on the White Bird, replicating to some extent God "who breathed into [Adam's] nostrils," thus endowing him with "the breath of life" (Gen. 2:7) Much to his father's delight, the bird is instantly transformed into his original shape, that of Genistan. Court festivities are organized to the joy of all, save the genie Rousch.

Unwilling to wed Polychresta unless Lively is given permission to remain his official mistress (the latter forgave the prince for losing his feathers as soon as she fully understood his situation), Genistan continues unabated his intoxicating sexual adventures, with stops every now and then to consult Fairy Truth. Although Polychresta represents common sense, devotion, and responsibility to family and state, and although Genistan is impressed with her wisdom, nobility, seriousness, and particularly penetrating eyes, he cannot face the destiny she represents for him—to live in a state of sexual denial. Lively, on the other hand, a hetaera type, is not only sensuality incarnate, but a superbly amusing entertainer as well.

Whether he is in denial or not, Genistan's awareness of his obligations causes him such distress that, rather than try to understand his needs and distinguish the source of his psychological problems, he finds the perfect scapegoat onto whom he can heap all the blame for his hurt. The arrow points toward the arrogant, duplicitous, and powerfully evil Rousch. Because Fairy Truth focuses on Genistan's naïve nature, she enlightens him concerning the positive aspects of Rousch's destructive powers. Negative acts in society or destructive impulses in humans may, for the discerning, point to ways and means of rectifying one's deficiencies and also enhancing one's lifestyle. Only with increased vision and maturity will Genistan come to understand the psychological meaning of the magician's idiosyncratically destructive acts—his mood swings, disguises, violence, and conflictual needs—and thereby adjust his own conduct and outlook on life. Couldn't the characteristics Genistan interpreted as evil be considered warning signs set to hurt vulnerable people such as he? Wasn't it his naiveté, narcissistic nature, and overemphasis on sexual matters that were being called into account? To protect Genistan, Fairy Truth renews her proclamations and laws against defamation of character, lying, and inequities in general. Any infraction of her newly stated ethics will result in banishment.

FAIRY TRUTH AS ANIMA. Fairy Truth is Genistan's anima or soul image (inner unconscious feminine attitude or personality). As his spiritual guide, she fills the psychological vacuum existing within him. Indeed, her educative potential is so significant that it, like the previously mentioned wand, it has transformative power over the one-sided, vacuous, and irresponsible prince. He has reached an impasse in his life, following years spent merely sowing his wild oats, equated in this regard with the prolongation of a childlike, identity-less joyful existence, that of the mindless *puer aeternus*, forever stuck in the same rut. Never did he attempt to adapt to his multiple environments; he remained oblivious to them, satisfied, like Don Juan, to hop and skip from one sexual game to another. Given to *affects*, or emotional explosions resulting mainly from his inability to adapt to new, and perhaps unpleasant or even dangerous situations, Genistan/White Bird sought out woman after woman for the never-ending magic of the sensations they afforded him. His transitory emotional ties not only did not release him from what was to become a condition of stasis, or self-perpetuating emotional enslavement, but would require their healing by the immediate and miraculous intercession of his guiding power, Fairy Truth (Jung 6, #807–11).

Unwittingly perhaps, nonetheless perceptively, Genistan described Fairy Truth as possessing "ancient traits," qualities inherent to many supernatural beings. Thus, they are revered, and called upon for help, by humans in moments of crisis. Because fairies as anima images have existed in the human psyche since the beginning of time, seemingly answering the needs of the individuals who project upon them, they have become manifest in countless forms ranging from goddess to harlot. Whatever image man projects onto the archetypal woman, the image constellates an unconscious aspect of himself. Fairy Truth's role is to point out to Genistan the realities of the life experience in general, and his in particular. Understandably, he consults her frequently, and in so doing, he unconsciously invites her to play the role she has actually performed in his life for all these years: agent of transformation. Hasn't she over and over again reminded him of his undifferentiated eros condition? his infantile search for immediate sexual gratification? and his inability or unwillingness to work toward more meaningful relationships? Although Genistan might never be capable of understanding a profound love experience, he could learn, perhaps under duress, to accept the obligations of a future Japanese emperor.

FAIRY TRUTH'S MAGIC TOUCH. After multiple humorous and off-color episodes typical of many of Diderot's narratives, the reader learns that, thanks to Fairy Truth's magic touch, Genistan finally is initiated into semi-adulthood, and, in time, will become, if not an ideal emperor, at least a relatively conscientious and thinking one. By agreeing to marry Polychresta, he will bring to his rule common sense, serious-mindedness, and down-to-earth qualities. His queen is dull, but she does award him numerous children, all of whom will become great achievers. As for the the law denying plural wives, Genistan proves himself to be above the nation's directives by choosing the beautiful, delightful, and voluptuous Lively to be his legal mistress. Diderot's irony rises to heights, when he has the queen, ruled by common sense, agree to Lively's presence at court. To finalize the situation, thus assuaging all distressed consciences, the entire matter is brought to the attention of the emperor's council. With tongue in cheek, Diderot further declares that, after having been authorized by the priesthood and included in the slates of several synods, the dual-woman situation has been resolved as follows: in keeping with certain saintly volumes and a special dispensation from the controlling religious forces, it has been decided that at a cost of one thousand ecus, Genistan will be allowed to have two wives. And so it comes to pass. No jealousy is manifested by either the queen or the mistress. To the contrary, the two ladies servicing the same man preserve a kind of wonderful happy ménage à trois. Only one question remains unresolved: the location of the White Bird's progeny born to the convent nuns.

THE WHITE BIRD'S PROGENY. In time, a group of fifty-two young people of both sexes endowed with white wings on their backs arrives in Japan, asking to be presented to its ruler. After permission is granted, their spokesperson utters the following:

> Invincible Sultan, do you recall the days when . . . you flew rapidly over immense territories, to finally arrive in China in the form of a pigeon and deigned to alight in the temple of the "fire-colored grande guenon," where you found a henhouse worthy of a bird of your importance? You now see before you, very prolific lord, the fruit of your brilliant youth and the marvelous effects of your warblings. The white wings decorating the shoulders [of these birds you see before you] leaves no doubt in your mind as to the sublimity of their origin. They have come to your court to claim their due. (*White Bird* 359)

Genistan not only recognizes all of his children, but awards them generous financial help. He believes that if their wings are clipped, they will resemble the children he has had with Polychresta and thus avoid jealousies, but despite frequent clippings, their wings grow back, each time increasing in beauty. Although differences between the two groups of children are noteworthy, they live in peaceful coexistence. Only one stressful situation still exists: Genistan asks to meet the son he had with Lively before he became emperor. To his chagrin, he is told that the lad has been taken by Fairy Coribella, the child's godmother, who spoils him excessivedly. After a long search, the son is finally located and brought to Genistan's court, but the educators fail to alter his self-indulgent nature. His debaucheries lead to the duel that ends the young man's life.

Diderot's ideas, which were dangerous in their time, were conveyed in *The White Bird* in coded, veiled, contradictory, and frequently mystifying terms. He allowed his unpublished text to be read in the privacy of some salons whose hostesses were open-minded and friendly to his cause. Nor had Diderot been the first to parody sacred dogma. An earlier heroico-comic burlesque, *Vair Vert* or *The Voyages of the Parrot of the Visitation of Nevers* by Jean-Baptiste Louis Gresset, depicted the arrival of a parrot in a convent and the ensuing pandamonium to which his presence gave rise. Not only was Gresset's burlesque published in 1734, but it earned him, incredibly, great success, to the extent that several editions were printed (Robert, *Le Conte de fées littéraire en France* 253).

Diderot's parody on the virginity of Mary, the fertilizing capacities of the Holy Ghost ("who carried the whole child into Mary's womb to be nourished there"), and the Pentecost ("the gift of tongues"), is replete with idiosyncratic paradoxes, digressions, and unforgettable semiotic devices, each enabling the author to air his ideas on religion, politics, ethics, and androcentrism. Banalities were rampant in licentious eighteenth-century literature and *The White Bird* is no exception. They were *willed* by Diderot to better underscore the ironies involved. For example, the ways in which the dove's priapism and the convent girls' hysteria were treated remain not only indelible mockeries of religious dogma, but critiques of specific maladies to which sex-starved women are prone. Nonetheless, by casting women in such derisive, fallable, and inconsequential roles, Diderot prolonged the commonly held misogynist belief in the intellectual inferiority of women.

It must be noted as well that Diderot cast his plea for openmindedness and balance by pointing up the absurdity not only of excessive religious asceticism, but of effete hedonism. The fairy tale allowed him the luxury of fantasy sequences of ascetico-erotico-masochistic mixtures, as was his habit in some of his other works. *The Nun*, for example, draws attention, via exaggeration and shock techniques, to the dangers of naïveté, persecution, repression, effetism, and hypocrisy in the society of his day. His purpose, to bring down the masks!

5

WAS JEAN-JACQUES ROUSSEAU'S THE FANTASTIC QUEEN MERELY A TONGUE-IN-CHEEK FAIRY TALE?

COMPOSED IN 1754, SEEMINGLY FOR THE HABITUÉS of Mlle Quinault's salon, *The Fantastic Queen* remained unpublished until 1758. A year later, after one of Rousseau's protectresses, Mme Dupin, expressed the wish to read the fairy tale, he acquiesced to her request, but downgraded its import. "It's a five-or-six page folly, which, having been written in a moment of gaiety, or rather extravagance, is not even worthy of being called amusing, and, in truth, should not be read by a person of common sense" (Rousseau, *Oeuvres complètes* II, 1909).

The opening sentence of Jean-Jacques Rousseau's *The Fantastic Queen* (1758), although on the surface banal, implies deep poignancy, but gives no hint of the satire and irony that will later appear. "Once upon a time there was a king who loved his people . . . and consequently was adored by them . . . the people blessed him" (Rousseau II, 1179). The bleeding embryonic psyche pleading for love, understanding, and togetherness, which lies buried in these preliminary words, suffuses *The Fantastic Queen* with contradiction, instability, and frustration. These first words present the reigning king as loving his people and being adored by them. Such feelings, not too far from the historical truth about Rousseau's monarch, Louis XV, at the outset of his reign; he was referred to by the French as "the well-beloved." But Rousseau's subsequent description of his fictional monarch as working feverishly, intent upon "making his people happy," is in sharp contrast to Louis XV, who spent little time attending to governmental matters, preferring a well-stocked larder of women (*Fantastic Queen* 1179).

Rousseau's parodic protagonists, neither poetic nor sensitive, emerge as puppetlike; instead of flesh and blood human beings, they are caricatures. Their exaggerated speech, harsh actions, ebullience, cutting humor, and mood swings are forever hyperbolized. Replicated in them as well are aspects of the author's own notional personality: his idealistic, but aggressively critical, even belligerent, views on politics, philosophy, and religion.

Fairy tale lineaments served Rousseau's purpose. They enabled him to convey via dissimulation, hiddenness, and exaggeration his so-called bent for virtue and transparency, the latter used in the moral sense of the word. On a more positive note, he also invested *The Fantastic Queen* with his ideas and ideals concerning the establishment of future utopian societies. Although pretense and misrepresentation ran counter to the reign of truth and virtue Rousseau ostensibly forwarded, their inclusion in his political, social, educational, and philosophical writings, including *The Fantastic Queen*, are in keeping with his discordant and chaotic inner nature. Acknowledging human frailty, wasn't he to write three years later in his celebrated novel, *Julie or The New Héloïse*, that "God himself had veiled his face," after separating himself from his creation (Starobinski, *Jean-Jacques Rousseau. La transparence* 144; *Oeuvres complètes* II, V, 594)?

ECTYPAL ANALYSIS

Rousseau's psychological instability and ideational inconsistencies were exacerbated both by his upbringing and by the swiftly changing times in which he lived. The eighteenth century, generally speaking, is alluded to as the Age of Enlightenment, for the emphasis its writers and philosophers placed on science and reason and their diminishing support of traditional values, divine monarchy, and church doctrine, as well as strong metaphysical, exotic, and romantic undercurrents, also sounded their strong rumblings. Understandably, Rousseau's thought is not entirely consistent in *The Fantastic Queen*. Hadn't he confided in his friend and benefactress, Mme Louise d'Epinay, in contradiction to his statement, "that God himself had veiled his face" to him, that at this juncture in his life he had been drawn to religion: "that in the silence of his study he had felt himself influenced by the the dialectics of the philosophes, but that the spectacle of nature had cured him of his doubts" (Robert, *Le Conte de fées littéraire en France* 244)?

Voltaire, Diderot, and Montesquieu, among other celebrated writers of the period, also sought to improve humanity's lot by struggling against religious persecution, intellectual repression, war, famine, high taxes, and exploitation of the poor. Because their values, along with those of the growing bourgeoisie, were frequently at odds with the regressive notions professed by the royalty and aristocracy, the tension between these factions aroused enormous energy and optimism in the nation, culminating, as we know, in the French Revolution.

Although the solitary and introverted Rousseau responded instinctively to the ills of society and sought to remedy them in his utopian writings, on a personal level he suffered from feelings of guilt throughout his life. In his *Confessions* he discloses to his readers that he was born "infirm and sick" in Geneva on June 28, 1712, the event taking "his mother's life" (*Oeuvres complètes* I, 6). His early years spent with his relatively unstable father, a clock maker and dancing master, had seemingly encouraged a similar unpredictability in the son. Father and son habitually spent long evenings together reading the plethora of sentimental novels in vogue, all the while bemoaning their cruel fate. This self-indulgence came to a sudden halt in 1722, following Rousseau senior's quarrel with Genevan authorities, his subsequent departure from the city, and his abandonment of the ten-year-old boy, who spent the next two years at Pastor Lambercier's boarding school. Henceforth on his own Rousseau spent the next four years working at odd jobs, including that of engraver's apprentice, after which he simply left his native city and received asylum from a twenty-eight-year-old "amoral" woman, Mme de Warens, whom he would call "chère maman." In the pay of the king of Savoy, her function was to convert Protestants to Catholicism—succeeding in Rousseau's case. For the next twelve years, the unstable young man wandered about, worked at different trades, and educated himself in a variety of disciplines: musical theory, and sciences such as chemistry, medicine, and astronomy. He presented his new system of musical notation to the Academy of Sciences in Paris in 1742. His liaison with a servant girl, Thérèse Levasseur, in 1745, resulted during the course of years in the birth of five children, who, it is believed, were abandoned to foundling homes.

In Rousseau's controversial but prize-winning *Discourse on the Sciences and the Arts* (1750), he claimed that the evolution of the sciences and the arts, rather than fostering moral progress, had engendered an increase in depravity and corruption. By 1752, he had authored a light opera *(The Village Soothsayer)*, a ballet *(The Gallant Muses)*, and a play *(Narcissus)*, which was produced at the Théâtre-Français. Following a brief stay in Geneva in 1754, he renounced Catholicism and returned to the Protestant Church. His polemical *Discourse on the Origin and Bases of Inequality Among Men* (1754), emphasizing the evils of divine monarchy and the social inequalities arising from a division of labor and a capitalist society, offered a back-to-nature cure based on the natural goodness of primitive man and his simpler notions concerning law and order. Rousseau earned a reputation among the philosophes and *encyclopedists*, such as Diderot, Condillac, Voltaire, and later Grimm, D'Alembert, and Hume, but his nostalgic, pessimistic, and simplistic approach to life, as well as his intransigeance in his political views, led to quarrels with erstwhile friends (Voltaire, Diderot, D'Alembert, and Hume; even with those who had befriended him, Mme d'Epinay and Mme d'Houdetot, in whose home he had been given lodging for months on end). He rejected theater as an art form because of what he believed to be its socially corruptive power and the immorality of its performers. Voltaire, who considered the theater to be a means of remedying social evils, took umbrage. That Rousseau had himself authored works for the performing arts, as mentioned above, is one of many examples of his psychological/intellectual inconsistency. Rather than plays to entertain the masses, Rousseau advocated such events as dancing around the maypole and local religious festivals to buoy up the people's spirits.

Inborn pessimism coupled with nostalgic visions of paradisaic societies became increasingly evident in Rousseau's writings, and his cantankerous and dyspeptic nature grew in virulence with age. Outside of his highly successful epistolary novel, *Julie or The New Héloïse* (1761), his other works did not fare well during his lifetime. His treatise on education, *Emile* (1761), was condemned to be burned by the Paris Parliament. His political opus, *The Social Contract* (1762), although forbidden to circulate in France and burned in Geneva, was nonetheless enormously influential outside of Europe, later attracting the attention of Mill, Emerson, Thoreau, Whitman, Kant, Hegel, Marx, and others. With the passing of years, Rousseau suffered increasingly from intermittent delirium. He attempted to justify himself to his readers in some of his most poetic works, *Rousseau Judge of Jean-Jacques* and *Daydreams of a Solitary Stroller* (1776-1778). He died at Ermenonville in 1778, at the home of the marquis of Girardin. In accordance with his will, his deeply subjective *Confessions* appeared posthumously.

Rousseau felt himself continuously hounded and victimized by individuals and by society—a condition defined by some as a persecution complex; by others as a bent for self-destruction. And perhaps his feelings of constant victimization had some justification. Hadn't *Emile* been burned? his *Social Contract* banned? and his home at Môtiers lapidated in 1765? It has been claimed that he suffered from chronic bladder trouble, and that he wore trusses to keep a hernia under control, adding to his sense of affliction. According to the autopsy report, the surgeons had "found nothing exceptional—neither in the bladder, in the urethra, nor in the testes of the spermatic duct." It was concluded that Rousseau's ailment and complaints were of psychosomatic origin (Ziegler, "Rousseauian Optimism, Natural Distress, And Dream Research," *Spring* 1976: 55).

Archetypal Analysis

The eighteenth century could boast of fairy, supernatural, and marvelously licentious tales by Voltaire (*Zadig* [1747], *Micromégas* [1752]), and Diderot (*The White Bird* [1747]) and sections of *The Indiscreet Jewels* [1748]). Satiric and frequently ironic, they included extraterrestrial events and appearances and disappearances of angels and other miraculous creatures. The subtext of Rousseau's *The Fantastic Queen*, like that in Voltaire's and Diderot's works, involves philosophical ideas and political concepts, but is more personal and subjective.

It is a tongue-in-cheek fairy tale, redolent with levity as queen, king, and Fairy Discreet play out their relationships—a perfect literary vehicle to mask Rousseau's own inner turmoil, discomfiture, and torment. Emotionally flayed by his mother's death nine days following his birth, he was increasingly haunted by guilt feelings. The all-important mother figure who, under normal conditions, would have seen to his psychological and spiritual nourishment and development, had been snatched from his world and left him with a gaping void in his life. Such psychological divestiture, C. G. Jung wrote, is life-long.

> The mother-child relationship is certainly the deepest and most poignant one we know; in fact, for some time the child is, so to speak, a part of the mother's body. Later it is part of the psychic atmosphere of the mother . . . and in this way everything original in the child is indissolubly blended with the mother-image. This is true not only for the individual, but still more in a historical sense. . . . It is the absolute experience of our species, an organic truth as unequivocal as the relation of the sexes to one another. Thus there is inherent in the archetype, in the collectively inherited mother-image, the same extraordinary intensity of relationship which instinctively impels the child to cling to its mother. (Jung 8, # 373)

Concomitantly with Rousseau's severe guilt feelings toward his genetrix, like so many other children bereft of their mothers at birth, he too experienced her disappearance from his world as a betrayal, accounting to some extent for the volatility in his relationships with women such as Mme de Warens and Mme d'Houdetot, among others. Rousseau's genius—his musical, literary, and scientific talents—had, fortunately, provided him with an antidote necessary to his emotional survival. Written when he was forty-six years old, *The Fantastic Queen* may be gauged in part as a compensatory device able to partially, and only temporarily, fill his sense of inner vacancy. His negative outlook on life and on humanity is likewise evident in the words Rousseau himself used to describe *The Fantastic Queen*: a "plotless, loveless, marriageless, and saucyless," yet "bearable," even "jolly" fairy tale (*Oeuvres complètes* II, 1177). His comment on this work is all the more telling to today's reader for the window it opens onto the author's psyche: the use of his creative instinct, perhaps unconsciously, to relieve his increasingly morbid condition. Sharply antipodal to his didactic and deeply meditative works, the fairy tale called into play the complexities and masking devices of humor and acerbic repartees, and afforded him the opportunity to cast aspersions on concepts and types he had come to abhor.

Set in a Middle Eastern background, an ambiance popular in eighteenth-century France thanks to A. Galland's memorable translation of the *Thousand and One Nights*, Rousseau's *The Fantastic Queen* bears traces also of Voltaire's and Diderot's remarkably pithy, ribald, and satiric style. Nor, as in the narratives of his predecessors, did his puppetlike caricatures fail to gyrate about his inner stage. Their evanescent traits, used by Rousseau to magnify a variety of human failings and dysfunctional concepts, were buoyed along by their verbal, rhythmical, and imagistic concatenations. Events, to be sure, pivoted around Rousseau's preternatural Fairy Discreet, who allowed the author to inject vigor and trenchant wit into the quasi-magical and puckish miscreants in his story.

KING/FATHER/PHOENIX. The name Phoenix, chosen by Rousseau for the king in *The Fantastic Queen*, was perfectly suited to his function. According to Herodotus and Plutarch, the life span of the phoenix, a mythical bird, was some five hundred years, after which it burned itself to ashes on a pyre, later to rise and live anew. In that French kings ruled by divine right, they, like the legendary phoenix, would also live on eternally, passing through the rituals of death and resurrection. Appropriate as well to Rousseau's monarch is the Greek origin of his name: the word *phoinix*, meaning purple, crimson, or blood-red, thus identifying the king with French royal colors. A stab at Louis XV seems obvious in the word, *phoinos*, closely akin to *phoinix*, when associated with the bloody murders occurring in the wars of the Polish Succession (1733–1735), Austrian Succession (1748), and Seven Years' War (1756–1763) fought during the French monarch's reign.

THE MOTHER/QUEEN FANTASTIC. Queen Fantastic, (Gr. *phantastikos*, indicating the presence of mental images identified with imagination), whose name appears in the title of Rousseau's fairy tale, was a far more complex personality than her spouse. Lacking her husband's stability and a realistic approach to life, she objectified her inner desires in sequences of dance-like mimetic poses. Depicted as "lively, dizzy, crazy in the head, wise in things of the heart, good in temperament, bad because of her capriciousness," she gathered conflict and volatility in her makeup. Whether Rousseau was targeting characteristics of Louis XV's queen, Marie Leszczyńska, and/or of some of his mistresses, Mme de Châteauroux or Mme de Pompadour, is not known. Nonetheless, Queen Fantastic emerged as whimsical, quixotic, and high-strung (*Oeuvres complètes* II, 1179).

Fantastic had inherited her name from a long line of female ancestors. Like a jigsaw puzzle, her bizarre personality was made up of whimsical, capricious, weird, and even eccentric pieces. An inner antagonism between her various traits made her alluring, yet coercive, intent upon controlling and shaping her world and the lives of her entourage. She was happy of disposition, yet had a morbid streak. "Very reasonable," she was her husband's "charmer," but she was also described as his "torturer" (*Fantastic Queen* 1179). That Rousseau should have described Fantastic in such antithetical terms indicates his double intent to amuse his readers by pointing up her endearing traits and to maim the personal mother image by underscoring her ungovernable and eccentric antics.

The personal mother is the first bearer of the child's *anima,* and Rousseau's had died before he even became aware of her existence. His mimetic visualization of her, although fragmented, was nonetheless deeply entrenched in his unconscious. Unable to integrate what could have been a source of wisdom, devotion, and nourishment into consciousness, he continuously projected his yearning for fulfillment onto the women to whom he was attracted, and onto the collective image of Mother Nature. Under normal circumstances, children usually learn to fend for themselves during the maturation process, but in Rousseau's case, he continued to transfer his mother-imago onto specific males and females, particularly those, such as Diderot, who showed him so much kindness and understanding, and with whom he shared similar intellectual goals.

FANTASTIC'S PREGNANCY AND ROUSSEAU'S MEMORY IMAGES. Saddened by her inhability to conceive, Fantastic indulged in scapegoat tactics, blaming those around her for her barrenness. In time, however, she adopted a relatively realistic attitude and began asking clergymen and doctors for secret remedies. After carefully listening to their recommendations, she dutifully filled each of their prescriptions and with equal rigorousness and a tinge of solemnity, just as she was about to ingest the required brew, as if mimetically fulfilling some ritualistic formula, she broke the spell in a moment of jocular madness by throwing the medicine at their faces. Rousseau's narrator, in a bantering mode, declares that since "instinctive processes" such as pregnancies almost always meet with difficulties, Fantastic's behavioral patterns were to be expected. The scenes of irritation and of vindictiveness played out by Fantastic when her attempts to become pregnant failed might be identified by today's psychiatrists as a fixation—or hypertrophy—of the maternal element.

Not easily dissuaded from achieving her goal, Fantastic consulted dervishes (members of a Muslim religious order noted for their devotional exercises), and Catholic prelates suggested a novena (nine days of devotion) and pilgrimages to expel the malefic forces that prevented her from conceiving. She was told that her wish would be fulfilled by emptying her coffers most generously into various houses of worship. (In this regard, Rousseau took the opportunity, as had Montesquieu and Voltaire before him, to confuse and satirize the miracle-performing rituals recommended by organized religions to make conceptions possible.)

Cleverly and with utmost guile, Fantastic advised her entourage of an impending trip she was making to the country to breathe some fresh air. Instead, she went to a monastery where she gleefully availed herself of the opportunity of entering the monks' cells and throwing their effects all about. Donning their vestments and their relics, the dramatically inclined queen appeared at court decked out in "most of their equipment," namely, their white belts, leather sandals, hoods, and scapularies. The thrills she derived by observing the peering eyes of onlookers during her bouts of "monastic masquerading," encouraged her to keep changing her "disguises," posing in some of these before the royal court painter and thereby retaining her image for posterity (*Fantastic Queen* 1180).

The narrator then declared that after Fantastic had carried out all of her devotions to the letter, "earth and heaven finally acquiesced to the queen's wishes," and she became pregnant. No sooner had the glad tidings been made known to the world than doctors and clergy alike attributed the queen's success to their individual fields of expertise: drugs, relics, and prayers; and, the king, most overtly, credited his "lovemaking" (*Fantastic Queen* 1180). The populace, naturally, conveyed its unbounded joy by declaring the event a miracle!

Once pregnant, the queen looked upon her husband as an accidental detail in her life-creating ability. Nevertheless, she was unable to focus on the natural course of her pregnancy, and she tended to extremes in her comportment and thinking processes, as well as in her propensity for violence and will to power. So exacerbated did her normally volatile and quixotic temperament become during the nine-month period of gestation that her tantrums took on a robot-like quality. Not only did she smash everything in her path, but she "embraced with indifference whomever she encountered; men, women, courtiers, valets, [and] if you just happened to be in her way, you ran the risk of being smothered" (*Fantastic Queen* 1180). Her joy at the thought of bearing a child was compounded, strangely enough, by sadistic visions of her whipping the child as she saw fit (*Fantastic Queen* 1180).

Do Fantastic's extravagant antics and actions reflect Rousseau's own secreted or repressed feelings of rage and frustrated power drive? Was he releasing his anger at what he might have looked upon as his mother's *betrayal* of him? If so, Fantastic's personality becomes an exaggerated mirror image of his own unpredictable, self-absorbed, angry and at times high-spirited nature. As a composite of unconscious, unlived tendencies in the author, Fantastic may be said to have taken on the veneer of a memory-image that allowed him not only to live out his inordinate attachment to the mother he never knew, but to expel his wrath against her, who, by dying, had abandonned him.

THE PROBLEMATICS OF AN EXPANDING UTERUS. Notwithstanding the glow radiating from Fantastic's entire being during her pregnancy, her husband grew increasingly opposed to her dictatorial and quixotic antics. It was evident to Phoenix, representative of the family, of the community, and of society in general, that his wife had usurped his prerogatives. Besides, another inimical power—over which the king had no control—was rapidly building up against him —the fetus, firmly lodged in Fantastic's expanding *uterus*.

Dichotomies within a family or a nation frequently unite its members, but may also cause a buildup of spheres of interest and of influence, which diminish the status of one or more members. In our case, the king not only was excluded from Fantastic's world—pregnant with excitement and expectancy— but he was downgraded by her as well. To regain his dominion would necessitate his breaking or reducing his wife's power. How best to succeed in this endeavor? By emphasizing her shortcomings. Occasions to denigrate either a husband or a wife are rarely lacking. Taking advantage of a meeting with the Greats of his government, Phoenix declared his desire that a prince be born, thus assuring the continuation of his patriarchal regime. Aghast by what she considered to be a wish/command, Fantastic took umbrage, declaring her husband's order that a son be born to be an outright usurpation of power. His words were not only out of place, she claimed, but were offensive to her as queen. "It appeared singularly strange," she announced with vigor, "that anyone would dare to dispute her right to dispose of something that incontestably belongs to her" (*Fantastic Queen* 1181). It is perfectly understandable that a pregnant woman consider her future child as a completion of herself. In Fantastic's case, she sought to transmit not only her talents and her personality but even her sex to her progeny.

Rejecting all her husband's reasons, Fantastic vehemently and unequiv-
ocally contended that childbearing was none of his affair. In keeping with her
behavioral patterns, she locked herself in her room and sulked for at least six
months.

The more Fantastic's uterus expanded, the more her maternal instinct
increased. Her awareness that she was the carrier of all aspects of life became
obsessional, paving the way for her belief in the sanctity and the miraculous
nature of motherhood, just as in parts of the Catholic world excessive veneration of the Virgin Mary finds expression in Mariolatry. Fantastic saw herself
as mystery: the arcana of childbearing residing in the woman's creative nature—an unknown and elusive power within her expanding uterus—which
took on great amplitude and manifested itself in her increasing outbreaks of
warped aggression and hysteria.

Rousseau's ambivalent feelings for the mother figure in general, as already cited, and for pregnant women in particular, are expressed in Fantastic's jarringly inconsistent behavior—sequences marked by contention, flux,
and moodiness—mirrorings of Rousseau's own behavioral patterns. The
mother-to-be's conduct ranged from the sublime love and shelter Rousseau
described in *The New Héloïse*—to a harshness and insensitivity that revealed
a deeply marred psyche.

That Rousseau poured his libido into the creatures of his imaginings is
clear. What is less evident, however, is his inability to differentiate or to objectify or rationalize these inner pulsions with respect to his own behavioral
patterns. His paucity of insight into his idiosyncratic nature caused him frequently to over- or undervalue the positive and negative personality traits of
his friends and acquaintances. His yearning, for example, to recreate paradisaic communities *(Discourses, Social Contract)*, or his depictions of angelic creatures *(The New Heloïse)*, served to obscure his world of actuality.

Rousseau's inflated view of himself at times became blatantly evident in
Fantastic's quixotic comportment. Her excessive likes or dislikes, her irra-
tionality and transgressions, her spitefulness and vindictiveness were, like
globules of cement, affixed to her character. While Rousseau for the most part
did not indulge in such extremes, preferring to escape his real and imagined
persecutors rather than confront them, he resembled Fantastic in that he
never came to terms with his ever-corrosive hurt. His guilt feelings toward his
mother, and perhaps his anger against his father for having abandoned him so
early in life, caused him to feel an expanding sense of emptiness, vacancy, and
foreboding, which haunted him increasingly during the latter part of his life.

FAIRY DISCREET AND HER PRAGMATIC APPROACH. Rousseau's emphasis alters with the presence of the minute Fairy Discreet, who, as representative of

discernment, judgment, prudence, and civilized comportment, brings new values to the willful and self-indulgent couple. As advisor to the king, and later to the queen, Discreet functions as mediator between husband and wife, her discernment alleviating to a great extent the reigning virulence and acrimony.

As representative of *logos*, Discreet symbolizes the drive in individuals to diminish primal darkness (or unconscious factors) by seeking the light of consciousness. The accomplishment of such a feat requires the continuous and unrelenting development of transparency, a recognition and/or illumination of everything that mars an individual's inner vision. A kind of warrior fairy, Discreet may be viewed also as a destroying agent, obliterating or rendering nonfunctional everything that veils or blocks inner sight.

Observing Phoenix in fervent, if not hysterical, prayer, and not knowing which saint to call upon to help him solve his dilemma, Discreet realizes that he cannot deal with the extremes of Fantastic's irrational behavior. Compassionate and understanding, and in keeping with her eponymic function, she cognizes the following syllogism: conflict stirs fire, fire arouses (as in emotions), flame provokes combustion on the one hand and light on the other. Adroitly, she counsels the king not to embark on an aggressive nor antagonistic course with regard to his wife, unless he seeks to go mad, but rather to opt for tenderness, understanding, and conciliation to gain his ends. He must, she advises him further, ask the queen to pardon him for his apparent aggression in expressing his "sincere wishes" to have a male child (*Fantastic Queen* 1181).

The king's immediate acquiescence to her suggestion prompts Discreet to explain a woman's goal during pregnancy: to diminish the male's arrogance toward the birthing process. Phoenix must, therefore, learn to play a more subtle hand to achieve his end: no longer must he trumpet his desires, but conceal—or veil—them via a semblance of courtesy and graciousness. Most importantly, he must divest himself of the "ridiculous hope of transforming his wife into a reasonable woman" (*Fantastic Queen* 1181). As soon as he alters his approach, Discreet cautions him, his wife will curtail her caprices and become the wiser.

Swayed by Discreet's rationalizations, Phoenix decides to penetrate the Queen's Circle to apologize to his wife for having contested her and to inform her that he really wants a girl baby to be born. He also tells her that henceforth he will rectify the causes of tension between them. Seemingly understanding of the physical and emotional changes taking place in the queen's heart during her pregnancy, he accepts the less important role in the creative enterprise they have undertaken together.

Although friction between husband and wife subsides, the psychological adventure that the infant's growing presence in Fantastic's uterus affords her, triggers in her an increasingly divisive attitude. Misinterpreting the king's apparent kindness as hypocrisy, and fearing it could boomerang and cover her with ridicule, Fantastic concludes that the king's arrogance is more overt than ever. However, she declares, as has always been her custom, she will once again accede to her monarch's wishes. "My prince and my husband having ordered me to give birth to a boy," she says with queenly elegance, thereby underscoring once again Rousseau's bent for irony. "I am too well versed in my duties not to obey" (*Fantastic Queen* 1182). In that her husband's tender words to her, she further notes, reveals greater love for his people than for his wife, she will "imitate his so very noble and disinterested ways" by asking the Sultan's Council for a document that states the number and sex of children a royal family should have for the good of the state. In this manner, she will be putting her best foot forward by conforming to state dicta, placing her country's needs before her own and, in so doing, "regulating her nightly conduct" accordingly. Needless to add, the narrator indicates the pains taken by the court officials to muffle their laughter during the queen's speech (*Fantastic Queen* 1182).

The breaches of sincerity or transparency in the king's alleged desire for wanting a girl point to the complexities involved in the royal couple's internecine feud. Given the fact that *being* (his desire to have a boy) and *appearing* (his false statement of wanting a girl) are at odds, dichotomies between the two still stand. Nonetheless, although hypocrisy, falsehood, and the mask all breed corruption, decadence, and sloth, Rousseau had contended numerous times, in his *Discourses* and other writings, that these same poisons possess their own subtle pragmatic or healing elements as well. While noxious indirection is a function of denial, it is also operative as an escape mechanism: both, being deeply entrenched in Rousseau's psyche, might have led him to use them to extricate himself from an unfortunate situation as a child. Wasn't he accused of lying when he denied he had broken the teeth of Mlle Lambercier's comb (the daughter of the family in whose care he had been placed)? (*Confessions* I. Book 1, 18ff.) Broaching in *Emile* the difficulties his protagonists had in their passion for each other, Rousseau wrote:

> He who seeks to preserve the supremacy of natural feelings in civil life is oblivious to what he asks. Ever in contradiction with himself, forever hesitating between his wishes and his duties, he will be neither a man nor citizen. He will be of no use to himself or to others. (*Emile* IV, 1, 249; Jung 6, #120)

FAIRY DISCREET'S ARCHETYPAL ANDROGYNE. Discreet, "whose sex and name contrasted sometimes so pleasantly with her character," judged the quarrel between the royal couple so pleasurable a pastime that she decided to amuse herself at their expense (*Fantastic Queen* 182). Such psychological androgeny as existed in *Discreet* was not of Rousseau's invention. Androgynous figures have existed in religious pantheons since time immemorial. Cases in point are the mustached Chinese Kuan Yin and the Japanese Kannon, both deities of compassion and forgivingness; and the Hindu's consoling and loving Avalokitesvara, the Buddha of the Present time cycle, appearing as male or as female to his devotees.

Rousseau adopted the image of the psychologically oriented androgyne to create a condition of harmony in the kingdom. Discreet's lucidity concerning the ambiguous and contentious situation, expanded the scope of her objective intelligence. Assuming the positive role of bridge builder between the two one-sided contestants, she directed them toward a broader understanding of their connected paths.

Like the all-inclusive zero, which incorporates odd and even numbers, the psychologically androgynous Discreet better understood the dichotomies between female and male emotionality and how to deal with them. Rather than being didactic in her approach, Rousseau's free-spirited, winsome, humorous, and wise fairy transcended her sexual framings, thus heightening the condition of oneness in those torn by antagonism.

How did Fairy Discreet set about her task? Through duplicity? Or did she have access to arcane truths hidden from ordinary mortals? After consulting the comets presiding over the birth of princes, she told Phoenix that he could rest assured that a baby boy would be born. Moments later, she assured the queen that her wish would be granted by the birth of a baby girl.

The deep-seated love the royal couple really felt for each other was *veiled* from them both, and more importantly, from themselves, by the jocular (or should we say "jugular") side of their personalities. Doesn't the veiling of truth arouse curiosity in some and awe in others? Was Rousseau's levity a means of circumventing or perhaps of ridiculing his own intransigeant credo of virtue, rectitude, integrity—and transparency? How else, except by deforming truth, or by dissociating what he considered to be truth from fiction, could he construct his anti-truth fairy tale? Aren't these poisons implicit in the very notion of creativity? Of *art* itself? (The word stems from *artifice*, dissimulation.) A fine dividing line, then, must be drawn between the greater truth of Rousseau's fiction—and the lies permeating the relationships between husband and wife. The humor Rousseau invested in his exaggerated and frequently farcical images, situations, and events was designed to point up Fantastic's madness, and the sequences may be viewed, to a great extent, as conveyors of pain and sorrow interspersed with moments of mimed mirth.

FANTASTIC'S DUPLICITY. The veiling devices used in *The Fantastic Queen* disclosed Rouseau's dependency on the layering process to highlight the dramatic elements, which destabilized the ideal condition of transparency for which he yearned, yet clarified the points he was trying to make. Having already used Plato's image of the statue of Glaucus in his *Discourse on the Origin of Inequality* to underscore its disfigurement "by storms and tempests, [which made him look] more like a ferocious animal than a god," Rousseau pointed to similar veiling processes during the course of human lives (*Oeuvres complètes* III, 122; Plato, *Republic* X, 11). With the passing of centuries, he maintained, people had not only distanced themselves from their original pristine purity, but from their souls, which concomitantly underwent a similar degenerative process. Carried a step further, Rousseau's analogy may be applied to Fantastic's extreme facial distortions when in the throes of passion—either love or rage making her equally unrecognizable.

Discreet's insights, coupled with her clever and winsome ways, worked some of their magic on Fantastic, yet the queen was still impulsive, particularly regarding the extravagant layette she ordered for the son her husband had told her she was to have. So extremely male was it, that it had to be restyled to suit the baby girl Discreet had secretly informed her she would have. Fantastic's peals of laughter at the thought of dissimulating the truth of the newborn's sexual identity from her husband were, for no apparent reason, transformed seconds later into their opposite, utter sadness. This was in startling contrast to her previous merry imagining of the "venerable Chancellor" donning his large glasses, bending down to verify the baby's sex, and her husband's expression of despair when told the news. Feelings of glee had flooded her system when fantasizing about her husband's remark, "But I thought. . . ," as "disorder and confusion" broke out at court (*Fantastic Queen* 1183). The court ladies would be sent into a tizzy, she mused, attempting as best they could to understand the unfathomable.

Fantastic, whose imagination and initiative functioned in a peculiar manner, believed that the best way to celebrate the blessed event would be to have the magistrates argue their cases at court dressed as newborn princes. Phoenix disagreed, reasoning that such a costume would degrade their title and cause, particularly since the infant had not yet been born. Taking the initiative as usual, Fantastic assured him that to let them harangue in court prior to the infant's birth would allow them to expel their foolishness beforehand, thus sparing the future prince from having to listen in his maturity to discourses that could drive him mad (*Fantastic Queen* 1183).

Although Fantastic had kept Discreet's secret as best she could, within three days everyone within the kingdom—except the king—was aware of the fairy's prognostications. As the termination date approached, the entire court observed Phoenix with eagle eyes. How, they wondered, would Discreet, despite her supernatural qualities, get herself out of the predicament she herself had created?

Ministers, senators, and royalty from other lands were summoned to celebrate the blessed event; the most important person, however, the obstetrician, had been overlooked and had not been called. Beside himself, the king "inadvertently" called on a midwife to proceed with the delivery. The unrestrained glee amid the court ladies triggered by his act added to the queen's good humor, transforming the early stages of the birthing process into the jolliest of events ever (*Fantastic Queen* 1184).

Fantastic's pains then increased and her screams intensified. Discreet's duplicitous prognostications would soon be known to all. The surprise birth of "a girl and a boy, more beautiful than the sun and the moon, who resembled each other so strongly that one could barely tell them apart," not only disculpated the fairy, but transported Phoenix into a state of rapture (*Fantastic Queen* 1185). Regressing into childishness, he ran to the balcony to announce to his people that Fantastic had given birth to a son, a father for the nation, and to a girl, for the queen.

But Fantastic was still unaware of the existence of the baby boy and wept at the thought of her husband's disappointment. Attempting to alleviate her sorrow, Discreet, whose supernatural powers enabled her to read into the hearts of humans, announced to her the glad tidings: the boy's emergence into the world. So happy was Fantastic at this news that her laughter grew into a hysterical faint, from which even Discreet had difficulty reviving her (*Fantastic Queen* 1186).

Discreet's genial idea, having been conveyed in word, then in deed, accounted for the court's change of heart toward her. Those who had formerly mocked her were now themselves derided—just vindication for one who had exhibited such profound kindness and wisdom (*Fantastic Queen* 1186; Starobinski 170).

FANTASTIC'S GUILT. What Fantastic had not counted upon was a sudden upsurge of guilt feelings: she regretted having not only tormented and derided her husband, but having denied him the joy of fantasizing about their future progeny together. So sincere was her repentance that, unaccountably, she came to love the baby boy more deeply than the baby girl she had so strongly desired. A similar and equally singular bonding between the king and his daughter also came to pass (*Fantastic Queen* 1186). Moreover, Fantastic's energy generated by the double births was such that she disregarded the custom of the times: unlike God, who had rested on the seventh day after his creation, she announced to her entourage that she felt perfectly well and would go out on the sixth day. In addition, unlike many court ladies who feared its deforming consequences, Fantastic would breast-feed her babies (*Fantastic Queen* 1187).

BREAST-FEEDING. For Rousseau, breast-feeding was indispensable. In his pedagogical writings, *Emile* and *Sophie* among others, Rousseau went so far as to reject the idea of a wet nurse, contending that such a substitute would deprive the mother of this uniquely joyful and meaningful experience.[1] Not only did Rousseau consider breast-feeding a natural function salutary for infants and thus for the nation, but he found that no analogue for it existed. He believed that "everything known to a new-born rests in sensation" (*Emile;* Garnier 97). Indeed, "sensation in the [infant] relates to nothing, constructs nothing, does not become idea: it remains image" (Poulet, *Etudes sur le temps humain* I, 201). In that life at birth is virtually limited to "pure sensation," it is understandable that Rousseau rejected the use of a wet nurse: "Women have ceased being mothers; they no longer will be; they no longer want to be. Even if they wanted to be, they might not be able to be" (*Emile* IV, I, 258). The bonding resulting from the closeness of mother and child during breast-feeding time created an indelible image for Rousseau of a loving family. The warmth, and tenderness that would pass between mother and infant would allow "women to become mothers again, and men to soon return to being fathers and husbands" (*Emile* IV, 258).

The symbol of the nursing mother, which played a crucial role in Rousseau's educational treatise *Emile,* was for him one of fulfillment. As a polyvalent symbol in many religions—Egyptian (Isis), Greek (Rhea; the many-breasted mother, Diana of Ephesus); Hindu (Kali); Christian (Mary); and Mexican (Mayauel)—this archetypal image features woman as creator and nourisher. Homer illustrated this same all-inclusive point in his *Odyssey:*

> At the sight of their mothers the calves skip so wildly that their pens can no longer hold them; they break loose, lowing all the while and gamboling. (X, 410–114; E. Neumann, *The Great Mother* 125).

The breast motif in Rousseau's fairy tale reflects the archetypal experience of the Feminine as an all-nourishing power. Breast-feeding may be a physical necessity for the infant, but the image conveys maternal solicitude and love for the newborn as well. Associated with feelings of containment and protection, breast-feeding came to symbolize a means of safeguarding an infant against the dangers of the outer world. The uterus with its potential for transformation is linked to water symbolism, and is also related to breast imagings, thus integrating the two processes in the one primordial womb of life, and eternalness in humans and animals. Understandably, then, such projections on Rousseau's part may have been felt so powerfully as to compel him to declare that any woman shying from this function has committed a villiany. Because he was deprived of a mother, the all-encompassing archetype of the Great Mother answered a deeply felt unconscious need in him. Indeed, it lived on as an eternal and active presence in his psyche. Since the visual factor had always been crucial to Rousseau, it might be suggested that the picture of the nursing Fantastic impacted on him with the power of direct psychic experience.

Fantastic, who maintained "that there is no more beautiful sight in a husband's eyes than that of a mother breast-feeding her children," triggered guffaws and ridicule from the sophisticated court ladies who attributed Fantastic's new fad to the capricious royal couple's latest obsession. Soon, however, their titters died down (*Fantastic Queen* 1188).

SUBLIMATION AND VENERATION OF THE FEMALE BODY. During Fantastic's pregnancy and breast-feeding episodes, the female body was sublimated, even venerated, but it was neither eroticized nor sexualized. Rousseau had glorified the breast, and breast-feeding in *The New Héloïse* and in his *Confessions*. In the former, Saint-Preux, Julie's lover, his eyes peering through her garment—unveiling her bosom, so to speak—conveyed both his shock and his delight at the "enormous amplitude of her breasts" (Eigeldinger, *Jean-Jacques Rousseau* 177; *Oeuvres complètes* II, 82). In his *Confessions*, Rousseau depicted Mme de Warens's beauty in terms of an "intimacy of the heart . . . more spiritual than physical; a pleasure forever troubled by a feeling of sadness" (ibid., 154; *Oeuvres complètes* I, 49–50). Although she was older than Rousseau and the one who had initiated him into love, his reference to her as "chère maman" indicates a psychologically incestuous relationship, despite the fact that he considered her a beatific and angelic presence in his life. Had he thought of himself as having transgressed society's incest taboo, his sexual relationship with Mme de Warens would have been an inhibitory sexual experience (*Oeuvres complètes* 154, 174). Although he did not mention overtly the breasts of Mme d'Houdetot, he alluded to happiness that could derive from that part of her anatomy in subtle, troubled, and embarrassed overtones. Nor did he express his happiness in terms of physical possession of Mme Basile's body, but rather in his awareness of the "intensity of [its] presence" (Starobinski 186). Was Rousseau a voyeur? Perhaps, since the voluptuousness communicated by the image of a woman's breasts was seemingly more powerful and more pleasurable for him than the actual touch sensation.

DISCREET, THE BESTOWER OF GIFTS. Fairies customarily bestowed gifts on those whose lives they touched. Prior to the baptism of the twins—"before the magical water removes them from my protection"—Discreet announced that the infants should be endowed with names that would best reflect the qualities needed by their nation. Since the king and queen knew their children better than anyone else, Discreet asked them to choose the names for the infants (*Fantastic Queen* 1188).

No sooner spoken, than Fantastic and Phoenix were at odds with each other. The queen claimed that she alone knew what best served the interests of her family and her country. She wanted pretty names suitable for children who were young that would delight her entourage. Whether the infants became dolts at thirty held no interest for her (*Fantastic Queen* 1189). The king, by contrast, realizing the meaningfulness of the choice of names, opted for ones underscoring reasonable and thoughtful outlooks on life. The arguments became so acrimonious that Discreet decided to let each parent name the infant of his/her sex, giving each the impression of having won the contest (*Fantastic Queen* 1189). Although the king grabbed the prince, and the queen the princess, their quarrel did not abate. Fantastic in fact was so annoyed that she asked that each child be endowed with the qualities of the parent of the opposite sex (*Fantastic Queen* 1189).

Unable to curb his anger at Fantastic's irrational behavior, the king yielded to her demands, stating that the boy infant he was holding should resemble her. She declared impetuously that the daughter she was holding should resemble him. Accordingly, having been endowed with the qualities of the girl, the prince was named Caprice, which means a sudden or seemingly unpredictable action or thought. As his opposite, the princess, endowed with the boy's qualities, was named Reason, implying a rational and intelligible outlook on life (*Fantastic Queen* 1189). Derisively, Rousseau refers to Caprice, and the topsy-turviness of this future successor to the throne, as having all the perfections of a beautiful woman. As for the girl, Reason, she will have all the virtues and qualities of a good king.

After taking his daughter in his arms ever so tenderly, the king said to her: "[W]hat good would even your mother's beauty be to you if you did not have her talent to take advantage of it? You will be far too reasonable to turn anyone's head!" (*Fantastic Queen* 1190). The "far more circumspect" Fantastic hugged her son and, although sadness marked her expression, she refrained from articulating her prognostications regarding his lack of wisdom.

Looking at both his children and his wife, the king realized, albeit too late, his mistake in the choice of names. Rather than blame himself for his temper surge, however, he made Fantastic the scapegoat. His errors, he stated categorically, were of his wife's making. Had she not intervened, their children would have surpassed their parents in intelligence and in rulership of the land (*Fantastic Queen* 1190). Fantastic, whose heart had always responded to her husband's pain despite her quixotic and dictatorial behavioral patterns, rushed to hug him and comfort him with words of solace: "At least they will love each other as much as possible" (*Fantastic Queen* 1190). Touched by his wife's understanding, Phoenix repeated what he had so frequently said to her in the past: "Natural goodness and a sensitive heart suffice to repair everything" (*Fantastic Queen* 1190).

THE PROGNOSTICATION. In time, the insightful Druid attached to the court prognosticated the following: Prince Caprice would be imaginative and filled with good intentions, but each time he might seek to introduce reforms to alleviate suffering among his people, he would instead bring increasing despair and blame others for his failures. Said the Druid:

> He will disrupt the kingdom while trying to reform it. In his attempt to make his subjects happy, he will drive them to despair, always blaming others for his own mistakes: unjust for having been imprudent, he will renew his mistakes when attempting to rectify past errors. Since wisdom will never be his guide, the good he seeks to accomplish will aggravate the evil already in place. In one word, although deep down he is generous, sensitive, his very virtues will do him disservice, and the slightest irresponsible act on his part, will make him more hated than had he planned a reasoned campaign of malicious acts. (1190)

As for Princess Reason,

> the new Heroine of the land of Fairies will become [so] prodigiously wise and prudent that, although without adulators, will be so adored by the people that each person will wish to be governed by her; her good conduct so advantageous to everyone, including herself, will serve to hurt her brother, whose unsound ways will forever be contrasted to her virtues; to the point of awarding him all the defects she does not have, even though he might not himself possess them. (1191)

Rousseau's extraordinary character analysis of Prince Caprice and Princess Reason aimed slings and arrows at the present monarchs of France, but may also be viewed as a mirror image of his own chaotic inner world. Like Rousseau himself, the prince was impulsive, unpredictable, inconstant, overly sensitive, and cantankerous. But Rousseau also possessed Princess Reason's extraordinary intellectual capacity—a brilliant, logical, theoretical, and philosopical mind. In expressing what he believed to be reasonable ideas in a reasonable way, however, Rousseau often entered into destructive and hurtful quarrels with his friends and acquaintances.

PATRIARCHAL OR MATRIARCHAL RULE? After the demise of Fantastic and Phoenix, the wise of the land debated as to whether it would be better for a kingdom to be awarded Caprice for a king or Reason for a queen. The patriarchs having won out, it was decided that "the most demented of men is preferable [as ruler]to the wisest of women," whether "the male or the first born be a monkey or a wolf . . ." (1191).[2]

The fairy tale's supernatural deus ex machina outcome, in accordance with the nature of this literary genre, refreshes the reader's memory by inviting Discreet to explain what might not have been divined: since the twins were physically identical and were always dressed in the same manner, errors as to their gender were not only possible, but probable. And so it happened that on that fateful naming day, the king, erroneously believing he was holding his daughter in his arms, and the queen, mistakenly thinking she was holding her son, had both erred in identifying the twins. Discreet, allowing or rather inviting such an error, did so in order that each of the infants would be endowed with the qualities that would best serve the interests of the state.

Thus, the princess had been Caprice; and her brother, Reason. Therefore, when he assumed the kingship after his parents' demise, he adhered to his duties, and acquired glory by refraining from participating in wars, by abstaining from committing violence against his subjects. His peaceful rule won the compliments and benedictions of his people—doubly so, for having carried out the projects his father had had in mind. So harmonious was King Reason's accession to the throne that the people did not even realize a change in rulership had occurred. As for Princess Caprice, after having driven so many of her lovers either mad or to death, she finally married a neighboring king, preferring him to the others since "he had the longest moustache and was the best hopper" (Fantastic Queen 1192).

The disapearance of Rousseau's mother divested him not only of her love, but of her acceptance, her wanting and valuing of him in his own right. Such severance had not only injured his earliest image of the maternal, but its development as well, impacting on both his conscious and subliminal spheres. His mother fixation was not only his lifelong preoccupation, but the basis of many of his writings, with their emphasis on, and quest for, values such as integrity, purity, and virtue. "Children who have suffered [through deprivation of a mother], live in a pathological inner state" throughout their lives (Harding, The Parental Image 10).

Rousseau's need for mother figures, his emotional dependency on them, his yearning for new beginnings and for, as he put it, the simplicity of primitivity indicated a failure on his part to subdue the monster within, whose positive qualities he was incapable of absorbing.

Had Rousseau shaped Fantastic's comportment according to what may be identified as mother-void? Was the cathexis (concentration of psychic energy) invested in the maternal image upon which he fixated forever alive in his unconscious? Rousseau's memory-images permitted him to resurrect a panoply of feelings which he then sifted, translated, revitalized, and verbalized in pithy and sardonic ironies within the context of *The Fantastic Queen*. Compensatory character traits in both Fantastic's and Phoenix's caricaturized personalities, although extreme, revealed their one-sidedness, and the author's as well. It was not without wise intent that Rousseau yielded the last word on the subject to Fairy Discreet (Lat. *dis*, apart; M.L. *discretus*, discern, separate, distinguish between). Discreet was the one who had shown good judgment in conduct and in speech, for she was capable, above all, of preserving prudent silence!

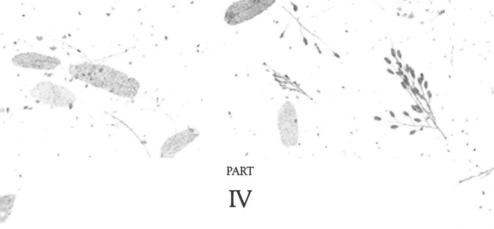

THE NINETEENTH CENTURY
"LE ROMANTISME"—
ESTHETIC AND UTILITARIAN

T HE FRENCH REVOLUTION, having put the *Ancien Régime* to rest, catalyzed in its place short-lived political panaceas: the Convention (1792); Robespierre's rule of Terror (1793-1794); the First Republic (1795), the Directory (1795-1799), the Consulate (1799) and the advent of Bonaparte, the future Emperor, Napoleon I (1804-1815), whose grandiose visions altered the face of Europe. France's external wars, including Napoleon's sixty battles, created a condition of virtually continuous turmoil until his abdication in 1814. Sequestration on the island of Elba, however, did not prevent his return to France, his defeat at Waterloo, and his imprisonment on the island of Saint Helena, where he died in 1821.

The restoration of the French monarchy, with the coronation of King Louis XVIII in 1814, led to the Treaty of Paris which allowed France to retain its 1792 frontiers. Ultra reactionary royalists began to dominate the scene again: the perpetration of murderous excesses in the south of France as in the White Terror (1816), and the assassination of the duke de Berry (1820), and so forth. The authoritarian rule of Charles X (1757-1836), unpopular from the very outset, ended with the July Revolution (1830) and the king's abdication two days later. Louis-Philippe's reign (1830-1848), while beginning on a liberal note, veered toward conservatism, concluding with his abdication at the outbreak of the revolution of 1848. The proclamation of the short-lived Second Republic followed in 1852, with the emperorship of Napoleon III. Although exercising absolute power, he encouraged industry and commerce, but his wars in Crimea, China, Austria, Mexico, and the last and most devastating with Prussia, forced his capitulation at Sedan in 1870. The Third Republic, proclaimed that same year, lasted until France's defeat by the Germans in June 1940.

The powerful confluences of mutating political, artistic, religious, and scientific currents unleashed in France during the turbulent decades of the nineteenth century, while polarizing some, unified the creative energies of others. Reacting powerfully against the constraints imposed by the monarchy, many welcomed Napoleon's meteoric rise, and even his wars that engulfed all of Europe. Others withdrew into themselves, activating their imaginations and a whole subliminal world of dreams, fantasies and spiritual yearnings. In all camps, the arts burgeoned. In the fore were painters, such as David, Delacroix, Géricault, Corot, Ingres, Courbet, Manet, Monet, Renoir, Gauguin, Cézanne, Van Gogh, Degas, Toulouse-Lautrec; writers, including Hugo, Balzac, Stendhal, Flaubert, Sand, Zola, Baudelaire, Rimbaud, Mallarmé; and composers, such as Boieldieu, Gounod, Berlioz, Massenet, Offenbach, Meyerbeer, Halévy, Lalo, and so forth. The sciences thrived as well: Cuvier founded paleontology; Champollion deciphered hieroglyphics, thanks to the Egyptian Rosetta stone. The pre-Darwinian Lamarck furthered transformism. Pasteur gained international fame for his discoveries in applied bacteriology and treatment for hydrophobia, inter alia. The Industrial Revolution made enormous strides with its foundries, mills, steam power, railway, steel manufacture, and electricity.

The immensely creative nineteenth century, strangely enough, never ceased being romantic in tenor, oscillating as it did between esthetic romanticism (1815–1830); social or utilitarian romanticism (1830–1852); and an innovative return to esthetic romanticism with Parnassianism and Symbolism capturing the attention of artists to the end of the century. What did the spirit of romanticism imply, that it encapsulated a whole culture for nearly a century? The word *romantic* reached French shores from England in 1776, in Pierre Le Tourneur's translation of Shakespeare. If one really wants to understand and appreciate Shakespeare, he advised his readers, one must wander and meditate along willow-strewn paths, in thickly forested areas, on seashores, in ethereal and *romantic* cloud-filled landscapes. This mind-set was further affirmed in 1807, when August Wilhelm Schlegel delivered a groundbreaking lecture lauding the northern movement of "romanticism" for its truth and passion, while condemning the southern movement of "classicism," for its overrationalizations.

What did the subjective spirit of romanticism imply? An escape from a present empirical and limited reality into a cosmic, visionary, ever-expansive domain, emphasizing one's solidarity with the universe—ideas already professed, but in a different form, by Diderot and Rousseau, among others.

These conflictual attitudes encouraged two approaches toward life and creativity: one of deep pessimism, and the other of great optimism. In the former, writers such as Chateaubriand, who saw themselves as small and powerless in contrast to the immensities of the universe, gave birth to a morbid condition identified as *le mal du siècle*. Others, such as Hugo, drawing strength from these very sources of universal power, opened themselves up to the visionary experience, going so far as to believe in the perfectibility of earthly existence.

CHARLES NODIER'S
THE CRUMB FAIRY—A SACRED
MARRIAGE OF SUN AND MOON

Nodier's unappeased thirst for fairy tales induced his monumental dream-reverie, *The Crumb Fairy* (1832). The fantastic adventures of the author's protagonists, the young Michel, incapable of adapting to society, and his beloved Crumb Fairy, are narrated mainly in flashbacks within the framework of a "lunatic" asylum in Glasgow (Scotland). Studies and inquiries concerning insanity and mental institutions were popular in the nineteenth century. In fact, the idea for Nodier's *The Crumb Fairy* came to him after having read a letter from the Duke de Levis to a Dr. A. in *La Revue de Paris* (May 1829) concerning new—but considered by Nodier inhumane—treatments used in Scottish mental institutions (Nodier, *Contes* 156).

The tale reveals the metaphysical and psychological dramas of two humanized cosmic principles: Michel takes on the personality of a Moon Man and becomes the receptor of indirect occult knowledge; the love of his life, a wizened Crumb Fairy by day, at night manifests herself as a Solar principle—who claims at times to be the beautiful Belkiss (another name for the Queen of Sheba; *Koran* 27:22), or her descendant. To lend credibility to this and to his other fairy tales and fantastic writings, Nodier wrote insightfully: "[Y]ou must first write something believable, and to make certain that others believe what you have written, you must first believe it yourself. Once this condition has been accepted, you may boldly say whatever you like" (Nodier, *Contes*, preface by Castex 170).

ECTYPAL ANALYSIS

Charles Nodier, born out of wedlock at Besançon in 1790, was not legit-
imized until 1791. His father, a rather dogmatic gentleman, had presided for
a short period over the criminal tribunal of that city during the Reign of Terror headed by the much-feared Robespierre. Memories of horrific experiences remained incised in the lad's mind throughout his life, and may have
accounted in part for his later hypertension, nightmares, and insomnia. Some
of the particularly excoriating spectacles he had witnessed as a child were interspersed in his short stories: rolling heads, pathetic cries, blood flowing
into gutters. Other reasons may have also triggered his bouts of morbidity,
his penchant for the fanciful, and the exotic as a would-be escape mechanism.
Ever since he could recall, family life had been unpleasant. His mother,
whom he never mentioned in his writings, had been a housemaid. He dis-
liked her for her ignorance, brusqueness, and lack of feeling. From her he inherited Addison's disease (a malfunction of the adrenal glands, characterized
by anemia and peculiar discoloration of the skin); he suffered also from periodic fevers, which did not abate with the passing of years. The opium he took
at times aggravated rather than alleviated his condition.

A Catholic by heritage, Nodier did not find salvation in a conventional
approach to worship. His needs being more complex, he turned to the writings
of mystics such as Jakob Boehme (1575-1624), Emmanuel Swedenborg
(1688-1772), Martinez de Pasqualis (?-1774), Claude de Saint-Martin
(1743-1803), and Jacques Cazotte (1719-1792). Not only did they stimulate his
imagination, but they helped him develop his own comforting credo as well.

Nodier married in 1808, and had several children, only one of whom,
Marie, survived. Beautiful and charming, she became the focal point of her
father's life. After the marriage of his beloved daughter in 1830, Nodier suffered a bout of depression—perhaps a better term would be a kind of post-
partum melancholia. He had lost the main attraction of his well-frequented
Salon and, more accurately, the *love of his life!* Unable to see his daughter
daily, he felt a void that gnawed at his very existence. More and more introverted, his dream world intruded increasingly and persistently into his empirical existence, bringing with it the momentary and necessary joys for
survival. It has been suggested that Nodier's death at home in 1844 had been
perhaps caused by a continuously diminishing interest in life!

An inveterate reader, the very learned Nodier wrote on a variety of subjects: natural history (*Dissertation on the use of Antennae Insects* [1789]); philol-
ogy (*Dictionary of French Onomatopoeias* [1808]); the occult (*The Army's Secret
Societies* [1815]); fantastic tales (*Smarra* [1821] and *Trilby* [1822]) to mention
but a few. Following his appointment as librarian of the Bibliothèque de

l'Arsenal in 1824, he invited and received the most creative people of his day at his Sunday night gatherings: Gautier, Nerval, Balzac, Hugo, Sainte-Beuve, Lamartine, Dumas, and others. A storyteller in his own right, he would regale his guests with tales by Scott, Hoffmann, and some of his own manufacture as well. He spoke in a clear and elegant manner, gesticulating from time to time, his long, slender hands enacting the dramatic events he recounted, while his face mirrored a sense either of excitement or of serene melancholy.

ARCHETYPAL ANALYSIS

The Crumb Fairy, a prolonged reverie of irrational images linked together in a relatively comprehensible pattern, mirrored to a great extent haunting and ecstatic imaged episodes in Nodier's powerfully active dream world. What better way, he may have mused, was there to give body to one's personal phantasms than in the fairy tale genre?

Nodier's penchant for the irrational led him to praise the tales of Ernest Theodor Hoffmann—*Devil's Elixir* (1816), *Night Pieces* (1817), and others—considering the author a visionary who brought to life an invisible and mysterious world hinging on the practice of magnetism and the occult. None better than Hoffmann knew how to usher in moods of nostalgia and malaise. He seemingly was endowed with a sixth sense that allowed him to understand both human beings and nature, obscure relationships, and invisible phenomena that escaped scientific explanation. (Humphrey, *L'Esthétique de la poésie de Gérard de Nerval* 52). Hoffmann's influence was clearly discernible in *The Crumb Fairy*'s atmosphere of disenchantment, gloom, and quest for the supernatural.

Scientific and metaphysical credos are also integrated into the fabric of *The Crumb Fairy*'s plot and the souls of its *dramatis personae*. Some of the issues developed in Nodier's tale revolve around monism, broached by Diderot in his *D'Alembert's Dream*; metempsychosis, by Cazotte in his tale, *The Devil in Love*; and palingenesis, the fruits of Leibniz's and Charles Bonnet's philosophical peregrinations. Under the guise of specific individuals and events, the universal domain is at issue in *The Crumb Fairy*. Two cosmic principles, male and female, participate symbolically in a *hieros gamos*, the alchemical formula for the sacred marriage of Sun and Moon.

NODIER'S REJECTION OF EMPIRICAL REALITY. Nodier's lack of realism and difficulty in adapting to the workaday world is not only evident in his comportment, but partially explains his mental leaps into time and space during periods of slumber, waking dream, and in his writings. Unable to face the ugliness of burgeoning industrial civilization, and longing to transcend the realm of appearances, he withdrew into his own inner domain, which was rich in spirits, fairies, and sorceresses. Like the German Romantics—Novalis, Schelling, the two Schlegel brothers, and Tieck—Nodier was convinced that humans could not know earthly happiness because their souls were living in exile, longing to return to the heavenly spheres of their origin. Humankind's fall from Paradise, as related in the Bible, the German Romantics contended, was tantamount to a separation from God. No longer *one* with divinity, divided mortals belonged to two spheres: the world of matter (the earth) and that of spirit (the divine realm). For the metaphysician, life on earth became a long search for a path leading to primordial unity with God, or a reintegration into the existence mortals had known prior to the Fall. Unity with divinity—the flowing into the All, or Universal Force—could be experienced at fleeting moments in a person's lifetime: in dream, ecstasy, illumination, or transcendence of one's identity via meditation or other devices (Birch, *The Disciples at Sais* 70).

Together with other esthetic metaphysicians who had established what has been called an "autocracy of the imagination," Nodier believed nature to be a living organism and not a mechanism capable of being reduced to its various components or elements. In opposition to the eighteenth-century philosophes and ideologues, he distrusted the world of appearances. He yearned for a deeper reality, achieved by communing with a profounder realm where God's presence could become manifest. Glimpsing God and/or eternity in these vast expanses, Nodier felt shorn of his finitude and basked in sensations of well-being.

It may be posited that Nodier's earthly existence consisted of an unending desire for oneness with God and/or with the Cosmic Soul. If life were looked upon as a separation from God, death, in this context, became a return to Him. Death, it follows, was not to be feared nor treated as something ugly. It was, rather, a *rite of passage*, an initiatory process into another frame of existence.

NODIER'S EMPHASIS ON SLEEP. Like death, the notion of sleep, with all of its transcendent visualizations was likewise mystery for Nodier. It opened him onto the unknown, and thus he believed it to be a source of creativity; he was mesmerized by its capacity to usher him into the dream. "The first perception which emerges from the inexplicable vagueness of the dream," he wrote, "is as limpid as is the sun's first ray when dissipating a cloud. . . . It is in this region that the immortal conception of the artist and the poet bursts forth" ("Quelques phénomènes du sommeil" in Nodier, *Oeuvres* V, 161).

The dream world imposed itself gratuitously onto Nodier's life, acting on all aspects of it. His linking of waking and sleeping states, he maintained, not only transformed reality, but was a rite of passage as well into the beyond, enabling him to communicate with other species, with the dead, with past civilizations, and also to anticipate future events. During sleeping hours, he claimed, thought made acute inroads into his unconscious, taking on its most lucid and pellucid forms to the point of developing and expanding his perceptions and insights.

Forays into subliminal spheres had additional value for Nodier. They helped him deal with a corrosive source of guilt and unrealized—or unconscious—terror: most specifically, his pychologically incestuous love for his daughter, Marie. That love was the very life blood of his creative efforts and his mental well-being, and gave rise to dreams and fantasies, which helped heal the breach between morality and the erotic.

"I ONLY WANT TO WRITE FAIRY TALES." The fantasies and obsessions described in Nodier's fairy tales released him from the pain and emptiness he felt throughout his life. "Until my death, which can come at any time," he wrote in a letter (Jan. 3, 1830), "I only want to write Fairy Tales."

Because of the conflicts beating within his psyche, Nodier, like Michel, the protagonist in *The Crumb Fairy*, longed desperately to experience the serene state of unity that the fairy world had made accessible to him. He lived in a world of extremes, enduring intense turmoil followed by sequences of sublime love that allowed him to recover some semblance of equilibrium. Such mood swings eventually banished Michel from the world of duality which, he sensed, would tear him apart. Aware of the incompatibility of living out a paradisiac state on earth, Nodier labeled his protagonist a *lunatic*, and confined him to a mental institution.

Further analogies between Michel and Nodier are in order. At about the age of twenty, the tense and nervously ill Nodier—as were many of his generation who had experienced the Terror—succumbed to moods of extreme elation. Had it been due to his opium intake? Or his imprisonment at Sainte-Pélagie during the winter of 1803–1804, following accusations that he had written the anti-Napoleon satire "La Napoléone"? At the time, some of his contemporaries judged him to be mad. In 1830 the pendulum swung to an antipodal condition of severe depression and melancholia. His periods of imbalance, interestingly enough, usually preceded his most creative moments (Castex, *Le Conte fantastique* 122).

MENTAL INSTITUTIONS. Prior to the nineteenth century, insanity in Europe was mainly not considered an illness, but a possession by the devil. The mentally deranged were cast into prisons and/or dungeons, where they were chained to the walls, flogged, starved, brutalized, and frequently killed. A cure, being effected only by moral and spiritual agencies, consisted in exorcising the individual. In the middle of the eighteenth century, the mildly insane were sometimes cared for at religious shrines, or were allowed to wander about the land, frequently starving to death.

In 1792, Dr. Philippe Pinel, director of a hospital for male "lunatics," Bicêtre in Paris, made one of the great breakthroughs in the treatment of the insane. Pinel's decision, despite negative press, to remove the inmates' chains, was, indeed, a heroic act (*The Encyclopaedia Britannica* XIII, 1898). To his detractors, Pinel maintained forcefully: "Citizens, I am convinced that the insane here (in Bicêtre) are highly untreatable because they have been deprived of fresh air and freedom" (Foucault, *Histoire de la folie* 249). Following Pinel's forward leap, insanity began to be treated principally as a disease, resulting in a diminution of cruelties heaped upon the unfortunate patients. By 1838, the move to transfer the insane from houses of detention, workhouses, and prisons to asylums constructed for the purpose, gained momentum. A similar movement of reform was started in England by William Tuke, a member of the Society of Friends, and chief founder of the "Retreat" (1796), or asylum in the city of York, for the nonviolent treatment, care, and cure of insane members of that sect (Foucault 249).

In Paris, Dr. Esprit Blanche, a friend of Nodier, was unique among medical men of the time in his treatment of patients such as Gérard de Nerval, a long time schizophrenic. Not only did Dr. Blanche dispense his care of the mentally ill with kindness and understanding, but used the most advanced treatments of his time as well. Believing that close contact with patients and the recreation of a family situation in a mental institution would be beneficial to them, he went so far as to make his home in a section of his clinic, a beautiful eighteenth-century building situated high above Paris—on Montmartre, where many windmills still dotted the horizon. Rigorous discipline in his clinic nonetheless prevailed: physical therapy, extensive exercise programs and, when necessary, Scotch baths (hot and cold showers used alternately). The latter were designed to shock patients out of their torpor or fury. Violent patients, under constant supervision by his well-trained staff, were placed on another side of the house. Only sometimes were straightjackets used. All forms of cruelties toward the patients were excluded. It must also be noted that Dr. Blanche's wife, who was always on the premises, comforting those who needed warmth and understanding, played an important role: she was a perfect mother image, with whom patients identified and to whom they responded (Knapp, *Gérard de Nerval* 101).

MICHEL'S "LUNACY." Prompted by his compassion for those suffering from emotional problems, Nodier visited Glasgow's "lunatic" asylum on a trip to the British Isles. It was there that his protagonist, Michel, was said to have been interned.

Considered ill-adapted, or mad, Michel fit Nodier's definition of lunatics: those "who spend their time busying themselves as little as possible with worldly matters, as if they had, in fact, descended from the moon, and spoke on such strange subjects, as could not have possibly happened in any other place, but on the moon" (Nodier, *Contes,* edited by Castex 175). Michel's transcendence of the barriers of logic—or of "sublime reason" as Nodier noted satirically—made him all the wiser. Unlike the ordinary well-functioning citizen, secrets barred to the rationalist were revealed to the "lunatic," whose psyche transcended the time/space continuum. The very word "lunatic" for Nodier, then, applied to individuals who experienced altered states of consciousness, which allowed them to see into worlds unknown or unimagined not only by the normal well-adjusted individual, but by scientists as well.

The "lunatic," (V.L. *lunaticus*), one who submits to the *moon,* was defined as an individual suffering from some kind of periodic bouts with folly or behavioral problems, and who was by nature capricious, fantastic, and disconcerting. The moon, visible only as a reflection of the sun's rays and deprived of its own light, has been considered since ancient times as the source of indirect knowledge or vision. The transformation of earth's only known satellite during the course of a month has allied it with the feminine and her biological rhythms. For Pythagoras, whose ideas Nodier admired, the three days during which the moon was either invisible or dead to earth people marked the passage from life to death and back again. With light flowing into the world of darkness came rebirth or renewal, a notion also applicable to "lunatics," who are susceptible to a sudden illumination, not of rational understanding, but of cosmic knowledge! Such persons, Nodier wrote,

> would occupy the highest degree on the ladder, which separates our planet from its satellite, and, since they communicate, as of necessity, with other intelligences, from this degree, with a world that is unknown to us, it is certainly natural for us not to understand them, and it is absurd to conclude that their ideas make no sense, and that they are not lucid, because they belong to an order of sensations and reasonings which are completely inaccessible to our understanding and customs. (Nodier, *Contes,* edited by Castex, "La Fée aux miettes" 176)

A "LUNATIC'S PEREGRINATIONS." The protagonist of Nodier's tale, Michel Charpentier, is from Granville, in Normandy. His mother had died shortly after his birth; his father was a businessman whose work had taken him to India, and so Michel was brought up by his uncle, a carpenter (Fr. *charpentier,* a trade that bestows civil status). A solitary lad, he made friends with a wizened two-and-a-half-feet-tall lady, whom the children of the district called the Crumb Fairy because she lived on the crumbs she was given. At times she claimed to be Belkiss and at other moments, a descendant of Belkiss (another name for the Queen of Sheba), and her goal in life was to settle in Greenock (Scotland), where she owned a tiny house. Michel gave her enough money to pay for her trip.

After his uncle's departure for the sea, Michel's lifestyle changed. He became increasingly detached from society, and in a spirit of self-abnegation, he gave the money he earned as a carpenter to the needy. Finding himself destitute one day, he miraculously found twenty louis d'or his uncle had sewn into his jacket and these saved him from starvation. Out of gratitude he went on a pilgrimage to Mont Saint-Michel, rescuing on his return none other but the Crumb Fairy, who was sinking into quicksand. The two became engaged. Since she had been divested of all of her belongings, Michel in another act of extreme generosity gave her his remaining louis d'or. In time, he discovered that his uncle had been declared insane because he claimed to be the superintendent of Princess Belkiss's palace, Michel went in search of him on a fantastic ship, *The Queen of Sheba*, with twenty-four smokestacks and twenty-four masts. Despite, or perhaps because of its surrealistic equipment, the ship sank, and once again Michel saved the Crumb Fairy who had secretly followed him. Miraculously, he found another twenty louis d'or tucked in his belongings, enough to pay for her return to Greenock. In exchange, she gave him a diamond-studded medallion with a portrait of her—as Belkiss, or the Queen of Sheba—imaged as the beautiful young girl she had once been. Continuing on his way, Michel eventually landed on the Scottish coast and, by chance, met the charming Folly Girlfree. So fractured in his mind were time and memory, that he did not even recall having met her previously (Lambert, "La Fée aux miettes: une autre dimension" 717, in *Hommage à Jacques Petit*).

Since no rooms were available at the local inn, Michel had to share accommodations with the bailiff, whose head reminded him of a Danish wolfhound. During the night Michel had a nightmare, the next morning he was found with the bailiff's wallet in one hand, a dagger in the other, and the dead bailiff beside him. He was summarily arrested. Although his lawyer pled insanity, Michel was found guilty and sentenced to death. The entire scene allegedly was inspired by—or duplicated—a similar episode recounted in Balzac's *The Red Inn* (1831). The fact that Nodier chose to include in *The Crumb Fairy* a murder, also perpetrated by a man in a semi-sleeping state, indicates the depth of his projection onto Balzac's tale.

THE NIGHTMARE AND ANIMAL SYMBOLISM. Michel's dream, a reenactment in symbolic form of an unconscious struggle within his subliminal realm, began with a cacophany of strange noises: creaking hinges, howling winds, and whispering voices. The auditive power of the ensuing horrific hallucinations depicted by Nodier not only heightened the dreamer's condition of extreme disorientation, but sent him on the course of his "lunacy." Archetypal images surged in his Dantesque inferno: four heads as if emerging from one body, a grimacing wild cat, a dog whose hair bristles and whose jaws oozed blood, a horse's head "half calcinated by the sun." Finally, behind these apparitions loomed a monstrous head, all the more terrifying since its facial traits and their functions were the reverse of normal ones (*Crumb Fairy* 248). As Michel's macabre dream scenario progressed, a hand suddenly jutted forth, brandishing the fearful head as though seeking to amuse a multitude. Immediately, Michel pushed to safety the bailiff's body which, inexplicably, fell on him like a cadaver. Moments later, Michel felt an arm as cold as ice gripping him around the neck. Believing this stranger wanted to steal the bailiff's money, Michel rushed toward him with his dagger, struck out in all directions, and finally sunk his weapon into the aforementioned monsters—the cat, the dog, and the horse—as well as into owls, serpents, and salamanders which suddenly invaded the room. "Triumphant," Michel seized the wallet and returned to his bed. The following morning the bailiff was found dead, and the wallet and the knife in Michel's hand along with the knife (*Crumb Fairy* 248).

Scholars and psychiatrists have commented on the cruelty of the knifings and the gore in Michel's hallucinatory images. Such subliminal activity, however, may be explained as an aftereffect of the guillotinings Nodier had witnessed at Besançon during the Revolution. These beheadings, mutilations, and aggressions, as previously mentioned, had a lasting traumatic effect upon the lad. The writer's detailing of such horrors not only created artistic effects, but by reaching out to them, he may have also learned how better to understand and thus deal with his fears and rages—imprints of the most primitive levels in his psyche.

The four terrifying images (a bristly dog, a wild cat, a calcinated horse's head, monstrous face) not only are important in themselves, but they evoke a numerical symbology. Since numbers are endowed with numinous qualities, they are to be considered transforming agents, able to change chaos into order. As compensatory forces, therefore, they may be said to have the capability of balancing out or releasing troubling elements within the psyche (Jung 8, #456). The number 4, paradigmatically, represents a totality, completeness, and the rational organization needed in empirical reality. But such a paradigm is inimicable to Michel's psychic makeup and he seeks to annihilate and/or transcend it.

The bailiff with "the magnificent head of a Danish wolfhound, " is able, in a strange connection, to communicate with Michel in the dream by bark-

ing at him, astounding the lad "by the precision of his language and the exquisite delicacy of his judgments" (*Crumb Fairy* 245). The bailiff's wallet holds
receipts collected from the Isle of Man, which may relate him to society with
its social structure and its materialism; but his barking head constitutes an
oddness about him. According to Platonic belief, a human being's head symbolizes his highest spiritual attributes, his divine intelligence, while the body
is his animal counterpart. Nodier, instead, suggests that the rational function
in people is not always their highest sphere, and he seems to indicate a desire
on his protagonist's part to break out of the constricting pattern imposed
upon society in its conventional relationships.

That the bailiff has a dog's head is significant in other respects. In ancient
Egypt the dog, as the God Anubis, accompanied the dead to the domain of
Osiris and Isis. In Greek mythology, Cerberus stood guard outside of Hades,
thus preventing the shades from leaving their abode. Dogs, as chthonic spirits
in China (Tien-k'uen) and in Norse mythology (Garm), are also identified with
the underworld. Perhaps the bailiff's function would then be to guide Michel to
the realm of the living dead as well. It may also be suggested that the dog with
bristling hair represents repressed bestial forces within the "lunatic." The cat,
the second animal to appear in Michel's dream, according to ancient Egyptian
lore is a moon figure, sacred to both Isis and Bast, considered the"guardians of
marriage." Frequently associated with woman because of its sensuality and its
mysteriousness, the cat lives in its inner world, exteriorizing its thought and feelings in secretive, unpredictable ways. In that the cat in Michel's dream is wild,
it may be said to represent vicious and destructive subliminal forces within the
female—a projection of Michel's own feminine nature, which seethes within
him and which he seeks to annihilate or liberate.

The calcinated horse's head in the third image of Michel's nightmare
presages a world of shadows. As the son of night, this animal, like the cat,
represents mystery. The image evokes the "pale" horse of the Apocalypse rid-
den by "Death," followed by "Hell," whose power to "kill with sword" again
emphasizes unregenerate murderous instincts—a primogenial chaos (Revelations 6:8). Horses such as Pegasus, when running at high speeds, are considered fire bringers, and thus they symbolize triumph. Their up-and-down
rhythmatics experienced by the rider of such an animal are usually associated
with sexual symbology. In that the horse's head alone, bereft of a body, was
visible in Michel's dream, the image seems divested of sexual inuendoes.

Although the calcinated head of Michel's dream horse is stripped of all
livingness, one may make an etymological association with *mare* (M.E. female
horse, demon), as in *nightmare* (G. *Mar,* incubus). The origin of the word
nightmare (OHG. *mara,* meaning "ogress, incubus, demon") relates it to an
evil supernatural being that causes nightmares (Jung 5, #370).

The dagger used by Michel to perpetrate the bailiff's murder, may be likened to the magic swords of heroes such as Roland (Durendal), Siegfried (Notung), and King Arthur (Excalibur). Used to destroy enemies, these cutting instruments identified their possessors not only as protectors of noble virtues, but as activators in the birth of new attitudes. In the hands of monsters such as Morholt, Goliath, and Grendel, the sword became the instrument for the destruction of a society's well-being and the serenity of its members.

Each of the above associations to the sword indicates Michel's unconscious need to cut ties with the world of instinct (the force he projects onto the animals in his vision), and with the society in the form of the bailiff and the materialistic social order he represents. The surprising brutality of the murder scenes suggests a state of unredeemed chaos within the dreamer's unconscious. He can face neither the archaic forms within him as symbolized by the animals, nor the constricting and limiting world represented by the bailiff. His subliminal desire is to destroy both, thereby gaining the freedom to live his "real" world of fantasy, or "lunacy," with his Crumb Fairy/Queen of Sheba.

A CHASTE MARRIAGE. During the course of Michel's trial for the bailiff's murder, a letter stamped with seven seals arrives unexpectedly from Belkiss. The plaintiff is ordered to choose between the portrait on the enclosed medallion, or its lavish diamond frame worth two million guinees. He opts for the portrait; and the judges divide the diamonds. Further obstacles are now set in Michel's path: unless a girl consents to marry Michel, he must die. Although Folly Girlfree establishes her willingness, he refuses on the grounds that he is already affianced and under no circumstances would he break his vow to the Crumb Fairy. Michel rejects the offer of Folly, who represents easy sex, or sexuality in general, even though the Crumb Fairy, who suddenly arrives on the scene, releases him from his engagement. But Michel prefers to die rather than break his vow. Suddenly, he is miraculously judged innocent of his so-called crime, inasmuch as, incredibly enough, the bailiff is still very much alive.

The story now switches to Greenock, where Michel and the Crumb Fairy are living together in what is analogized to a doll house. Blissful contentment pervades their existence. By day, the wizened Crumb Fairy tends to all of Michel's earthly needs; by night she comes to him as the beautiful Belkiss/Queen of Sheba, embellishing the medallion.

> She was not a woman as I had understood her to be; nor a divinity as I had imagined her to be. . . . She was that radiant woman endowed with an undefinable expression, the mere sight of whom filled my heart with a more complete and more perfect felicity than all the fantastic felicities my imagination could conjure. And I lost myself in this contemplation, as does the

ecstatic worshipper for whom heaven's mysteries have just been opened. (*Crumb Fairy* 226)

Although refusing herself physically to Michel, their union is complete, until another cloud emerges on the couple's horizon. Michel is advised that unless he finds a singing mandrake, the miraculous plant that can return youth to the Crumb Fairy, she will die within six months. To be sure, Michel leaves immediately to search for the mandrake, which he finds at an herbalist's shop in Glasgow. After the owner assures him that mandrakes are plentiful in the Glasgow lunatic asylum, Michel heads straight for the asylum, where he is summarily interned. Here he cultivates the plant, describing it "as the laughing mandrake within which are hidden the secrets of my last illusions" (*Crumb Fairy* 185).

THE ANDROGYNOUS MANDRAKE. Was the mandrake yet another obstacle set in Michel's path by his Crumb Fairy, who for reasons of her own might be attempting to banish him from paradise? Or was this another step in his initiation process leading to transcendence? The answers are moot. The "fairy plant," as the mandrake was frequently called, was considered by certain mystics to be a positive force, representing the first degree in the elevation of matter to spirit (Le Rouge, *La Mandragore magique* 24).[1] The poisonous and healing properties of the mandrake add other attributes to the mysteries associated with this medicinal plant. Used as an aphrodisiac in medieval and renaissance times, for Michel it had the opposite effect. After all, hadn't he banned from his life, the sexually awakened, permissive, or *free* woman—as indicated by her name, Folly Girlfree—opting instead for the joys of an enchanting love lived out in his dream world?

The plant that the Greeks called Circe was associated in the Middle Ages with magicians and sorcerers as attested to by references such as "the hand of glory" (Fr., *gloire*), or that of *gorre* (Fr. sorcerers)—suggesting that hidden treasures, identified with those feeding Michel's dream, exist in this plant (Le Rouge 28). Adding to the mystery of its androgynism, Theophrastus saw the mandrake as half man and half woman—its forked roots embodying both sexes—and claimed that it was self-reproductive. As a symbol of Michel's androgyny, the mandrake serves to illustrate an inability to identify with either sex, leaving him in-between, or a complete and self-sufficient individual in need of no other. The androgyny of the mandrake may explain in part Nodier's antithesis to society's much-admired masculine hero types (Roland, Bayard, Napoleon) and his greater identification with so-called nineteenth-century French Romantic figures (René, Adolphe, Obermann).

The mandrake's ascribed ability to sing and speak unknown languages not only humanizes this supernatural plant, but invited Michel to relate to it in a manner that may disclose aspects of his own ungraspable personality. The superstitious belief that this mysterious plant sings with pleasure and screams with pain when uprooted from the ground renders it paradigmatic of Michel's world of infinite joy and protracted sorrow. Mentioned in the Song of Solomon in the Bible, the mandrake became synonymous with the king's passion for the Queen of Sheba, whom he invited to the vineyards where "the mandrakes give off a smell and at our gates are all manner of pleasant fruits, new and old, which I have laid up for thee, O my beloved" (Song of Solomon 7:13). Because the mandrake was believed to endow the person bearing it the power to foretell the future and to command armies, Joan of Arc, so the legend goes, was said to have traveled with this plant hidden under her breasts (Jung 8, #456).

The vermilion, flamelike, pale, and bloody color tones of the mandrake described in *The Crumb Fairy* may symbolize what alchemists allude to as the Philosophers' Stone, defined at times as the elixir of life or the *élan vital*. The mandrake, like the Philosopher's Stone, would therefore be able to spiritually regenerate human beings. To achieve such a goal, the alchemist had to transform the imperfect substance upon which he was working (a condition of imbalance) into a perfect combination (a condition of balance or harmony)—a process that required a reblending of nature, a reforming of matter, and a reshuffling of inner contents.

In that the mandrake, like the Philosopher's Stone, belongs to the world of absolutes, it is inimicable to empirical existence. Indeed, it is the very antithesis of the energetic or life process that is based on opposition, causality, and acausality. To conceive of the reality of the mandrake or the Philosopher's Stone was surely an attempt, in Michel's case, to shy away from the workaday world, to escape into an Edenlike atmosphere, or to regress into an infantile state—or "lunacy."

Endowed with narcotic values by such physicians as Hippocrates, among others, it could extend Michel's beautiful fantasy world and help him forget or repress what detracted from it. It was fitting, then, that the Crumb Fairy should ask Michel not only to fetch the plant for her, but to cultivate it in the lunatic asylum, for she knew that if Michel's hallucinatory dream world were not sustained, his vision of her would perish, and her existence would never again be evoked. The implication is that in the protected atmosphere of the asylum, where the inmates live out their illusions, the mandrake symbolized utopia—where love flourishes eternally.

THE HIEROS GAMOS: THE SACRED MARRIAGE OF SUN AND MOON. It is within the framework of Michel's hallucinatory illusions—or insanity—that

Nodier broaches the cosmic problem of the warring male-female principles and the *hieros gamos*, or marriage of sun and moon. In conventional alchemical practice, as already noted, the sun is considered the male principle, representing spirit, order, and illumination, the purest and highest thinking processes known to human beings. The moon, by way of contrast, viewed as feminine, is thought of as fickle, dark, and enigmatic, and, therefore, frequently dangerous. In *The Crumb Fairy*, interestingly enough, the situation is reversed. The sun becomes the feminine force, a composite of two anima figures—the ancient and wizened Crumb Fairy, who typifies wisdom in its most active form, and the passive Belkiss, who emerges at night and represents chaste passion. Although double, they are *one*—functioning as the regulator[s] of Michel's life.

Michel as the moon figure, the "lunatic," not only incorporates certain aspects of the feminine personality (purity, tenderness, gentleness, generosity) but is also under the dominion of these. Having no identity of his own, he functions only as a reflection, and not an instigator of the two anima figures. He is what psychologists term a "medium" personality, that is, influenced by outside events, by the feelings and sensations generated by others. Physically he is male; psychologically he is female. As a composite of male and female characteristics, he may be referred to as a hermaphrodite, one of the most archaic archetypal images known—a being that existed, according to Platonic and Kabbalistic belief, prior to the division of the sexes.

MICHEL, THE MOON MAN—"LUNATIC." Since nothing in the universe is exempt from change, it may be said that change rules the universe. Implicit in all phases of life, perhaps most acutely in the sexual domain, exists the power struggle between male and female principles.

Prior to the identification of the moon with woman (after the advent of patriarchal societies), the sun in many societies was female: and Sun Goddesses regulated cosmic activity. The ancient Sabbeans in Yemen worshipped the sun as the Goddess Shams; the tribal Arabians, as Shamshu; the Japanese, as Amaterasu; the Egyptians, as Hathor, whose right eye was the sun, and left eye the moon. In the Babylonian and Assyrian pantheons, both the moon (Sin, Nana) and the sun (Utu, Shamash) were male. The sun was worshipped as female by the Celts (Sulis), by the Germans (Sunna), and by the Norwegians (Sol).

With the advent of patriarchal civilizations, the woman yielded her power to the man and became associated with the moon, whereas male qualities were attributed to the sun. Psychologically, such a change in religious power mirrored a concomitant trend within the human psyche: male figures, in the ascendancy, became identified with the sun (the most powerful force on earth), while female forms were relegated to what was considered a lesser sphere, the moon. Nonetheless, the female element was still a potent force.

The process of counting, for example, was based on the rhythmic life of the moon. This astral body also stood for love and fertility. In that it caused climatic changes, such as rains, storms, floods, and tidal waves, it influenced nature's growth. Understandably were the Moon Goddesses of antiquity (Isis, Ishtar, Hathor, Artemis, Selene, etc.) worshipped as regulators of life on earth, and considered instrumental in the continuation of the great death-rebirh cycles, playing the prime role in dismemberment mysteries such as those associated with Pentheus, Orpheus, and Osiris.

Michel's lack of sexual identity is apparent in the moon-and-sun imagery which is at the heart of Nodier's tale. In archaic times these astral bodies were personified, as previously mentioned, each taking on the personality traits and sexual configurations of the Gods and Goddesses with which a society identified. During the course of centuries, the pendulum swung in favor of male domination, while the the female struggled for recognition and ascendency, each in turn seeking to attain his or her goals. In nineteenth-century France a rigid patriarchal system was giving way to matriarchal forces. Nodier translated the change of emphasis into sun and moon imagery in his tale.

Understandably did Michel—as "Moon Man"—identify with the astral body that most fully replicated his unconscious and conscious yearnings. The moon, or the earth's planetary satellite responsible for outer disturbances (storms and tidal waves, as indicated previously) is accountable as well for inner, or psychological traumas: moonish tensions and mental chaos, generators of turmoil and of hyper- or diminished emotional activity cause destabilization in some, and insanity in others. Described in ancient times as irradiating an eerie light in darkness, the moon dulls harsh illumination and may produce visions, as illustrated by the Moon Goddess Hecate, also alluded to as Antea, who was called "The Sender of Nocturnal Visions." Her son, Museos, the Muse-Man, was called "The Son of the Moon." During waning, waxing, or full moons, feats of magic, swoons of ecstasy, and intuitive insights allegedly released forces—for better or for worse—within the most archaic regions of the human being (Harding, *Woman's Mysteries* 109).

In alchemy, the moon is associated with silver. Although highly placed within the hierarchy of metals and chemicals for its purity, silver illuminates only partially, and thus is considered less dazzling and less perfect than gold, which is associated with the sun. Fantasy, fear, and the dream are born, alchemists contended, within the moon's penumbra. In the semidarkness of its silvery tonalities, intuitive forces, analogized to those residing in shadowy corners of the mind, emerge if summoned. Because silver is subdued and mobile in coloration (it tarnishes, darkens, lightens, etc.), it represents hidden, enigmatic aspects of the personality. Since it stirs up ineffable, and intangible—or creative—motifs, it is understandably identified with poets.

Michel, according to Nodier, functions solely in the realm of feeling and intuition. Fantasies and strange ideas surge within him. The description of his physical and spiritual makeup are comparable to those used by poets to describe the moon: he is "pale," his eyes have the "transparency" and liquid "gaze" of a person from whom the fire of the sun has been "eclipsed." His world, bathed in darkness and in ambiguity, is lost in the illusions of the imaginary world (*Crumb Fairy* 180–81). His loving and compassionate personality hovers, like the moon, solitary in the vast expanse of blackness surrounding him.

To become a Moon Man requires a long period of gestation. In alchemical tradition, a rite of passage had to be endured and transcended before a higher spiritual state of consciousness could be reached. Unlike some eighteenth-century Cartesian rationalists who believed reason to be the supreme form of consciousness, Nodier, in accord with the alchemists, was convinced that the realm of logic alone could not lead to greater knowledge. Higher consciousness was to be found in "obscure movements," in a variety of impulses buried within the depths of being, made manifest in moments of clairvoyance, illumination, intuition, or other nonrational forms.

The Gnostics associated the moon with the divine Sophia; for Nodier, she likewise symbolized "the fallible aspects of God" (Jonas, *The Gnostic Religion* 176). In ancient days moon people were considered the spokesmen of the gods, the possessors of some divine power, but they were nonetheless fallible (L. *falere*, to deceive). One listened to their statements and prognostications with awe and trepidation, since they, unlike Gods, could err. Moon-thinking might open new insights and fresh orientations to those who could see!—but could entrap as well.

Michel, capable of divining and understanding more deeply than the socalled rational or normal person, occupied "a higher degree in the ladder" separating the moon from the sun world. He ranked among the privileged—the elect—because he possessed the mystery of inner coherence. Free from the constrictive time-space limitations imposed upon ordinary individuals, his thoughts could traverse cosmic spheres in order to access greater wisdom. "And what will prevent this indefinable state of mind, which ignorance labels folly, to lead in time to the supreme form of wisdom via a path unknown to us" (*Crumb Fairy* 310).

A price must be paid, however, for divining cosmic secrets. Divested of identity when among his peers, solitary and unable to communicate, Michel was, in Nodier's view, a *superior* being, set apart from the collective. That he lived exclusively in a world of fantasy prevented him from falling in love with a flesh-and-blood woman. When the Crumb Fairy appeared to Michel as the beautiful Belkiss on the medallion, he said that "her mysterious voice spoke to my soul, the celestial smile on her lips and gaze answered my very thought" (*Crumb Fairy* 231). As the divine Belkiss, she lived fixed in his unchangeable reality.

THE CRUMB FAIRY/BELKISS: SUN WOMAN. As a supraterrestrial spiritual power, the ancient Crumb Fairy represents what Michel had lacked in life: a positive mother figure, wise, understanding, gentle, loving, and tender. "My affection for you," she says to Michel, "is greater than a mother's affection, and is imbued with its chasteness" (*Crumb Fairy* 280). Since he had first set eyes on the Crumb Fairy when he was twelve, he experienced, he confessed, the love and security denied him since birth. Her presence in his life had inspired in him feelings of "tender veneration and almost religious submission, tending toward another order of ideas and sentiments" (*Crumb Fairy* 193). She was Michel's "guardian angel" during his school years, going so far as to help him and his friends with their studies (*Crumb Fairy* 275).

A type of miracle worker, she was the helping mother par excellence, and would continue to play this role throughout his life—at least as long as Michel needed her. "I had the joy of advising you, of helping . . . and you have not reached the point of being able to get along without me" (*Crumb Fairy* 201). That the Crumb Fairy/Belkiss/Queen of Sheba realizes Michel's ideal love indicates his desire to remain under the dominion of his vision of the Eternal Feminine throughout his life. The prolonged kindness and solicitude of a mother may, however, become destructive inasmuch as growth in the face of the realities of the world. The fine line that distinguishes a loving mother from a possessive one is tenuous. Examples of proprietary mothers have existed since antiquity: the son of Cybele, Attis, and the son of Ishtar, Tammuz, died after unsuccessful attempts to escape an overpowering mother-influence.

Michel's relationship with his ideal feminine image necessarily leads to not only a condition of stasis, but to a withdrawal from the existential world, understood as a regression into an archaic and/or infantile realm. There, serenity and security are afforded by the uterus during the paradisaic stage of the unborn. At the tale's conclusion, the very foundations of Michel's personality had been undermined, his every need having been answered by the Crumb Fairy's dominion over his fantasy world. Psychologically, we may suggest that his sense of fallibility quickened the disintegration of his ego. Defined as the center of consciousness, the ego stands as a mediating force between the inner and outer worlds, its function being to adapt to both. In Michel's case, his ego had lost its ability to act outside of the world of fantasy. Why should he battle out his existence on an external level when all was so beautifully cared for in his inner domain?

Belkiss or the Queen of Sheba, the beautiful, sparkling, and youthful side of the Crumb Fairy, symbolically representing an archaic sun figure, appears in all of her perfection only after Michel passes the first stage of the initiation process: from son-mother motif to son-lover. In Arab legends, many of which Nodier had read, Sheba, known under the name of Nilqis or Balqis (Belkiss), came from the sun-drenched land of Yemen, where the people practiced Sabbaean cult worship: the adoration of the sun as a supreme cosmic force. Michel's reference to his "divine Princess of the South" is in terms of the solar disk: pure sunlight–gold! (*Crumb Fairy* 213).

When his passion was aroused, she became, both physically and emotionally, fire and flame. "Moved, agitated, palpitating, ready to bound forth, to join her lips to mine. I felt that the warmth of her kiss poured torrents of flames into my veins" (*Crumb Fairy* 234). At night, she was that radiant sunlight, that celestial illumination around whom "all torches lit at the same time" (*Crumb Fairy* 306). "Sovereign of all unknown realms of the Orient and of the South, she had inherited Solomon's ring, scepter, and crown" (*Crumb Fairy* 239). As fire, Belkiss radiated sparks as powerful as solar conflagrations, becoming a dangerous force. Like Circe, she had the power to entice, hypnotize, mesmerize, and eventually destroy. In time, Michel became her passive instrument, her victim.

By rejecting the flesh-and-blood woman, as exemplifed by Folly Girlfree, Michel became progressively engulfed in Belkiss's image, eventually, to drown in it. Like the novitiate who loses him- or herself in prayer, or the mystic in contemplation, or the artist in his creative endeavor, Michel united with his sublime collective figure–Belkiss/the Queen of Sheba. As the woman in front of whose image he knelt, and whose "mysterious voice" spoke to his soul, Belkiss was Michel's spiritual bride, like Dante's Beatrice, or Mary as the Bride of God/Christ, and the Queen of Heaven (*Crumb Fairy* 226, 231, 296).

EARTH FORCE: MISSING MATTER. The third force, *earth* (or matter; the others being fire, water, air), which would have solidified the union between solar and lunar principles, was missing from the quaternity.[2] Michel's rejection of the terrestrial sphere in the form of Folly Girlfree, despite his attraction to her gentle manner, indicated that the two did not "live in the same region." Paradigmatically, it suggested that no bond between them could ever be sacralized, and that Michel would never know "love for any earthly creature" (*Crumb Fairy* 54).

Even though the *hieros gamos* had been constellated between sun and moon, and personified as well by the protagonists, only a trinity emerged. The fourth force—earth—which would have given balance and substance to the union, had been rejected, leaving the *hieros gamos*, as experienced in *The*

Crumb Fairy, one-sided. A cosmic union of this nature, by its very limitations, could never lead to spiritual regeneration. The earth principle, crucial to the conflict of opposites, that hastens the growth process was lacking. Identified with the alchemist's *nigredo,* or blackening process, Michel as Moon Man represented chaos, a *massa confusa,* a psyche that existed prior to the separation of the elements. Psychologically, Michel lived in a state of unconsciousness, of somnolence, during which the human mind is unaware of conscious conflicts, needs, and desires. In this state of wholeness or *uroborus* (the image of the serpent eating its own tail), "Primal Darkness," according to both Gnostic belief and Jung's collective unconscious, Michel existed as a child prior to his separation from the parents, prior to his experiencing himself as a conscious individual. At this stage, he remained unknowable and undifferentiated, existing as within an arcane substance—in a state of continuous reception. Thanks to "Princess Mandragore," he was released from imprisonment in the rational world, married the queen of Sheba, the light of his life, and became emperor of seven planets—never to be seen again! (*Crumb Fairy* 329).

What most strikes contemporary readers of *The Crumb Fairy,* is Nodier's need to unify what was divided—sun and moon—in a *hieros gamos.* That an androgynous figure such as Michel pervades the literary scene evidently answers a need in Nodier and in other creative spirits of the age (Gautier, Nerval, Balzac) to rectify an imbalance in the contemporary social structure—to reshuffle the system. Because the rigid patriarchal tradition in which reason, logic, and rational attributes personified in the masculine sun principle prevailed, the world of feeling, tenderness, understanding, and Eros embodied by the feminine moon principle, having been neglected, was to be restored. For sensitive people such as Nodier, and the French, English, and German Romantics, the dichotomy between these two ways of life had grown so wide that the soul or anima was lost in the stiff, unbending clarity of consciousness.

THEOPHILE GAUTIER'S PARAPSYCHOLOGICAL HETAERA/FAIRY ARRIA MARCELLA

H AD A REAL MUSE/FAIRY triggered the parapsychological experience that allowed Théophile Gautier's protagonist, Octavius, to reenter the past and resurrect a Pompeian beauty? Or was his exploit the result of an opium induced dream? Or had it simply been a normal dream? Whether or not Arria Marcella, the love figure in Gautier's short story, was a *real* fairy, she nonetheless fits *Webster's Ninth Collegiate Dictionary* definition of a "mythical figure of romance . . . having magic powers."

ECTYPAL ANALYSIS

Gautier (1811-1872) found it difficult to adapt to his century, to the ugliness of the newly created industrial cities, and to the utilitarian world. His double obsession—the cult of beauty and preoccupation with death—both triggered his fertile imagination and intensified his powerful yearning to escape the present and flow back into the past. He accomplished this feat in *Arria Marcella* (1852) by revivifying Pompeii, a city that had been destroyed by the eruption of Mount Vesuvius in 79 C.E. Upon Octavius's return to a long since vanished culture, he thrilled at the reality of Arria Marcella's beautiful physical presence, and to the ancient city he visited tactilely, visually, and auditorially. His reentry into a past time offered him the imagined pleasures that had eluded him in his empirical world. Indeed, these privileged moments convinced Octavius, and by extension Gautier, that linear time could be transcended and that terrestrial restrictions could be bypassed, albeit momentarily, but long enough to alleviate his gnawing sense of solitude.

Although he was born in Tarbes in the south of France, Gautier's family moved to Paris three years after their son's birth. He frequented the Lycée Charlemagne and studied art with the painter Louis-Edouard Rioult, who taught him such techniques as brushing on pigments and applying rub-on overtones to heighten the emotional value of certain areas on his canvas. Following a modeling session in Rioult's studio, however, Gautier inadvertently voiced his disappointment in both the model who had come to pose and in the entire learning experience: no matter how sublime the human form to be reproduced, a work of art should improve on nature. Years later, he confessed: "I always preferred the statue to the woman and marble to flesh" (Bergerat, *Théophile Gautier* 242). His negative reaction to traditional art modes was to take on amplitude in the philosophical and esthetic stand voiced in his future artistic credo: "Art adds something to even the most perfect natural form." Art for Gautier would henceforth imply *artifice*.

His literary career began officially with the publication of a slim volume of *Poems* (1830), in which his yearning to escape the finite world was already revealed. Because of the exotic elsewhere for which he incessantly longed, his happiness could only stem from, and flourish in, an atmosphere of dazzling beauty, guiltlessness, and serenity in love. Such ineffability was lived by him fleetingly when he attended certain theater pieces and ballets; when he visited the studios of specific painters and sculptors at art exhibits of his choice; and, to be sure, through his own writing. During the creative process, he allowed his imagination to take flight, to escape the constrictions of linear time, and, convinced that he had penetrated a fourth dimension—a space/time continuum—he felt he had targeted and connected with the cosmos as a living organism.

Gautier's early contributions, *Albertus* (1832), a theological legend in which a young painter damns himself for a witch, and *Les Jeunes-France* (1833), a volume of humoristic short stories, did not attract many readers. By contrast, his novel, *Mlle de Maupin* (1836), satirizing virtue, journalism, and the bourgeois in general, won the attention of many, perhaps because of its racy scenes and androgynous protagonist. As a believer in "Art for Art's Sake," Gautier declared that art should be divested of all morality, and that everything that is useful is ugly. Beauty alone is worthy of enduring: plastic beauty of form, contour, harmony of lines, and color tones. His celebrated poetic work, *Enamels and Cameos* (1852–1872), discloses his metaphysical beliefs in a world of *secret affinities*, and sets down his stylistic credo: a poem should be labored over as a sculptor does his stone, as a goldsmith does his precious metals. The word, like a hard object, must be hammered, chiseled, and melted down to suit the artist's vision. To create a work of art, he maintained, is physically and emotionally arduous. The contrivance of what had never before existed was particularly taxing for Gautier, who was perpetually haunted by an ideal of perfection and beauty.

Despite his flagrant disregard for morality in art and his craving to escape into a world of beauty, Gautier was, nonetheless, of his time. Like many of his "Romantic" contemporaries, he sought to flee from what he saw as a moneyed and materialistic world. Extreme distaste for the empirical environment fostered in him the impress of different personality traits: melancholia, fantasy, and the proverbial *mal du siècle*. Around the middle of the nineteenth century, many had become profoundly disaffected from modern Western civilization and from Christianity, and longed for a return to polytheism or, as it was termed in those days, "Paganism." Poems, such as "Myrtho" and "Delfica" by Gautier's friend, Gérard de Nerval (1808–1855), captured the spirit of an ideal realm of beauty and harmony with which the ancient Greeks were familiar. The "mystical pagan" Louis Ménard (1822–1901), who reinterpreted Greek legends in the light of contemporary society, believed polytheism to be the nurturer of the republican form of government, and Catholicism that of absolute monarchy. In *Ancient Poems* and *Orphic Hymns*, Leconte de Lisle (1818–1894) sought to recreate in his images the perfection the Greeks had achieved in their temples and sculptures. Insofar as religious ideations were concerned, he set in contrast polytheists, as incarnated in the beautiful philosopher martyr, Hypatia, and the Christian group of ignorant and superstitious converts who stoned her to death. Gautier too, longed for a return to Greek modalities, which he idealized, looking upon Greece as a society whose goal was esthetic and not utilitarian, and whose religion was based on beauty and not repression.

Illuminism, Buddhism, and alchemy had also become popular panaceas offered to those unable to accept the increasingly industrialized contemporary world. Gautier, in this regard, was haunted by a sense of mystery and awe for the occult and a delightfully titillating fear of the unknown. Like Charles Baudelaire (1821–1867), who had dedicated his *Flowers of Evil* to him, he believed in universal correspondences, mesmerism, transmission of thought, vampirism, sympathetic magic, and the *déjà vu*. According to his son-in-law, Emile Bergerat, Gautier was extremely superstitious. Indeed, he seemed to be superstition incarnate, convinced of the truth of divination, premonitory dreams, signs, omens, and magic. His daughter, Judith, added that he was convinced that occult forces dictated his destiny, and that he could influence them in certain secret ways.

Gautier, in many of his short stories evoking antiquity—*The Golden Chain* (1837), *One of Cleopatra's Nights* (1838), *The Opium Pipe* (1838), *The Fairy* (1843), *Jettatura* (1856), *Avatar* (1856), and *Spirite* (1866)—launched into the supernatural realms where fairies, spirits, succubi, and incubi co-habited. Other writers had similar outerworldly inclinations. Charles Nodier dramatized arcane realms, as we have seen, in *The Crumb Fairy*, as well as in *Smarra*, and *Infernalia*; Gérard de Nerval concretized esoteric happenings in *The Enchanted Hand*, *The Green Monster*, and *The Devil's Portrait*; Balzac dealt with the supernatural in *The Wild Ass's Skin*, *The Red Inn*, and *The Unknown Masterpiece*. In Hugo's *Our Lady of Paris*, sorcerers and grotesque monsters came to life side by side with beautiful young maidens. Gothic tales imported from England were in vogue in Paris: Horace Walpole's (1717–1794) *The Castle of Otranto*, Ann Radcliffe's (1764–1823) *The Haunted Chamber*, Matthew G. Lewis's (1775–1818) *The Monk*, Dr. John Polidori's (or Byron, 1788–1824) *The Vampire*, and Mary Shelley's (1797–1851) *The Dream*. These and many other similar works sent chills coursing through the spines of readers in search of phantasmagorias. E. T. Hoffmann's preoccupation with animal magnetism, astrology, and all types of occult forces as revealed in his narrations *The Devil's Elixir*, *The Educated Cat*, and *The Violin of Cremona* were even more popular in France than the Gothic tales. Science likewise aroused the imagination of the vulnerable populace. Clinical studies on hypnotism, mesmerism, magnetic sleep, som-nambulism, posthypnotic suggestion, witchcraft, spiritism, satanism, animal magnetism, and lycanthropy had been published by medical men such as Alexander Betrand, J. P. F. Deleuze, and Armand M. J. de Puységur, to mention but a few. The discovery of the unconscious, and the invisible world it conjured came into its own in musical works such as, *inter alia*, Weber's *Der Freischutz*, Berlioz's *Fantastic Symphony*, Meyerbeer's *Robert the Devil*, Tartini's *Devil's Trill*, and Liszt's *Goethe Festmarch*.

ARCHETYPAL ANALYSIS

ARCHAEOLOGY: A YEARNING FOR THE PAST. The setting for *Arria Marcella* is Pompeii, a city dating back to the eighth century B.C.E., which had been oc-cupied by the Etruscans, influenced by the Greeks, and was subject-ally of Rome. Gautier's thirst and idealization of antiquity, coupled with the birth of scientific archaeology in the nineteenth century, made Pompeii the ideal decor for a lover of "Art for Art's Sake."

The term archeology (Gr. *arkhaios*, ancient; *logos*, discourse), introduced in the seventeenth century by Jacques Spon of Lyons, referred only to the "classic" elements of the past, namely, art and history. Renewed interest in Egyptian culture and the studies of antiquities was fostered by Napoleon's invitation to 171 scientists to accompany his army on their military campaign in Egypt (1799–1801), a venture instrumental in the discovery of the Rosetta Stone (a decree written in Greek, Egyptian hieroglyphics, and Demotic) and its decipherment in 1822 by the Orientalist J. F. Champollion.

Although the collecting of antiquities in Pompeii, Herculaneum, and Stabiae began in Italy as early as the fifteenth century, it was only after 1748 that excavations of ancient sites were carried on in a systematic way. These once-flourishing artistic and commercial cities had been buried in 79 C.E. under a layer of lava erupting from Mount Vesuvius; their population, estimated at 20,000, had been decimated. When the much-admired naturalist, Pliny the Elder, rushed to Stabiae to rescue his friend Pomponanius, he too was overwhelmed by the vapors emanating from the lava. Despite the irreparable damage Pompeii suffered, some edifices, mosaics, sculptures, paintings, utensils, and paved streets were saved, at least in part, from complete annihilation.

Whenever the name Pompeii was mentioned in conversations among the young "Romantics" in nineteenth-century France, its lavish and sensual life style, the beauty of its artistic wonders, its elegance, and, strangely enough, even its commercial activities triggered feelings of longing in many, including Gautier and the hero of his *Arria Marcella*, Octavius.

OCTAVIUS. The name Octavius brings to mind the Roman Emperor Augustus, who was so called prior to his adoption by Julius Caesar as his heir. Rome's power and grandeur reached its apogee during the Augustinian age, which boasted of authors such as Horace, Virgil, Titus-Livius, and Ovid.

More important for our purposes, however, is the numerical indication in the name Octavius (Lat. *octavus*, eight). The digit 8 may be identified with the notion of infinity (as imaged in the double zeros, or two intertwining circles), suggesting the inexhaustible, or transfinite, possibilities of the protagonist's mind. Thus, the name Octavius is admirably suited to Gautier's intensely imaginative hero. As applied to the musical octave in the Dorian mode, the number eight embraces the "two tetrachords grouped around the mese (middle)" (Cannon, Johnson, Waite, *The Art of Music* 20). The melodic progressions and rhythmical interchanges that become operational in the Dorian mode—musical equivalents of Octavius's highly affective nature—serve to accentuate the dynamic principle in *Arria Marcella's* composition and evocation. Each note/word in its own way may be said to be moving toward a point of orientation.

The eight in Octavius's name may be said to revolve around Pythagorean astral calculations, such as his concept of the "music of the spheres," his computations involving eternal time, and his metaphysical beliefs in the immortality and transmigration of the soul. The numerical equivalent of Octavius's name undeniably constitutes the ideal paradigm for his successful attempt, during the course of his peregrinations in Pompeii, to regress into a cyclical or timeless frame—the *eternal present* of Pythagoras, Plato, Aristotle, Empedocles, and others.

Historical time, commonly alluded to as eschatological, as opposed to cyclical or mythical time, is present in *Arria Marcella*. The former, philosophically and historically speaking, having arisen with consciousness, or with socalled "civilization," is the antithesis of primordial (unconscious) time, measured in terms of cyclical events. The ancients considered each day not only as a conquest over night, but as a cycle, or circle, to be understood and experienced to its fullest. Since there was no beginning and no end, the concept of past, present, and future was nonexistent. In that the ancients lived closer to nature than modern dwellers in industrial societies, they were *one* with the cosmos and placed themselves within its endless series of cycles. No split, therefore, existed between them and nature; they had no consciousness of themselves as separate entities from the forces surrounding them and from the world of phenomena. In this regard, death was part of organic phenomena or of seasonal changes. Because death was not seen as a separation nor as an end—it simply gave entry into another world—the hereafter did not inspire fear.

When Gautier wrote in *Arria Marcella* that "nothing dies, all exists always; no force can annihilate what once was," he was reiterating Platonic, Pythagorean and Empedoclean doctrines (Gautier, *Contes fantastiques*, "Arria Marcella" 245). He continues:

> Every action, every word, every form, every thought which has fallen into the universal ocean of things produces circles which grow increasingly large until they encapsulate the confines of eternity. Material figurations disappear only to the eyes of the vulgar; for others, continuously detaching apparitions people the infinite. (*Arria Marcella* 245)

For Gautier, humans live on eternally in the endless variety of forms of nature's transformatory process.

NAPLES' ARCHEOLOGICAL MUSEUM. *Arria Marcella* begins with Octavius's visit to the Naples archeological museum, housing since 1790 one of the largest collections of antiquities from Pompeii and Herculaneum. Accompanied by two of his friends, Max and Fabio, Octavius stops to admire the frescoes, bronzes, mosaics, textiles, varieties of glass, and other artifacts displayed. He finds himself inexplicably riveted in contemplation of a large fragment of petrified lava outlining a woman's bust and thigh. Marveling at the thought of what she had once represented, and the fleeting empires that had emerged and vanished into oblivion since her day, Octavius imagined the horror experienced by those buried nearly two thousand years ago under Vesuvius' ash. How strange it was that this particular exquisitely rounded form before him had been exhumed from the home of M. Arrius Diomedes in Pompeii, thus sparing it from obscurity! Aware that Octavius had suddenly become lost in his meditations over some ancient fragment, Fabio and Max ushered him gently back to reality by reminding him that if they did not hurry they would miss their train for Pompeii.

The museum, a symbol of an enclosed and protective uterine area, had catalyzed Octavius's collective unconscious. The deepest layer of his subliminal spheres became accessible to consciousness via archetypal images, allowing him to *recall* specific mythological, architectural, and cultural motifs, as well as the archetypal *feminine principle*—in his case, Arria Marcella. This upsurge within him of potent forces, unmanifested at the outset of the tale, led him along a pathway going back to a former level of existence, to a world in which he longed to participate.

According to André Malraux, the phenomenon of the museum was a creation of the occidental world stemming, he noted in *The Voices of Silence*, from a human need to halt the march of time; to create limits and categories; to make order out of disorder; to fix the fluid; and to transform the ephemeral into the eternal. By *containing* the fleeting and disparate components of worldly existence, humans seemingly felt more secure and less isolated. The museum's function, then, was to arrest time via the work of art. When Octavius saw in the Naples museum the stonelike piece of lava that had retained the configurations of a female form for nearly a thousand years, past and present suddenly fused. The museum, reaching across centuries and embracing a period in history to which Octavius related, succeeded in renewing a bond. The piece of lava in question, like a fetish or hierophany, assumed extraordinary importance for him and would pave the way for his inner trajectory into the past. This parapsychological experience or "supranormal" happening may be understood as a paradigm of what can occur to someone "predisposed" to certain situations, or to a person in a "psychologically receptive state" (Jung, "A Letter on Parapsychology and Synchronicity," *Spring* 1960, 205).

POMPEII. A mood of levity pervaded the thoughts and actions of Octavius and his friends as they arrived in Pompeii. Striking them as ludicrous was the anachronistic blatantly modern and ugly railroad sign—"Pompeii Station"—as set against the remains of the beautiful ancient Greco-Roman city (*Arria Marcella* 217). As they made their way across a cotton field, Octavius observed a seemingly outerworldly glow hovering over the countryside—the brilliance of the sun's "golden" luminosities, the "transparency of the air," and the blues, violets, and pinks of Vesuvius' once-blazing volcano. As his gaze wandered about the fragmented shadowy formations looming here and there, he was struck by portentous feelings of reality. Had he opened a window onto another sphere of being? As he peered at the thin, striated vaporous lines issuing from the volcanic center of Mount Vesuvius, his dreamy imaginings were, to use Jung's words, creating a kind of "magnetic field," or "center of energy" within his psyche (Jung 5, #344). Would he undergo some kind of transfiguration?

Why, the reader may wonder, did Gautier personify nature's forms and colors, for example, encapsulating the Pompeian hills in the distance in "undulating and voluptuous lines," and those closest to him in the contours of a woman's thighs? Why, as the blue-green sea came into focus, shining "placidly" under the city's ramparts, did he muse about the biremes and triremes that had once docked in the harbor. Had the color tones, working in consort with the nearly two-thousand year-old fragments of lava he saw in the museum, removed part of the "shroud" hiding certain ancient mysteries (*Arria Marcella* 218).

Gautier's imaged personifications led to a sharp increase in overtones, feelings, and ideas, and intensified the *sensation* and *distillation* of his spiritual notions. Like the sculptor working in stone or marble, Gautier, the writer, transmuted the rapid or prolonged hand strokes of the artisan into deft verbal gyrations, creating an intellectual and emotional climate that shifted about in keeping with Octavius's compositional and psychical inner drama.

After gazing into distant spaces, Octavius scrutinized within the ancient city the large paved Roman streets before him, marveling at the "cyclopean" polygonal blocks on which heavy vehicles had left their imprints in the form of deep ruts (*Arria Marcella* 218). In awe of the modernity of these ancient roads, he focused admiringly on the astuteness of the city planners who had thought of using stepping stones to protect pedestrians from the dirt and mud of the main thoroughfares. The state of preservation of some of the inscriptions on the signs dotting the walkways, most notably the painted red letters announcing future theatrical performances, gladiator fights, the layout of seats, and votive formulae, gave Octavius the impression that everything advertised was still occurring.

Had time stopped? What arcana, he wondered, lay hidden beneath the masses of half-destroyed or collapsed roofs? What secrets were embedded within the crumbling walls? Historians failed to note domestic details in their volumes, he complained. As for the vestiges—the forum, fountains, columns, carved architraves, sculptures, temples, shops, marble counters, and cabarets—they all seemed to be awaiting an *awakening*, a change in their condition of stasis. Visibly excited at the sight of the amphitheater, Octavius and his friends, romantic youths that they were, climbed its stone steps and from the summit declaimed their favorite poems.

Following their descent to street level, they continued their walk, empathizing all along with the victims of the destruction wrought by the volcanic ash and the centuries of neglect that followed. Tree roots, for example, had burrowed their way into the roofs of the half-buried houses; disjoined tiles, semi-crumbled walls, broken columns, and faded colors—once "marvels of art"—had obliterated the memory of this formerly thriving metropolis (*Arria Marcella* 220). The more he observed the dismantled fragments strewn about him, the more he lamented the original harmonies of Greco-Roman art and architecture that now lay beneath layers of dross. What was the city's actual layout? which was the cardo? the decumen? the placement of Fortune Street, the House of the Bronze Bull, the House of the Faun, the Pharmacy, the Surgeon's stall, the temple of the Vestals, Albinus's Inn, the Tombs (*Arria Marcella* 220)?

On the dismemberment surrounding him, Octavius superimposed a unified vision of the Pompeii that once had been. Excision of an existing reality engenders affective tension between past and present. Buffing, shining, and burnishing what lay embedded in Octavius's mind's eye gave his intuitive powers full sway, and allowed purity and beauty of design, form, and color to surge and activate him in a past time. After all, Gautier had suggested, "Nature is the painter's invention" (Gautier, *Pochades et paradoxes* vii). As long as the sun cast its clear and trenchant light over the city, all seemed cohesive and rational to Octavius. No sooner was mention made of the Tombs, however, he experienced an inexplicable mood-change. Indeed, it was as if a door had opened and led to some secret realm bathed in obscure shadowy moon tones!

SUN/MOON/TOMB. As in Nodier's *The Crumb Fairy*, so in Gautier's *Arria Marcella* the archetypal image of the sun, identified with conscious, masculine, and linear realms—the world of reality—was an energetic power for Octavius that aroused him to judge his thoughts, senses, and feelings in terms of their cosmic and esthetic amplitudes. But, the sun's shifting, mind-altering luminosities stirred up also in his consciousness indeterminate oppositional or contrasting realms. Quadrangles, circles, and squares, and the fearful, triangular Mount Vesuvius in the distance came into sharp relief. As long as the sun emitted its light, Octavius remained an inhabitant of the rational, and temporal world. No sooner had he entered Pompeii's Street of Tombs, than his outer, and by extension, his inner climate altered dramatically.

In the absence of the sun, lunar tonalities invaded the scene. The land of the dead, of the unconscious, and of the feminine, took precedence.

Octavius's psychological orientation slipped into dimness, into haunting, mysterious, and lusterless nether spheres. Fragmentation and dross were obliterated. Was Octavius reliving an Orphic mystery—a descent into the timeless realm of Hades? or into his mysterious inner self, which he was projecting onto his own as yet unlived darkness?

His musings over the dichotomy between ancient and contemporary religious ideations, particularly those revolving around death, opened him up to increased dissatisfaction with the latter. Unlike the Christians, the Greco-Romans did not consider death to be "lugubrious," "sad," or "terror-provoking." The ancients, rather than conserve a "horrible cadaver" in a cemetery, Octavius noted, created sepulchres decorated with beautiful and lively-colored images based on daily life. As for the human remains within the tomb, they consisted merely of a pinch or two of ashes, underscoring the ancients' "abstract understanding of death" (*Arria Marcella* 221).

Continuing on his way, Octavius stopped briefly in front of the tomb of the priestesses Mamia and Tyché Novoleja , then walked up a low hill to the monument of L. Ceius Labeo. After looking at the tomb of M. Arrius Diomedes, he approached what had once been this man's suburban villa, one of the largest and most lavish in Pompeii. Gautier describes it as follows:

> One ascends the bricks as if by degrees, and once having stepped beyond the door flanked with two small lateral columns, one finds oneself in a court that resembles a *patio,* like those at the center of Spanish and Moorish homes, referred to by the ancients as *impluvium* or *cavaedium:* fourteen brick columns, covered over with stucco form a portico or covered peristyle on the four sides, similar to those convent cloisters under which one could walk without being afraid of rain. The pavement of this court is made of a mosaic of bricks and white marble, its effect being gentle and soft to the eye. In the middle stands a quadrilateral marble basin that had once received rain waters draining from the roof of the portico, and is still intact. (*Arria Marcella* 222)

The villa's exedra, or summer living room, opened on to the sea, inviting ancient and modern visitors to receive the fresh breezes that alleviated the heat of the burning summer months. From one marvel to another: the basilica; the white marble terrace giving onto gardens and sea; the nymphaeum with its yellow painted walls, stucco columns, mosaic floors, and marble tubs; a tetrastyle or recreation room, a cubiculum, or sleeping compartment intended to induce dreams; a chapel to the *lares* (household deities); closed spaces housing archival materials, a library, museum, and the women's apartments. Although they were all in lamentable condition, to Octavius's delight he was able to discern traces of forms and colors in the paintings and arabesques adorning the original walls. On the lower level of Arrius Diomedes' villa, Octavius saw eight more rooms painted in antique red and a cellar containing eight amphoras, possibly filled with Cretan or Falernian wine.

Gradually the declining rays of the sun blocked out the water's emerald and topaze hues. As Octavius penetrated another enclosure, he felt himself increasingly enveloped by the shadowy forms of seventeen unearthed skeletons, including that of the lady of the house whose imprint in lava he had first seen in the Naples Museum. She had been wearing gold rings at the time of Vesuvius' eruption, and bits of her finely woven tunic garment adhering to the now-fixed ashes had retained their form. Fascinated by the sight, Octavius asked the guide to show him exactly where these "precious remains had been discovered" (*Arria Marcella* 224). So deeply moved was he by what he labeled his "introspective love" for the lady who had perished nearly two thousand years ago, that he turned away, and his friends, Fabio and Max, failed to see that he had shed a tear.

OCTAVIUS'S INNER/OUTER NIGHT JOURNEY. Although Octavius dined with his friends, he realized that he had been taken by "an impossible and mad passion" reminiscent, Gautier noted, of Faust's for Helen. Her "form, invisible to the eyes of the vulgar, still subsists in time and in space" (*Arria Marcella* 228). Just as Helen had played the role of eternal feminine for Faust, similarly would the Pompeian lady impress herself on Octavius. Anima figures had dominated Octavius's world prior to his visit to Pompeii; indeed, he had been captivated by an entire harem of female powers—Semiramis, Aspasia, Cleopatra, Diane de Poitiers, Jeanne d'Aragon. So taken was he by beauties of the past that on one occasion, when visiting Rome and observing archaeologists exhuming a thick clump of braided hair from an ancient tomb, for some unknown reason he felt deliriously moved by the sight and feel of it. Following his instinct, he bought three stands of the hair, paying a high price for these, and then asked a medium to evoke the shadow of this dead woman. Because too many centuries had passed, Gautier was told that the conductive fluid in the strands of her hair had lost its energy, preventing the "apparition" of this dead woman from becoming manifest—that is, "from emerging from its eternal night" into Octavius's daylight (*Arria Marcella* 229). Ready once again to invoke an anima or soul figure from the realm of the dead into his contemporary world, Octavius invited the Pompeian lady's soul to transmigrate from Titus's century into his own (*Arria Marcella* 229).

So engulfed was he in his vision that Octavius, unlike Max and Fabio, did not return to their hotel after dinner. His ego (center of consciousmess) no longer in command, he yielded to the urgings of his subliminal domain, which guided him according to its own dictates. Acting like an automaton, Octavius found himself at the entrance of the "City of the Dead," where he opened the gate and penetrated among the rubble.

Now, on this paradoxically nocturnal day, Octavius viewed Pompeii in a slow-motion interplay of silvery and bluish moon tones. No longer did the sun's brilliant lighting effects and their shadowy counterparts mark contours of destroyed buildings, mutilated columns, cracked façades, and sunken roofs, which filled him with feelings of vacancy and absence. Under matte moon rays and their halftones, he felt bathed in sensations of completion and unity of purpose. No longer was Pompeii the "fossilized city" he had seen during daylight hours; rather, it was restructured and resurrected as a living reality. Vague forms peopled the avenues, stirring "strange," perhaps even heady feelings in him (Arria Marcella 230). Was he entering into another time zone? Returning to the Octavius/Augustinian age?

Because linear time has been identified with consciousness and masculine power, its trajectory is irreversible. Cyclical or dream-time, however, associated with the feminine moon force, is allied to the unconscious. In keeping with Jungian psychological theories, the unconscious is composed of both personal and collective domains: the latter "does not represent merely a psychic appendage of 'archaic remains' . . . but *the* living creative matrix of all our unconscious and conscious functionings, the essential structural basis of all our psychic life" (Franz, *Number and Time* 4).

Timelessness, simultaneity of events, universal landscapes—everything experienced by humankind coexists in the collective unconscious. Thus, Octavius advanced into Pompeii for the second time, under matte moon rays, revealed to him—in tact—the buildings, columns, ochre walls, roofs, bronze statues, and paintings he had seen during his daylight tour. Nothing bore any sign of destruction or mutilation. How could the restoration of a city have taken place so rapidly, he wondered? Even the shafts of moonlight now streaming onto the city enclosed it in a singular glaze of scattered rose, violet, and azure tints. The entire image seemed enveloped in a complex of pale disconnected yet continuous hues.

No longer did Octavius feel he was walking through a "dead, cold, cadaverous city," but a revivified, ancient living metropolis, bustling with activity in its daylight hours. Yet, when he looked at his watch it indicated midnight. How could it be, he asked himself? Was he dreaming? He looked around again. The roads and paths were filled with people dressed as they had been in Titus's era. Some even slackened their pace, and looked at him quizzically, perhaps wondering why his dress was so different from their own. Had time receded? Was he living a mirage? a dream? a somnambulistic event?

an optical illusion? a hallucination? or was he going mad? That he had crossed the time barrier, of this he was certain!

TIME RECEDES. Octavius decided to live out the experience as fully as possible. Having determined that the date of his entry into time was prior to August 24, 79 C.E., the day of the Vesuvian eruption, he hazarded an otherwise impossible thought. Couldn't the lady, whose captivating imprint he had seen in the Naples Museum, still be alive? If so, might it not be possible to see her? After all, had not Faust succeeded in conjuring Helen and Paris?

Gautier was not alone in evoking part II of Goethe's *Faust* (1808-1832) and the resurrection of previous eras. E. T. Hoffmann (1776-1822) had done in his *Night Pieces*; Gérard de Nerval in *The Enchanted Hand*; and Charles Nodier in *Smarra*. Goethe's approach to the convergence of past, present, and future, however, seemed more scientifically and metaphysically based than that of the other *conteurs*.

Octavius's night journey into the past is comparable in certain ways to Mephistopheles' suggestion to Faust that he descend to the "Realm of the Mothers" (or to the archetypal universe; to the Goddesses; in psychological terms, to the collective unconscious). Faust does so, but frightening shadows form and reform about him. Both to allay his fears and to encourage his entry into time, Mephistopheles resorts to magical rituals and objects, and, to facilitate his journey, gives him the "Cup" and the "Key." The Cup, indicating "spiritual baptism" according to the fourth sermon of the Thrice-Greatest Hermes Trismegistus (the father of alchemy and of "hermeticism," as his name indicates), "becomes irradiate with Life and illumined with Light." The Key fills the possessor who has learned to transcend corporal limitations with "Gnosis" or "beatific vision." Having accomplished this feat, Faust hubristically displays his achievements by touching the "Cup" with "the still glowing Key," thereby bringing a mist into being (Raphael, *Goethe and the Philosopher's Stone* 150). Faust has not only "unlocked the doors of matter—an accomplishment of nuclear fission which to us is no longer a mystery—but he is now engaged in bringing certain atoms together and shaping them anew into man and woman" (Raphael 150).

Reborn from death (or disintegration), Helen and Paris appeared to Faust as, virtually, flesh-and-blood human beings. The moment he saw her kiss her lover, who then lifted her up to carry away, Faust, unable to contain his rapture, seized Helen, who promptly faded. No sooner had he touched Paris with the key, than Paris exploded. Having committed the unpardonable sin of attempting to change history or facts, Faust found himself alone lying on the ground (Raphael 151).

In keeping with the tenets of Astralism, a cult flourishing in Greco-Roman times (associated by some with Pythagoreanism), and of which Cicero was a member, human souls after death went not to Hades but to another sphere located below the moon. Accordingly, Helen is not to be considered an apparition, but rather an *eidolon* ("a sheath or covering of the soul"), visible to Faust in moonlight. Having touched her as an *eidolon*, he had endowed her with enough "vitality," or life, to make her visible to him (see Plutarch, *The Vision of Aridaeus* 22; Plato *Timaeus*; Raphael 145). May we assume that Octavius would live out a similar drama, on a far more simplified scale?

OCTAVIUS'S REENTRY INTO TIME PAST. Applicable to Octavius's reentry into time past are Heraclitus's words: "Awake, men have but one world common to all, but during sleep, each one returns to his own universe" (Brun, *Héraclite*, fragment 89, 65).

Pursuing his walk along the streets of ancient Pompeii, Octavius observed male pedestrians going about their daily activities, beautiful young girls gathered around a fountain, patricians walking nonchalantly in their togas. Interestingly, he noticed a shop selling amulets to ward off the *jettatura*—evil eye. Continuing on his way, he happened upon a young man of his age wearing a safron tunic over which a finely woven white woolen covering had been draped. Addressing him in Latin—*Advera salve*—a language that had been dead for so long, but which Octavius had studied in the *lycée*, he began conversing with him. A humorous note is interjected into their conversation when the Pompeian, aware of Octavius's linguistic difficulties, suggests they speak in Greek. Octavius demurred. No sooner had he told him that he was a Gaul from Lutèce (the ancient name for Paris), than the Pompeian pridefully revealed that his ancestors had fought in the Gallic land under Julius Caesar. Overlooking the preposterousness of Octavius's ridiculous disclosures—that emperor Titus had been dead for nearly two thousand years and that the "Nazarene" had replaced the wonderful Gods of the Greco-Romans—he offered to act as his city guide (*Arria Marcella* 237). As they passed the Temple of Isis, the Pompeiian pointed to the Odeon, where Plautus's farce, *Casina*, was being performed, and recommended to the Gallic "barbarian" that he see the presentation. Octavius accepted the suggestion and entered the amphitheater, which Gautier describes in detail, together with the play, the masks worn by the actors, the audience's dress, and the tickets made of slim pieces of ivory on which numbers indicating the seats had been inscribed (*Arria Marcella* 238).

Was Octavius living a waking dream? Were these figures, conversations, and architectural constructs real—that is, material, in the sense of an *eidolon*? Let us note that Democritus and Leucippus, pre-Socratic atomist philosophers, had referred to unsubstantial images or phantoms as *eidola* (sing. *eidolon*), or lower souls. Reality for Democritus consisted of "indivisible" atoms, in their materialized form. Dreams, visions, and hallucinations similarly may be said to be *eidola* made up of individual atoms grouped together in certain forms and shapes, attracted to each other by atmospheric or energetic conditions, and looked upon as visual and/or thought perceptions. In either case, they influence and are influenced by those who project upon them (Franz, *Number and Time* 68).

The *eidola*, or infinite particles of matter, that Octavius may have encountered in Pompeii were so forceful that they seemingly had the power to redirect his libido into happier eras. His awareness of the existence within him of these potent surges of forms and feelings affected his body rhythms as well. The resulting emotional reactions inspired sexual and spiritual beatitude. The quasi-divine pleasure of having met his possible soul mate, Arria Marcella, in the Naples museum in the fragment of lava, and the hope of seeing her as a composite of human and/or divine female figurations, encouraged him to further his quest.

Scanning the faces of the spectators in the theater, Octavius noticed an extraordinarily lovely lady seated in the woman's section. Her eyes, virtually instantaneously, focused on his. He was as if struck by "an electric charge"; his heart began to throb (*Arria Marcella* 240). The folds of her dress, he noted, and the lines of her face, bearing an "undefinable expression of voluptuous sadness and passionnate ennui," were so exquisite that she could have inspired the works of two Athenian sculptors, Phidias (500 B.C.E., statue of Athene) and Cleomenes (statue of Venus), who probably lived in the Augustan age) (*Arria Marcella* 240). Identifying her as the woman whose form he had seen molded in the fragmented lava at the Naples museum, Octavius was certain that seeing her at this moment was *no* dream. Rather, he reasoned, he had transcended the wheel of time!

Once the performance had ended, Octavius made his way to the entrance of the amphitheater. He felt an arm stop him. It was that of Tyché Novoleja, informing him that she was the servant of Arria Marcella, daughter of Arrius Diomedes. "My mistress loves you," she said, "follow me" (*Arria Marcella* 242). Just then, a palanquin borne by four hefty, half-nude Syrian slaves passed by; a small curtain was parted at its window, and he saw a ringed hand beckoning him to follow. Guided by Tyché, Octavius made his way through the intersecting roads, noticing splendors of Pompeii that archaeologists had not even begun to discover.

ARRIA MARCELLA'S VILLA/TEMENOS. Octavius's out-of-time experience that had brought him to the villa of Arrius Diomedes' villa, would pave the way for his Orphic descent into his past and his renewal. Psychologically, villas, houses, huts, and such protective areas have been since ancient times considered preservers of wisdom, memories, and traditions: as *temenos* (sacred space). The enclosed and closeted area represented by Arrius Diomedes' villa , symbol of the womb, of the "darkness of night," of the "Realm of the Mothers," or Goddesses, to use Goethe's imagery, would enable Octavius to confront *woman* both as earth principle and as *anima* figure—in both cases, an aspect of the feminine principle that still remained unintegrated in his conscious life. His world revolved around "beauty" and its replication in art form and he yearned for renewal. To receive inner nourishment required withdrawal into self, where he, like Orpheus, God of music and poetry, and other great creative spirits, had made contact with their inner matrix or fountainhead. Octavius's universe dilated during his march inward, allowing him to experince what Pythagoras had called "the music of the spheres," or that creative inner femimine principle living incandescently within his being. Would Octavius, unlike Orpheus who failed in his attempt to resurrect his beloved Eurydice from death, succeed in bringing Arria Macella who once inhabited Arrius Diomedes' villa back to life?

The first step in his Orphic descent had been constituted by the museum episode, the second, his entry into Pompeii, and the third, his visit to Arrius Diomedes' villa, which struck Octavius by its architectural and ornamental beauty: its Greek Ionic marble columns, painted to midpoint in brilliant yellow and ornamented in matte reds and blues enriched with garlands of large green-leafed *aristolochia*; colorful wall frescoes of fantasy landscapes; and arrays of plants decorating the basins of water. Tyché led Octavius to the bath. As servants prepared him for his cleansing ritual, he had time to observe the beauty of this enclosed area: its brightly toned ceiling decorated with images of Mars, Venus, and Love; its friezes of deers, birds, rabbits; and its mosaic pavement, so expertly rendered as to remind Octavius of the art work of Zosimus of Pergamon.

The reader may wonder why Gautier went to such lengths to describe architectural details in *Arria Marcella*. According to Pythagoras, numbers, as previously mentioned, were closely allied not only to music ("music of the spheres") but, when understood in terms of spatio-temporal intervals, to architecture as well. It follows, then, that numbers may be appreciated both as beautiful living rhythms, and as "anthropocosmic harmony." Likewise was proportion in architectural constructs, such as in the Parthenon, mentioned several times by Gautier, crucial in maintaining cosmic balance and harmony (Brun, *Empédocle* 22).

THE PARAPSYCHOLOGICAL HAPPENING

The Mystery of the Darkened Room. No sooner had Octavius penetrated Arria Marcella's cavelike room, than sensations of ease and wonderment, harmony and serenity, burgeoned within him. Although the room was dimly lit, it revealed griffon-shaped tables encrusted with silver, ivory, and mother of pearl; gold and silver tables heaped with exquisite foods, exotic fruits, flowers, and wines. Musing that he would no longer, as his religion commanded, sacrifice instinct to obligation, joy to sorrow, nature to spirit, earthly existence to an illusory heavenly domain, Octavius, unbeknown to him, would experience the *mystery* of matter, in a death/rebirth ritual. As hierophant, his nocturnal moon-world experience would return him to his origins, to the very *principia vitae*. Union with his anima figure, in this case, the hetaera, as muse and fairy figure combined, would reveal secrets to fill his parched notional world with the thrill of inspiration.

Arria Marcella—Hetaera/Fairy. The *hetaera*, or courtesan, associated with Aphrodite worship, was beautiful, entertaining, and charming. Introduced into Greek society by ordinance of Solon, her function was to see to the pleasures of unmarried men, thereby preventing any threat to the structure of marriage.

Upon entering Arria Marcella's room, Octavius saw his *hetaera/fairy* leaning voluptuously on her arm on a *biclinium* (bed for two people). Serenity marked her pale, exquisite features. "Her shoes embroidered with pearls were lying at the foot of the bed, her beautiful naked feet, purer and whiter than marble, were extended to the edge of a light blanket" (*Arria Marcella* 244). Her loosely fitting garment, and her adornments—pearl earrings, a gold necklace, and an ebony-colored headband, a gold and gem-studded arm bracelet in the form of an asp—made Arria Marcella irresistible.

As a *hetaera/fairy*, she filled a psychological void in Octavius's life. She beckoned him to lie beside her on the biclinium. He did so, after which he partook of food brought to him by a servant with an intensity and pleasure previously unknown to him. Arria Marcella's sips of "dark purple wine" brought life-blood back to her pallid cheeks. Octavius, raising his goblet to drink, touched her arm, which he described as icy, "like the skin of a serpent! or the marble of a tomb" (*Arria Marcella* 245). Sensitive to his shocked reaction, Arria recalled to him his visit to the Naples museum, and his soul's instantaneous "leap toward her" despite the fact that her *beingness* appeared to exist only in the petrified ash. Perhaps by way of comforting him, she told him that her soul, "floating about as it did in this world, was invisible to those devoid of inner sight." Nonetheless, she affirmed, "One is truly dead only if one is no longer loved. Your desire to restore my life, and your heart's powerful evocation of me did away with the distances that separated us" (*Arria Marcella* 245).

Uncertain as to what he was experiencing and ignorant as to whether Arria Marcella had come to him in a dream, or whether he had been the "plaything of a vile magical feat," Octavius knew only that she was his first and last love. "May Eros, son of Aphrodite, hear your promise, she said to Octavius, resting her head on his shoulder" (*Arria Marcella* 246) Having for so long remained incarcerated in the icy world of the unloved, Arria yearned for the burning ardor of his embrace.

PLATO'S MEMORY AS RECOLLECTION. How may one explain Octavius's return to a living past? Plato's belief in the transmigration of souls, expressed in terms of memory, distinguishes between two types of excursions into the past: *anamnesis*, a recollection of events experienced in the existential world based on rational recall, comparable to eschatological time; and *mneme*, or "primordial memory," which summons up anterior existences. The latter, identified with cyclical or mythical time is, for Plato, the sign of true wisdom. He writes:

> But if knowledge which we acquired before birth was lost by us at birth, and if afterwards by the use of the senses we recovered that which we previously knew, will not that which we call learning be a process of recovering our knowledge, and may not this be rightly termed recollection by us? . . . . either we had this knowledge at birth, and continued to know through life; or, after birth, those who are said to learn only remember, and, learning is recollection only. (*Phaedo*, trans. Jowett, 210)

Octavius's parapsychological experience may be looked upon as an example of Platonic recollection: the revivifying of some aspect or understanding of an anterior existence. Like Plato, Empedocles too believed in the transmigration of the soul and the continuity of life; in *Purifications* he declared: "I once was a boy, a girl, a bush and a bird, a mute fish in the sea." Similarly, Pythagoras was described as "an extraordinary man of science" because "he saw with ease what he had been ten and twenty human existences back" (Brun, *Empédocles* 187). Pythagoras also believed that, because of the cosmic alliance between numbers, planets, musical rhythms and sonorities, and architecture, the souls of the living and of the world soul enjoy sympathetic correspondences with one another (Brun 23).

Gautier found even greater support for his belief in the notion of reincarnation and in the capacity to return to anterior existences in the Far Eastern and Greek doctrines of the Akasic Record, a brand of mysticism that had also impacted on Goethe. It affirmed that everything that happened on earth and within a human's mind had been indelibly recorded on the Akasa, a type of *ether* believed to encircle the world. If individuals disciplined themselves in the practice of clairvoyance for many years, Astral Light would help them to perceive certain revealing signs within the Akasic Record. To believe in the Akasic Record was to conquer death. According to *Divine Inspiration*, by the eighteenth-century theosophist Dutoit-Membrini, *gnosis* of this nature may be disclosed through a kind of sensorial experience that permits exposure to sidereal influences, thereby laying the foundations for divine inspiration. "Just as the outer core of the body was formed by the powder of the earth," he suggested, so it is prone to the influence of astral substances. Stars and planets have the power to impact strongly on certain individuals, most specifically, "the less impure, and those disengaged of passions," to the point, although rarely, of bringing them to a state of ecstasy. The intuitions thus gleaned may reveal to them not only "astonishing truths," but influences that may determine the outcome of their own existences (Raphael 123; Viatte, *Les Sources occultes du romantisme* I,117f). Analogously, Octavius entered a fourth dimension and succeeded in resurrecting, via certain images and symbols, his hetaera/fairy figure—that eternally appealing, eternally alluring, and eternally fascinating woman.

POLYTHEISM VERSUS MONOTHEISM. Most unexpectedly, just as Octavius and his hetaera/fairy were on the threshold of basking in voluptuous ecstasy, a "severe looking old man" appeared at the door. He was wearing a cross and was dressed like a Nazarene. His face etched with groovelike lines was the result of his prolonged self-inflicted macerations and punishments. There was no doubt in Octavius's mind that he belonged to one of the new sects—the recent disciples of Christ.

A negative father image for Arria Marcella, he epitomized the pain, guilt, and punishment intrinsic to the Christian credo. Octavius, instead, believed in the beauty, form, and balance of personality implicit in Greek understanding. Body and mind for the ancient Greeks were not antagonistic; rather, they worked together as soma and psyche blending into a harmonious whole.

For the Greeks, as for Octavius who rejected his Christian-oriented upbringing and the society it had produced, the universe was peopled with Gods and Goddesses, and heroes, but also with traitors. As concretizations of the inner world of humans, each deity stood out as a reflection or manifestation of an *état d'âme;* each incorporated human qualities and defects. As combinations of carnal and sacred powers, each, like mortals, was the plaything of the Fates, destined to reward people for their good deeds, and punish them for their transgressions.

In Arria Marcella's case, her only *sin*, if one may refer to it in a Christian context, was the hetaera/fairy role she played in life. Understandably, at the sight of the Nazarene, she hid her face under her cloak "as a bird [does] its wing upon facing its enemy" (*Arria Marcella* 247). Castigating her for her "infamous loves," the old man assaults her.

Can't you leave the living alone in their sphere? Your ashes have not yet grown cold since the day you perished under the rain of molten fire from the volcano—and without repenting. Two-thousand years of death have not even calmed you? Your voracious arms attract to your heartless marble breast, the poor and the senseless, inebriated with your love potions. (*Arria Marcella* 247)

With the birth of Christianity, an alteration of focus occurred within society: not beauty and joy, but "weakness, suffering, poverty, and failure [were] given special dignity" (Edinger, *Ego and Archetype* 153). These characteristics, stressed as an aftermath of Christ's credo, were "given supreme representation in the crucifixion itself where God is degradingly scourged and dies the shameful death of the criminal on the cross" (Edinger 153).

The presence of the Nazarene in Arria Marcella's inner chamber sharpened the simmering conflict between Greco-Roman and Christian values. The intrusion of such a negative father image—that of the Nazarene—at the climax of Gautier's story, banished Octavius's new-born feelings of joy, superimposing instead a mood of confusion, fear, and "horror." The Nazarene spewed words of reproach at the couple, calling their love sordid and infamous. As representative of a patriarchal religion for Octavius, he was the harbinger of doctrines of sin, guilt, and "austerity" (*Arria Marcella* 248). Asceticism was his doctrine: self-flagellation and punishment for any inroads into earthly happiness, his path.

Begging the Nazarene to desist from his exhortations, "in the name of this morose religion that was never mine," Arria Marcella affirmed that the ancient Gods "loved life, youth, beauty, and pleasure," and that she refused to be submerged by this credo of "pale nothingness" that the Nazarene was flaunting. Condemning her gods and demons, and execrating her past impieties with her "Asiatic, Roman, and Greek lovers," the Nazarene enjoined her to return Octavius to his century. "Never," replied Arria Marcella. As she spoke, she embraced her stunned lover, her "sparkling eyes, dilated nostrils, trembling lips . . . radiating with a supernatural glow." It was as if she sought to indelibly engrave in his memory the image of this "supreme moment" (*Arria Marcella* 248)

Now addressing Octavius, the Nazarene ordered him to rid himself of this "larva," and not fall victim to her "impure seductive ways" (*Arria Marcella* 248). While the atmosphere tingled with bitterness and rage, the flesh-and-blood individuals participating in this drama seemed to vanish, the struggle being taken up by two cosmic principles: Greek and Christian. Seeking to impose his vision, the adamant Nazarene would have recourse to "great means," that is, to exorcism. Unlike Christ, who had exorcised "many that were possessed with devils, and . . . cast out the spirits with his word" (Matt. 8:16), the Nazarene compelled Arria Marcella to relive the agony she had known when first her body had been cleaved asunder, then burned, by Vesuvius' flaming fire (*Arria Marcella* 249). As for Octavius, the "nocturnal wanderer," he lost consciousness.

The following morning, after Fabio and Max had entered Octavius's hotel room to discover that he had not slept in his bed, thinking that he might have returned to Pompeii to copy a painting, they retraced their steps to the area of the ruins they had visited together the previous day. There they found Octavius in a swoon in one of the rooms in Arrius Diomedes' villa. After awakening, unwilling to share his experience with his friends, Octavius simply told them that he had wanted to see Pompeii by moonlight and he must have fainted. Upon his return to Paris, Octavius, weighted down by feelings of "mournful melancholia," never divulged his secret to anyone, not even to the loving wife he married.

Was Arria Marcella actually a *hetaera/fairy?* Had Octavius's return to a resurrected Pompeii actually occurred? Or had his imagination been activated by a growing interest among European medical practitioners, mystics, and charlatans in the mysteries of the unconscious? We may also ask whether the sophisticated preternatural happenings in Gautier's tale were dreamed or were examples of cryptomnesia? hypnosis? agnosia? somnambulism? Hadn't Arria Marcella made her presence known to Octavius at a time in his life when he was undergoing severe emotional distress and loneliness? Certainly, she, like other fairies and/or miracle workers in French lore, had the capacity to move through time and space to bring a sense of excitement and feelings of well-being to an ailing malcontent.

Could such an excursion/transformation into time past have been possible? Only *time* will tell!

8

COUNTESS SOPHIE DE SEGUR'S ROSETTE
A MANICHEAN MERRY-GO-ROUND!

S OPHIE DE SÉGUR, born Rostopchine (1799–1874), was one of the best-known and most popular writers of fairy tales and of children's literature of her day and ours. Whereas the protagonists in the fairy tales of Perrault, Mme d'Aulnoy, and Georges Sand, among others, were figures who evolved in thought and understanding during their adventures, Mme de Ségur's children were generally unthinking. Rarely did they reason, reflect for themselves, or weigh possibilities for worming their way out of problematic situations. All good or all bad, the two warring Manichean principles constitute the makeup of Mme de Ségur's creations.

Might the negative extremes described in *Rosette* (1856) reflect the psychological bruisings the author herself had undergone as a child? Could her mother's icy personality have induced the young Sophie, unconsciously to be sure, to contemplate inflicting sadistic scenes on her future readers? Even as she preached love and kindness, she would flesh out scenes of hatred and vindictiveness: children subjected to verbal and physical beatings, life-scarring accidents befalling evildoers, and similar calamities. In her narrative, *The Model Little Girls*, a child, Sophie, is beaten so brutally by her stepmother, Mme Fichini, that the birch stick used for the purpose splits in two. Brutalities are cumulative in Mme de Ségur's writing: Mme Fichini having been beaten by her husband, she in turn beats Sophie, and so forth. Mme de Ségur's editors insisted she delete the passage, but the author refused, claiming that such descriptions were based on the true-to-life beatings her mother had administered to her (Diesbach, *La Comtesse de Ségur* 183). The caning scene in *A Good Little Devil* features the inhumane Mme Mac'Miche beating the orphan, Charles, to the point of impairing his walking. When called upon to defend herself before the justice of the peace, she describes the lad as "[b]ad, given to tempers, a liar, lazy, stubborn; finally all vices are his" (Mme de Ségur, *Oeuvres 2*, 1157).

Whether Mme de Ségur understood the psychological and sexual ramifications of the scenes of violence peppering her works (*The Misfortunes of Sophie, The Model Little Girls, Rosette*, etc.) is less than evident; that she derived pleasure from writing these descriptions, experiencing a kind of cleansing of her conscience in so doing, is likewise moot. Nonetheless, the repeated delineations of punishments and cruelties lend moments of great satisfaction to the punishers—or healers of souls—in her penitential scenes.

Corporal punishment certainly was common practice in France at the time but, as entertainment for the young of her day, the lengths to which Mme de Ségur carried episodes of brutal brandishings to extract repentance or gain redemption give the reader pause. A writer's penchant for describing cruelties, particularly toward children, may be a projection of the author's repressed and unconscious sadomasochistic tendencies. Self-identification with the victim or with the aggressor in *The Model Little Girls* or *A Good Little Devil* would allow Mme de Ségur to release onto her victim her anger, hatreds, and unredeemed yearnings, in the misguided unconscious belief that suffering, repentance, atonement, and sacrifice would lead to the child's salvation—ergo, hers.

Let us note in this regard that the word *penance* (L. *poenitencia*, indicating "punishment," "penalty") as, for example, in an act of contrition, although considered a "disease" by the psychoanalyst, was looked upon as a cure by the medieval church. Indeed, "the sacrament of Penance" was believed to be a significant factor in healing ailing souls. Since a "diseased" soul, it was reasoned, needed a "cure," penance became a "medicine for sin." The medieval Flagellants in Camaldoli and Fonte Avellana in Italy, among others in Europe, scourged themselves in public view, at times drawing blood with crooked hooks in an *imitatio Christi* (Cowan, *Masochism, A Jungian View* 19). Moderns may have difficulty understanding "what bloody passion drove these Flagellants, what frenzied desire could reach consummation only in torn flesh and self-degradation" (Cowan 21).

That there is an aesthetics of masochism is evident in "ritualistic—and one might add, artistic and religious fantasies of those who feel that everything must be 'right' to achieve the effect." Theodore Reik indicated that "verbal masochists" derive "titillation" from certain words "which must be spoken with certain emphases and in a certain tone of voice." He continues:

Dialogues during the masochistic phantasy are pretty frequent. Certain accents or expressions are deemed very important, the cadence of a certain sentence is tasted voluptuously. . . . In one case a sentence used by the patient's father—"Be careful you don't do it again"—became the content of such a phantasy scene and had to be repeated again and again with a definite melody. The son, who had to be on his knees, would ask with a certain fearful expression, "May I get up?" (Cowan 54; from T. Reik, *Of Love and Lust* 216)

ECTYPAL ANALYSIS

Born in St. Petersburg, Sophie was the daughter of Count Fiodor Vassilievitch Rostopchine, a charming, well-educated, and enterprising young man on whom a fortune would settle. Empress Catherine II gave her blessing to his marriage with Catherine Petrovna Protassov in 1796, which, according to hearsay, was a love match, at least on his side. The count was impressed by Catherine's fine education and virtuous behavior, and, strangely enough, he was drawn to her haughtiness, inner strength, rigor, and icy demeanor. Disinterested in idle chatter and in socializing merely to while away the time, Catherine spent long hours reading mainly religious literature.

In 1799, the couple moved to Fiodor's father's estate, Voronovo, where Sophie spent much of her childhood. Catherine had to contend with Rostopchine senior, a brutish, debauched, and boorish man. During the long cold winter months, she faced the perils of howling wolves and hungry bears roving dangerously close to the family's palatial home. Count Fiodor, unlike his father, was kind and thoughtful toward his family, and banned any form of corporal punishment to his 1,700 serfs, or "souls," as they were called. Catherine, by contrast, treated her servants and serfs most harshly. Seemingly insensitive to the suffering of others, she was herself a determined individual who walked the straight and narrow path—as she conceived it. When, for example, a smallpox epidemic raged in the area in 1807, many inhabitants feared and refused vaccination. To convince them to be vaccinated, Catherine had her infant, Lise, vaccinated by the village doctor not with the recommended vaccine, but with the living virus taken from a sick child. Although Lise lay close to death for months, she finally did recover (Ergal and Strich, *La Comtesse de Ségur* 82).

Sophie and her siblings had a harsh upbringing: they wore light clothes in winter, slept on hard beds at night, and when the few blankets allotted them proved insufficient, they were allowed to use paper to supplement them. Their food intake was sparse. At times, starved for food and water, Sophie would go to the stables to steal the horses's bread and drink the dog's water, relating some of these happenings in her more or less autobiographical *The Misfortunes of Sophie (Les Malheurs de Sophie)* (Diesbach, *La Comtesse de Ségur* 36).

Whether the Rostopchine family lived in St. Petersburg, Moscow, or Voronovo, tutors were engaged to teach the children. At five years of age, Sophie spoke French, Italian, English, and Russian. Having secretly converted from Russian Orthodoxy to Roman Catholicism in 1806, Catherine felt it incumbent on herself to take charge of her children's religious education. When she finally revealed her conversion to her husband, who considered her act a betrayal of the confidence he had always placed in her, he sobbed, and refused to talk to her for a week. Fiodor's marital relationship henceforth soured (Ergal and Strich 84ff.).

Strangely enough, Catherine's conversion increased her inner rage, bitterness, and bigotry. This misguided ascetic apparently did not know kindness. Conversion had transformed the Countess Rostopchine into "an object of fear and terror." Her granddaughter Lydie wrote that "the devil played a very great role in her conversations," thereby "indicating that they were tightly bound in a very solid friendship, she being aware of his tastes and the manner in which he considered things" (Diesbach 244; from Lydie Rostopchine, *Les Rostopchine* 155).

Sophie was close to her father, whom she saw as a hero. Following his appointment by Czar Alexander I to the post of Governor of Moscow, he ostensibly ordered the evacuation and burning of Moscow the day Napoleon's army marched on the city (Sept. 14, 1812). Nonetheless, it was her mother's presence in her life that formed her personality, accentuating perhaps, via her example, Sophie's incipient despotic, austere, and opinionated manner (Ergal and Strich 124). It has even been speculated that Sophie's conversion to Roman Catholicism in 1815 took place under rather ambiguous circumstances.

By 1815, Count Rostopchine, suffering increasingly from insomnia and nervousness, possibly psychosomatic in origin, decided to travel to Europe, hoping to assuage his emotional distress. So taken was he with Paris that he and his family moved there in 1817. Two years later, Sophie married the handsome Eugène de Ségur (1819) who, despite his dearth of finances, came from an illustrious family, including a grandfather who had held an ambassadorship and had sat in the House of Peers; and an uncle, a general in Napoleon's Great Army who had, coincidentally, participated in the taking of Moscow (Diesbach 91). Although Eugène fathered seven children, he enjoyed many extramarital affairs. Having finally been made aware of her husband's betrayals, Sophie looked to her mother-in-law for comfort, but failed to receive any from the unfeeling lady. Funds being scarce and Sophie finding her cramped Parisian quarters distasteful, she asked for and received from her father 100,000 francs, which she used to buy a castle, "the Nouettes," in Normandy. It was there that she chose to live most of her life.

Her parents, disenchanted with France, moved back to Russia in 1823. Sophie never ceased corresponding with them and with the siblings who had likewise returned to their native land. In time, she learned that despite her sister Lise's refusal to leave the Russian Orthodox Church, their mother, unbeknown to her husband, had her converted *in extremis* on her deathbed in 1824. Because Count Rostopchine, who loved his daughter deeply, had her buried according to Russian Orthodox rites, the mother refused to attend the funeral. Having learned that the Countess Rostopchine had not only taken to beating her servants, but had sent more serfs to Siberia than all the other landowners in the region, the count altered his testament in 1826. In his first will, drawn in 1812, he had left all his possessions to his wife. In accordance with his last will in favor of his son, he not only gave Catherine the minimum required by law, but relieved her of her administrative tasks on the estate as well. Upon the count's death in 1826, the trusted friend appointed as executor of his will freed the house serfs of Voronovo. As for Mme Rostopchine, she refrained from attending her husband's funeral (Diesbach 111). The increasingly religious countess lived on to be detested by those around her, including the remaining serfs whom she brutalized: "[A]ll her love having gone to Christ, nothing remain[ed] for humans" (Diesbach 133). Except, according to Lydie, she found consolation in her pet parrot, "which is understandable," she commented. "An unaffectionate and ungrateful animal, rebellious to all caresses, the parrot understandably takes the place of dogs and cats in this heart which is so dry as to reject caresses, considered something immodest and perverse" (Diesbach 224; from *Les Rostochine* 213).

Albeit to a lesser extent than her mother, Mme de Ségur was intransigeant with those surrounding her and with herself, particularly in matters of religious devotion and personal relationships. One of her closest friends and advisors was the Catholic writer Louis-François Veuillot (1813–1883), a powerful supporter of the pope, and editor in 1843, then editor-in-chief in 1848, of the ultra-Montanist newspaper *The Religious Universe*. Like Mme de Ségur, he despised liberal and lukewarm Catholics, not to speak of heretics. The many books he authored including a biography of Pope Pius IX (1863), *Rome's Perfume* (1865), and *Paris' Odors* (1866), brought him admiration from rightist quarters.

Mme de Ségur, as the mother of eight children—one of whom died in infancy, another who, after having become a priest, went blind, a daughter who became a nun and died of tuberculosis at an early age, and the others, who simply married and bore children—believed she had a great deal to teach young mothers about child care. At fifty-six, she decided to impart to mothers in need her knowledge of simple and inexpensive ways of coping with child-hood diseases. To this end, Mme de Ségur wrote *Children's Health* (1855), which she had printed at her own expense.

In 1852, the publisher Louis Hachette, whose flair for business was highly developed, set up "A Library for Railroads," the concept being that passengers should purchase a book to read on the train. The idea became so popular that, by 1857, he decided to publish for the "Library" Mme de Ségur's *New Fairy Tales for Young Children (Contes de fées pour les petits enfants)*, which she had dedicated to her granddaughters. Many more volumes followed: *The Model Little Girls (Les Petites filles modèles* [1858]), *Memoirs of a Donkey (Mémoires d'un âne* [1860]), *Sophie's Misfortunes (Les Malheurs de Sophie* [1864]), and others, all of which became best-sellers. What came to be known as Mme de Ségur's "Pink Library Collection for Girls," and her religious works such as *The Acts of the Apostles,* (1867) and *A Grandmother's Bible* (1868), were also available to travelers.

Though Mme de Ségur lived mainly on her estate in Normandy, whereas her husband resided in Paris, or at his brother's home, they were not estranged. Love, or attraction for one another, had simply vanished. Following several strokes, Eugène de Ségur died on July 15, 1863. His wife also died from heart problems on February 9, 1874.

ARCHETYPAL ANALYSIS

Since the extremes of Good and Evil are emphasized in her thematics and/or in the actions of her protagonists, Mme de Ségur's writings have been labelled *Manichean*. Imprisoned in a world of extremes, her characters are dominated more by hatred than by love, by sorrow rather than joy, by tears and pain instead of exuberance and pleasure.

For a better understanding of Manichean extremes in Mme de Ségur's work in general, and in *Rosette* in particular, the main doctrine of this religious sect may here be briefly defined. The essence of Manicheanism, a school founded by Mani (216–277 C.E.) in Persia and deeply influenced by Zoroastrian beliefs, lies in the conflict between two cosmic powers: Light (goodness, the spirit of humankind created by God) and Darkness (chaos, evil, Satan, the creator of the body). Christianity, having drawn on Manicheanism and its ancestor, Zoroastrianism, gives us a clue to the dichotomies implicit in Mme de Ségur's fairy tale, as well as to the psychology of the convert. One may better understand why Mme de Ségur passed on to her protagonists the rigidity, asceticism, and sadomasochistic penchants of her mother, Countess Rostopchine.

Seeking punishment on the road to forgiveness, and sacrifice on the way to atonement, the lives of many of her characters revolved around contrition and repentance. Didactic rather than esthetic, her fairy tales reflected her understanding of Roman Catholic values, duties, and social behavior. Her construction of plots and formation of characters were, however, designed not only to edify but to entertain as well.

The Story of Princess Rosette, one of Mme de Ségur's New Fairy Tales, focuses on the overpowering hatred for the newborn Rosette, on the part of a king, queen, and their twin daughters, Orangine (orange toned) and Roussette (Dogfish). Unlike the rest of her family, Rosette had been born good. More importantly, she had a godmother, Fairy Powerful, to protect and to guide her, while her sisters had no one but their parents. Jealous of what they considered Rosette's boon, the twins could not help but despise their younger sister. Her parents' favoritism prompted them to send the newborn away, to be cared for by a nurse in the country, where Rosette spent the first fifteen years of her life in joy, contentment, love, and serenity. Her total faith in her nurse made her secure in the knowledge that strict obedience would bring her happiness. Her parents sent the nurse small sums of money for the child's upkeep, but they never invited her to visit them, never inquired about her, never provided for her education. Had it not been for Fairy Powerful, who supplied tutors to teach the child how to read, write, sing, and speak foreign languages, the child would have remained illiterate. Rosette's innate goodness, kindness, and love for her nurse and for Fairy Powerful were so complete that never was there a need to scold, reprimand, or punish her. Nor did she at any time long to see the parents she had never known.

THE REJECTED CHILD. Rejected children frequently bear grudges, develop hatreds and phobias, and are prone to aggressive behavior. In Rosette's case no flaws or irritants altered her complacent and accepting disposition. Never having experienced sorrow and suffering, however, she was unversed in conflict and decision making, which are crucial to the maturation process. By obeying her loving nurse unquestioningly, never pondering the outcome of her commands or the ethics involved, and, even more significantly, by heeding Fairy Powerful's wise counsel blindly, she remained perfectly secure and steady in her daily existence. She lived out Voltaire's "best of all possible worlds." Not required to reason, choose or dispute, Rosette would continue to be cared for, and remain out of harm's way, simply by obeying, or, in terms of religious dogma, by performing the required rituals.

That questions of ethics were never broached during the first fifteen years of Rosette's life is understandable in view of the child's place in the home in the nineteenth century. But that no questions on any subject were ever posed or discussed reveals that instant obedience to adult directives was Mme de Ségur's rule of thumb. Such placidity or, as one might define it, inactivity of a child's reasoning powers, may be considered stultifying, even dangerous, at the age of fifteen. Obstacled in her understanding of life, Rosette lived in a world of "childish illusion," suggesting that her unconscious was nonfunctional. As Jung wrote:

> Psychology can no longer afford childish illusions of this kind; it must ensue the truth and declare that unconsciousness is not only no excuse but is actually one of the most heinous sins. Human law may exempt it from punishment, but Nature avenges herself the more mercilessly, for it is nothing to her whether a man is conscious of his sin or not. We even learn from the parable of the unjust steward that the Lord praised his servant who kept a false account because he had "done wisely," not to speak of the (expurgated) passage in Luke 6, where Christ says to the defiler of the Sabbath: "Man, if indeed thou knowest what thou doest, thou art blessed: but if thou knowest not, thou art accursed and a transgressor of the law." (Jung 10, #676)

What Jung suggested in the above quotation was his belief that the more an individual develops his or her consciousness, the more meaningful that person's life experience becomes. The fifteen-year-old Rosette received a proper education thanks to Fairy Powerful, but she learned by rote. Never had she been taught the art or science of reasoning, probing, and thinking. Rarely does obedience alone give rise to consideration of ethical principles.

THE MESSENGER. Seated on a bench in front of her house one day, Rosette was approached by a man in braided uniform who asked to speak to Princess Rosette. Having identified herself, she was handed a letter from the king, her father, informing her that her sisters, now eighteen years of age, were ready for marriage. Princes and princesses had been invited from distant lands to choose husbands for her twin sisters. The family felt that she, at fifteen, was old enough to attend the parties. The king would send for her in eight days and she would spend three days at the castle. "I won't send you money for your dresses," the king wrote, "because I have spent a great deal on those for your sisters; besides which, no one will look at you, so dress as you wish" (*Rosette* 101).

Delighted at the thought of meeting her parents and sisters, attending the parties, and then returning home, Rosette ran to her beloved nurse who decided she should wear the white percale dress she saved for feast days. Observing that what was appropriate for the country was not necessarily so for palace balls, the nurse spent the following days freshening the dress as best she could. She then packed everything Rosette would need for her journey in a small wooden chest, including some flowers to ornament her hair.

No sooner had the nurse closed the chest than Fairy Powerful appeared on the scene to examine the clothes Rosette would be taking to the parties. Upon glancing at them, a smile came over her face: "I want my Rosette's wardrobe to create a sensation: these clothes are not worthy of her" (*Rosette* 102). Opening a small bottle, she sprinkled three drops of liquid on the packed garments which, surprisingly, were transformed into the ugliest of ragged clothes. She then placed in the chest a necklace of nuts and bracelets garnished with dried beans, after which she kissed the shocked Rosette and vanished. Whereupon, the nurse and Rosette burst into tears, the former suggesting that Rosette not attend the festivities, claiming illness as an excuse, but the young girl was confident that her future visit to her parents' castle would turn out well. Putting her wardrobe out of mind, she went to bed and fell asleep.

OBEDIENCE AND TRUST IN FAIRY POWERFUL. The uncalled-for rejection and fifteen-year-long separation of a child from its parents marks an abnormal psychological situation from the very start of Mme de Ségur's fairy tale. What made the king and queen so protective of their older, perhaps less beautiful twin daughters that they rejected the infant of their own flesh for so many years? Why did her sisters rebuff her? Heartless rigidity? Anger? Rage? Jealousy? Guilt? Envy? A blend of all may perhaps have been functional in their psyches.

Having been denied a real mother for unknown reasons, Rosette spent her early life with a kind and loving nurse who answered her innate need for love. That she had never attempted to fathom the reasons for her rejection is, nonetheless, strange. Acceptance, obedience, and faith remained her commandments. And why not? The nurse fulfilled the biological mother's role to perfection, responding to Rosette's craving for love and tenderness. Another protective device was Fairy Powerful whose name, onomastically, conformed to her infallibility in making everything wonderful happen to the girl, as long as blind obedience and submission were forthcoming. Had Rosette not been a fairy tale figure, the path of such a "mindless" child would have been paved with danger. George Sand or Mme d'Aulnoy would not have proposed such a passive behavioral pattern for the characters in their fairy tales. Deleterious inactivity, nonparticipation, send the wrong message to young readers.

As a savior figure, Fairy Powerful is a force for the good: uncorruptible, knowing what is best for Rosette, and like a personal mother, she wants her obedient child to reap all of life's joys.

INTRANSIGENCE: THE PSYCHOLOGY OF THE CONVERT. The intransigence and extremism implicit in many of Ségur's characters are not unknown among converts. Indeed, Jung suggested that at the outset of a change of religious allegiance, the proselyte has a tendency toward fanaticism. Since the emotional aftereffects of the rituals and beliefs of his or her former religious persuasion have not as yet been completely "relinquished, [they have] merely disappeared into the unconscious, where [they are] constantly at work as a counter-irritant" to his or her newly chosen religion. For this reason, new converts frequently feel obliged to "defend fanatically" their new credo. The same may be said, writes Jung, of the "paranoiac, who feels compelled to defend himself against all external criticism, because his delusional system is too much threatened from within" (Jung 3, #462).

It follows that compensating powers breaking into consciousness are frequently distorted. What is of no further use, the convert reasons, is discarded from consciousness. Nonetheless, the transfer into new but uncontrollable subliminal spheres is not so simple. "Such material includes all those forgotten infantile fantasies which have ever entered the minds of men, and of which only legends and myths remain" (Jung 3, # 463).

Mme de Ségur's either/or—Manichean—approach to life had become her reality. Never did she waver from the straight and narrow path. For her, rigidity, predictability, punishment, and hurt always preceded redemption.

> And labour, working with our own hands: being reviled, we bless; being persecuted, we suffer it:
> Being defamed, we intreat: we are made as the filth of the world, and are the off scouring of all things unto this day. (I Corinthians 4: 12-13)

That terrible emotional stresses occur in the life process is a truism; the extremes to which Mme de Ségur carried suffering and punishments into the fabric of her writings verged in many instances, including *Rosette*, on the pathological. Hope for the individual was always a possibility, for the Fall, in keeping with Christian doctrine, did not destroy "man," but only "deformed" or "corrupted" him. Thus, his restoration was possible "through God's grace"and through devout comportment.

Unlike the protagonists of Perrault and Mme d'Aulnoy, the all-good Rosette, as previously mentioned, never had to think out her every move during her moments of trial; nor, therefore, could she even begin to understand or seek to probe the reasons for her banishment from the world of her parents. We might go a step farther and suggest that because she had not been endowed with an *anima rationalis*, she never suffered the split of her personality required to even set out on the individuation process. Her despicable other half, however, having become manifest in her parents and her sisters, functioned at high power! (Jung 11, #71).

ROSETTE'S ARRIVAL AT COURT: THE FIRST DAY. Having covered in two hours the six leagues separating the child's farmhouse from the king's domain, Rosette was surprised that her parents were not there to greet her. Instead, a page took her into a small building the back way, through long dark corridors, and up multiple staircases, to a tiny and sparsely furnished servant's garret room. Embarrassed by the paltriness of the quarters assigned to Rosette, the page explained that the other rooms had been reserved for royal guests. She then asked the page most "timidly" to see the queen. She could do so, he responded, at the reception. Meanwhile, he added, he would call for her in two hours. The uncomplaining Rosette opened her chest of clothes, combed her long blond hair, which she then arranged beautifully, and donned her ragged clothes and country boots. Looking at herself in the mirror, she was stunned at the sight! Her dress was now of gold brocade embroidered with rubies; her boots, of white satin with ruby buckles; her stockings, of the finest silk; and her necklace and bracelet, of radiant rubies and diamonds. Overjoyed, she thanked her Fairy Powerful for having rewarded her so lavishly (*Rosette* 107).

When Rosette made her appearance at the magnificent reception given by the king and queen, all eyes were fixed on the unknown girl. The king looked at her with "comic surprise," and asked: "You are probably a great queen or a great fairy . . . whose unexpected presence here is both an honor and pleases us greatly" (*Rosette* 108). Bowing before her father, she told him she was his daughter, Rosette. The shocked queen responded: "Rosette, you are more richly attired than I have ever been!" (*Rosette* 108). Who gave her the magnificent dress and jewels? she inquired. Rosette responded candidly that it had been her fairy godmother. After curtsying, she requested permission to kiss her mother's hand and to meet her sisters. The queen extended her hand perfunctorily, and the sisters greeted her disdainfully. No sooner had Rosette tried to embrace them than they backed away for fear she might smudge their makeup. Orangine had had to apply her powder thickly in order to hide her yellow skin; as for Roussette, she used a great deal of rouge to cover her freckles.

Rosette now found herself surrounded by many ladies and princes of the court who were duly impressed by her fine education and her ability to speak several languages. The more she was feted, the more her family's jealousy mounted. What most disturbed them was King Charming's visible attraction for Rosette. Indeed, he who headed the most beautiful and largest kingdom of them all seated himself next to Rosette at dinner and remained at her side in rapt attention.

Following the repast, Orangine and Roussette proposed that the three sisters each sing a solo. Since Rosette had been brought up on a farm, they took it for granted that she would not have learned this art. Hoping to humiliate her, and thereby attract suitors to themselves, the sisters decided they would perform first. Not only did Orangine and Roussette sing beautifully; they accompanied themselves on the harp with dexterity, and were loudly applauded for their efforts. What they did not know was that Rosette had been taught music and was an accomplished performer. No sooner had she begun singing and playing the harp than the sisters, aware of her superior musicianship, almost fainted from spite. "Transported with admiration," King Charming approached Rosette with tears in his eyes, and verbalized his emotions: "charming and amiable princess, never have I heard a voice as pleasurable to my ears. I would be happy to hear you again" (*Rosette* 111).

Aware of her sisters' jealousy, Rosette, complaining of fatigue, excused herself and retired. King Charming, having intuited the real reason for her departure, admired her the more for her sensibility. Once in her room, Rosette removed her magnificent attire, placed it carefully in the chest, and although she was distressed by her parents' coldness and her sisters's jealousy, the image of King Charming in her mind's eye effaced all traces of sorrow. Whereupon, she went to sleep immediately.

Rosette's magnificent clothes, her *persona*, was an externalization of what would only later become visible: her hidden inner beauty, refinement, and inborn elegance. More and more guests found themselves gravitating to this *puella*, dazzled at first by her outward beauty, not yet discerning her purity of character. One may aver that Rosette's magnificent attire had, paradoxically, unmasked her inner being. By contrast, her sisters' wealth, their costly gowns, their expertly applied makeup, served to mask the contaminants festering within their unhealthy psyches.

JEALOUSY AND THE HATRED FIXATION. Psychoanalytically speaking, fixations (L. *fixus*, from *figere*, to fasten, to secure, to make firm, stable, or stationary)—hatred or love attachments—usually imply a pathological condition: "persistence of the libidinal or aggressive cathexis of an object of infancy or childhood into later life" (Campbell, *Psychiatric Dictionary* 286). Such a condition suggests that "the amount of energy retained at the infantile level is greater than is seen in the normal person, who never fully abandons an object or mode of gratification that was strongly connected with psychic energy" (Campbell 286). A relatively normal person may still retain earlier levels of gratification, but may concentrate upon higher levels of psychic energy as well. In *Rosette*, a persistent concentration at earlier levels of psychic energy predisposed the royal couple and their twin daughters to obvious neurotic or nerve function disorders (Campbell 475).

The family's fixated hatred, as related to aggression, may be identified with a desire to destroy, as in the death instinct. Instinct predominates, consciousness never having the power to intrude in order to teach adaptation or normalization of behavioral patterns. Hatred, envy, and rejection, as experienced by the king, queen, and the twins, like other fixations functioned as "unconscious blind emotionality" with regard to Rosette (Franz, *Shadow and Evil in Fairy Tales* 271).

From the very outset of Rosette's visit to her family, hatred was manifested by her parents' uncontrollably hostile desire to humiliate her by lodging her in a garret room, thus segregating her from what they feared might *contaminate* or displace their power and prestige. Gradually, the family's aggressivity increased; the twins resorted to humiliation, as in the singing episode. So imperiled did they feel by their inability to destroy—even kill—her to achieve their ends, that their *ardor* or *libido* increasingly fixated on what appeared to be the threatening agent (Campbell 20).

As for Rosette, since neither an increase in consciousness, nor a driving force for sublimation or individuation were manifest, she remained a *puella aeterna* throughout her stay at the palace, and no doubt throughout her life. Never probing her joy—not even King Charming's attraction for her—never questioning the orders given her by Fairy Powerful, Rosette continued to proceed by rote, passively, allowing herself to be manipulated.

STRATEGIES FOR DESTRUCTION. Enraged by Rosette's success at court, the twins blamed their father as the cause of their humiliation. The king protested that it was not he who had recalled Rosette; it was, rather, Fairy Powerful. Jealous and unable to see themselves as they were, the twins rationalized erroneously that Rosette's attraction lay in her breathtaking fineries. Why had their parents not provided them, too, with similar dresses and jewels? Or with a fairy godmother? In the latter's defense, the queen revealed to them that Fairy Powerful had chosen Rosette as her godchild. In an attempt to calm the dissension, the father decided to alter his strategy by focusing on the elimination of the irritant, namely, Rosette, thereby making it impossible for King Charming ever to see her again. In complete accord, the queen would see to the removal of her fineries and then her immediate return to the farm, where she would remain for the rest of her life.

Whereupon Fairy Powerful threatened in thunderous tones, audible only to the family, that if Rosette were not kept at the castle and allowed to attend the receptions, the king, queen, and the twins would be the targets of her *anger*. Revealing her *shadow* or destructive side for the first time, Fairy

Powerful warned the parents further that, if they countered her command, they would be transformed into frogs, and their "detestable" daughters into vipers. Terrified by her words, but still harboring rage in their hearts, they complied with Fairy Powerful's orders.

THE SECOND DAY. Wishing to be alone during her magical clothing metamorphosis, Rosette dismissed the servant sent by her parents to help her dress for the hunting party. As she looked for the ebony case that contained her magnificent wardrobe, she found instead an old box with the written message "wear the clothes you had brought from the farm" (*Rosette* 115). Having donned them, she combed her hair, looked into the mirror and to her astonishment saw herself garbed in the "richest" of blue velvet riding habits adorned with pearl buttons. When the time came to leave her room, the page knocked at her door and whispered into her ear: "Rosette, don't ride any other horse but the one that King Charming will give you," after which he accompanied her to her parents (*Rosette* 116). Rosette's initial concern was transformed into joy when, moments later, King Charming asked if he could be her protector during the forest hunt. The page then led her toward a beautiful black horse. In Plato's image in *Phaedrus,* the black horse represented ubridled destructive instinct. In Rosette's case, had destiny not intervened, the black horse would have meant her demise. King Charming, knowing the animal to be wild and unruly, warned her not to mount it. Although there is significant doubt that Mme de Ségur had ever read Plato's *Phaedrus,* an analogy with this dialogue is nonetheless in order.

In Plato's myth, the soul was divided into three parts: a charioteer, representing *reason*; a white horse, representing good ("lover of honor, modesty, and temperance, and follower of true glory . . . guided by word and admonition"); and a dark horse ("the mate of insolence and pride . . . hardly yielding to blow or spur"), a paradigm of evil (*Works of Plato* 413). One may suggest that the white horse was sensitive and reasoned, and thus represented order and clarity of purpose, while the black one, dominated by impulses, unconscious urges, and instincts, was vowed to destruction. The question now remains as to which horse Rosette would choose? Would it be the black one the page had been ordered to bring her? Since the page had forewarned her in secret, as had King Charming, the obedient girl again followed her true and tried behavioral pattern: she waited patiently for King Charming to bring her another horse.

The beauty of the handsome snow-white horse that was now brought to her was enhanced by its blue velvet saddle embroidered with pearls. As she was about to mount it, the horse knelt before her, rising only after she had seated herself firmly on the saddle. King Charming mounted his horse, and when the king and queen saw them ride away together, their hostility surged insanely. Setting themselves apart from the others, Rosette and King Charming chose a secluded forested area in which to ride, then to walk, basking in the serenity of Mother Nature's protection. It was here that she decided to tell him about the farm on which she had been raised and about her nurse and fairy godmother, while King Charming listened with "tender compassion" (*Rosette* 120).

The bejeweled gown worn by Rosette that evening created the effect of the sun bursting forth in the reception hall. Indeed, she was surely a personification of Gnostic radiance and light. King Charming focused his attention exclusively on her, which increased the royal family's rage. Somewhat naively, he failed to understand her family's dastardly treatment of Rosette, but wishing to spare her more distress, he sought her advice as to when it would be appropriate to ask her father for her hand. Rosette promised to seek counsel from Fairy Powerful.

That evening, the twins, with ten years of dancing lessons behind them, and seeking again to humiliate Rosette, performed their twirls with expertise, after which they insisted that their younger sister perform as well. Aware of Rosette's unwillingness to do so, King Charming offered himself as her dance partner. Should she be uncertain of her steps, he would lead her, he whispered. The two danced with such grace and lightness of step that the audience could not contain its admiration. So agonized were the two sisters by Rosette's success that they fainted outright; on their faces, the marks of envy and rage served to intensify their inherent ugliness.

The same night, Rosette drew from an ivory sculpted case with turquoise nails another magnificent dress with appropriate jewels. Fairy Powerful now advised her how she should answer King Charming's marriage offer: "Because I wanted you to meet King Charming, I forced your father to invite you to the castle" (*Rosette* 125). Everything having been prearranged, she was to accept his proposal. Once in bed, Rosette felt two "maternal and protective" kisses on her cheeks, and fell asleep in complete serenity.

MATERNAL AND PROTECTIVE FAIRY GODMOTHER. Fairies usually use their good magic to protect the downtrodden, no matter their ilk, from oncoming conflicts or disasters. As Franz explained:

> Mankind has always used [good magic] against the onslaught of the destructive powers of evil and psychotic dissolving impulses from the unconscious. There is nothing to be said against it, except that, through this, the conflict is not fully suffered and therefore there is no conscious realization of what it is all about. (Franz, *Individuation in Fairy Tales* 88)

The magical powers or inner voices Rosette had heard throughout her life in moments of crisis, while representing psychological activity, did not, as previously mentioned, gird her with any inner armor of her own. Incapable of deploying any defenses, as in battle, or as in searching for purpose, she never developed nor evolved. Rather, she lived in a condition of emotional stasis. Her robotlike behavioral patterns helped her deal with the problems at hand and parried immediate dangers, but did not stave off future on-slaughts of cruelty. She embedded herself more and more deeply in her pro-tective, idyllic, paradisaic domain, even as the king, queen, and the twins retreated ever more monomaniacally into their stereotypes.

Rosette's fairy godmother was named Powerful (Low Latin, *potere,* to be able), indicating someone in control, in possession, an authority figure. She was endowed not with a highly developed consciousness, but a highly devel-oped *conscience.* Thus, Rosette was the ideal patient for this expert practi-tioner of magic. As Jung explained:

> Magic exercises a *compulsion* that prevails over the conscious mind and will of the victim: an alien will rises up in the bewitched and proves stronger than his ego. The only comparable effect capable of psychological verifica-tion is that exerted by unconscious contents, which by their compelling power demonstrate their affinity with or dependence on man's totality, that is, the self and its "karmic" functions. (Jung 911, 216)

Like a seasoned puppeteer, Fairy Powerful knew just how to direct Rosette's every move, every thought, every feeling. As a higher principle, or guiding force, she extracted complete obedience for her services. Fairy Power-ful conducted Rosette toward a happy destiny, but did not succeed, nor even try, in establishing a connection between her godchild's conscious and/or un-conscious domains. Rosette's understanding of morality was split, revealing a severe personality dissociation. Good veered to the right, and evil to the left—with no mutual concession, no uniting, no reconciliation.

THE THIRD AND LAST DAY. A single strategy was left the royal family: to kill Rosette. Since a chariot race was to take place on the third day, king, queen, and twins were determined that the two horses chosen to draw Rosette's car-riage would be so uncontrollable that they would infallibly cause, if not Rosette's death, then at least her disfiguration. Another superb riding outfit awaited Rosette for her participation in the chariot race. It was embroidered with diamonds, emeralds, sapphires, opals as large as eggs, and a hat gar-nished with white velvet decorated with feathers of a thousand colors.

In the great hall, King Charming was impatiently awaiting her and Fairy Powerful's answer to his marriage proposal. Rosette was told to follow the dictates of her heart, and she did, adding that she would "consecrate her life to him as he would give his to her" (*Rosette* 128). Prompted by Fairy Powerful's admonition that if they did not marry as soon as possible Rosette's life would be in danger, King Charming was determined to ask the king for Rosette's hand that very day following the chariot race. Mysteriously, Fairy Powerful added: "I will not be able to watch over her for eight days, beginning at sundown tonight" (*Rosette* 129).

Wisely, King Charming henceforth was never to leave his beloved's side. When the time came for her to step into the chariot her mother had ordered for her, he was there once again to restrain her, warning her that the horses chosen for her chariot were so fierce that they could barely be held in place by the four strong grooms in charge of them. At that very instant, a small chariot of mother-of-pearl drawn by two beautiful white horses appeared before Rosette. Not knowing whether it was another trap set by her family, King Charming hesitated before allowing Rosette to step into it, but he propitiously heard Fairy Powerful's voice confirming the safety of both the horses and the carriage. A moment of terror did occur during the trajectory, however, when a massive chariot driven by a veiled woman collided with Rosette's. Had it not been constructed by fairies, Rosette's chariot would surely have been destroyed, and Rosette crushed. Instead, the heavy chariot was *magically* overthrown, and the veiled lady ejected from it. Rosette, recognizing Orangine immediately, now that her veil was torn and she was lying on a pile of stones, instincively wanted to help her, but the voice of Fairy Powerful commanded her to remain inside her chariot. Seconds later, another massive chariot hurtled her way, and its driver, Roussette, suffered her sister's fate. Immediately, King Charming jumped into Rosette's carriage and, having been told by Fairy Powerful that Rosette "has to be in your kingdom before nightfall," drove away (*Rosette* 130).

And so it went. Rosette arrived safely at King Charming's kingdom, thanks to Fairy Powerful's wise advice and to her beloved's dexterity in driving at high speeds to avoid her father's murderous henchmen sent in pursuit of his daughter. King Charming's courtiers greeted the couple with joy, and Rosette was shown an apartment furnished in the finest of taste. Fairy Powerful reiterated the need for haste—every minute diminishing the power of which she would be divested for an eight-day period. The reception preceding the nuptials having been *miraculously* or *magically* prepared prior to their arrival, the lovers celebrated their marriage in the chapel with only one hour to spare.

DID FAIRY POWERFUL'S PUNISHMENT FIT THE CRIME? How could Mme de Ségur—in the guise of Fairy Powerful—not carry out her inborn penchant for destruction, humiliation, and cruel punishment of the evil forces in her fairy tales? The moment of retribution had arrived, and she would take full advantage of it to cut her victims down to size.

If we measure the wickedness of the twins by the ugliness of their personae, it comes as no surprise that while the lacerations on their faces resulting from their accidents during the chariot race had healed, and might have disappeared, Fairy Powerful chose to have the scars remain in full view and at all times as physical reminders of the twins' spiritual disfigurement. So, too, were their once-elegant clothes transformed into those of lowly farm servants, thereby teaching them humility via humiliation. That they were awarded brutal grooms as husbands, "whose mission was to beat them and mistreat them until they experienced a change of heart, which [would] probably never take place," was to inflict on them the experience of a Christian hell (*Rosette* 134).

To have the king and queen transformed into "beasts of burden," to have them ordered to fulfill demeaning and demanding tasks, and to have them assigned to horrific masters, was to consign them to an earthly hell. Thus they would be, Fairy Powerful evidently believed, *expiating* their villainous acts through hard labor and mortification. "I neither want to nor must I pardon wicked people whose heart is vicious and incorrigible" (*Rosette* 134). The only consolation for this formerly royal couple would be biting and/or kicking each other, allowing them, she perhaps believed, to vent their rage, and thus expel their aggressions. That they were ordered to bring their masters to Rosette's wedding ceremony was perhaps the most venal of all punishments.

Like Ixion, who had been fastened to a wheel that turned endlessly, or Sisyphus, who had been ordered to roll a stone to the top of a steep hill only to see it roll down into the valley the next day, so Rosette's parents and sisters were sentenced to equally ignominious tortures. Would these punishments change their characters? As Fairy Powerful noted: "They were supposed to return to their original form once their hearts had changed. It is said that they remained as they were for six thousand years" (*Rosette* 136). Within the parameters of Fairy Powerful's abilities, she had functioned to the enhancement of good. "I have just punished each in keeping with what they deserved," she maintained (*Rosette* 133).

Fairy Powerful generously transported the farm on which Rosette had spent the first fifteen years of her life to the park adjacent to King Charming's castle, thereby allowing Rosette to see her nurse on a daily basis. Also brought to the castle were the ebony and ivory cases containing the gowns and jewels Rosette had worn on those memorable days when she met King Charming, with whom she lived in harmony and in tender love for the rest of their lives.

Fairy Powerful made one request of King Charming: never must he disclose to his bride the kind of punishment she had meted out to Rosette's family. Such secrecy on Fairy Powerful's part suggests unconscious feelings of shame at keeping her godchild's parents enslaved and in bondage. King Charming kept his secret: when Rosette inquired about her sisters' well being, he simply told her that they were married, and that she need not worry about their welfare. That she never again asked about her family comes as no surprise, since she had never before questioned anyone's order, act, or advice. Closure on a disturbing past had been effected.

The reasons forwarded for the punishments of the evildoers in Mme de Ségur's fairy tale are to a certain extent valid, but the sado-masochistic aspects are not. Fairy Powerful's cruelties revealing the unredeemed *shadow* side of her personality is reminiscent of a denatured mother figure, or of those old-time hangmen who, inured to daily executions, rationalized that the punishment fit the crime. Was Fairy Powerful, as Mme de Ségur's spokesperson, seeking to reenact her own mother's deprivations, humiliations, beatings, and hurts and thereby exact retribution from her evil protagonists? Was she so bound to the idea of penance, contrition, and mortification as cure-alls for sins, which, in her and her protagonists' cases, cured nothing?

What is of great interest are the reasons why Mme de Ségur divested Fairy Powerful of her magical capabilities for eight days—not as a punishment, but rather as a preventive measure. This indicates the lower place Fairy Powerful occupied within the supernatural or divine hierarchy, for the limitation makes it quite plain that a distinction had to be made between the former's finite capabilities and God's infinite powers. Understood psychologically, such a restriction prevented an all-too-human and frequent sense of *hubris*, or arrogance, that takes possession of individuals after knowing fame and joy. Mme de Ségur was simply warning readers that even Fairy Powerful was fallible. Children particularly, for whom this tale was written, must be alerted to the ups and downs of destiny.

With the animalization of the king and queen, and the debasement and suffering inflicted on their twin daughters, Fairy Powerful/Mme de Ségur had, unbeknown to her, launched another round in the "phenomenon of evil." She did not cure bad consciences; rather, the evil deeds remained in the unconscious, unrecognized by the doers for six thousand years (Franz, *Shadow and Evil* 169). The cruel punishments did nothing to alter the personalities of Rosette's persecutors. In certain cases, kindness and generosity may further *consciousness* in the evildoers, leading in some cases to an enhancement of their thinking processes. Similarly, Rosette's attitude of blind obedience to her fairy godmother and her innate kindness, which was as extreme as was her sisters's viciousness, were noxious in that they led to the deprivation of any and all capacity to reason.

The sage advice given by Fairy Powerful to Rosette throughout her early years, and to King Charming prior to his marriage, embodied Mme de Ségur's own inner voice: her extreme capacity for good, and its opposite, evil. Both good and evil existed in Mme de Ségur's character, but unfortunately, it may be suggested, no connection between the two was made in her psyche. Rosette pursued her one-sided paradisaic life with King Charming, and her parents and sisters continued their painful destinies for more than six thousand years, thereby leading to the continuous fixity of rigid polarities, and to an unalterable condition of stasis. As reflections of their author's unbending and limited understanding of both her religion and of humanity's behavioral patterns, her protagonists were the recipients of her genes as well.

Like robots, each character reacted automatically, and thoughtlessly, sweeping reflection and interiorization by the board. Acts and reactions, like simple mathematical problems, were beaten down, as if by *polichinelle's* stick, resulting in an artificial construct—puppets enacting the directives of the almighty puppeteer—the author.

Mme de Ségur's "crippled creatures," endowed with "schizophrenic personalities" and singleness of purpose, were simplistic in their onesidedness. They would continue *ad infinitum* to pursue the sameness of course—through eternity. But perhaps sameness is a fact of life? Has humanity really altered its course? Are not evil and good still potent forces with which individuals must—but mainly fail to—reckon? But then, hadn't these polarities been willed in the beginning, when God created the angel *Lucifer.* (L. *lux + ferre,* meaning light bringer)?

As Jung wrote:

Myths and fairytales give expression to unconscious processes, and their retelling causes these processes to come alive again and be recollected, thereby reestablishing the connection between conscious and unconscious. What the separation of the two psychic halves means, the psychiatrist knows only too well. He knows it as dissociation of the personality, the root of all neuroses: the conscious goes to the right and the unconscious to the left. As oppposites never unite at their own level *(tertium non datur!)*, a supraordinate "third" is always required, in which the two parts can come together. And since the symbol derives as much from the conscious as from the unconscious, it is able to unite them both, reconciling their conceptual polarity through its form and their emotional polarity through its numinosity. (Jung 9 11, #280)

9

GEORGE SAND'S THE CASTLE
OF CROOKED PEAK
THE TOPOGRAPHY OF
MEMORY MANIPULATION

EORGE SAND'S MOTHER referred to her daughter's earliest "literary attempts" as the outpourings of a highly emotional child "whose passion for inventing tales seemed endless and dull." Not in the least mortified, Sand simply assured her mother that her future writings would not be "pedantic," but would convey her feelings in the simplest of ways (Sand, *Oeuvres autobiographiques* I, 808). Her grandmother, by contrast, eager to learn about the marvels constellated in a child's world, encouraged Sand's creative efforts, but since she was a rationalist, she "would have demolished," Sand wrote later, "without remorse and pitilessly, the entire enchanted edifice of my imagination" (Sand I, 630).

ECTYPAL ANALYSIS

Born in 1804—the year Napoleon was crowned Emperor of France—George Sand lived through the glories and ignominies of the Empire, the revolution of 1848, the 1851 coup d'etat, the rule of Napoleon III, the 1870 Franco-Prussian War, and the proclamation of the Third Repubic. She died in 1876. With the downfall of the aristocracy and the growth of the bourgeoisie during her tumultuous era, wealth replaced rank, not only accentuating the already potently forceful effects of the Industrial Revolution, but creating as

245

well an industrial proletariat with its increasingly urgent and excoriating problems. A century fraught with difficulties, it struggled with France's hope of living in peaceful coexistence with its European neighbors and its attempt to find, if not a solution, at least ways of relieving the economic suffering of its masses.

Creatively, as previously noted, the entire nineteenth century was Romantic in its outlook, thrust, syntax, and vocabulary. Hadn't Victor Hugo in one of his more flamboyant phrases uttered: "Je mis un bonnet rouge au vieux dictionnaire"? Inspiration and affectivity led the way for genius! Even as the century grew older, and more cerebral Parnassians, Symbolists, Positivists, and Actional Naturalists held sway, it still remained Romantic. Utopians, visionaries, and mystics in multiple disciplines—literature, economics, politics, religion, esthetics—absorbed and haunted the thoughts of writers, composers, and artists. Sand was no exception.

As participant in, or simply bystander of, some of the philosophical schools emerging in nineteenth-century France only to vanish a short time later, Sand sang out her own unique hymns to life, joy, sorrow, nature, and love. Her writings, the scholar Ernest Renan wrote, "are the echo of our century." Endowed with a vibrant, independent, and passionate personality, she indulged in many amorous adventures, the best known being her involvements with Musset, Chopin, Mérimée, and, probably, Marie Dorval. Her numerous friends counted illustrious figures such as Balzac, Nodier, Hugo, Sainte-Beuve, Michelet, Flaubert, Dumas fils, Fromentin, Liszt, Meyerbeer, Berlioz, Chopin, Turgeniev, la Malibran, and Pauline Viardot.

A feminist in dress and in heart, Sand preached not only psychological and economic independence for women, but love of humankind as well. Although entranced by an ever-renewed world of illusion, she was also in touch with the realities of life. A composite of both empirically and spiritually oriented worlds, she often injected into her protagonists her own aspirations, torments, and joys, underscoring these in verbally painted images set in dramatic sequences. Alexandre Dumas conveyed his feelings for his friend in verbal images: "A daylight somnambulist, she wanders, looks, listens, without really knowing what she has accomplished. . . . At night, this woman restores to the world of soul and spirit everything she has received from the invisible material world" (Dumas, Preface to the *Fils naturel*).

Author of novels, short stories, essays, plays, and autobiographical works, Sand also created sensitive and charmingly disarming fairy tales, one of which, *The Castle of Crooked Peak*, was published in *Tales of a Grandmother (Contes d'une grand'mère)*, a volume, written expressly for her beloved grandchildren, Aurore (Lolo), born in 1866, and Gabrielle (Titite), born in 1868 (Sand, *Histoire de ma vie* II, ch. 12 and XV).

What emerges in Sand's remarkably penetrating fairy tale, *The Castle of Crooked Peak* (1873), is the protagonist's attempt to acquire wholeness of personality. For a better understanding of this work, significant references to the author's life will be introduced into our text. George Sand (Aurore Dupin) was the daughter of Sophie de Laborde, a loving and charming grisette, and Maurice Dupin de Franceuil, who traced his lineage back to Frederic Auguste de Saxe, King of Poland. During the course of a successful army career, Maurice was sent to Milan where he met his wife-to-be, Sophie, then mistress of his superior officer. Although she was five years older than Maurice, and already a mother, he married her in 1804, without his family's knowledge. Aurore, born two months later, spent much of her early years at Nohant, on her grandmother's estate. At four years of age, Sophie took her daughter to Madrid where her husband was stationed. Upon her return to Nohant, she gave birth to a blind boy who died shortly thereafter. That same year, 1808, Maurice was killed in a riding accident. In time, discord between Sophie and her mother-in-law became so great that they agreed that Aurore would remain with her grandmother at Nohant,while her mother would move to Paris and receive a stipend of 1,000 francs a year.

That Aurore had been divested of both father and mother must have been traumatic for the child. Her grandmother, a highly rational and seemingly cold individual, could, evidently, not fill the void in the child's heart. Aurore was enrolled from 1818 to 1820 at the Convent of English Augustinians in Paris, where she allegedly underwent a mystical experience. A year later, her grandmother died, but not before telling her that she was losing her best friend. Although Sophie had arranged for Aurore to live with friends in Paris, much to her mother's chagrin, her daughter married Casimir Dudevant. The couple took up residence at Nohant, which Aurore had inherited from her grandmother, and a year later she gave birth to Maurice, and, in 1828, to Solange. Dudevant having married Aurore for her talents as a homebody, it is not surprising to learn that the couple separated in 1830.

Words, fantasies, feelings, dreams, sensuality, and a highly active and lyrical imagination were Sand's lifeline to the world. Many of her works—*Indiana* (1832), *Lélia* (1833), *Consuelo* (1842–1843), *The Haunted Pool* (*La Mare au diable*) (1846), *Little Fadette* (1849), *Francis the Waif* (*François le Champi*) (1850), *Story of My Life* (1854), *Tales of a Grandmother* (1873)—became and are still household names. Enraptured, particularly at the outset of her writing career, by Rousseau's *The New Héloïse*, Goethe's *Werther*, Chateaubriand's *René*, and Senancour's *Obermann*, Sand committed herself wholeheartedly to humanitarian causes, focusing frequently on the emancipation of women and the rehabilitation of wronged girls.

Feminism weighed heavily on her: having had to earn her own living early in life, she readily understood the difficulties involved for women in general, and the writer in particular. A striking example is offered by her dealings with *La Revue de Paris*, whose administrative board paid her less for her articles than they did their male contributors. Elizabeth Barrett Browning, in her sonnet dedicated to Sand, expressed her disenchantment with the fact that women writers had to use male pseudonyms in order to have their works published. "True genius, but true woman, dost deny,/ The woman's nature with a manly scorn. . . ." Hadn't George Eliot and the Brontë sisters, among others, adopted pen names (Currer Bell, Acton Bell, Ellis Bell) in order to find publishers for their works, thereby accepting restrictive existences imposed upon them in patriarchal societies? By masking their gender, they opted for duplicity and androgyny.

Not to be omitted are the influences on Sand's writings of well-known political and social thinkers of her day, namely, the theologian F. R. de Lamennais (1782-1854). Advocating freedom of speech and press, this man of the cloth, at odds with conservative royalists and Gallicans, went to Rome in 1832 to plead his cause before Pope Gregory XVI. His condemnation in the encyclical *Mirari Vos* led the excommunicated Lamennais to retire from public life for two years, and to the publication of his *Words of a Believer* (1834) in which he preached his mystical brand of socialism. Impacting on Sand as well were the writings of the influential social reformer, C. H. de Saint-Simon (1760-1825), who not only had foreseen the rapid growth of an industrial society but advocated a division of labor that would ensure social harmony. In his writings such as *New Christianity* (1825), he preached the notion of brotherhood as the basis for all scientifically oriented industrial organizations. The works of Pierre Leroux (1797-1871), with their flavor of Pythagorianism—*On Humanity, its Principle, and Future* (1840), and *Project of a Democratic and Social Constitution* (1848)—influenced Sand as well. Leroux's brand of mystical and humanitarian socialism fed her appetite for certain popular trends of the day: metempsychosis, reincarnation, and Masonism. Understandably, she embraced the eventual unity of all peoples and classes through equality and fraternity in nonviolent socialism.

Once Sand moved to Paris in 1831 and began writing for popular consumption, she voiced her social and psychological platform clearly and loudly and adopted her pseudonym: "I and I alone made my pseudonym . . . after the fact, by my labor alone" (Sand II, 140). Taking a further step in self-liberation, she wore men's garb: trousers, a morning coat, a cravat, and metal-tipped boots. Her conduct and lifestyle likewise altered to suit her needs and inclinations toward independence. High on her agenda was militant opposition to

France's Napoleonic code, which forced woman to submit financially, ethically, intellectually, emotionally, and morally to their husband's wishes.

With age, the "good lady of Nohant," as she came to be called, pursued her writings, humanitarian activities, and gracious entertaining. Her awareness of the weaknesses of others made her increasingly understanding of the vagaries of human nature.

ARCHETYPAL ANALYSIS

CORAMBE: SAND'S ANDROGYNOUS DIVINITY. Sand's creation, around the age of ten, of her own androgynous deity answered a profound psychological need: to confide her sorrows to a higher principle, thereby alleviating her suffering. Empathy (Gr. *empatheia*, affection + pathos), a vital factor in her makeup, helped her relate to the world around her. As a self-healer, she learned when living on her grandmother's estate as a child to exteriorize her solitude through the medium of fantasy. By endowing giant trees, windswept flowers, clear streams, and/or turbid mudholes with lives of their own, she penetrated nature's multiplicity of moods, cohabited spiritually with its cyclical rhythms, even while also resisting its sometimes destructive powers. Attunement with the visible world's life cycles taught her to assess and to deal with the death of her father when she was four, the departure of her mother for Paris when she was five, and her grandmother's demise when she was nineteen. Each exit in its own way left her with a deep sense of bereavement. Nor did her displacement at age fourteen to a convent in Paris help heal her wounds. Nonetheless, the yearning and the will to fill the *vacuum intus*—within—produced positive results: it triggered the workings of a fertile imagination and strengthened her determination to become economically and spiritually independent.

Sand's need to relate to nature's relatively secure forces—such as trees and rocks—developed in her psyche a belief in nascent animistic powers. Her ability to communicate with plants, sun, moon, opened her up to their languages, moods, and temperaments, which, seemingly, corresponded to her own. The luminescence of a fiery sun making its way across a brilliant sky, although casting its shadow on earth, led her to observations on life's dichotomies—and her own inner light/dark patternings. Alone, after sunset, in the darkness of a forest might have caused fear had she not been attuned to nature's traps and temptations as reflections of her own anxieties and a whole world of unknowns. She had learned early in life how best to cope with a universe of imponderables.

Having fed on ancient mythologies, Christian lore, and the fairy tales of Perrault among other works of fantasy, Sand gradually became antagonistic to

Catholic dicta. Nor did her mother's rote recitations of prayers stimulate her belief in Christianity or any other organized religion. The original birth-bond existing between mother and child was increasingly loosened by her mother's continuous belittling of what she referred to as her daughter's "sovereignly dull . . . and interminable tales," and her denigration of their inordinate length and digressive plot lines (*Oeuvres autobiographiques* I, 542). Yet, paradoxically, it had been her mother, Sand maintained, who introduced her to a world of glimmering marvels. Her grandmother was an outspoken Voltairean deist—deprecating the superstitions of Church miracles and the divinity of Jesus—yet her actions belied her words, and revealed a pusillanimous and hypocritical cast. Hadn't her grandmother, fearing personal social reprisals during the Restoration, adhered to the Church's dictates? And for the same reason, had she not insisted that her granddaughter make her first Holy Communion? While her grandmother, Sand wrote years later, had tried more or less to turn her into a *tabula rasa*, she parried this remark: "A child is never a *tabula rasa*," she wrote, because a child "comments, interrogates, doubts, searches, and if one gives it nothing with which to build a house, it will build its own nest with the straw it can gather" (*Oeuvres autobiographiques* I, 811).

During periods of stress, the unconscious of children, and Sand's was no exception, comes to their aid. In 1818, the fourteen-year-old, deeply divided child had an archetypal dream—or *annunciation*—in which her divinity, Corambé, became manifest. It was to this divinely sent mediating God/Goddess that Sand confided her feelings and thoughts (*Oeuvres autobiographiques* I, 840).

All Gods/Goddesses, Judeo-Christian, Hindu, Buddhist, Muslim, or Shinto, have not only their mysteries but their androgynous aspects as well. Sand's transpersonal Corambé, reminiscent in certain ways of Plato's myth of the androgyne *(Banquet)*, was also male and female. The configuration of a sexually complete primordial being, or divinely unified entity, understood on a psychological level, indicates a need for melding of oppositional forces within a personality. Corambé fulfilled Sand's unconscious call for the healing of her emotional split. Gentle, kind, and loving, her nutritive deity—or cosmic cult figure—represented a *fruitful coexistence* of opposites in her psyche. At odds with the ruling consciousness of her family, despite its apparently matriarchal cohesion, the incipient feminist revealed not only a need for love, but an unwillingness to compartmentalize her world by adhering to stultifying gender limitations. These modalities of behavior having been imposed by proxy on both her mother and her grandmother, recipients themselves of an ingrained patriarchal society, Sand refused to follow the same well-worn path.

Like the ancients, Sand worshipped her deity in natural surroundings, hiding it amid a cluster of three maple trees. There, in its own hiddenness, she built a temple to honor Corambé and an altar to make sacred its androgynous nature. The recipient of her mother's artistic talents, Sand decorated Corambé's natural house of worship with beautifully colored pebbles, a variety of shells, fresh green moss, ferns, ivy, birds nests, and a crown. Seated on the moss in front of her divine figure, she created a theogony based in part on Greek, Roman, and Judeo-Christian tales. As an offering, she poured out her heart in the private tones of her nascent personality. "Corambé was endowed with all the attributes of physical and moral beauty, the gift of eloquence, the all-powerful charm of the arts, above all, the magic of musical improvisation; I wanted to love it as a friend, a sister, and, at the same time, revere it as a God" (*Oeuvres autobiographiques* I, 813). Conversations with her deity, interwoven with ritual, figured in what Sand referred to as her "book" or her "song" (*Oeuvres autobiographiques* I, 812, 819).

Sand's serene and peaceful dream-created cult figure was shattered when a neighbor child happened upon her *temenos*. Taking the altar dedicated to Corambé for a *Corpus Christi*, the intruder made light of Sand's sacred world and privileged moments. Believing her religious mystery to have been desecrated, Sand, like those persecuted for their religion, refused to let it into enemy hands, and destroyed it herself, along with the temple and altar dedicated to Corambé's memory (*Oeuvres autobiographiques* I, 821). Not yet the stoic that she was to become, Sand sobbed during the entire night. No more "sweet dreams. Corambé remained mute." Nonetheless, the hidden deity—like the *deus absconditus* of the Gnostics and Jansenists—produced within the future author a course of healing for the continuously tormented child (*Oeuvres autobiographiques* I, 858).

THE TALES OF A GRANDMOTHER. Sand's adored granddaughters, Aurore (Lolo), who stayed with her at Nohant in 1866, and Gabrielle (Titite), in 1868, brought the writer unparalleled joy. Their beautifully intelligent, happy faces and their responsiveness added to the charm and excitement of a household filled with friends, devotees, and relatives. With her magic wand, the writer opened her granddaughters to a universe of sprites, fairies, and genies (*Contes d'une grand'mère* 6).

Although Sand had first begun composing fairy tales for her daughter, Solange, in 1837, it was not until 1873, and posthumously, in 1876, that her thirteen masterful *Tales of a Grandmother* were published. Having always contended that outside of La Fontaine, Mme d'Aulnoy, and Perrault, literature for the very young was not only sparse, but filled with "foolishness," she determined to remedy the situation by writing her own. Tales, she believed, should not seek merely to entertain, but also to trigger the imaginations of listeners, to enlighten them as to life's pleasures and its dangers, and to educate the young by stressing an awareness of responsibility, integrity, love, and camaraderie in human relationships. Amid the glitter and excitement of fantasy constellated with dreams, premonitions, animistic sorties, cosmic interplays, suspenseful events, and creative dialogic interchanges, tales must include a moral as well. Although imperceptible to children on a conscious level, its impact in time would subtly infiltrate their subliminal spheres.

Having previously used the word *empathy* to describe Sand's makeup— defined as "the imaginative projection of a subjective state into an object so that the object appears to be infused with it" (*Webster's Ninth New Collegiate Dictionary*, 1983)—we repeat it, in order to underscore the manner in which the author felt toward the protagonists peopling her literary treasure trove. Children—and I might add adults as well—listening to or reading her tales could not but identify with, and be emotionally moved by, the creatures of her fantasy. In keeping with the level of a child's psychological development, each in her or his own way would assimilate its lessons and profit from the feelings aroused.

THE CASTLE OF CROOKED PEAK. Sand's fairy tale begins as the eight-year-old Diana and her forty-year-old father, M Flochardet, a handsome, wealthy, and sought-after painter, are traveling by horse and carriage to his villa in Arles. Because Diana had been suffering intermittent fever for the past three months in her convent-school, the doctor has recommended that she be taken home. Rather than going directly to Arles, father and daughter detour to visit a relative, and are scheduled to spend the night at Saint-Jean-du-Gard.

During their journey through the rugged, thickly forested, and mountainous Lozère region, the driver, Romanèche, pointed with pride to the once-beautiful castle of Crooked Peak in the distance. The French words *pic* (peak) and *tordu* (crooked), if interpreted onomastically, give the impression of something askew, distorted, and peculiar, making readers aware that something is seriously out of joint with regard to the giant castle.

In that it had been built on a high and isolated mountain, the castle of Crooked Peak was not easily accessible, in keeping with an important requirement of medieval and early Renaissance builders: protection from enemy attack. To gain entry into these formidable structures was dangerous. On a symbolic and/or psychological level, their penetration required specific character traits: *perseverance, wisdom, drive, and a sense of aloneness and separateness.* These were incipient qualities in Sand's heroine, Diana.

That the castle of Crooked Peak stood on such a high and remote mountain identifies it with the notion of transcendence: of going beyond the limits of normal experience and human knowledge. Indeed, the reader is lured into a sphere that surpasses the material universe and infiltrates the world of the imagination. Here spirits, fairies, and genii cohabit and extrasensory perception, metempsychosis, and hallucinatory experiences take on reality. As in a religious *mystery*, the acolyte entering the portals of the Castle of Crooked Peak, will be ushered into the deepest arcanum—a nonreferential level of experience.

By detailing the castle's Renaissance construction, a period known for its restoration of Greek and Roman culture, Sand attests to its ancientness. Such sixteenth-century edifices in France may blend various architectural styles, as in the Castle of Crooked Peak, which included medieval cloister-like pavillions and halls, as well as baths replicating antiquity's own. That the castle was in a state of ruin—a stereotypical image for romantic writers (as in the Gothic tales of Walpole, Radcliffe, and Lewis) and painters (H.Robert), suggests that a once functional edifice had become disused and ill.

Poor road conditions created severe difficulties for Romanèche, and the incessant jolting of the carriage and the damp coldness of the night air led to a recurrence of Diana's fever. Understandably, Flochardet was impatient to reach the inn in which they planned to spend the night. Both to allay the father's fears, and advertise the historicity of his home territory, Romanèche related to his passengers that the Castle of Crooked Peak, although originally owned by a wealthy and powerful noble family, was at present in a state of decay. Having fallen on difficult times, the descendents no longer had sufficient funds to make the necessary repairs. That the entire area had been set ablaze by a smoldering volcano centuries earlier did not improve matters. The fiery image referred to by Romanèche may apply to Sand's own "sacred flame," her "primitive energies," and her explosive inner fire that she instilled, then ignited in her fairy tale/*revelation* (Berthier 9).

Having nearly reached the Castle of Crooked Peak, Romanèche warned his passengers that the detritus, including large blocks of stone fallen from the castle and from other ancient monuments that were scattered about the road, would make it virtually impossible to reach the inn by nightfall. Moreover, the long drive up the mountain would be not only difficult but perilous. Concerned about Diana's welfare, Flochardet decided to leave the carriage and carry his daughter up a crumbling stairway to the terrace above, leading directly into the Castle of Crooked Peak.

DIANA: A MOON FIGURE. The protagonist's name, Diana, adds further luster to Sand's scenario. From the beginning of recorded time, divinities, such as Diana/Artemis, Isis, and the hyperdulian Virgin Mary have been associated with the moon. Birth, death, renewal, the rhythms of its waxing and waning, and alternating seasonal fertility were identified with aspects of the eternal feminine. The moon's dark, shadowy, and chthonian sides, symbolizing a woman's occult, hidden, and subliminal spheres, are not, in Diana's case, to be associated with any sinister powers. Rather, it symbolizes an inner topography—an active and compensatory dream world.

Unlike the ancient Roman Diana and the Greek Artemis, Sand's protagonist leads the life neither of an undaunted huntress, nor of an archer, nor is she Goddess of Wild Animals. Similar to her namesake, however, is our protagonist's love for, and identification with, nature's fertile and undefined spaces. Indeed, her psychological well-being rests largely on the connections she would make between her empirical and her spiritual existences. In keeping with the mysteries identified with the moon Goddess, Sand's heroine, as we shall see, practiced equally hermetic behavioral patterns. From her prepubescent years, continuing through her adolescence and early maturity, she was prone to nightly visitations and annunciations. Under the sway of these mysterious visual interludes, she entered into dialogue with transpersonal figures, particularly animated statues, inanimate carvings, and the dead. Each visitation and/or annunciation, which may be considered psychologically as a foray into her collective unconscious, yielded greater insight into herself and the necessary strength to surmount immediate obstacles facing her.

At the Attic festival, the Brauronia, celebrated at the temple of Artemis at Brauron, a period of seclusion was required during which girls ranging from seven to fourteen years of age cut a lock of their hair, removed their girdle and their maiden garments, and donned instead saffron robes to perform "the act of the bear" *(arkteuin)*. Similarly, Sand's Diana would withdraw into a room in the Castle of Crooked Peak, or, psychologically, into herself, where she would contend with her demons, as she inched along in her ceremonial rite of passage. The ordeals she had to overcome prepared her for entry into a social system based on specific concepts of justice, equity, harmony, and balance (Vidal-Naquet, "Recipes for Greek Adolescence"179).

PSYCHOSOMATIC FEVERS. That Diana was unable to cope with the difficulties plaguing her life becomes evident to the reader when mention was made of her repeated bouts of fever at the convent. Not an "illness itself," her fever was "but a purposive reaction to the organism." Because her elevated temperatures had "meaning and purpose," they neither were nor are to be considered a "neurosis," "antinatural," or "pathological" (Jung 4, #415). The greater the disparity between what she imagined the ideal familial world to be, the more painful became the reality of her true-to-life situation, the increasingly disturbed she grew, and the more her fever peaked. In Jung's words:

> The more one-sided [her] conscious attitude is, and the further it deviates from the optimum, the greater becomes the possibility that vivid dreams

with strongly contrasting but purposive content will appear as an expression of the self-regulation of the psyche. Just as the body reacts purposively to injuries or infections or any abnormal conditions, so the psychic functions react to unnatural or dangerous disturbances with purposive defence-mechanisms. (Jung 8, #488)

Becaused Diana's fever was again to peak during the course of her trip to the castle, it suggested that the thought of returning home, having become unaccepceptable to her conscious mind, had again impacted on her body/psyche complex. Her inability to solve her mysterious problems caused her to react physically to her anguish with episodes of *fever, hallucinations,* waking and sleeping *dreams.* The convoluted symbology of the preternatural happenings victimizing her were interpreted by her as facts of life. Like an archeologist, she would in time have to study the meanings of the events occurring in her nightly peregrinations and interpret these in keeping with the dictates of her morality, personality, and perceptions. So, too, will the reader of Sand's tale be made privy to the material remains—or fossilized semiotic relics—interwoven in the geological folds of Diana's unconscious.

THE STAIRCASE. Although stairs—as in the biblical Tower of Babel, the step pyramid in Egypt, the Japanese heavenly ladder in Shintoism, or the twelfth-century Byzantine icon of the "Heavenly Ladder" by John Klimax—have been associated with ascension and transfiguration, Flochardet's reaction to them differed considerably. The act of carrying his daughter up the broken, unsteady, and hazardous stone steps leading to the castle's terrace indicated not only love for his child, but his desire to protect her from the rigors of life, by lifting her out of the struggle—about which the reader knows nothing as yet.

On the other hand, Flochardet feared his daughter would be scratched by the thorns growing on either side of the shaky steps he was climbing, an anticipation, perhaps, of the pain that she would have to face during the course of her initiation. That he was largely responsible for that pain—as manifested in her former and present bouts of fever—is accounted for by the fact that, although unbeknown to both of them at this time, father and daughter were at odds in personality and in temperament. He, for example, found ugliness in their immediate surroundings: cracked and dismembered statues, misplaced stones, helter-skelter plant growth, and uprooted trees that had become detached from the once-symmetrically laid flagstones. She, by contrast, as if stepping into a Garden of Eden, marveled at what she saw as lordly elegance in the sometimes faceless, headless, or armless statues on the terrace; wild flowers of variegated colors, and unusually shaped tree trunks and stumps, and other untrammeled vegetation. Still very much of a child, she lived close to the earth, related and relating to the variegated manifestations of the Great Mother's abundance from which she drew sustenance.

To be sure, the age differential beween father and daughter accounted to some degree for the dissimilarities of their likes and dislikes. Nonetheless, it went deeper than that. A painter adulated by the bourgeoisie, Flochardet reacted positively only to the finished, the polished, the new, and the ordered aspects of life and art. Accustomed to luxury and to an easy and prosaic lifestyle, he reacted negatively to nature's unprogrammed and disorderly manifestations, which disturbed him and posed both emotional and physical difficulties for him because they disrupted his staid life course. Indeed, whatever interrupted the smooth-running sameness of his routine world—as artist or in the empirical domain—became a negative concept from which he shied.

With a setting sun, Diana's upward climb—or ascension—to the castle's terrace gave her both a better view of the countryside and increased perspective as well. She was able to scan the environs from her new vantage point, alerting her to a world brimming with excitement and anticipation! For Flochardet, the climb and the delay spelled danger and discomfort. He fretted, for example, about how Diana would fare alone while he descended the stairs to decide with Romanèche whether they should continue their course in the dimming light of dusk. To allay his agitation, Diana—a motherly type—comforted her father by suggesting he lend her his coat to keep her warm while she rested on the terrace until his return. No need to worry, she assured him! Somewhat heartened, he left, returning shortly afterward downcast, informing his daughter that since the carriage needed repair, they would have to spend the night in some niche in the castle.

Again, antipodal reactions were forthcoming from father and daughter. Diana's attunement to the locus seemed to have released in her a whole realm of heretofore repressed and unrequited feelings. Had the castle and all it represented embedded itself as a living corpus in her psyche? In sharp contrast to Flochardet, who constantly complained about the discomforts of a night spent in the rundown Castle of Crooked Peak, Diana relished each moment of mystery that such an unexpected event would accord her. Wise for her years, she advised her father that since darkness had already set in, it would be safer to spend the night in the castle rather than risk a serious accident by traveling on those poor roads in sheer darkness.

THE ANIMATED STATUE. Diana stunned her father by telling him that, during his brief absence, she had *heard* a lady call her by name and, looking in the direction of the voice, she saw the arm of a statue hidden in the bushes on the terrace move and point toward the castle. The resonance of the lady's voice, together with her accompanying gesture, had reverberated so deeply in the folds of Diana's psyche that she understood these signs to mean she should enter the castle's portals. Flochardet considered his daughter's reasoning absurd and, not unreasonably, asked to know the lady's identity.

How may one explain Diana's extrasensory visualization? Clearly, her recurring fever had been a somatic symptom, an outspoken *cry* on the part of her body, for help in healing some mysterious wound. The unknown affliction that caused her soma such distress, although physically sensed by her, had not yet been made cognitive, thus could not be articulated. The reader senses only that Diana must have experienced some kind of alienation, some unresolved familial problem. Disturbances of this kind in one who lives in harmony, or in primary identity with Mother Nature, may be transliterated— and were, in Diana's case—via the dream and/or active fantasies.

Somatic signs evident in Diana's fevers, would now become manifest in psychic signs. "Don't you see the lady?" Diana questioned anxiously. No, he did not. Was it because the child, in touch with her unconscious or Moon self, could *see*, and was made privy to the humanization of inert matter, and related to it in an outerworldly female form? Darkness interspersed with moon glow gave an impulse to her dream world. For her father, daylight encounters alone were real; all else remained either invisible to him or explainable in terms of the painter's technique of optical illusion.

For the moon-oriented and intuitive Diana, the animated statue took on the contours of a gracious lady, whose elegant, beckoning gesture expressed in an arcane language the the invitation to enter a *secret inner space*. Gently and firmly, Diana would insist on following the statue's directives. Penetrating the vast and unknown spaces within the castle was tantamount to the discovery of her own inner riches buried deeply within her inner castle/psyche.

What you take for a lady, Flochardet said in the only language he knew, wrenching Diana out of her dream, is simply a stone statue, an allegorical replica of the famous *Hospitality*. But fearing another flareup of her fever, he went along with her wish to enter the castle. If nothing else, he reasoned, it would at least provide them with shelter for the night.

As the two made their way through the "superb" Renaissance peristyle, which gave on to a vast court overrun with all types of vegetation, Romanèche appeared with a lantern to dispel the pervading darkness. He ushered them into a pavilion modeled on a Greco-Roman *thermae*, affirming that with the exception of a broken column here and there, the doors, ceilings, and walls were structurally sound.

Flochardet, having once again misread his daughter's desires, erroneously believed she needed reassurance and took her on his lap, failing completely to fathom her joy at the prospect of entering an ancient castle. Viewed psychologically as a complex of intertwining archetypal treasures stored in the child's psyche, to step into bygone centuries is also to penetrate structures of memory, which, if depicted in linear terms, are reminiscent of many Piranesi's etchings.

Sensing her father's anxiety over her well-being, Diana assured him again in motherly fashion that she was no longer feverish but hungry, which for her was a healthy sign. The little mother/wife that she was, she proceeded to help Romanèche in setting up the provisions they had brought with them for their evening meal. Noticing that her precious doll had lost an arm during the trajectory, she almost began to cry, but quickly reasoned herself out of an act she deemed ineffectual to alter the situation. Delighted by his daughter's hearty appetite and spirited mood, Flochardet judged it the ideal time to put her to bed. Agreeable to the suggestion, Diana settled onto the cushions Romanèche had brought up from the carriage and arranged in a corner of the room in bedlike design. Her father's coat, in lieu of a blanket, would keep her warm.

Flochardet, thinking Diana asleep, queried Romanèche about the legend connected with the Castle of Crooked Peak. Unbeknown to them, she was listening attentively to every word of the saga, and learned that, according to some people of the region, the "Veiled Lady"—the very statue that had gestured to Diana to enter the castle—was considered the guardian of this once great Renaissance edifice. Wearing a period costume, this "Veiled Lady" was not dead, but was very much alive and, as the living spirit of the princess who had inhabited the castle long ago, she returned to her home nightly. Despite her courteous nature, Romanèche affirmed, she occasioned some kind of road accident to those to whom she beckoned and who refused to enter. Although she had been heard to scream "*leave*," the "Veiled Lady" was considered a good power by the local inhabitants. Flochardet confided to the driver that his daughter had heard the voice of the "Veiled Lady," but he personally did not believe in such "nonsense" (*Castle of Crooked Peak* 43).

In harmony with a rising moon, Diana's body now sank into a kind of stressless sleep, and unshackled her from the turbulent—still secreted, for the reader—anxieties corroding her psyche. Would she strike at the root of her fever and succeed in abating, if not eradicating it in the no-man/no-woman's land in which she now floated?

MOON DOMINANCE. Diana, now resting comfortably on her makeshift bed, awaited sleep. The moon, just beginning to mount in the heavens, illuminated the frescoes on the ceiling and the walls encircling her resting place. Engraved above the door were the words "Diana's Bath." In this scene, Sand must certainly have had in mind the famous canvas bearing the same name, by the Renaissance painter François Clouet.

Unlike the sun, viewed as a male principle in the West, as already noted, thus representative of spirit, order, illumination, and the highest of rational thinking processes, the moon was identified with an enigmatic, occult, and vacillating feminine world. Understandably, as Diana advanced into the heart of her lunar domain, that is, into her unconscious, she became acutely perceptive of hidden moon tones. Unlike the sun, identified with consciousness, the moon acquires visibility when set against darkened skies, its alternating contours embodying dream or mythical schemes.

By releasing Diana from her anxiety-riveting reality, the moon had endowed the statue that she had earlier observed on the terrace of the castle with increasing power over the child's dream world. Each of the "Veiled Lady's" future avatars—Greco-Roman nymph, fairy, and so forth—would help answer a specific need in Diana's psyche and direct her toward a better understanding of her distresses—each in its time.

THE PERSONAL AND THE ARCHETYPAL MOTHER FIGURE. The reader now learns that Diana's childhood had been a lonely one, her mother having died soon after her birth, and her father having remarried shortly thereafter a pretty, but flighty and superficial, young lady, Laure. Her stepmother's interests focused exclusively on showy apparel and social activities; she displayed only momentary inclinations toward Diana's well-being, thus setting the stage for the child's earliest torment. Nor was her father's behavior any more commendable, yielding as he did to Laure's desire to rid their home of the bothersome child by sending her to a convent school. Living under a cloud of rejection and alienation, Diana craved love and relatedness from a father who demonstrated shows of affection only sparsely, and only when alone with his daughter. Since she had been brought up earlier by a loving, but uncommunicative governess, Diana had learned to internalize her sorrow. Compelled to fend for herself on an emotional level, she faced the problematics of the divisive void within her.

During Diana's pre-slumber musings in the Castle of Crooked Peak, she had overheard the conversation between her father and Romanèche, and feasted visually on the decayed frescoes of the pavilion. Still discernible were images of birds flying about painted garlands in their attempt to catch larger than life fluttering butterflies, and colorful nymphs holding hands in their circular dance. The arms, legs, and faces of some of the dancing figures had been eroded by the ever-encroaching mold and mildew, but in no way was Diana's attraction to the images constellated about her diminished. Her attention was drawn, however, to one dancing figure in particular, whose head had been obliterated by the the ravages of time, but whose gleaming green dress glittered. Based on the conversation between her father and Romanèche, Diana was convinced the figure on the wall was in some way related to the Veiled Lady.

As she mused about the reality of her vision, a glowing blue luminosity pervaded Diana's semi-dream world. Bathed in these gentle color tones, the Greco-Roman dancer of the fresco took on life, emerged from the wall, and glided toward Diana. Not at all frightened by the luminescent figure approaching her, she was only disappointed by the effulgence of the veil wrapped about the lady's head, which hid her facial contours. Visible were only two pale rays of light emerging from the area of the eyes. Revivified by the extraordinary beauty and warmth of this ethereal form bending to kiss her forehead, Diana instinctively opened her arms to envelop the tender presence. Much to her surprise and disarray, however, she realized she was embracing only a shadow. "Are you made of fog, that I can't feel you?" she asked the nymph. "At least speak to me, that I may know if you were the one who spoke to me before," she pleaded, alluding to the stone statue. "It is I," the Veiled Lady/Greco-Roman nymph/Fairy all in one responded, after which she invited the child to join her in a walk (*Castle* 47). Before acquiescing, however, the child, placing her father's needs first, asked her to take her fever away, explaining that this would allay his chagrin. The Veiled Lady/Greco-Roman nymph/Fairy extended her hand to the child; Diana's fever dropped.

"Don't you wish to enter my castle?" the fairy asked, adding that only those unauthorized by her see it in a state of decay. The child joyfully acquiescing, as the two penetrated its vast portals, the edifice was transfigured into its former glorious elegance. Music and dancing couples filled the richly decorated halls. Overwhelmed by the reigning mood of merriment and abandon, Diana jumped and ran with glee from one gold, pastel, and silvery toned room to another. She observed the gorgeousness of the women's gowns, jewels, and exquisite fineries, and then her eyes rested on the magnificently arranged platters of food—especially the endless sweets. No sooner did she inquire about the frescoes on the walls of the room than figures emerged and became alive before her eyes. After observing the delights of a restored past, Diana, complaining of the heat, asked her fairy figure to take her into the garden. Finding herself on the terrace, she saw that there, too, everything seemed to have been transformed. No longer growing helter-skelter, the colorful plants were arranged in orderly fashion. Rather than a single statue, there were several, singing in unison a canticle in honor of the moon. Diana, who had once perused a book on mythology, asked to see the deity whose name she bore. Her wishes were realized: the Goddess Diana appeared before her in the form of a silver cloud in the sky, tall, larger than life, holding a brilliant bow in her hands. Suddenly, she seemed to diminish in size, becoming so small that she might be taken for a swallow, yet, as one approached her, she again increased in size.

Delighted, Diana expressed a desire to kiss her Greco-Roman Nymph/Fairy/Veiled/Lady, who, interpreting her words as a desire to sleep, responded by taking the child in her arms. "When you awaken, make certain you don't forget anything I have shown you," she admonished, after which Diana fell into a deep and nutritive slumber (*Castle* 50).

Deprivation since earliest infancy of the personal mother image and of the natural, free-flowing symbiotic relationship between mother and child, caused Diana unconciously to seek out an archetypal mother figure, manifested for her in the Veiled Lady, the Greco-Roman Nymph, and the Fairy. Education or explication may help alleviate certain psychosomatic disturbances, but Diana's were less likely to be assuaged, given the habitual behavior of her unconscious and its nearly "irresistible demands for fulfillment (Jung 8, #720). Jung further explains why, in the absence of a personal mother—the collective mother image, or Mother archetype—takes on such importance.

> The mother-child relationship is certainly the deepest and most poignant one we know; in fact, for some time the child is, so to speak, a part of the mother's body. Later it is part of the psychic atmosphere of the mother for several years, and in this way everything original in the child is indissolubly blended with the mother-image. This is true not only for the individual, but still more in a historical sense. . . . Thus there is inherent in the archetype, in the collectively inherited mother-image, the same extraordinary intensity of relationship which instinctively impels the child to cling to its mother. . . . Consciousness only recognizes contents that are individually acquired; hence it recognizes only the individual mother and does not know that she is at the same time the carrier and representative of the archetype, of the "eternal" mother. Separation from the mother is sufficient only if the archetype is included, and the same is true of separation from the father. (Jung 8, #723)

In view of a child's closeness to its mother, it is not unusual for one such as Diana to live out a painful deprivation through projection. The collective or archetypal image of the Veiled Lady, the nymph gliding forth from the fresco, and the good fairy in the background—the three being one—plays the role of healer, confidant, and loving mother, releasing Diana to a certain degree from the corrosive anxieties that usually preceded her fevers. As constellated by the child's unconscious, the archetypal Veiled Lady/ Nymph/Fairy was associated with comfort, beauty, and joy and could provide dance, music, beauty, and laughter—nature's healing balms!

Diana's suffering had set the stage for what were to become her increasingly frequent projections—or autonomous visions—identifiable with a "psychoid archetype":

> The "psychoid archetype" is an unknowable factor which arranges both psychical and physical events in typical patterns, much as the axial system

of a crystal preexists in the mother liquid of the crystal, although it has no material existence of its own. The psychoid archetype lies behind both psyche and matter and expresses itself typically in synchronistic events . . . an acausal principle which stands behind such events as telepathy, clairvoyance, etc. (J. M. Spiegelman, "Psychology and the Occult" 108)

The emergence of the "psychoid phenomena," and Diana's belief in the reality of the Veiled Lady/Nymph/Fairy—spirits transcending both psyche and matter—are called into being in answer to her pressing subliminal needs. Given the relative popularity of premonitory visions and conversations with angels, which the Swedish theologian, philosopher, and scientist Emmanuel Swedenborg (1688-1772) had both written about and experienced, it comes as no surprise that Sand likewise introduces in her fairy tale dialogues with outerworldly beings. An associated notion is that of *correspondences*, which permeated the works of Nerval, Balzac, Baudelaire, Hugo, and so many other nineteenth-century creative spirits of the era who were convinced of the vast and subtle interpenetration of everything in the universe—organic, inorganic, plant, animal, mineral, and human. The vibrations or varieties of energetic patterns emerging from each entity in specific frequencies may be understood, psychologically, as types of behavioral patterns distinguishing one individual from another.

It may be forwarded that since Diana's emotional, spiritual, and psychological brain waves, amplitudes, or frequencies were at variance with those of her father, her fantasy world or transcendent function was more attuned to extrasensory phenomena and thus more accessible to various planes of the mind/psyche complex. Although she was uaware of any mystical schools or theological ideas on the subject, her energy centers, heightened by fever, sleep, dream, or meditative states, activated the vibrations experienced in these various situations, making them operational. Understandably, then, she became highly receptive to whatever illuminated her darkness.

The relatively frequent apparitions of Diana's positive, forceful trinitarian archetypal mother figures, and their effect on her soma and psyche, enabled her in time to acquire greater consciousness of her needs and wants. Encounters such as the one at the Castle of Crooked Peak may even be considered a kind of unconscious apotropaic device enabling her to cut through layers of defense mechanisms she had unconsciously erected for her own protection since her mother's departure—or abandonment—from this world.

Once implosion of the mind had taken place, and Diana had begun digging deeply into her archetypal or primordial past, that is, into the mystery of her own being, she would herself discover visible and audible healing powers in the vastness of her own inner spaces. The tripartite Veiled Lady/Nymph/Fairy existed first in the visual world as *image* and *gesture*; secondly, as *voice* and *echo*, conveyed as a *mouthpiece* emanating from the child's and humanity's collective unconscious. No longer simply a passive *sign*, as when Diana's healing process started to take root, voice and echo were beginning to actively integrate unconscious happenings into the young girl's life experience, snatching covert dreams or hallucinatory spannings from a timeless past, present, and future, and actively clarifying what lay hidden in darkness. The struggle between Diana's *soma and psyche* would in time lead her to better awareness of her own feminine nature in its development toward wholeness, and would set in motion the individuation process.

Childhood, usually a happy period, had been one of sacrifice, pain, and illness for Diana. Fantasy images, such as that of the Veiled Lady/Nymph/Fairy, stored for preservation in her memory, now would expand and/or contract in response to her emotional needs. Questions centering on her mother were compounded by those relating to her father's rapid remarriage after his first wife's demise; his attraction to a woman endowed with a pretty face, a flighty disposition, and no maternal feeling; and his reasons for never having taken any overt steps to protect his child from the negative mother figure that Laure was. Had his insight into his own deficiencies become so limited that he simply glided from one wife to another? Only Diana's symptoms (fever) brought him a certain amount of awareness of his daughter's needs. An undifferentiated adolescent consciousness is excusable at the age of eight, but not at forty.

THE MIRROR/MUSE. The morning after the Veiled Lady/Nymph/Fairy's visitation, Diana awoke refreshed and fever-free. So delighted was she by the memorable images she had called up during the night that, prior to their departure, she asked her father for a mirror in which to look at herself. Knowing his daughter to be careful and wise, he provided her with one but admonished her not to venture with it outside the castle.

The introduction of the mirror image on the morning of their departure indicates a desire on Diana's part for self-knowledge. The inner sight she had gained passively, via unconscious lunar rays during the night hours, she now sought to examine actively and consciously by solar light. The mirror was considered in medieval times a compendium of all knowledge, or a drawing table showing the relative positions of the planets. The concept brings to mind the act of pondering or reflecting, and therefore indicates curiosity and/or doubt about the subject encapsulated in the mirror—in Diana's case, her face.

By observing her face (Fr. *visage*; L. *visus)*, Diana would learn not only to discern her very special character traits, including her strengths and weaknesses, but also to *face* her situation with boldness and courage. It has been claimed that only via the image and its reflection in the mirror may one begin to know oneself—that is, the mystery of being. Diana's mirror experience not only revealed an increasing interest in herself as an individual, but disclosed a powerful latent urge to ask for paper and pencil so that she could replicate in line drawings a whole richly furbished inner realm. Copying—or *mirroring*— from memory the frescoes visible in her dream the previous night, she delineated a beautiful nymph dwelling in deeply forested mountains, and cascading waters glistening under the brilliance of the morning sun's fresh rays, reflecting the glories to which she had been made privy. Marking a step forward in her initiation ritual, Diana identified the nymph with a Muse, one of the nine sister goddesses in Greek mythology presiding over the arts and sciences. The Muse, henceforth, would be her guide and inspiration. With this in mind, she penciled in other scenes, not serenely, however, but frenetically, as if determined to carve out her future.

Even if the images she set down on paper were blurred or blotched, they may be envisaged as precious mementos of Diana's efforts to apprehend aspects of her being, and to snatch segments of her past to integrate into her present and future. Although undecipherable for others, and disparaged by her father as "scribblings," the drawings orchestrated a whole symphonic tone poem for her. In time they would become a tool to probe her hitherto elusive inner domain.

Were her early "scribblings" an attempt to rival her father as an artist? Although he himself was lauded by his clientele as a great portrait painter, Flochardet had not only never given his daughter any art lessons, but had repeatedly dismissed any thought that she might have talent. His single aim was to bring up his daughter as a lady, that is, Sand wrote, "knowing how to dress and babble" (*Castle* 54). Despite his obvious affection for his daughter, providing she did not tread on his turf nor on his wife's, Flochardet became increasingly identified in Diana's unconscious with a negative father image.

Prior to her departure from the Castle of Crooked Peak, hoping to revisit the unforgettable sites that had emerged in her dream, Diana again entered the vast rooms within the edifice. But the world revealed to her in broad daylight jarred her sensibilities inasmuch as structures of memory images possess their own reality, summon their own souvenirs, trigger their own energies. The statue that had taken on the glow of livingness in her dream, she now saw as mutilated, cracked, and pockmarked. Even its mobile arm, extended toward the castle the previous night, was lifeless and silent. How could it have spoken to her? she questioned. It had no mouth, nor face, only a kind of drapery around its hair. Still, upon further scrutiny, she comforted herself somewhat with the thought that it bore a resemblance to her good fairy. Had she perhaps dreamed it all? Hadn't she been told that during her bouts with fever, her thoughts and behavioral patterns were sometimes wanting? or irrational, to use the contemporary term.

So deeply had Diana felt the mystery of the previous night's excursion, so lingering had its evanescence become that, before leaving, she stooped down to pick up some tiny pebble-size mosaic fragments, which she then slipped into her pocket. This tangible evidence of a past and a present, and anticipion of a future reality, brought a smile to her face. She even toyed with the idea of remaining in the castle a while longer. Impractical, she reflected, for there was no water.

A ten-year-old girl, Blanche de Pictordu, the daughter of the marquis who owned the castle in which Diana had spent the night, arrived on the scene unexpectedly and happily told her she was to lunch at her home nearby. The reader learns that the once wealthy family of Pictordu had fallen on hard times. Sensitive to the girl's embarrassment at her poverty, Diana asked her father for permission to offer her a small turquoise broach. Flochardet agreed.

HER PERSONA DOES NOT FIT. The Latin word *persona*, for the actor's "mask" or "public face," represents the attitude or image that mediates between one's inner and outer worlds. Since the persona includes some of the individual's personal characteristics, as well as aspects of the family's or the society's expectation of her or him, it both hides and protects the person seeking to adapt to the workaday world. Difficulties arise, however, with an unconscious rejection of the persona (Edinger, "An Outline of Analytical Psychology" 2). An ill-fitting persona may cause an overwhelming sense of alienation or may mask a burgeoning but still weakly structured ego, either stifling it, and/or leading to its eventual eclipse.

For the first few days after Diana's return home, Laure busied herself enthusiastically and virtually exclusively with the child's wardrobe. The two shopped for new clothes and presents galore, including a new doll. Hours were spent deciding on the appropriate frock for a specific occasion, on hair styling, and so forth. Guided by all the latest fashions, Laure intended to embellish the child to fit the persona she had in mind.

Such frivolous attention so palled on Diana that she soon grew weary and, bored, she yawned, and was scolded. Hers was a serious breach of etiquette, Laure maintained, but the guilt feelings she sought to instill in the child failed to take root. Interiorizing the criticism, Diana remained outwardly silent on the subject, and yearned only to find some serious outlet that would enable her to grow and find fulfullment. Uppermost in her mind was a desire to learn how to draw.

It was not to be. The more Laure inflicted her persona on Diana, the greater grew the child's distress at the artificial environment imposed upon her. Soon, as expected, Diana's fever returned. Taking matters into her own hands, Laure gave the child drugs which not only did not lower the fever, but aggravated it. The concerned father finally called on his old-time friend, Dr. Féron, who quickly recognized the root of the problem—the hostility between Laure and Diana—and ordered all medication to be stopped. Advising Flochardet not to force his daughter to occupy her time doing things she detested, he predicated that she be allowed to find her own direction. Why force her to become "a little model," to try on dresses all day long, and wear her hair in fashionable and constricting styles, when she detested this routine (*Castle* 61)? As for Laure, she must resume her heretofore active social life. Flochardet carried out the doctor's recommendations to the letter.

Hardly had Diana been given her freedom, than her color reappeared and her temperature dropped. When she asked her father to let her draw in a small corner of his atelier, her wish was granted. With burgeoning understanding and interest in the pictorial arts, she studied her father's paintings. Impressed by workmanship and technical artistry, she realized that art does not consist of mere scribblings and scrabblings, but is a serious discipline. Her newly discovered knowledge inspired her to reject pencils and paper and to spend her time *dreaming*. Not stasis! Not wasted! She knew instinctively that if she were to grow as an artist, she would have to allow fantasy free rein. Unbeknown to her, reverie served as a protective device against her father's derogation of her linear efforts. Hadn't he reiterated her lack of talent? Hadn't Laure's opposition to her ventures into art been equally overt? To remain mute about her future plans might be the best solution for the moment. Silence might even invite her unconscious, in the form of dream images, to participate in finding an answer to her gnawing problem. The Veiled Lady/Nymph/Fairy, now referred to as Muse—might once again point the way!

BACCHUS/DIONYSUS. Not long after Diana's return home, she looked at one of the mosaic fragments she had picked up outside the Castle of Crooked Peak. Curious about its contours, she noted that its hardened sand casing had become detached. Upon closer scrutiny, and much to her amazement, she discerned a beautiful marble head that, she thought, must have once been part of a statuette. So entranced was she by this tiny sculptured form that she could not stop focusing on it, holding it to the sunlight, then shading it, each displacement disclosing another of its exquisite facets.

Doctor Féron,who happened to be visiting, asked her what she thought the figure represented. Perhaps Cupid (Gr. Eros)? she replied. Rather, "a young Bacchus" (Gr. Dionysus), he interjected. After examining the head more closely, he attested to its beauty and to its ancientness. Not knowing the meaning of "ancientness," Diana took it upon herself to define the term: "Something which is no longer stylish today?" Diana told the doctor that, unlike Mother Laure, she considered everything new ugly. Flochardet, having joined them and having glanced at the sculpture, declared it to be debris and not a work of art, adding that it resembled one of his daughter's play dolls. Annoyed by the superficiality of his response, the doctor labeled him a "frivolous artist, knowing only laces, and mantles—nothing of real life" (*Castle* 63).

Although usually protective of her father and deferential to his ideas relating to art, Diana mustered sufficient courage to express her own diametrically opposed opinion and her love for antiquities. The Bacchus head clearly had roused her esthetic feelings. We may question her reasons for immediately accepting the doctor's apellation of Bacchus, rather than clinging to her initial choice of Cupid. As God of the vine, Bacchus represented joy and laughter—nature's unbridled side—the aspects of which had not only remained undeveloped in Diana's world, but were virtually nonexistent. The Attic cycle of festivals in his honor emphasized nature's abundance in the luxuriance of vineyards and trees. Kindly and gentle toward his worshipers, this God was the harbinger of joy and blessings. He healed the body, gladdened the soul, and obliterated pain. Frequently called, the "loosener of cares," Bacchus was known to have inspired diligence and labor as well as merriment. Toward his enemies, however, he could be ruthless (Seiffert, *Dictionary of Classical Antiquities* 191).

As the days flew by, Dr. Féron taught Diana ways of distinguishing between living and dead art. The former is realized by a duly trained artist who pours out his inner vision onto an object, or transliterates a figment of his imagination into free-flowing lines and colorations on canvas or paper. Dead art, devoid of imagination, is merely a question of technical proficiency. The latter type of artist, he continued, waxes in routine, in perfunctory replications of what he or she has observed. Using the head of Bacchus to exemplify his philosophy of art, Dr. Féron noted that, although divested of a body, the head is alive, the artist having endowed it with the will, the science, and that undefinable something—genius—to bring it into being (*Castle* 65).

Aware of Diana's fascination with Bacchus's bodyless head, Dr. Féron admonished her in ambiguous terms not to *lose her head* in the learning process. Not to worry. "I love it too much," she noted emphatically. "It comes from one whom I shall never forget" (*Castle* 65). (Although the reader may not know to whom Diana is referring at this time, it becomes clear that it is her mother.) When he was querying her on the meaning of her words, the reticent Diana, having feared mockery on the doctor's part, was reassured by his gentle ways, and shared with him the content of her vision of the Veiled Lady/Nymph/Fairy. Fascinated by the psychological aspects of the child's feverish meanderings and by her predisposition to the poetics and marvels of art, Dr. Féron in no way attempted to destabilize Diana's belief in the reality of her mysterious encounters in the castle. His compassion and respect for art brought Diana ineffable joy and formed the basis for a solid and beneficial relationship with him.

Sensitive to her needs, the doctor invited Diana to his home, showed her his collection of antique statues, medals, cameos, and engravings and, after listening to her reactions, realized that "this little girl was a born artist" (*Castle* 66). The empathy between the two generated an inner excitement in Diana, imbuing her with the Bacchic fervor needed to draw out those living, moving, speaking elements within her soma/psyche. Her "facile illusions having been all but dissipated," she was no longer satisfied with simple scribblings. The good doctor inculcated in her an understanding of the demanding discipline that art—or any creative work—imposes upon the artist (*Castle* 66). Inexplicably, although not to Diana, she again ceased drawing, supplementing her bouts of daydreaming with salubrious walks in the countryside, immersing herself in Mother Nature's strengthening fold.

MOTHER. During the summer months, Diana's family moved to the country, to an area Diana loved. Walking in the garden on one occasion, she overheard a particularly hurtful conversation between Laure and a neighbor. Not only did her stepmother denigrate her, but called her an "idiot," unable even to tie a ribbon in her hair. Even more destuctive were her father's words about her, which Laure repeated to the neighbor, declaring Diana "to have no taste" and "no understanding about painting" (*Castle* 68). Initiation rituals, whatever their goals, require as we know, suffering. But such verbal brutality was too much for Diana to bear.

Running hysterically from the spot, she fell to the earth weeping, calling to her mother for help. Seconds later, as if the mother figure dormant within her for so many years had been revivified, she heard a tender voice emanating from the lilac bushes next to her: "Diana, my darling Diana, my child, where are you?" (*Castle* 69). Rising suddenly, the panic-stricken young girl ran hither and thither. "Here, here, I am here!" Again the voice called to her. Diana's frantic efforts to reach the yearned-for source were in vain. Her inner world, temporarily blocked by the power of the devastating remarks, failed to image her mother's voice in her mind's eye.

Hallucinating, she saw herself in a river, peacefully astride a silver-eyed, golden-finned dolphin, observing sirens picking flowers from the watery depths. Mood and placement having altered, she now observed herself standing on a mountain near a large snow statue, which spoke to her. "I am your mother, come and kiss me!" (*Castle* 70). No sooner had Diana attempted to carry out the command than she, too, was turned into a snow statue, broken in half, unable to move, powerless. Then she felt herself rolling into a ravine. The comforting image of the Veiled Lady having again made her presence known, Diana cried out to her in desperation: "Let me see my mother" (*Castle* 70).

That a lake emerged during Diana's hallucinatory episode is significant. The water element—which the Greek philosopher Thales considered the principle of all things, and which psychologists identify with amniotic fluid and with the collective unconscious—indicated the dreamer's need to absorb and reabsorb the creative and protective powers of the pre-formal state of existence. A fluid condition would help Diana to reconstitute her now paralyzed relationships and reconsider her priorities. The reappearance of the castle of Crooked Peak and flower-picking nymphs revealed a need for beauty, dream, and malleability in her rigidly constructed environment. Flowers, identified with the ephemerality, transience, and change of the creative process and of Mother Nature's living world, suggest that if she was seeking to become a living and not a dead artist, Diana would have to dig beneath the surface, into her creative, ever-fertile, living amniotic fluid.

The vision of herself transformed into a snow statue, broken in two and slipping into a ravine, brings to mind aspects of ancient and modern dismemberment (Gr. *sparagmos*) rituals, as in Euripides' *The Bacchants* and Claudel's *Break of Noon*. The shock of being unable to move—stricken with paralysis because of her untenable situation at home—is evident. Her division into two parts indicates a cutting up of previously nonfunctional, so-called *solid* attitudes. The duality of overt opposition and confrontation are positive events in Diana's initiation. In proper assessment, duality paves the way for greater lucidity on the child's part, particularly in dealing with Flochardet, and with Laure by extension. The breaking-up or restructuring of the ouroborus, a child's sense of "original totality and self-containment" existing "prior to the birth of consciousness," had to be brought about in Diana's case. Such a change required the dismemberment of her previously passive infantile attitudes, including her own rigid fear of hurting her father. To mutilate the ouroboric stage would destroy the faulty ruling conscious principle dominating her life, thereby releasing her from her psychologically oppressive mind set.

That Diana had been privileged to see herself astride dolphins—symbols associated with rebirth, salvation, wisdom, and prudence—attests to the furtherance of her psychological growth as woman and artist. Admittedly, the Veiled Lady's appearance and the pronouncement of Diana's command—"Let me see my mother!"—marked a turning point, but they did not denote a resolution of her problems. At this moment Diana felt someone kissing her forehead. Unable to discern between sleeping and waking worlds, she soon realized that it was her governess who, having sought and found her, had bestowed this tenderness on her.

As the two wandered back to the house, Diana again took the initiative—this time in the world of reality. She questioned her governess about her real mother, now in heaven. How does one reach heaven? Only through kindness and patience, the governess replied. Did her mother love her? Yes, she adored her. Diana's misfortune was to have lost the most "wonderful woman in the world," but she could "repair this misfortune by being kind and wise—as if [her mother] were looking at [her]" (*Castle* 71).

Despite a high fever that night, Diana felt comforted by the thought of having seen her mother and of knowing that she was watching over her. When the Veiled Lady appeared in another dream that same night, Diana had no qualms about asking to see her mother again. To Diana's amazement, her mother revealed herself as the Veiled Lady.

> "Really? Oh?" Diana said, "Then remove your veil so I can see your face"
> "You know very well that I don't have one any more!"
> "Then, alas! I shall never see it?
> "That depends on you. You will see it the day you return it to me."
> "Oh! My God, what does that mean and how will I go about it?
> "You will have to find it yourself. Come with me and I will teach you many things." (*Castle* 72)

Taking Diana in her arms, she proceeded to show her a series of beautiful images of Goddesses and Muses.

THE MAKING OF THE ARTIST. The preceding visions had revealed Diana's urgent need for change—from passivity to activity. What seemed to have motivated the turn of events were the drawings she had made in a corner of her father's studio. The origins of her configurations—amalgams of interlocking lines—were embedded in mystery, but her linear outpourings responded to certain psychic rhythmic patternings that served to fuse subject with object, thereby activating mood-altering sequences. Differences between authentic creativity and facile societal art, as exemplified by her father's renditions, were working their way into Diana's increasingly receptive *thinking* world. The partnership of subliminal, or irrational images in Diana's hallucinatory fantasies and dreams, considered by some as examples of primitive formlessness, had catalyzed an increase in her awareness of the visual arts in particular, and of the creative principle in general. Although an admirer of her father's talents and techniques, she took umbrage with his slave mentality, caught up as it was in the parameters of stylish nineteenth-century portraiture. Her expanded consciousness brought increased objectivity toward her father as artist. Nor was his goal—to appeal to his customers and thus make money—her sole criterion. Her decision was not to follow in his footsteps, but because the unconscious is loath to reveal its secrets, she could not yet pinpoint the direction she ought to take. First she would have to develop her cognitive and technical skills, then learn how to transform the richness of the unfathomable—the veiled and shadowy forms in her mind's eye—onto paper or canvas.

Recognizing Diana's psychological progress through the medium of her drawings, Dr. Féron saw them now no longer as a hodgepodge of fleeting designs, but rather as an active search on her part for the *rebirth archetype*. His support gave her courage; his counsel to channel her inner energies into acquiring knowledge and depth enhanced her self-understanding; and his advice to retain independence in her home environment was also of great help. Under his tutelage, Diana focused on what she believed to be vital: to recall, thus to visualize, her real mother. The Veiled Lady, existing as a living and active image in her unconscious, would help Diana take her first step toward psychological independence as woman and as artist. Because the Veiled Lady/Nymph/Fairy/Mother still remained *veiled*, and thus unseizable, as already noted, her lack of availability both pained as well as energized Diana, driving her on to actively seek out her mother's *face!*

THE SURROGATE FATHER. How best could she reach her goal? Convinced that Diana would never acquire the instruction she craved under the benevolent despotism of her father and the mindless domination of her stepmother, Dr. Féron suggested that he become her mentor. Having gained Flochardet's assent, he arranged that Diana and her governess should spend their days at his home, and their nights at Flochardet's. To allot sufficient time to his teaching, he would devote only two hours daily to his most urgent medical cases, leaving the remaining ones to his beloved adopted nephew, Marcelin.

That Flochardet accepted the idea of surrogate fathership for his daughter may have revealed his unconscious sense of failure as a guiding principle in Diana's life, or/and, an unwillingness to devote his own time to her needs. His virtually inoperative ego, masked by his friendly, affable, and charming manner, had divested him of the courage needed to curb both his wife's material urges and his own narcissism and self-indulgence. Just as psychological stasis conditioned Flochardet's empirical existence, so it shaped his art. The sameness, repetitiveness, and surface prettiness that marked his every artistic endeavor saved him from the harrowing torments of dissatisfaction. He had no urge to peer into the linear involutions, play of lines, or rhythmic formations. Exilarated by his slight painterly depictions, he shrank from any pictorial ventures or adventures. His needs were pedestrian—skin-deep. An inability on his part to peer *intus*, however, spared him the suffering and doubt experienced by great artists. Absorbed in what he considered to be his achievements and his active social life with Laure, he found little time to feel guilty about his neglect in furthering Diana's artistic education. More importantly, his passive/aggressive denigration of his daughter's talents and an unconscious rivalry with her prevented him from building up her continuously eroding self-esteem. Indeed, he fostered its diminution.

The day Dr. Féron became Diana's surrogate father, the principle of complementarity—symbolized by the number four—became operational in Flochardet's household. Analogized by mystics with the earth, with the four letters in Adam's name, the four authors of the Gospels, and so forth, the magic number four has come to symbolize the notion of completion, wholeness, earth, and stability. The prevailing inoperative trinity—a natural father, a deceased mother, and a stepmother—would be replaced by a new working dynamic by the addition of a fourth.

The doctor's highly developed thinking function and his scientific acumen coupled with maturity, generosity, and strength of character, would actively help redress the prevailing negative play of opposites. Although Diana's natural mother was absent from the household, she was, paradoxically, present in the form of the Veiled Lady who both pointed the way into the castle and played an active role as her daughter's nurturer and healer. Not to be minimized, however, was the catalytic role played by the ever-present, flighty, domineering, and disruptive Laure, who would bring matters to a head.

Diana's inborn self-healing principle, again being called into play, would see her through the next stage of her development: that of a functioning and independent adult. To this end, Dr. Féron's scientific and logical approach to history, art, and culture in general were instrumental, as were his sensitivity and, most importantly, his unselfish love for her. As a doctor, he was capable of healing her physically; as a psychologist and altruist, he instinctively knew how to stir in her a sense of renewal and purpose. Rather than teaching by rote, as was the custom of the time, he strove to trigger her imagination and enthusiasm for life. Taking her on a tour of his collection of ancient art objects, he stressed their livingness, beauty, and cultural significance, arousing, in so doing, her intellectual and emotional excitement.

Diana's fulfillment as woman and artist required that she learn to think for herself, even while studying humanity's anthropological, philosophical, and spiritual development. Such a goal would clearly force her into an impasse. Hadn't she always responded instinctively and positively to artifacts and to antiquities—as attested to by her excitement when she first entered the Castle of Crooked Peak? To transcend her parents' resistance to her approach to the creative principle would oblige her to confront them by articulating her ideas on art and other topics. Taking sides in a cultural debate would teach her to consider a value system of her own. Nonetheless, even confrontation would prove to be an insufficient educational tool. She would have to be taught to distill the elements in modern, as well as in past eras, to which she could relate and from which she could benefit emotionally and spiritually.

Still painfully evident, albeit diminished on the surface, contention continued in Diana's household, particularly in the domain of art. Dr. Féron sensed a whole undeveloped side behind the pretty little pictures Diana drew. Her father, however, judged her efforts to be poor. A hypertophy of ego-consciousness divested the latter, as we know, of a sense of compassion, but even more significantly, of any objectivity in his appraisals of her drawings. Bleeding inwardly from her father's continuous castigations, her self-image would have continued to erode had it not been for her mentor's encouragement. His positive attitude toward her efforts during this interim period so bolstered her self-confidence that she was able to formulate and verbalize judgments of her own. A case in point revolved around her ability to understand and accept the doctor's lack of technical expertise in matters of art, even while she lauded the depth of his critical ideas. Was it not he who had instilled in her a sense of the beautiful in art? What he could not teach her, she realized, was the means of apprehending, then transmuting on to paper or canvas, the visual sensation and/or the visionary experience. She *alone* would have to take that giant step of giving concrete shape to sensation and perception by submitting to, and thereby mastering, nature's multivalent forms, textures, and colorations.

The greater Diana's insights into the pictorial world, the more she distanced herself from her father's work. Although her judgments, she now realized, were antithetical to his, she still interiorized them, fearing, perhaps, their devasatating impact on him. Or was she unprepared to cut the umbilical cord? And to deal with his possible destabilization if she should hurt him by articulating her real thoughts? Even more crucial, would she be strong enough to bear her guilt? No matter the answers, her father, in her eyes, was no longer a deity. He was beginning to take on human dimensions.

A step forward does not negate regression. Fearing her father's assailing remarks, Diana secreted her sketches. Each day she rose very early to draw until the rest of the household was astir. Severe sleep deprivation undermined her health to the point of provoking renewed bouts of fever and hallucinatory dream sequences. To the concerned doctor, she admitted to being under the dominion of an *idée fixe:* her mother's words as uttered by the Veiled Lady: "I am your mother and you will recognize my *face* after you have drawn it" (*Castle* 78). The discovery of her mother's face and the drawing of something she had never previously seen drove Diana to a frenzy of activity. No matter her efforts, her mother's face still eluded her. Although dominated by feelings of failure and defeat, to her credit, she persisted in reaching for her goal.

She *alone*, the doctor repeated could discover her mother's face; she alone could delve into the deepest folds of her psyche to educe her reality. Nor did he minimize the difficulty of such a quest, and the effort, time, and patience it required. By way of assurance, he mentioned the existence of a miniature cameo of her mother in her father's possession. Why had Flochardet never mentioned it to her? Was it because, as the doctor suggested, he had never liked it? Or, was it because he had not painted it? Diana opted not to look at the portrait. To do so would be a travesty—to take the easy way out.

Mother Nature at times forces the vulnerable to take detours. In Diana's case, she was again harassed by visions of the Veiled Lady. This time, she again signaled her to follow her into the now-crumbling castle of Crooked Peak. By some extraordinary show of fate, neither was hurt by the falling rocks. "Let us look for my face!" she said to Diana. "It must be somewhere inside. It's up to you to recognize it. If you don't succeed, it is your misfortune. You will never know me!" (*Castle* 80). Instead of destroying Diana's sense of purpose, the threatening cast of her mother's voice energized her search for the hard-to-attain treasure. As she made her way through the debris of engraved stones, reliefs, shells, antique masks, and other artifacts scattered about, she again heard the voice command her, "Hurry up. Don't amuse yourself looking at all this. It is I alone you must find" (*Castle* 80). Meanwhile, Diana, who had inadvertently picked up a small carnelian stone, was stunned by the beauty of the profile carved in it, the star embedded on its forehead, and its hair pulled back and held in place by a ribbon. Although the object seemed very small, the more she looked at it, the larger it grew. "Finally!" the object itself cried out. "Here I am. It is really I, your muse, your mother, and you'll see that you are not mistaken!" (*Castle* 80). Just as she was about to remove her veil, however, the image of the carved lady faded, and Diana awakened.

That Diana had not been bruised by the falling debris in the crumbling castle indicated that whatever tragedy were to befall her, she would have the resiliency, the fortitude, and the direction to see herself through her ordeal. Strengthened by her vision and decision, when the doctor brought her the little box containing the miniature cameo of her mother, thinking it might cheer her up, Diana resisted looking at it, and pushed it away. "No, no, my good friend! I must not look at it yet! She does not want me to. I have to find it myself. If not, she will abandon me forever" (*Castle* 80). Diana hid the unopened box in her secretary.

THE FACE REVEALED. A few years having passed, one day Diana was drawing mindlessly—or automatically—perhaps in an attempt to expel the demons that had kept her awake the night before. She wept silently, as if from the depths of her soul, having learned that Laure's thoughtless spending had led to her father's financial ruin. The tears she shed, unlike those in times past, were not due to her ordeals, but from concern for her father's peace of mind. At that very moment Diana felt a warm breath flowed through her hair, and she heard a feeble voice exclaim: "I am here, you have found me" (*Castle* 86). She looked around. No one was there! Mechanically, she gazed at the drawing she had just penciled, examined its profile, and, to her amazement, discovered it to be a duplicate of the one imaged in her archetypal dream recounted above. Continuing to flesh out her design on paper, she improved its rhythms, its nuanced interplay of shadowy lightnesses and the solidity and depth of the lines. She endowed them with a special livingness as well. Had she succeeded in casting off the limitations imposed upon artists working in the concrete or empirical world? Had Diana finally gained access to some substratum—some previous, residual experience echoing and rechoing in her psyche that she was calling up?

Diana's governess entered the room, looked at her drawing, and complimented her on the accuracy of her copy of the miniature. But she had not looked at her mother's picture, Diana protested. "Then it's a miracle," the governess replied, and called the doctor, who likewise affirmed its extraordinary resemblance. He, too, praised Diana for her excellent workmanship and her fidelity to the original. Flochardet, who also entered the sacred precincts, marveled at the accuracy with which Diana had rendered her mother's traits. "It's quite remarkable," he said. "Not one of my students is capable of doing as well" (*Castle* 88). Nor could he believe his daughter had never set eyes on the original.

So overwhelmed was Diana by the praise, particularly her father's, that in order to avoid their gaze, she turned and walked toward the window. Bedazzled by the brilliance of the sun's glare, she had a *visitation*:

[S]he saw a great, marvelously beautiful white face, set off by a greenish dress radiating emerald-like dustings. It was the muse of her dreams, her good fairy, the Veiled Lady, whose face was no longer hidden by a veil, that she now saw floating around her like a nimbus, and her beautiful face . . . bearing the exact likeness of the one Diana had drawn. (*Castle* 88)

Without knowing why or how, Diana found herself extending her arms toward this now-smiling radiance, and heard her fading image say: "You will see me again !" (*Castle* 88). In a state of virtual ecstasy, she cried out her joy. Going to her room, she opened her precious box, kissed the miniature, closed her eyes, recalled her dream vision, then looked at the face for the first time. It was the same: "that of the muse, the cameo, the dream, and her mother as well; it was reality discovered through the poetics of feeling and imagination" (*Castle* 89).

The configurations that had emerged on paper had leaped forth spontaneously from an unknown collective unconscious—a universal, if not cosmic heritage. As if by a play of magic, Diana had succeeded in integrating the essence of her mother's face into the structural vitality of the whole picture; that she had experienced the *numinosum*—or transpersonal reality—allowed her to bestow an aspect of the infinite unknown onto the world. Diana was a mediating power or bridge from one world to another; she revealed the mysteries of the unmanifest!

THE CROSSROAD. For the next two years the humble and sensitive Diana pursued her art, not only affirming her own taste, but revealing undercurrents in her drawings that had heretofore remained hidden, unrealized, unformed, and uncognized. Thanks to the doctor's lessons, her understanding of ancient art was looked upon as resurrected complexities and associations to which she could connect. Affinities with the past, via not imitation but kinship, led her to new interpenetrations of vitalistic organicism that spoke to her beyond linear time schemes. By fusing what lay beyond—and within—the reach of the mundane artist—as in the works of French Renaissance painters, such as Jean Clouet, Jean Cousin, those of the Fontainebleau School; and the intuitions of the nineteenth-century artists David, Delacroix, Ingres, and Géricault—Diana gave emotional expression to her feelings.

Art for her was incarnation: the reenactment of archetypal imprints in the psyche. Just as light shifts in the outside world, so similar phenomena cast their mobile illuminations within her. It was now incumbent upon Diana to saturate, then transmute the objects envisioned by her imagination/dream into visibly palpable forms, intensities, shadings, and gradations. Only then would she be able to call up those seemingly forgotten memories—which actually have been extant ever since humans took stone in hand to trace or mark their earthly sojourns.

Although her search continued for new ways of conveying authentic constituents of her feelings of love and fantasy, she, like her father, retained a basic notion of verisimilitude. Unlike him, however, she explored varieties of natural and mutable forms and tones—her linear involutions unwinding themselves not merely in pictorial representations on flat surfaces, but as if imbricated in some deeply indeterminate spatiality. By connecting with elements that flowed beyond the picture per se, Diana was resourcing herself with some primordial and eternal imprint. In the atmosphere, evanescence and musicality of her subjects—mostly portraits—she transcended her creative milieu and, like the prophets of old, anticipated new trends. Her outerworld orientation had, it may be said, turned inward, inviting her to see beyond the mundane, grounding her, as it were, in a continuously expanding psychic center stretching into a timeless reality.

Diana's time for artistic musings would, however, be drastically curtailed. She was forced to focus her attention on her father's financial catastrophe. Besides Laure's spending, his sudden loss of clientele was also to blame. Fashions had changed. Elegant simplicity was now the rage in the pictorial arts, decor, fashion, even hair styles. Constriction and ornateness were passé. Flochardet's unwillingness or inability to alter his techniques in order to follow the trend, caused him to lose his popularity. That his wife had returned to her parents' home served to increase Flochardet's depression. Diana's ability to function positively under such severe pressure could be ascribed in large measure to Dr. Féron's presence, the lessons he taught her, and, now, his financial expertise. Not only did he show her how to reduce expenses; he offered her a business arrangement designed to settle debts with her father's creditors. For her part, Diana, in the hope of relieving her father's distress but not wanting to vie with his style, decided to limit her salable drawings to children's portraiture. So charming were the faces she penciled that she rapidly built up a modest clientele.

THE SEARCH WITHIN. Although on the surface Diana seemed relatively happy, within, she felt uncertain and doubtful of her efforts and goals. Had her creative energies atrophied? Had financial matters desiccated her instincts? Was she starving for lack of creative nourishment? Doubt, or the reshuffling of ideations and emotions, may at times pave the way for births and rebirths. As she pondered her woes, and feelings of desolation impinged upon her existence, she came to the conclusion that even though beauty permeated her portraits, she had failed to apprehend and make visible the magic world of analogy: *truth in color!* To analogize (Gr. *analogos,* proportionate) would help her discern resemblances in particulars, thereby to connect with universals. Herein lay the deepest secrets of the human soul! Automatically, and without any preconceived rational cause, Diana went to the secretary where she had placed the carving of Bacchus's head for safekeeping, and lovingly pondered this exquisite object. She then asked this God—this demiurge—for inspiration. Would he teach her the secret of great art?

No longer doubt-*less,* Diana felt doubt-*full.* A sense of renewal flooded her psyche. She would expand both her vision and her medium. Never before had she worked in pastel. She would try it. The results were breathtaking. Her soft, nuanced, matte faces captured what lay beyond the visible world—as essences, powers that she found herself articulating linearly for the first time. The unmanifested had become sign, reflecting its endless reverberations in her mind's eye. Gradually, her reputation grew by word of mouth; parents brought their children to her studio. So thrilled and moved were they by Diana's depictions that they in turn had themselves painted—in a different medium and style, to be sure—by Flochardet.

After several years of Spartan living and continuous work, Diana succeeded in liquidating her father's debts. Laure returned, but this time, it was Diana who laid down the conditions.

A PILGRIMAGE TO THE CASTLE OF CROOKED PEAK. Blanche de Pictordu, whose father had invited Diana and her father to lunch after their night's stay in the Renaissance castle, was now Viscountess of Crooked Peak. Visiting Diana, she extended a return invitation, which Diana acepted with joyful anticipation, for she now understood that the vison of the Veiled Lady in the castle had been the source of her inspiration.

Diana arrived at the Castle of Crooked Peak at four in the afternoon. The still-shining sun cast its oblique rays on the terrace, the very place where she had first glimpsed her beloved Veiled Lady, whom she remembered as gigantic in stature. Now, to the contrary, she appeared to be of only average height. Nor was her beauty exceptional as it had seemed to her at the time. Whereas Diana had lived almost exclusively in the domain of fantasy as a child, thus connecting to her tap root, she no longer needed such a fulcrum. Her ability to analogize, then evaluate dimensions, colorations, and appearances in her drawings, indicated her solid grounding in reality—an ability that would enable her to both anticipate and to deal with future empirical events.

She and Blanche made their way to the thermes—the seat of Diana's "memorable night." Diana observed, much to her dismay, that the entire area had been restored, but, looking out the window, she discovered to her delight that an outer staircase remained in its former state. The idea of apprehending the treasures retained in her image-memories motivated her to visit the spots that were still intact and which revealed that the detailed inner recordings of the images stored in her mind at the age of eight were not only inviolate, but had been carefully integrated into her present reality. By linking new perceptions or psychic connections with memories, she created, "islands of consciousness . . . like single lamps or lighted objects in the far-flung darkness" (Jung 8, #755). Unlike her earlier memories, the ones she now perceived "contain[ed]," in Jung's words, "a new, very important series of contents belonging to the perceiving subject . . . the so-called ego" (Jung 8, 755). Over the years, "the ego contents" or "the so-called ego complex," having acquired energy of its own, generated its charges into Diana's feeling world of "subjectivity or 'I-ness" (Jung 8, 755). It may be said that she had reached the stage of psychological differentiation, of separation—of *identity*.

The calm of the splendid moonlit darkness set the stage for a recapitulation or review of the effulgent events Diana had experienced long before. Her childhood pain, isolation, dread, and anguish, as well as the exaltation that had enveloped her as a child, she now realized, had served to open her up to mystery. As waves of memory-images flooded her rational processes, they concomitantly revealed a new truth to her: a "secret power" in her soma and psyche. Only sensed at first, its presence was audibly confirmed by a voice—her mother's—urging her, as individual and as artist, to "overcome" the obstacles confronting her, for only in so doing would she be able to accept her familial and societal "duties," even while fulfilling her "noble ambition" (*Castle* 107).

Throughout Diana's hazardous journeys into self, whenever anguish threatened to overwhelm her and decimate her creative élan in the process, her protective inner mother arose within her. It was she who "had bequeathed to her that secret and precious energy inhering in patience" (*Castle* 108). Diana had come to realize the crucial importance of biding her time in her artistic endeavors. Yearning for more guidance, she asked her mother's "protective soul to enter her being." Must she abandon all thought of advancing in her artistic vision? Of penetrating uncharted territories? The vocal vibrations emanating from the statue reached her in audible sounds.

> Leave the care of your future to the maternal soul that watches both within you and above you. Together we will find the ideal path. It's simply a question of accepting the present as a stage [in one's development] which, even as you rest you are still working. (Castle 108)

THE RAPTURE OF COLOR. Before leaving the Castle of Crooked Peak, Diana walked to the top of the nearby mountain at sunrise. Ever-alternating sunrays shed their glittering luminosities on a cascading stream. Diana was sheathed in an interplay of seemingly infinite tonal vibrations and nuanced gradations of pinks, greens, beiges, and browns. Reverberating against a background of fields of colored flowers, the ineffable dramatic grandeur of the scene impacted on her with unexpected violence, as if colors and forms had wrenched her out of her ego-preoccupied world, launching her into cosmic spaces. And suddenly, as if plunged into mystical delirium, she knew what she had never before known—"the rapture of color" (*Castle* 110). A world beyond knowledge and esthetic contemplation had now revealed itself to her!

Prior to her departure from the castle, she stood before the statue of the Veiled Lady and thanked it/her mother for having taught her how to feel and to see! To her, Diana owed the "the true secret of life" (*Castle* 110). Nor did she omit paying homage to the small head of Bacchus and thanking him for the marvels he had revealed to her: love, laughter, and abandon—qualities she would henceforth draw upon for sustenance.

An aware and responsible Diana returned home, where she was increasingly esteemed by Laure and by her father. The wealth she accumulated as a successful artist was used for necessities and for deeds of charity as well. She married Marcelin, Dr. Féron's nephew, who had loved her since childhood. The "noble soul" that she was lived in harmony and togetherness with her family—and with her art!

The vision of Diana's personal mother, absent in her empirical life, answered a desperate need for the eight-year-old child. She emerged in Diana's dream in the form of a sculpture, that of the Veiled Lady/Nymph/Fairy, taking on the collective values and energies of the Great Mother archetype. As the impact of this nurturing, loving, gentle, yet forceful mother figure increased in Diana's unconscious, her influence in that child's empirical existence grew in tandem, thereby helping her firm an identity for herself. As participant in an animistic world existing both within and outside of Diana's soma and psyche, the personal and the archetypal Mother, each an aspect of the other, had finally revealed to Diana the rapturous use of color, which in turn enabled her to render on canvas her sacred life experience as woman and artist! Concomitantly, she protected her against the devouring side of the feminine principle, represented by Laure, who utterly disregarded Diana's needs. Her fundamental animosity, although distressing, did not depress the child, who grew in understanding with the passing of years. The role Mother/Nature played in Diana's active subliminal realm was an inspiration for her to seek out ways of unblocking, and thus fluidify her relationships and understanding of the art process as a mirroring of her personal and collective inner topography.

The mother figure, who revealed the healing power of indirect knowledge, or moon, to Diana, wisely showed her own face only when she judged her daughter to be sufficiently prepared to assimilate its meaning. The analogy between human and astral spheres is increasingly clear since the word *face* also indicates the face of the moon in French. Diana had to transcend the limited, mundane, unimaginative domain of her family environment in order to grapple with one of the most poignant unveilings of all, that of her mother's face, to be regarded as the unveiling of her own. To shear those barnacles from her fear-ridden psyche, to fluidify or dislodge the stumbling blocks that had prevented her access to inner sight, required her mother's disclosure. The metaphor of Bacchus's head, encrusted with earth, did not reveal its gleaming beauty to her until she herself had removed its detrital encasement. No longer a passive recipient, Diana became instrumental in her developmental process. Her inner search, activated by feelings of radiance and release inspired by the image of the moon/mother during her second visit to the castle of Crooked Peak, strengthened the impulse to make manifest what previously had been hidden—the face that was her mother's!

Paul Gauguin's words on the subject (1888) are pertinent:

> Painting is the most beautiful of all arts. In it, all sensations are condensed; contemplating it, everyone can create a story at the will of his imagination and—with a single glance—have his soul invaded by the most profound recollections; no effort of memory, everything is summed up in one instant—complete art which sums up all the others and completes them. (In Chipp, *Theories of Modern Art* 61)

10

MAURICE MAETERLINCK'S PELLEAS AND MELISANDE
THE DYING COMPLEX

O F METAPHYSICAL DIMENSION, Maeterlinck's fairy tale, *Pelléas and Mélisande* (1893), dramatizes the birth and burgeoning of the passion of love and its ultimate destruction of the protagonists. As a theater piece based essentially on what psychologists have labeled the "dying complex," the personages appear within a framework of signs and sensations, of occult forces and shadowy moods. The resulting stage language, divested of nearly all verbal motion, unfolds in slow, ritualistic sequences; each restrained verbal gesture is a sign, analogy, or symbol of some hidden and mysterious reality. In direct contrast to the fairy tales already studied in this volume, the near stasis reigning in the text of *Pelléas and Mélisande* conjures an array of supernatural forces. An atmosphere weighted with tension hovers over the protagonists as they slowly and painfully acquaint themselves with their karma.

ECTYPAL ANALYSIS

Maurice Maeterlinck was born in Ghent, the capital of Flanders, in 1862. His father, a notary, whose worries revolved around business investments and the collection of rents from his tenants, rarely had time to read a book. His mother, Mathilde, the daughter of a wealthy lawyer, understood her son's literary needs and encouraged him in his creative undertakings, going so far as to lend him money to have his first book printed. The product of a parochial school education, as was the custom at the time, Maeterlinck confessed his childhood terror of the priests' excoriating teachings of hell and purgatory. Later, he grew to despise Jesuit bigotry; he especially resented the joyless "seven years of narrow tyranny" he had experienced at their Collège of Sainte-Barbe.

Although Maeterlinck had opted for a litererary career, his father forced him to study law and, being a dutiful son, he enrolled at Ghent University Law School. After attaining the title of Doctor of Law in 1885, he persuaded his father that a trip to Paris and exposure to the Palais de Justice with its famous barristers would broaden his legal education. What Maeterlinck senior might not have known was that Paris, at the time, was the mecca of the arts. Under such circumstances, how could his son in all good conscience limit himself to the study of law? Nor did he!

Symbolism was in its heyday. Baudelaire's *Flowers of Evil* had inspired creative writers to reach beyond the world of reality, to immerse themselves through the senses in a transcendental sphere that would put them in touch with the entire cosmos. The Promethean Rimbaud—the modern fire-stealer, as he was called—had shocked the literary establishment with his violent, hallucinatory, and distorted visions that made up the bulk of his *Season in Hell* and his *Illuminations*. He advocated savage rebellion, and a concerted distortion of the senses. Verlaine, the author of imagistic and melancholy verse, felt most acutely the conflict between flesh and spirit. Mallarmé, the dean of French Symbolists, despised the ugliness of the industrial civilization of which he was a part, and longed to experience cosmic consciousness. His poetry was hermetic, a distillation of complex thoughts that he enclosed in words and in unusual and revolutionary syntactical procedures. His works were enigmatic, obscure; they captivated by the sheer beauty of visual and musical evocations and the density of the thoughts. And there were other Symbolist poets—Laforgue, Villiers de l'Isle Adam, Huysmans, and so forth.

Following his return to Ghent in 1886, Maeterlinck began leading a double life—writing poetry by night, in which the influence of the above-mentioned geniuses was discernible—and practicing law by day. He sent his first play, *Princess Maleine* (1889), to Mallarmé in Paris, who gave it to Paul Hervieu, who in turn sent it to Octave Mirbeau. In the latter's review of it, appearing in the *Figaro*, he labeled it "an admirable and pure and eternal masterpiece, a masterpiece which can immortalize a name . . ."(Maeterlinck, *Bulles Bleues* 202-207). Although little financial remuneration was forthcoming, the review served as catalyst for Maeterlinck.

His remarkably innovative plays—*The Intruder* and *The Blind* in 1891; *Pelléas and Melisande* (1893); *The Interior* (1894); *Ariadne and Bluebeard* (1901);

and *The Blue Bird* (1909), to mention but a few—were complemented by many long essays—including *The Life of the Bee* (1901); *The Intelligence of the Flowers* (1907); and translations of Ruysbroeck's *The Adornment of Spiritual Marriage* (1889) and of Novalis's *The Disciples at Saïs* (1895). Among the honors awarded Maeterlinck was the Nobel Prize for Literature in 1911. He and his wife spent World War II in New York, returning to France in 1947. He died of a heart attack on May 6, 1949. As an agnostic, he had requested there be no religious ceremony. Following a civil ceremony, his body was cremated.

THE STAGING OF PELLEAS AND MELISANDE. Directed by Aurélien Lugné-Poë, *Pelléas and Mélisande* was first produced on May 17, 1893, at the Bouffes-Parisiens. A devotee of Symbolism, Lugné-Poë was the ideal director for Maeterlinck's innovative play, for not only did he emphasize its fairy tale quality, but stressed its mystical, symbolic, eerie, and outerworldly dimensions as well.[1]

Lugné-Poë's penchant for the ambiguous, the evanescent, and the unclear in his staging of *Pelléas and Mélisande* was an outgrowth of his admiration for a group of painters known as the Nabis. Taken from the Hebrew word meaning "prophet," the Nabis group included such painters as Pierre Bonnard, Edouard Vuillard, Xavier Roussel, Félix Valloton, Paul Sérusier and Maurice Denis. These artists, having left the Académie Julian in 1890, rejected its conventionality, formality, and stereotyped vision.

Neither character nor infinite detail were of import to the Nabis, nor to Lugné-Poë at this juncture in his career. As noted by Maurice Denis, the spokesman of the group, after looking at one of Gauguin's canvases: "Thus we learn that all art is a transposition, the impassioned counterpart of an experienced sensation." He continued: "Remember that a picture before being a battle horse, a nude, an anecdote, or what not, is essentially a flat surface covered with colors assembled in a certain order." The Nabis painted on cardboard and blended turpentine with their pigment, thereby lending a "matte" effect to the surface. They applied cool colors and warm tones, rather than brilliant and harsh hues. Vuillard advocated indecisiveness, quoting Verlaine's famous dictum: "Où l'indécis au précis se joint." Muted tones, neutral colors, and a vagueness of atmosphere were their goal (Raynal, *History of Modern Painting from Baudelaire to Bonnard* 93).

Lugné-Poë in many ways applied the Nabis's conception of painting to his theatrical productions. His innovative procedures with regard to *Pelléas and Mélisande*, for example, caused a stir in the theater and art worlds. The flat and muted tones he chose emphasized the fairy tale quality of the drama. Contrary to custom, the stage was substantially bathed in darkness. Only diffused and dim rays shone here and there on the proscenium. The footlights were also eliminated in order to create a closer rapport between audience and actors. All extraneous accessories and sets were banished. A gauze veil was placed across the stage, which emphasized the play's spiritual quality, its dreaminess, and its mystery (Crawford, *Studies in Foreign Literature* 10).

The vagueness, ambiguity, and outerworldly impression achieved by such a technique aroused the admiration of one of France's leading writers, Octave Mirbeau, Maeterlinck's earliest champion, as previously mentioned. The coloring onstage, he wrote, was "graduated in muted tones of dark blue, mauve, and the blue-greens of the actors's costumes." The dim nuances, reminiscent of the canvases of the French pre-Raphaelite artist, Puvis de Chavannes, were evocative, suggestive, and not explicative. Theodor de Wyzewa's descriptions of Puvis de Chavannes's paintings may be applied as well to Maeterlinck's drama: "We are struck by a thirst for dreams, for emotion, for poetry. Satiated with light, too vivid and too crude, we longed for fog. And it was then that we attached ourselves passionately to the poetic and misty art of Puvis de Chavannes" (Rewald, *The History of Impressionism* 163).

ARCHETYPAL ANALYSIS

The strange or semi-earthly encounters of Maeterlinck's characters emphasize the powerlessness of humans to decipher arcana beyond their understanding. That fate dominated their earthly trajectories mirrored a *fin de siècle* fear and preoccupation with death. In this regard, Maeterlinck drew an analogy between humankind and the wooden marionette: both are manipulated by outer forces; both are unaware of the controls to which they are subject. The marionette is directed by the puppeteer; humankind is the plaything of God. Like marionettes, the creatures in *Pelléas and Mélisande* give the impression of being wooden, remote, passive, helpless, and impersonal, each in his or her own way yielding unabashedly to the forces of destiny. The stage became a microcosm of the macrocosm.

The play's atmosphere conveyed a sense of finitude, helplessness, and distress, particularly vis-à-vis the protagonists' inability to determine the problematics of their future. It underscored that humans were merely pawns in the hands of universal forces or of a higher being who imposed its will upon the world. Images, metaphors, personifications, associations, and correspondences conveyed Maeterlinck's deeply pessimistic view that humans were unable to order the events of their own lives.

The fairy tale genre, an ideal literary vehicle for Maeterlinck, allowed him to exteriorize his subjective world in structured patterns. Under his deft pen, linear time was abolished. Superimposed on his metaphysical universe of nonhuman essences was a sense of timelessness and of repetitiousness. The fairy tale structure with its obstacles, inexplicable appearances and disappearances, and its unaccountably lurking dangers, helped both cementation of emotional bonds (Eros) and their severance (Anteros). This genre also allowed him to emphasize the archetypal aspects of the *dramatis personae*: their timelessness, their intangibility, their repetitive answerings, and the increasingly portentous power of *mystery* that they shed throughout the performance.

MAETERLINCK'S MYSTICS. The writings of the German Romantics, (F. Novalis, C. M. Brentano, Achim von Arnim, E. T. Hoffmann) and of German mystics (Meister Eckhart and Jakob Boehme, among others), clearly impacted on Maeterlinck's writings in general, and on *Pelléas and Mélisande* in particular. The German Romantics had dug deeply into their inner world—a timeless realm of essences—and had transcribed their visions and insights for the world to read. Indeed, their ground-breaking works opened Maeterlinck up to the domain of the occult and of death—themes that were to haunt him for the rest of his life. The German mystics whose works Maeterlinck had read and admired encouraged him to penetrate cosmic spheres; where feelings and sensations were no longer phenomenologically restricted; where those who made the effort could experience the *true* world of reality—the eternal present, the cosmic soul, and God. In the words of the fourteenth-century mystic Johannes Eckhart: "There is in the soul something which is above the soul" (Taylor, *Maurice Maeterlinck* 22). Eckhart was convinced that the spirit living in each individual, after proper discipline, could be liberated and flow freely into the plenitude of the cosmos, where both the being and his or her essence would become one with God. The seventeenth-century German mystic Jakob Boehme, in his *Confessions,* wrote: "For I have seen and have known the essence of all beings, depth and nothingness (Boehme, *Confessions* 9). He believed that within the timeless universe there existed a dynamic dual structure: light and darkness, good and evil, love and hate, which could be overcome via a spiritual ascension. The Godhead could be reached and experienced thanks to the practice of special disciplines that, with God's grace, would liberate humans from their earthbound habitat and restore them to the luminous realm of divinity.

The cosmic element that came into play in northern regions—where *Pelléas and Mélisande* takes place—were conducive to the stimulation of his imagination and his sensibilities. They inspired him to surround protagonists and events with an aura of nebulosity never before seen in theater. He bathed the stage in a foggy and misty climate permeated with shadowy and contrasting lunar illuminations.

For Maeterlinck, the material or readily visible world was merely a reflection of the primordial, undifferentiated unity of God's domain prior to creation, prior to the emergence of good and evil. His view diverged from that of the nineteenth-century mystic Edouard Schuré, who believed that "the evils which devour men are the fruit of their choice: and that these unhappy ones seek far from them the good whose source they bear" (Schuré, *The Great Initiates* 329). To the contrary, Maeterlinck was convinced, as previously indicated, that humans were virtually powerless in directing their destinies.

EROS VERSUS ANTEROS. The dual concepts of Eros and Anteros underlie the mystery, enchantment, fear, and belligerency in *Pelléas and Mélisande*. Eros, understood philosophically, represents love, the attraction of one person toward another. Symbolically, it stands for a unifying force in nature. By contrast, Anteros, Eros's brother, the God of unrequited love (habitually bitter and anguished), seeks revenge; he is known as the agent of discord, the dismemberer of all that is linked in the cosmos. According to Pythagorean metaphysics, which Maeterlinck had studied, the world (or any product of creativity) was born out of Discord or Chaos (Anteros), evolved under the dictates of Eros, and in time became barren, thus paving the way for the spirit of Anteros to again prevail, and separate what had been unified, thereby making rebirth and renewal possible. Accordingly, there are periods in history as well as in human relationships when Eros (relatedness) dominates, and other times when Anteros (discontinuity) holds sway.

Eros and Anteros are the forces and counterforces that make for the peripeteia and lysis of the fairy tale *Pelléas and Mélisande*.

WASHING AWAY FATED EVIL. The play opens with a loud knock at the door of Arkël's castle. "Open the door," the servants cry out, announcing their arrival to the Porter outside. They have come to wash the large doorstep leading to the castle (I,i). Since the Porter is uncertain whether he has the strength to open the rusty hinged door, he tells them to come in through the side door. They insist that he open the main door. Trying unsuccessfully, he finally asks for their help. The screeching hinges, the Porter warns, will awaken everyone in the castle. No matter! The mood suddenly alters. The servants are delighted to see the sun that has just burst through the cracks of the door, in sharp contrast to the misty, dismal, and shadowy atmosphere in the castle. Joyful bursts are heard, panegyrics in praise of this ball of fire that casts its rays into the darkness of the distant sea. As the door slowly swings open on its corroded hinges, life seems to have been replenished.

The blissful birth of a new day—a *renovatio*—is quickly expunged by the reality of the task facing the servants, who soon realize that they will never succeed in cleansing the vast expanse of the castle's threshold, doorstep, and porch. They call for more and more water. To no avail. The sharp contrast between the brilliance of a newborn sun and the centuries of detritus heaped upon the stone points up the melancholy and defeatist mood of the servants and preludes the oppressive events to come.

Water, so frequently a metapoetic image for purity, rejuvenation, creativity, and source of beauty, is here juxtaposed to decay, disintegration, abandon, and unworkability. The metaphoric opening image gives audiences their first clue of one's powerlessness over the forces of destiny. Despite the large amounts of water supplied, and the diligence of the the servants' scrubbing, the discouraged and insightful Porter foresees that they "will never be able to wash all of this clean," the impurities on the threshold of Arkël's castle being too deeply embedded.

That the virtually unworkable door finally opens suggests the antithesis between the illness and decrepitude that reign within the castle, and the outside world in which sun, hope, and renewal are possible. The inhabitants inside the medieval stronghold seem to resist light, fresh air, and healthy open relationships. They languish in a psychologically deleterious condition, their introverted and stagnant attitude toward life resting on misconceptions, deceit, and blindness as to their own motivations.

THE HUNT IN THE FOREST. Following the servants' unsuccessful attempt to clean the doorstep of the castle, the audience and reader are introduced, in typical fairy tale manner, to a dark, archaic, primeval forest where chaos reigns (I,ii). Usually, such confusion is put to right in medieval epics and tales of wonder by a hero's or heroine's determined action. This is not so in Maeterlinck's drama. His protagonists live in a world of progressive obliteration, denial, and rational depletion. Theirs is the black, underworld domain of the unconscious; they are unable to see clearly into themselves, or into their forgotten memories. That the forest belongs to the domain of the Great Mother adds another dimension to our story. A remote and chaotic realm (see chapter 1), the forest may be identified with the most primitive level of the psyche, the collective unconscious. As a maternal shelter, it will bring the protagonists together for a certain period of time, and perhaps even hold them in thrall.

Golaud, the grandson of Arkël, lord of the castle and king of Allemonde, is in the forest hunting, a popular sport in medieval times, as we saw in *Mélusine*. The usual hunter, intent on killing his prey and delighting in doing so, returns to his castle in possession of his trophy, or proof of the pursued animal's death—and a validation of his strength, virility, and power over himself and the world. Hunting was frequently associated in medieval times also with a magico-religious quest, identifying it with the achievement of spiritual goals.

The death of Golaud's wife, his anima figure, has been experienced by him unconsciously as a divestiture of his feeling function, which she not only represented, but which she alone knew how to elicit.[2] Attempting to replenish the emptiness of his inner spychic space, he was prompted to ride out of his now maimed world. Unthinking, disoriented, and having no direction, he has forged ahead, searching unconsciously for a guiding purpose that might allow him to replenish his present empty life. States of directionless wandering or madness were known by heroes of old—Perceval (Parzival) in the Grail legend, or Roland in Ludovico Ariosto's *Orlando Furioso*—and may be interpreted as a metaphor for the hero's own irrational mode of behavior.

The wild boar he hunts represents intrepidness—a metaphor for Golaud's own dauntless but also aggressive nature. Unlike the rational hunter who stalks his prey, studies every clue left by the animal, its footprints in the grass or earth, and recognizes and acts upon its habitude, Golaud simply forges ahead. Unthinkingly, he follows his instinctual behavioral patterns in his relentless urge to fill the void in his heart and psyche. A lapse of attention on his part allows the boar to escape from sight, thus leading the hunter astray.

Unlike many kings and knights of old, Golaud is not master of his mount. Having unconsciously allowed the beast he was hunting to lead him off track—out of familiar hunting grounds into unknown and untried forest areas—indicates a loss not only of outer sight, but of his inner path as well. Traces of splattered blood convince him that he has killed his prey, but Maeterlinck's fairy tale atmosphere suggests that the blood is in fact a premonitory image of some future aggression or violence. Strangely and ambiguously, Golaud claims that his hunting dogs have suddenly vanished from sight during his forest trajectory. They "can no longer find him," he iterates. What could have persuaded these highly trained animals to follow another scent elsewhere? Have they really lost their master? Or has Golaud's personality changed to the point of destroying his animals' ability to track one they knew so well? Has his scent (L. *sentire,* feel), or feeling function, been wrenched from him, or died within him following his wife's demise? The loss of his anima has, psychologically speaking, impaired his vision and his understanding and, even more damaging, has created a void within his psyche that has paved the way for the release of his repressed killer instinct!

Determined to retrace his steps in search of his dogs, Golaud is again led astray, this time, however, by the sounds of crying. Looking for its source, he sees a young girl at a fountain.

THE GIRL AT THE FOUNTAIN. Pictorial and literary images of beautiful young girls standing or seated near fountains are virtually banal; Maeterlinck's delineation, by contrast, is unique. His Mélisande, unlike the Mélusine of the medieval tale (ch.1) is more an apparition than a flesh-and-blood human being. She is huddled at the fountain, weeping and wailing.

Tears in general, and Mélisande's in particular, may be identified with many watery and/or liquid images: weeping willows, rivers, lakes, seas, mountain cascades, or any transformative substances. Fountains, wells, and springs have since ancient times represented the infinite possibilities open to one starting out in life or on a creative venture. Water may be considered a nourishing, beautifying, and beatific force, as imaged in clear flowing streams in the manifest world. Like uncontaminated water, Mélisande is pure, naïve, transparent, fluid, and graceful, reminiscent of the intangible and distant women depicted by the pre-Raphaelite painter, Burne-Jones. Within her exists mystery. Was it by some feat of magic, or in some dream or trance state, that the youthful, and even childlike, Mélisande has revealed herself to Golaud in the forest?

Startled by his presence, and afraid of his intentions, she cries out: "Don't touch me or I will drown myself!" (Pelléas 6). Golaud, commenting on her beauty, reassures her and asks whether someone has hurt her. "Yes! Yes! Yes! Yes!" she answers, sobbing anew, but refusing to divulge her origins, her identity, or those responsible for her hurt. He learns only that she has fled from a distant land and has lost her way.

Happening to glance into the waters of the fountain, Golaud spies something shining in their depths. Mélisande admits only that it is her golden crown, the one "he" gave her, and that it has fallen into the fountain while she was crying. Although Golaud offers to retrieve the crown, she rejects the idea, spelling a desire to dissociate herself from her past, and with childlike petulance threatens to throw herself into the fountain in its stead. Evoking Ophelia (Hamlet, III, 1), Maeterlinck illustrates the suicidal temptation of water for utterly formless—or unformed—adolescent personalities (Bachelard, L'eau et les rêves 111). Like other abandoned, rejected, or fleeing maidens, Mélisande seems afloat on dangerous waters. In that her personality is still fluid, that is, unformed, her emotions seem to be in a perpetual state of flux. Like water, she represents a world in potentia; before form or rigidity have solidified her disposition. A dynamic and motivating force linked to the feminine, she may be looked upon as a future mother image, water being understood in this context as a nourishing agent: the fons et origo of all life. Could her forest meeting with Golaud, like a baptismal ceremony, act as a renewing and regenerating power leading possibly to her rebirth?

Now comforted in the knowledge that Golaud will neither touch nor hurt her, Mélisande, the unjudicious and imprudent child, questions him about his origins, then tactlessly comments on the gray hairs on his temples and in his beard. Is he a giant? she may have wondered. He, in turn, notices something strange about her: she never closes her eyes. She protests that she does so at night. The fact that her eyes remain open during the day indicates on the one hand her ability to face conscious occurrences without resorting to filters or screens (closing and opening of the eyes); and on the other hand, it suggests a need to block out or protect her unconcious from overinvolvement in real life situations. During the night, however, when subliminal spheres are preponderate, her psyche might feel greater ease in facing both inner and outer worlds.

Not lacking in forthrightness, Mélisande asks Golaud what has brought him to the forest; he confesses to having lost his way while hunting wild boar. As the chill of night descends on the forest, Mélisande shudders, and Golaud invites her to follow him, for she cannot remain in the forest alone: "The night will be very black and very cold" (*Pelléas* 10). Prior to their departure from the sacred sylvan realm, Mélisande asks him where he intends to go. "I don't know . . . I am also lost," he responds (*Pelléas* 10). Both Golaud and Mélisande are lost souls in a profound state of psychological distress and alienation.

Golaud and Mélisande exit from the forest and face the empirical world with its conventional standards, in which it becomes increasingly difficult for both to retain their delicate psychological balance. Profound affective reactions—denial, rejection, sublimation, or any other so-called protective psychological devices—once broken down, will make them prey to the dangers of the wild—those shadowy, evanescent pulsations lurking about in subliminal spheres.

MEMORY LOSS. In the case of both Golaud and Mélisande, memory loss may be attributed to painful psychopathological experiences that they had unconsciously sought to blot out. In Golaud's case, the death of his wife, as previously mentioned, has led to the sudden loss of his anima image, or what it represented in him. In Mélisande's case, however, the reader is unaware of the exact reasons for her inability to process or to recall the horrific experience that had led to her amnesia—a period when the ego (sometimes only momentarily) has been divested of its ties with consciousness. Memory, nonetheless, goes beyond mere registration, retention, and recall of the past, and includes complex processes of perception, aperception, differentiation, and understanding of previously learned responses. In that memory traces had apparently eradicated all connections with past conditionings and feelings, Mélisande gives the impression of behaving and speaking like a robot, as if unable to encode the slightest emotional event that had given rise to her trauma. Unlike Proust's characters who recall a past via sensation, Mélisande feels only the hollowness of her dank earlier years. Benumbed by some seemingly harrowing experience, she remains emotionally stunted, transformed in effect into inert matter. Memories, like sensations, having hidden themselves in the darkest corners of her psyche, they have virtually dismembered her past. Her power of recall, like so many retreating phantoms, has been reduced to nil. Understandably, she and Golaud speak in monosyllabic sequences.

Golaud's loss of memory is limited to a certain decrement of "energetic value" of conscious contents. Having fallen "beneath the threshold of consciousness" through perhaps "intentional forgetting," whatever incidents have been obliterated may be said to have been repressed. Under such circumstances, his rejection of what could be labeled "dead hours" has brought on their memory-dissolution (Jung VI, #614).

THE CASTLE. The medieval seaside castle ruled by Arkël, the aged grandfather of Golaud and his brother, Pelléas, is a containing image as enigmatic as the forest. Its thick, sturdy, and protective walls foster a sense of security and well-being in some of its inhabitants, while impacting on others as imprisoning and sisnister. This hermetic complex of opposites spells other polarities: light versus darkness and redemption versus damnation. Whether Arkël's castle holds the hard-to-attain treasure, which in Jungian terms stands for the highest of spiritual values, or whether it accommodates within its crumbling walls inner pollutants, molds, and other decaying agents remains to be seen.

As the scene opens (I,iii), Geneviève, the mother of Golaud and Pelléas by different fathers, is reading a letter from the former to his brother, describing his chance meeting with Mélisande in the forest and his marriage to her six months ago, adding that he knows nothing more about her past than he did when he first met her, and that he has refrained from questioning her further for fear of provoking more tears. Golaud awaits his beloved brother's return to the castle before announcing his marriage to Arkël. Pelléas's endearing and diplomatic ways can placate his grandfather's anger over the marriage, which does not fit this patriarch's political and economic plans. If Arkël should agree to receive Mélisande as he would his own daughter, Pélleas should, three nights after the reception of the letter, light a lamp atop the castle's tower, which will be visible to Golaud from his ship at anchor in the waters nearby. If Arkël's reply is negative, he, Golaud, will continue on his journey, never to return.

The tower, an emblem for elevation and ascent, indicates both a tendency toward higher realms from which a broader view of empirical situations is obtained and, psychologically, an expanding conscious attitude. In Golaud's case, he hoped the monarch would be sufficiently broad-minded to accept his marital folly. Such an eventuality would not only relieve him of his anguish, but preserve him from the fate of the Flying Dutchman, doomed to wander. Golaud similarly yearned to stabilize his moorings, thereby finding renewal. He felt a need to reconcile himself with his family, and especially with the patriarchal hierarchy. His escape into darkened subliminal spheres, as represented by the forest sequence, or his roaming of the seas since his marriage to Mélisande, suggests a failure to come to grips with his destiny in the real world. By openly announcing his marriage, which spelled danger and uncertainty, he sought now to shed his formerly secretive and masked existence. That he had asked his brother to light a lamp atop the castle's tower, would also serve to highlight, perhaps for the better, a whole previously concealed existential domain.

The patriarch Arkël accepts Golaud's request, admitting that "since he has never seen into himself with clarity, how could anyone believe him capable of judging the actions of others?" Unlike many monarchs in fairy tales or myths, whose governing principle and judging factors wavered or became flawed with age, Arkël saw himself as a physically and spiritually defunct/sterile force, no longer a leader nor a maker of paths, but rather an instrument of decadence and ruination. Unlike the ill Amfortas in *Parzival*, or the distracted or senile King Lear in Shakespeare's play, or the Hindu ruler Dasaratha in the *Ramayana*, who "had never studied his mirror properly," and thus had had "no occasion to scrutinize himself . . . or engage himself in any introspection" (R. K. Narayan, *The Ramayana* 35), Arkël understood that a new power must reign.

Seemingly having learned from past mistakes, Arkël asks Pelléas, who was supposed to leave on a journey to visit a dying friend, to remain at the castle with his father, Geneviève's husband and the present king, who suffers from a life-threatening illness. Even more significant are the famine and disease raging throughout the region; people are dying and agitation and rebellion are rampant. Prevalent aridity and chaos in fairy tales usually indicate the unproductivity or barrenness of the land's ruling forces. Dissatisfied with the status quo, the populace expresses a need for change. Renewal, the only means of stemming further decay, becomes an imperative. Anteros, as previously mentioned, must break up the stratified, ingrown, and sterile conditions in both physical and spiritual domains.

MELISANDE. As long as Mélisande remains an anima figure for Golaud, she will never become a person unto herself. Instead, she will remain a mirror image, or reflection, of the "other." Her presence fulfills Golaud's unconscious yearnings for beauty, radiance, tenderness, and luster. Projecting his unconscious needs—deficiencies—onto Mélisande, he is powerless to differentiate between his vision of her and the reality—if any—of what she is. Imprisoned in superficial and unsatisfactory abstractions, his relationship with Mélisande can never evolve. Mélisande's comment in the forest scene on Golaud's graying hair, as previously mentioned, symbolically preempted the course of their relationship: father-daughter (creator-creation), precluding a husband-wife alliance (based on mutual understanding). Nor would Mélisande take on reality for the other protagonists in Maeterlinck's drama. She simply is not related to this world.

When Geneviève first meets Mélisande (I,iv), she is enthralled by her purity, gentleness, and delightful childlike qualities. Indeed, like the primordial Eros of Greek mythology, Mélisande has the power to draw together disparate factors in nature and society. As a *medium* type woman, psychologically speaking, she is "permeated by the unconscious of another person," and therefore can make others believe she answers their needs (Castillejo, *Knowing Woman* 67). She magnetizes rather than relates to them on a conscious level. On a one-to-one basis, they see her with loving delight as the archetypal little girl.

Geneviève alone has reservations about introducing Mélisande—this stranger (L. *extraneus),* foreigner, alien creature—into the family enclave, feeling she will disturb the harmonious familial balance. Although she might have understood a rash act on the part of Pelléas, she found it inconceivable that Golaud, who since the demise of his wife Ursule had devoted himself completely to his young son Yniold, could have behaved so mindlessly and impulsively. Might Geneviève have divined that Mélisande, the *strange stranger,* would be responsible for introducing *estrangement* into the castle's equilibrium?

PELLEAS, THE LIGHT-BRINGER. The brother motif, dual aspects of a single figure, is common in fairy tales and myths (Cain and Abel, Osiris and Set). Pelléas and Golaud, although offspring of the same mother, did not share the same father, accounting in part for the differences in their personality traits. Golaud, the hunter, was aggressive and extroverted. He set forth to "catch" his prey—that is, his bride. Pelléas, by contrast, was passive, sensitive, emotional, and introverted. Submissive and obedient, he renounced, his mother's and Arkël's request, his idea of visiting his dying friend in order to remain at home both to care for his mortally ill father and to carry out his brother's appeal to light a lamp in the castle's tower. Pelléas's acquiescence indicated a heightened sense of responsibility and a benevolent generosity, particularly toward Golaud, who was seeking to rejoin his family. Golaud's return to his home—to his *foyer* (L. *focus,* hearth, fireplace)—would spark the play's lysis, but Pelléas would become the light-bringer—the catalyst responsible for igniting the destructive blaze that would in time bring down the ancient castle and its inhabitants.

In their first conversation, the personalities of Pelléas and Mélisande merge in unexpected ways (I,iv). In his company Mélisande is neither submissive nor fearful nor withdrawn, as she was with Golaud. To the contrary, she becomes a dominant in their relationship. As his anima figure, she responds to his need of the little girl archetype: provocative, seductive, and playful, she elicits in him feelings of well-being, and provokes his laughter. She even taunts him in her subtle games. On one occasion, for example, in the park of the castle, despite Pelléas's repeated warnings, she plays with her wedding ring right above the fountain. Alluring, mesmerizing, and dangerously charming, she takes on certain attributes of the siren for the seemingly naïve Pélleas.

Siren myths and fairy tales are plentiful in medieval bestiaries as well as in the works of Aristotle, Pliny, and Ovid. Indeed, the French have their own siren figure, Mélusine (see ch. 1), and one may underscore, in this regard, the similarity between the names Mélusine and Mélisande. In patriarchal societies, sirens have come to represent what the male considers to be woman's inferior force: ability to entice, but inability to fulfill the act of love. Psychologically, woman, remaining imprisoned in the most primitive levels of existence, is powerless to develop and mature. Inevitably she causes not only her own destruction, but the male's as well.

In that the siren is associated with the water principle (unconscious) rather than with the rational factor (conscious), we may suggest that Mélisande is governed by the moon, her favorite habitat being darkness rather than light. Her attraction toward water, identified with the moon, as previously noted, serves also to explain her presence near fountains, first in the forest, then in the castle's park (I,i).

Pelléas and Mélisande meet and converse near the the castle's ancient and abandoned fountain, which is bathed in an aura of mystery. It is alluded to as "the miraculous fountain" and "the fountain of the blind," its magical powers enabling the sightless to see into invisible realms. As the source of life, activity, and potentiality, the fountain in the thirty-sixth Psalm has been associated with life: "For with thee is the fountain of life: in thy light shall we see light." A realm *in potentia*, individuals and societies seek out the fountain when their world becomes arid and troubled.

Immersion in water is the equivalent of regression into a preformal state, to infancy, to a fresh start, to rebirth. In John we read, "Except a man be born again, he cannot see the kingdom of God," and, "Except a man be born of water and of the Spirit, he cannot enter into the kingdom of God" (3:3,5). Golaud, at the crossroads in his life, was in the forest hunting, hoping to find that which would give a new turn to his life. He came upon Mélisande, the source of what he thought would be his future renewal and rejuvenation. When the relationship went askew, he opted for a return home, believing the warmth of family life would restore harmony and balance. Unbeknown to him, he was to become fertile field for Anteros.

Mélisande, too, sought to be rebaptized, to be initiated into another existence upon meeting Golaud at the fountain. Once in the castle, however, she would undergo another kind of baptism (II,i). Complaining to Pelléas that her "hands [were] sick," indicating that her "active" or worldly outlook was nonfunctional, she felt herself changing under his gaze. The more he projected on her, the more tantalizing and irresistible he became to her. Conversely, the inciteful and wily Mélisande captivated Pelléas as she continued to play with her ring which, predictably, dropped into the water.

Why the emphasis on Mélusine's wedding ring? The loss of her gold band is to be regarded not only as a rejection of her marriage to Golaud, but of her previously unsatisfactory experience of wedlock—as indicated symbolically by the crown she had dropped into the fountain prior to Golaud's arrival in the forest. The circular shape of both the wedding ring and the crown may be seen as symbolic of eternity and wholeness, and, psychologically, as an infantile state: when the ego is still identified with the self, prior to its development, differentiation, and consciousness. Twice Mélisande had been married. Twice she had tried to evolve from the archetypal little girl figure to the mature woman. Twice she had failed!

THE SYNCHRONISTIC EVENT. Maeterlinck, who believed in extrasensory perception and in synchronistic events, gives us an example of how linear and spatial time concepts are transcended. Golaud, hunting in the forest, is thrown from his horse at the very instant that Mélisande's ring drops into the fountain (II,i).

Golaud's fall, his bloodied face and severe chest pain—as though his horse had fallen on him—necessitate bed rest. External wounds sometimes may be expressions of inner lacerations. "I thought my heart had been crushed," he tells Mélisande (II, ii). She tries to be helpful by offering him another pillow, asking him if his suffering is not too great. Suddenly, she begins weeping. She, too, is ill, she tells him. "Has anyone hurt you?" Golaud questions. "No, no. No one has hurt me in the least." Perhaps unthinkingly, or perhaps purposefully said, Mélisande chooses this occasion to utter the most jarring news. "I can no longer live here. I don't know why . . . I would like to leave, to leave! I shall die if I stay here." Shocked to the marrow, Golaud asks her whether Pelléas has caused her any sorrow. Denying such a possibility, she tells him she must leave. Golaud's response is couched in personifications and in chiaroscuro color tones which convey his sentiments: "It is true this castle is very old and very sombre. . . . It is cold and deep. . . . And the countryside seems very sad, too, with all of its forests, all of those old forests without lights" (II, ii). But he will do all in his power to make her happy.

When Golaud discovers the loss of Mélisande's ring, he is overcome with grief: "I would have preferred to have lost everything I own, rather than to have lost that ring" (II, ii). The ring had become for him a hierophany—that is, a sacred object, a manifestation of divinity, a concretization of his anima, his soul, everything he projected on to Mélisande. Loss of the ring means the severance of his union with his wife or, in psychological terms, the cleavage of what in his mind had been unified, the destruction of his projection, of the visualization of his ideal.

Mélisande lies to Golaud as to how and where she lost the ring, claiming to have lost it in the grotto by the sea. He sends her there forthwith, ordering her to seek Pelléas's company in this dangerous venture to retrieve the ring. Heavy-hearted, fearing the dank darkness of the treacherous subterranean passageways marked by deep ravines on either side, and the high tide that floods the area each night, she is aware of the perils awaiting the unwary every step of the way.

As the two make their way into this starless and as yet unexplored grotto, attempting to find a ring they know is not there, Pelléas comments on the stalactites "resembling plants and men" (II,iii), and the "tenebrous blues" that fill the depths of this dark. secret realm. "Great treasures apparently have been hidden" in the immensities of this labyrinthian grotto," Pelléas continues (II, iii). The two now penetrate into the blackness of the underground recesses—symbols of the "heart" and of the unconscious—which contain hidden "treasures" or spiritual values. The searcher—hero or heroine—who, by dint of effort, penetrates deeply into dangerous undergrown recesses in search of the self, may find riches of the heart and mind. If they are properly assimilated by the conscious mind and fruitfully channeled into one's existential existence, healing may result. If improperly accessed and understood, however, destruction may ensue.

Although released from their ordeal thanks to increasingly bright lunar rays which directed them to outer realms, neither Pelléas nor Mélisande has at all evolved in the knowledge of self.

THE TOWER WINDOW. From the depths of their despair in the dank, damp, underworld grotto, identified with their dread of Golaud, Pelléas and Mélisande experience the heights of jubilation in the release of their love during the window scene (III,ii), which is reminiscent of the balcony scene in Romeo and Juliet.

As Mélisande leans out of her window in one of the towers, she allows her incredibly long blonde hair to fall on Pelléas, standing on a level below. Hair, having become the conduit of her passion, contains all of her virtues as well. As a symbol of her most intimate self, it may indicate timelessness: the still-slumbering physical and metaphysical essences in her past, present, and future, experienced in an eternal present. Demure and saintly in her beauty, she is reminiscent of iconographic depictions of the former prostitute Mary Magdalene, by Pietro Perugino (1445–1523).

Just as Mélisande had played with her ring over the fountain and had allowed it, advertently or inadvertently, to fall into its waters never to be recovered, signifying rejection of any future bonding with Golaud, so she now offers her hair, an ever-growing life force emerging from her very being, to her new love, Pelléas. The playful little girl turned *agente provocatrice*, transgressing legal and moral codes, now tempts fate by allowing her hair to fall on Pelléas standing below, even thought she knows Golaud to be only a stone's throw away.

Equivocal as well is Pelléas's position in the dangerous game of love. Whether knowingly, or not, whether dominated by fate or by an enfeebled will, he likewise transgresses social bounds by wrapping Mélisande's long tresses around his neck. Overwhelmed by their loveliness, he kisses and talks to her hair as though it were a living being. "It is lukewarm and tender, as if fallen from heaven. . . . Look, look at it, my hands can hardly contain it" (III,ii). Inundated by the fragrance and beauty of her tresses, he becomes their pawn, receiving them as a metonomy, in lieu of her. Rapturously, he cries out, "I hold them in my arms, I put them around my neck." Like water, their texture changes, becoming "lukewarm and tender" (III,ii). Increasingly excited, he palpates her thick tresses, which have become transformative agents. Exclaiming that their power has blanked out the sky, in trancelike enumerations he personifies each strand: it "shudders, incites, palpitates." Her tresses " love him, they love me a thousand times more than you!" (III,ii)

Suddenly, Golaud comes upon the lovers. Although suspicious of their antics, he internalizes his feelings: "You are children. . . . Don't play this way in the dark" (III,ii).

THE SUBTERRANEAN VAULTS. Corrosive anger, when repressed, eventually will ignite. Golaud, with latent intent to kill Pelléas for what seems to be a transgression, takes his brother into the castle's subterranean grottos. The chiaroscuro in these dark, treacherous areas, depicted as a conglomerate of eerie pits, inner water beds, and seemingly endless abysses, reflects the protagonists's fearsome subliminal thoughts and feelings. The strange happenings, described in visually and verbally halting poetic progressions, increase the harrowing suspense of the episode, paving the way for a whole new orientation in theater.

Although Pelléas proceeds haltingly, Golaud is familiar with the insalubrious labyrinth and its ravines. While seething with jealousy, he restrains himself. The criminal act will have to wait. By holding Pelléas's arm to prevent him from slipping into a gully, he, at least overtly, conveys his friendship and concern. Pelléas, dominating his impulse to reveal his love for Mélisande, feels stifled and breathes with difficulty, a physical manifestation of his psychological state. The increasing intolerability of the subterranean vaults indicates his growing awareness of the danger of continuing his relationship with

Mélisande. As though reading his thought, Golaud warns him outright to stay away from her: "the least emotion could bring about misfortune," inasmuch as she is expecting his child (III,iv).

Pelléas's premonitory sensation of doom prompts him to leave the fetid regions of Arkël's castle, and venture forth to some distant land where he may lead a life of his own. Prior to his departure, however, he asks Mélisande for a final meeting at the fountain in the park.

YNIOLD'S INADVERTENT TREACHERY. Far from assuaged by the announcement of Pelléas's leave-taking, Golaud's anger and terror at the thought of losing Mélisande to his brother convince him that he must learn the truth. To this end, he questions Yniold, his young son by his first wife. Only after protracted interrogations does Yniold, a gentle and loving child who spends his time at Mélisande's side, inadvertently reveal her trysts with Pelléas (III,v). For all his innocence, he nonetheless becomes the fateful power leading to the lovers' undoing.

THE FOUNTAIN. The climax of the play is constituted by the lovers' confession of their passion for one another. As they verbalize their feelings, they seem, as if by some magic feat, to retreat into their subliminal worlds. Or have they lost consciousness of the perils surrounding them? Like children playing out a *regressus ad uterum*, they progressively withdraw from the world of reality, and enter one of *poesis*. Pelléas compares Mélisande's voice to water; he does so metonymically, likening it to abstract personality traits—"Your voice! Your voice . . . is fresher and more frank than water. . . ." (IV, iv). Attempting to save from oblivion the image he has formed of her, he aks her to come into the light, away from the shadow of the trees. Being a moon figure, she prefers obscurity, and a sense of turmoil, foreboding, even panic is ushered into the scene by the interplay of light and dark—as if sun and moon were vying for dominion in domains controlled by Thanatos. As long as darkness prevails, love (Eros) permits Pelléas and Mélisande to dwell in their undifferentiated and boundless world of childhood. In a moment of abandon, they embrace. Golaud surprises them and kills Pelléas. Mélisande takes flight (IV,iv). Anteros rules.

Unlike Cain, who murdered Abel in all innocence (it was the first murder on earth and the consequences of this type of violence were not yet known), Golaud was aware of his destructive act. Perhaps he believed he was paving the way for renewal. It was not to be. Mélisande's second loss of memory, prior to the premature birth of a daughter, prevents her from recognizing Golaud, her environs, or her own identity. Before dying, with her remaining strength she asks but one question "Why am I going to die?" (V, ii).

The doctor's oracular pronouncement—"She [Mélisande] was born for no reason . . . to die; and dies for no reason"—sums up humankind's ignorance of final causes (V,ii).

The tragic love motif in *Pelléas and Mélisande*[3] has been compared to the devastating passions experienced by Tristan and Isolde and by Paolo and Francesca da Rimini, as well as to Othello's blind love for Desdemona, and the unparalleled attachment of Poe's child lovers in "Annabel Lee":

> I was a child and she was a child,
> In this kingdom by the sea,
> But we loved with a love that was more than love—
> I and my Annabel Lee.

Like creatures in fairy tales, the archetypal *dramatis personae* in *Pelléas and Mélisande* are as ambiguous and as formless as Maeterlinck's space-time concepts. Mute and intercalated between occult forces, they are drawn together, then apart, as though in an invisible network of fatality. Never clearly defined, they are reminiscent of Plato's shadows in his "Allegory of the Cave," or those depicted in *The Adornment of the Spiritual Marriage* by the Flemish mystic Jan van Ruysbroeck the Admirable, whose work Maeterlinck had translated into French. Attempting to confront and create their own destiny, but powerless to do so, they withdraw farther and farther into themselves until they are no more.

Archetypal images as used by Maeterlinck—castle, tower, forest, water, sun, moon, and fountain—become supernatual protagonists of the drama. They compel certain vital forces into activity, their power resting on a whole network of associations and sensations that affect every aspect of the drama for those who either view or read it. Spinoffs of Maeterlinck's characters, objects seem to glide in and out of events, as though driven by some extraterrestrial force to birth, growth, and death in life's eternal round.

No magic brews or natural forces intrude in Pelléas and Mélisande. Fate, the arcane force termed *heimarmene* by the Gnostics, compelled the childlike protagonists to weave their web around Eros and Anteros. Eros predominated, irrationally and lustfully; blindness reigned, barriers vanished, and codes and ethics were forgotten. Anteros's wrath, aroused, brought death to an already preestablished miasmic condition. Like many a fairy tale, *Pelléas and Mélisande* is invested with a sense of eternity. It takes place in some nebulous past, probably during the Middle Ages when forests, castles, and large bodies of water dotted Europe's landscape; and where vast land masses and high mountain ranges were barely discernible, so thick was the fog, so portentous the atmosphere. Maeterlinck's *dance macabre* found fertile field then as it does today!

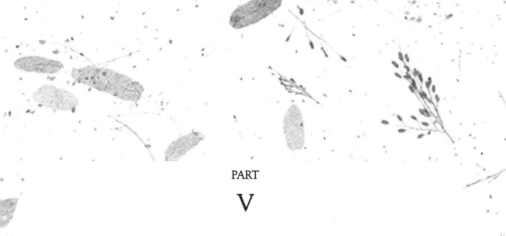

THE TWENTIETH-CENTURY
SLAUGHTER/SCIENCE/SPIRITUALITY

THE THIRD REPUBLIC, which came into being on September 4, 1870, was unable to surive France's defeat by the Germans in June 1940, but was fortunate to have had men of integrity in its ranks. One of these was the eloquent and passionate fighter for justice Georges Clemenceau— referred to as "The Tiger." A radical leftist early in his career, by 1917 he had broken with the Socialists to devote himself exclusively during World War I to France's struggle against Germany. At its conclusion, he negotiated the Treaty of Versailles. Raymond Poincaré, as President of the Republic (1913-1920), ordered the occupation of the Ruhr in an attempt to force Germany to adhere to the Treaty of Versailles. Extreme rightists and ultra-nationalists, such as Maurice Barrès and Charles Maurras, who was condemned in 1945 to perpetual reclusion for collaboration with the enemy, were, however, gaining ground in France. Socialists such as Léon Blum undertook to counteract the increasingly ultraconservative movement by establishing his "Front populaire" (1936), initiating such positive measures as the revaluation of the franc, the rearmament program, reinforcement of a mutual assistance pact with Russia and Great Britain, dissolution of the fascist Croix de Feu, and so on, to little avail. On September 7, 1937, Hitler declared his intention of "annihilating" France, after which he would begin the *Drang nach Osten* (Shirer, *Berlin Diary* 86). Joseph Goebbels, seconding Hitler's plan, wrote in his diary that France's borders would be pushed back to those of 1500, when Burgundy was part of Germany (*The Goebbels Diaries 1941-1943* 18).

France, divided by inner strife, was blinded to the reality of Hitler. Many even sought a rapprochement with Germany. Defeatism, nihilism, and pan-Germanism permeated many French circles: H. Béraud, J. Doriot, etc. When Hitler's *Anschluss* began on March 11, 1938, and Nazi troops seized Austria, the French government did not react. The reason was simple: there was no government. Blum had tried to form a coalition, but his hands were tied. Rightists dissociated themselves from him and what he stood for. Paul Reynaud, a friend of Charles de Gaulle, who likewise fought for a refurbishing of the French army, was virtually the only one in parliament to advocate a "renovation" and modernization of the army. Trying to talk sense to the various members of the government was to no avail. Pierre-Etienne Flandin advocated "a good neighbor" policy with Hitler. Edouard Daladier, the premier, and Georges Bonnet, the foreign minister, spoke on behalf of peace with Germany at almost any price (Shirer, *The Collapse of the Third Republic* 550). The Big Four—Mussolini, Chamberlain, Daladier, and Hitler—met at Munich on September 29 and 30, 1938 and agreed to the demise of Czechoslovakia in exchange for peace.

On June 14, 1940, Paris was declared an open city. The swastika waved in the cool wind on the Eiffel Tower. Marshal Pétain succeeded Reynaud and asked for an armistice, which was signed in the historic railroad car in the Forest of Compiègne. It was in the same *wagon-lit* coach that Marshal Foch had signed another kind of armistice with the Germans on Nov. 11, 1918. Marshal Pétain now took charge of the French government at Vichy, a fascist state controlled by the Germans. Pierre Laval operated behind the scenes. France had become an occupied country. General de Gaulle, having already fled, set up a French National Committee (Free France) in London. He and other members of the French army and navy who had also escaped continued the fight.

The Fourth French Republic, declared in June 1944, lasted until 1958. De Gaulle, who had become head of the French Provisional Government in Paris (1944–1946), retired in 1953 only to return to power with the proclamation of the Fifth Republic (1958–1969). Mention must be made of some of the presidents who followed: Georges Pompidou, François Mitterand, Valéry Giscard D'Estaing, and Jacques Chirac.

The twentieth century began in an explosion of creativity. Artistic movements such as Cubism, Fauvism, Art Nouveau, Futurism, Dada, Surrealism, Constructivism, Purism, Suprematism, Minimalism, Abstract Expressionism, to mention but a few, revealed intensely original vision. Innovative painters captured the world scene: Modigliani, Matisse, Picasso, Braque, Dalí, Delauney, Dufy, Derain, Van Dongen, Rouault, Miró, Ernst, Utrillo,

Rousseau, Marie Laurencin, Léger, Derain, Vlaminck, and more. French writers, dramatists, theatrical directors, and composers also dominated the world stage: Apollinaire, Gide, Breton, Valéry, Colette, Cocteau, Rolland, Duhamel, Romain, Mauriac, Claudel, Proust, Malraux, Queneau, Giraudoux, Martin du Gard, Saint-Exupéry, Bernanos, Char, Giono, Céline, Giraudoux, Sartre, Beauvoir, Camus, Robbe-Grillet, Bonnefoy, Butor, Simon, Genet, Ionesco, Beckett, Duras, Sarraute, Chedid, Atlan, Copeau, Dullin, Poulenc, Messiaen, Debussy, Aubert, Ravel, Jouvet, Artaud, Vilar, and so many others.

The twentieth century—age of the machine, of technocracy, of war—witnessed the birth of the European community as well. But then, hadn't Victor Hugo prophesied it all in an autograph found on the wall of the room in which he died, Place des Vosges in Paris:

I represent a party which does not yet exist: the party of revolution, civilization.
This party will make the twentieth century.
There will issue from it first the United States of Europe, then the United States
Of the World.

11

JEAN COCTEAU'S BEAUTY AND THE BEAST

THE "PLUCKING OF A ROSE"

J EAN COCTEAU ASKED his audiences to have faith in the supernatural when viewing his version of *Beauty and the Beast* (1946), one of the most beautiful and moving filmed fairy tales in modern times.

> Children have implicit faith in what we tell them. They believe that the plucking of a rose can bring disaster to a family, that the hands of a half-human beast begin to smoke after he has killed, and that the beast is put to shame when a young girl comes to live in his house. They believe a host of other simple things.
>
> I ask you to have the same kind of simple faith, and, for the spell to work, let me just say four magic words, the true "Open Sesame" of childhood: "Once upon a time. . . ." (Cocteau, *Three Screen Plays* 185)

Eschewing vagueness and nebulosity, Cocteau searched for exactitude, for sharpness of image, for precision in the story line, for acting, costuming, and use and placement of accessories—techniques that paradoxically would cause the world of enchantment and make-believe to dominate in the psyches of the audience. Only when precision and fantasy meet does illusion become reality for Cocteau; the miracle, actuality; the sleight of hand, truth; and abstraction, physicality. "Mystery exists only in precise things," in verism,

Cocteau wrote, as it does in the reality of the "documentary" style (Cocteau, *Beauty and the Beast. Diary of a Film*, 1972 vii). Like the Surrealists, he sought to "show things" rather than to "tell" about them. The concretization of objects endowed them with an existence of their own, thereby "changing [the viewer's] phantasms into undeniable facts" (*Diary* vi).

Cocteau's *Beauty and the Beast*, like many fairy tales, may be understood on a variety of levels, the most poignant of which is its identification with the Orpheus myth. The poet must make the mutually exclusive choice between his devotion to the world of art and that of love. For some, the allegory of the Oedipal myth may be woven into a young girl's transference from an endogamous relationship (love of a personal father) to an exogamous connection (love of a husband). The rite of passage she must perform as she crosses from unmarried to married state requires a probing of self, a development of feelings for others, and an understanding of one's direction in life. The ability to confront and deal successfully with obstacles does not imply a conquest of self, as many have suggested, but rather a comprehension of the outer and inner forces at work and an ability to maintain a delicate psychological balance during troubling times. Because a patriarchal approach to womankind has been in effect for millennia, the focus on purity (virginity) being the sine qua non of a girl's existence, her defloration in marriage has come to signify for many contemporary women an example of socially condoned rape. Images of sexuality outside the "sanctity of marriage" are considered ugly, sinful, evil, and beastly. Audiences were surprised and delighted by Cocteau's novel—and strictly personal—approach to the question.

ECTYPAL ANALYSIS

The name of Jean Cocteau (1889–1963) evokes a dynamic and sizzling age; his works, a world of fantasy, mystery and excitement. During his early years, Cocteau's wealthy bourgeois parents lived in a private home with his grandparents at 45 rue La Bruyère in Paris. For him, this house became a dazzling magical world. The upper floors of the mansion, occupied by his grandparents for whom he felt genuine affection, seemed filled with intrigue. The silver pipe with its resounding gong tones each time water flowed into it was a source of endless fascination; the books that ornamented the shelves, the Greek busts, drawings by Ingres, a painting by Delacroix, vases from Cyprus, and several Stradivari violins, provided endlessly enthralling stimuli for all sorts of fantasies and visions.

In *Portraits-souvenir*, Cocteau recounts how as a young boy and adolescent, nourished by an ever-dynamic imagination, he was swept up by the matinee idols of the age: Madame Réjane, Sarah Bernhardt, Mounet-Sully, de Max; the diseuse Yvette Guilbert; the clowns Footit and Chocolat—the last three immortalized by Toulouse-Lautrec. In 1906 de Max organized and paid for a public reading of Cocteau's poems at the Théâtre Femina. A shocking occurrence, however, terminated the young man's budding glory when Henri Ghéon, seconded by André Gide, wrote a stinging appraisal of Cocteau's poems for *La Nouvelle Revue Française*, warning him of the treacherous consequences of facile success. Serge Diaghilev, founder of the Russian Ballet, whom Cocteau had met in 1912, discouraged him from seeking instant adulation. He must learn to toil over his writings in order to reach his evanescent inner depths, then to verbalize and visualize these in the work of art.

Cocteau introduced Picasso to Diaghilev, and from this meeting was born the fabulous ballet *Parade* (1917), whose argument was written by Cocteau, the music composed by Erik Satie, and the sets and costumes designed by Picasso. The audience's reaction? Shock. The jarring colors and bizarre shapes of the sets and costumes, the atonal music, and the ambiguity of meaning in the argument were taken by the audience as insults. Cocteau noted prophetically: "I was never to know anything but scandals, a reputation for scandals, the luck and bad luck that come with scandals" (Lannes, *Jean Cocteau* 30). Cocteau would pursue a life mainly of successes/scandals: ballets, such as *The Do-Nothing Bar* (1920); plays, including *The Wedding on the Eiffel Tower* (1921), *Orpheus* (1926), *The Human Voice* (1929), *The Infernal Machine* (1934), *The Knights of the Round Table* (1938), *The Two-Headed Eagle* (1942); novels *Thomas the Impostor* (1923), *The Children of the Game* (1929); films *The Blood of a Poet* (1929), *The Eternal Return* (1944), *Beauty and the Beast* (1945), and *Ruy Blas* (1947). In addition, he produced a plethora of essays, poems, letters, and artistic endeavors: drawings, prints, decorated plates, ties, chapels—the list is long.

The greatest sorrow of Cocteau's life occurred in 1923, with the death from typhoid fever of his beloved lover and counselor, Raymond Radiguet. Shattered in body and in mind, Cocteau turned to opium. Although he tried to rid himself of this habit and spent time in detoxification clinics, cures were only temporary.

Cocteau's immediate inspiration for *Beauty and the Beast* was the fairy tale of Jeanne-Marie, Leprince de Beaumont, (1711–1780), who had herself adapted it from a work created by Mme de Villeneuve (1695–1755). Mme de Beaumont was an advocate of women's education and a teacher of young children in France and in England. Her teaching was geared to the needs, ideas, and yearnings of young women; it emphasized moral and intellectual qualities with the aim of helping those in her charge to become well-functioning and thinking women of the future. To this end, she sought to trigger her students' imaginations, believing strongly in their intellectual acumen or brain power (Sartori, *The Feminist Encyclopedia of French Literature* 399). Cocteau's alteration of some of Mme de Beaumont's plot lines, namely, the tightening and slimming down of her loosely worked structure, enabled him to focus on "the realism of the unreal" instead of diffusing the impact of fantasy with the inclusion of extraneous material.

ARCHETYPAL ANALYSIS

Beauty and the Beast, featuring Cocteau's lover, the actor Jean Marais (Beast), and Josette Day (Beauty) earned worldwide success A fairy tale imbued with love, power, tension, poetry and the religious flavor of ancient archetypal myths—Cupid and Psyche, Orpheus, Oedipus, Jesus—struck a universal and eternal chord in its viewers. *Beauty and the Beast* dealt with human nature in the raw, with creatures living conflictual lives, yet struggling for self-enlightenment. At once actual and fairylike, its themes were philosophical and moral; its archetypal creatures incorporated metaphysical qualities; others, imprisoned in their stereotypic halters, were like marionettes jiggled by the strings of destiny.

Cocteau added a new character to those of Mme de Beaumont: that of Avenant (Comely), thereby paving way for a metaphysical finale designed to provoke viewers to ponder their own poetic and imaginative inner universe—their individual *état d'âme.* By deleting the earlier platitudinous happy conclusion, Cocteau substituted a religious transfiguration which enhanced the fairy tale's mythic and spiritual qualities. Banished as well from his fairy tale were, surprisingly for some, all fairies, equipped or not with magic wands. The remaining visual scenes, pared down to their essentials, were reminiscent of the genre paintings of the seventeenth century—those of Vermeer, de Hooch, and Le Nain—and of the highly imaginative and sometimes grotesquely terrifying engravings of the nineteenth-century artist Gustave Doré. Although the themes depicted in the canvases of the above artists suggest dichotomy rather than unity, a timeless, time-ridden, and universal factor comes into view as well.

Cocteau's unique mélange of pictorial representations plunges readers and audiences into the suspense of a dual world in which good and evil, night and day, truth and the lie, sexuality and puritanism struggle for supremacy. Only one protagonist, the Beast, is physically masked, making him enigmatic to the extreme, perhaps even deceitful, if one relies exclusively on his *persona* to cast judgment. The other characters remain fully visible in their flawed or flawless natures and in what society considers their morally admirable or reprehensible characteristics. All are endowed with emotions; and act according to their obvious or concealed archetypal patterns.

Parallel to Cocteau's illusory world, over which his protagonists seem to have no control, there prevails another deceptively concrete functional world in which they participate as well. Objects, at once real and exact, take on at times the powers of ritualistic symbols, *hierophanies*—endowed with a life of their own in both empirical and transpersonal spheres. They enter and/or exit, like flesh-and-blood human beings, enhancing their prestige when necessary by acting as passive backdrops or animated sculptures, and intertwining a variety of elements in what is considered Cocteau's unique rendition of the French fairy-tale genre.

CHAOS IN THE HOME: A MICROCOSM OF A MACROCOSM. *Beauty and the Beast* opens onto a house divided: a microcosm of a macrocosm. Had Cocteau unconsciously underscored the divisive elements reigning within a family so as better to replicate the climate of uncontrollable forces that had been unleashed beyond France's borders? The harrowing days, months, and years of deprivation, disorientation, and sickness during and following World War II (1939–1945) had taken their toll on Cocteau. So physically weakened was he that during the filming of *Beauty and the Beast* one could say that his body had been virtually eaten away by boils, sores, eczema, and lesions caused by an assortment of infectious diseases, necessitating his hospitalization at the Institut Pasteur in Paris. Understandably, disarray, discomfort, sadness, and morbidity are implicit at the outset of the fairy tale. Even its conclusion waxes in the chance factor that rules human destiny (Cocteau, *The Screen Plays* 71ff.).

A condition of primal disorder and abysmal darkness is established at the outset of *Beauty and the Beast*: viewers learn that the merchandise-laden ships of the once-wealthy Merchant have been sunk at sea, leaving him impoverished and despondent. His material dispossession, symptomatic of his psychological diminution, suggests that a once-flourishing father-directed household or world is now in a state of decay. Confusion in the home, having given rise to undifferentiated, undirected, and disorderly affects, has paved the way for the rule of anthropoid, or undeveloped and unthinking behavioral patterns. No mention being made of the Merchant's wife nor of any other mother figure in the scenario, it is to be assumed that she died some time earlier.

The weakly structured son, Ludovic, and his equally empty friend, Avenant, are gamblers, drunkards, and unethical ne'er-do-wells. As for the daughters, split-offs of the nonexistent mother figure, only the youngest, Beauty, is loving toward her father and generous and kindly toward her siblings, Félicie and Adelaïde. The latter two are egotistical, vain, materialistic, and acquisitive. Whenever frustrated, they are given to temper tantrums.

Unlike Beauty, her sisters are devouring, instinctual forces of nature. Jealous, distrustful, and envious, they represent murderous and destructive *vagina dentata* types. The family enclave is divested of a central ruling principle, as well as all goals and values. Antagonism and aggressiveness prevail.

We also learn in the opening images that the Merchant, unwilling to accept his fate, has gone to town to adjust his financial affairs. During his absence, a battle royal is fought out over primacy in the art of archery between Ludovic and Avenant, who accuse each other of cheating, and downgrade each other's talents as archers. Taking their bows and arrows outside, they aim for the target, so badly missing the bullseye that one of the arrows flies into the window of their home. "Hooligans," the older sisters shriek: "You could have hit us in the eye!" (*Beauty* 198). A glimmer of feeling, however, is manifested by the "boys" who rush into the house, concerned over Beauty's welfare. Angered by the attention focused on their younger sister, and in an immediate assertion of their power and social superiority, Félicie and Adelaïde order Beauty to wash the floors, adding that, if they did not rush along, they would " be late for the duchess" (*Beauty* 198).

As the mood of jealousy and reprisal mounts, the bacchantic sisters direct their rage toward Ludovic and Avenant, flinging invectives of murderers, drunkards, womanizers, and cheats, answered by "sluts," "bitches," and "the laughing stock of society" (*Beauty* 198). Antagonisms mount as the sisters turn to castigating the peasants employed by their father for their laziness, drunkenness, and filth. The last scene of this sequence features the "ladies" being carried to their rendezvous on sedan chairs to the accompaniment of Ludovic's cursings.

MIRRORED TRANSPARENCY IN A CLIMATE OF IMMORALITY? OR, PERHAPS, AMORALITY? Without explanation, the handsome Avenant enters the house to find Beauty polishing the floor. Although his words to her seem banal, they are, nonetheless, redolent with the magic power of love. Kneeling beside her and proffering empty words of endearment, he tells her she is not made for servant's work; then, with sheer delight, he points to the shining floorboards, which highlight her exquisite features: "Even the floor would like to mirror you" (*Beauty* 200).

The mirroring image, a metaphor for the mirror as object, becomes a visual transposition of Beauty's inner nature, disclosing her purity and spiritual goodness. As an anima image par excellence, she is a soul figure, an unblemished being whose heart and actions reflect both inner and outer harmony. She is an ideal that exists in the male's unconscious universe.

By incorporating the world of objects into the action, Cocteau effects a unity between the inanimate "floorboards" and their actively mirroring effects. In so doing, he lends to his cinematographic frames a paradoxically real, yet illusory, dimension. Like talismans or fetiches, the inanimate objects—the floorboards and, later, statues, candelabra, gates, trees, and leaves—assume transpersonal powers. In that everything seems visually mobile on screen, all becomes related to the world of make-believe, thus giving audiences access to the protagonists' dreamscapes.

Unlike Beauty, Avenant is immature, irresponsible, dissolute, and unethical. Nonetheless, he possesses one redeeming feature: he loves Beauty and would like to to marry her. He is drawn to her crystalline qualities, which in himself are veiled and nonfunctional. His words of love, although sincere, are, understandably, both sexually motivated and irresponsible. His dissolute behavior belies the sincerity of his words of love. Unable to understand Beauty's ingrained sense of responsibility, he cannot persuade her to bond with him. Until he learns to act out his promises in real life, that is, to work rather than gamble and drink, his verbiage remains vacuous, devoid of substance and meaning.

Beauty represents an ideal for Avenant. Her feet are firmly implanted in the real world. She deals overtly with her daily chores. Her acts, like Cocteau's mirroring floorboards, *reflect* her intimate thoughts. No conflicts of envy or jealousy assail her. Straightforward, she knows that her father's ships have been lost at sea, that he is ruined, and that she must do the housework, reasoning in her graciously endearing and generous way that her sisters' hands are too beautiful and too white to mar.

When the adolescent Avenant, still indissolubly linked to Ludovic in his immoral escapades, attempts to take his beloved in his arms by force, Beauty's brother storms into the house to protect her. In a surprisingly commanding voice, he orders: "Take your hands off her, or I'll smash your face in!" (*Beauty* 201). Although Ludovic's ego is undeveloped and his behavioral patterns are clearly immoral, his sterling qualities are actuated in defense of someone he treasures. Having cognized the polarities between good and evil, he is aware of what he must do, but lacks strength of character. "I know I am a scoundrel, but I won't have you marry one," he affirms to his sister in stentorian tones. Then, turning to Avenant, he orders him out of the house. In his uncontrollable outrage, Avenant, just as he had resorted to brute force to express his love for Beauty, strikes Ludovic, who staggers, then falls to the floor (*Beauty* 202). Beauty, the peacemaker, the family's love-object, runs to help her brother.

BEAUTY AND THE FATHER. Many psychiatrists and psychologists, including Bruno Bettelheim, declare Beauty's rejection of Avenant—"I must stay single and live with my father"—to be a paradigm of the Oedipal situation (*Beauty*

200). Not until Beauty is able to effect a transference from father love to husband love, the Oedipal contingent argues, will she succeed in separating herself consciously and unconsciously from the archetypal father image dominating her psyche since birth. By contrast, that her love for her father might be unconsciously incestuous seems to be less of a factor in Beauty's loyalty to her father than formerly thought.

Considered unclean and unholy, and punishable by death in many societies, incest may be understood, psychologically, as the force that impedes new blood, new ties, new contacts from taking root (see chapter 2). The incest as depicted in the Oedipus myth continued the pattern of endogamy considered dangerous for the well-being and future development of a group and therefore had to be stopped. Psychologically speaking, endogamy in an Oedipal situation presupposes productive energy flowing back into the family cell, rather than outward. The incest taboo forced individuals to reach beyond what they had, to discover exciting worlds, and enjoy new biological family ties. It fostered aggressivity and expanded horizons; it spurred efforts and strengthened the ego in the experiences to be lived out.

Beauty was certainly deeply attached to her father, more so after her mother's death or departure, and similarly bonded with her brother and sisters. She was also profoundly in love with Avenant. Acutely aware as well of Avenant's immaturity, self-indulgence, and even narcissism, she had the good sense to hold him at bay, refusing to even entertain any thought of marriage. She loved and respected her father, who had replaced the mother figure in the household, inclining us perhaps toward an Oedipal explanation of Beauty's situation, with one great difference: whereas Oedipus was *blind* to his acts, she was fully cognizant of hers. The depth of her awareness of her place and responsibilities in the household served to increase her already acute suffering.

Soon after the struggle between Ludovic and Avenant, the Merchant returns with three gentlemen to announce to the family that since his ships have come to port, they will once again be rich (*Beauty* 202). The still-angry Ludovic now accuses Avenant of aspiring to his sister's future wealth through marriage (*Beauty* 203). As undeveloped psychologically as the two younger men, the self-serving egotistical father is unheedful of Beauty's welfare: "So you want to leave me?" he questions. She responds reassuringly: "No, father, I'll never leave you" (*Beauty* 203). The parlance of young people, and frequently of old ones as well, rarely reflects the notion of linear time, but addresses some undefined future. As they peer into their timeless universes, the aura of distant possibilites takes on the luster of reality. Beauty's reply to her father, divested of all experiential notions, consists in well-placed words that serve to dispel his anxieties. More significantly, however, they underscore a miasmic universe replete with hidden truths and noxious motivations.

Before leaving to return to his business in town, the Merchant asks his daughters what they would like him to bring back. The sisters, having spent a dismal afternoon at the party hosted by society people who ignored them, reveal their unabashed aggressive and possessive drives by asking for brocade dresses, fans, ostrich feathers, a monkey, and a parrot. What would Beauty like? A rose, she responds, "for they don't grow here" (*Beauty* 204). She already knew unconsciously that she would have to go *outside* her family enclave to live a different, difficult, but essential learning experience. Cocteau's world of objects again intervenes to unmask hidden movements of the soul and heart.

A usurer arrives on the scene. The now half-inebriated Ludovic, convinced of his father's imminent restored wealth, and having already borrowed large sums of money to pay his debts so as to avoid jail, is encouraged by Avenant to incur further financial obligations. Little does Ludovic realize the enslavement such borrowings will cause him: he mindlessly signs over to the usurer the legal right to seize everything in the house if accounts are not settled.

Melodramatically, the scene shifts to town. The Lawyer informs the Merchant that creditors have already seized everything on board his ships. Not a farthing remains. Not even enough to pay for a hotel room. It is night. The Merchant fears he will lose his way on his return home through the forest. Heartlessly, the lawyer retorts, "Well then, get lost" (*Beauty* 205). Whereupon the Merchant mounts his horse and leaves.

THE FOREST AS KATABASIS. Implicit in the maturation process is, as readers know, the forest experience, which so many heroes and heroines of old have had to face. Judging from the Merchant's pusillanimity vis-à-vis his children, and from his utter dependency on Beauty for running his household, it comes as no surprise that he failed to solve his business problems logically and/or realistically. He was, therefore, a perfect candidate for the traumas a forest situation engenders. The Merchant must, paradoxically, *lose* his way in the forest in order to *find* his direction in life.

The *katabasis* ("to go within"), or initiation into adulthood which adolescents experience when they begin severing their ties with their parents, seems to have been bypassed by the Merchant. The katabasis process amounts to a descent into self—the passage from one level of consciousness to another, until the deepest spheres within the psyche have been reached. Such a trajectory frequently succeeds in reconnecting the initiate with his or her own past and concomitantly with his collective unconscious, or humanity's primordial existence. This kind of quest into the unknown is considered paradigmatic of the search for greater knowledge—the searing effort required to open the initiate to broader perceptions, new understanding, and awareness of life's multiple choices.

In the forest, rather than walking through a manicured garden with its ordered, planned, and restricted vegetation, the initiate faces the domain of the Great Mother, as already described in the chapters on *Mélusine, The Blue Bird,* and *Pelléas and Mélisande.* Alone, he pursues a hazardous course into remote realms left in their natural, chaotic state. More importantly for the Merchant, Cocteau's forest will expose him to Mother Nature's possessive, destructive, and devouring side, or, psychologically, to those fearsome, frequently denied, aspects of an individual's subliminal world.

The Merchant's obliviousness to his ineffectiveness as both a father and businessman, has led not only to the stunting of his children's lives, save Beauty's, but to his own as well. Having failed to teach his children the essentials of integrity, he heaps material gain upon them, endeavoring to retain their affection. Nor are Beauty's high principled—anima, or ideal—qualities present in the Merchant's real or oneiric world. If sufficiently terrifying, the forest encounter could possibly shake him to such a degree that the energy catalyzed by the churnings of his emotions would serve to dislodge latent, and heretofore unaccessed qualities within his psyche. Such activity might perhaps open a window into his locked-in center—or seed bed!

The more deeply the disoriented Merchant makes his way into the uncharted forest, the thicker grows the darkness surrounding him. A flash of lightning—in fairy-tale style—suddenly reveals a magnificent castle looming ahead of him. The Merchant takes heart, dismounts, and makes his way through some thick underbrush, across a courtyard, observing amazedly the tree "branches silently clos[ing] in behind him" (*Beauty* 206). No sooner does he reach the inner gates of the castle than "they open before him." He releases his horse's reins and the animal walks through the gates, which close immediately, leaving the Merchant stranded on the outside. Terrified at his seeming helplessness that underscores the reality of his psychological stasis, he runs back across the courtyard, crying out: "Is there anyone there?" (*Beauty* 206) In desperation, he climbs a now-visible wide stone staircase, walks through an open door in the castle's wall, and inquires once again if anyone is there. Since no response is forthcoming, he forges ahead into an ineffable spectacle.

Throughout *Beauty and the Beast,* Cocteau stresses what he considers to be the hermetic nature of art, that is, the necessity of keeping the poet's secrets unrevealed. Only an arcane world can ensure the mystery and excitement engendered by the creative process. Emotions such as solitude, fear, and trembling, vital ingredients in the initiatory process, will open the Merchant up to the next step of his inner enlightenment—a course filled with pitfalls.

A NEW WORLD OF OBJECTS COMES INTO PLAY. In his *Essay on Indirect Criticism* (1932), Cocteau had evoked Giorgio de Chirico's calm and restraint, his mysticism, and the exactitude of his draftsmanship in rendering the ghostly silhouettes of objects. It was as if "Death [were] the only player that circulated freely and in any direction on Chirico's chess-board," Cocteau had written (Cocteau, *Oeuvres complètes* X, 31). De Chirico's paintings, he was also quick to emphasize, were not abstractions, but, to the contrary, ultrarealistic renditions. His reality differed from that of the primitive painter in that de Chirico "show[ed] us reality by removing it from its usual surroundings." Objects (a head, an arm, an arch, a mannequin, a globe, an egg, a fish) are placed in the most unlikely places, as evidenced in de Chirico's tableau "The Seer," which features a mannequin seated in front of a painting. In another canvas, "The Melancholy and Mystery of a Street," the strange and starkly lit environment casts an ominous shadow over the area portrayed, thereby destabilizing the viewer who not only loses all sense of well-being, but is overcome with feelings of ominous foreboding. Because things are just not what they should be or what is customary, fear intrudes, setting up a whole new dynamic born of tensions created by the alteration of relationships, tempos, and sonorities.

Few artists have been able to express underlying chaos or cosmos with such economy of means as did de Chirico. The same may be said of Cocteau's decors in *Beauty and the Beast*. The extreme control he exercised over his object-laden scenes lent a sculpturesque simplicity to the atmosphere, and a freshly found virtual rigidity of form to his imagings. The outcome of such a carefully planned object-universe was to endow each entity with hauntingly mysterious and metaphysical power.

How would the Merchant respond to the unseen forces embedded within usually immobile but now mobile concrete objects? Would he be caught up in their magic spell? And how would audiences react to visual conjunctions of ancient and up-to-date mechanical *things* emerging from within a historically traditional background? Once the Merchant passes through the door of the castle, he is confronted by a row of human arms holding candelabra, showing him the way along a corridor to a large hall. He stops and stares in disbelief. Two of the human arms release their candelabra, which remain magically suspended in space. Awed, the merchant backs into a room with a huge fireplace. A clock on the mantelpiece strikes eleven. He turns around to look from the fire to a dining table sumptuously set with food and drink.

> He puts his hat on the table, sits down and removes his gloves. A marble bust, which supports one end of the vast mantelpiece, slowly turns its head toward him. At the other side of the fireplace, its counterpart, breathing smoke through its nostrils, also moves its head around to look at him.

The merchant reaches for a silver globlet. A hand appears from the candelabra in the middle of the table. The merchant starts back. The hand takes hold of a wine decanter, fills the goblet, and returns to a candelabrum. The merchant lifts up the edge of the tablecloth and peers underneath it. He stares at the candelabrum on the table, stands up and turns to look once more at the row of candelabra leading out of the room.

He sits down again, picks up the goblet, sniffs at it suspiciously, and drinks. He falls into a deep sleep. The marble busts turn their heads again.

The merchant slowly wakes up. His hand is resting on the wooden arm of his chair, which is carved in the image of a lion's head. The lion's head comes to life under his hand and roars.

The merchant leaps to his feet and grabs his gloves. The marble bust breathes smoke. The candelabrum on the dining table extinguishes itself.

The merchant takes a last look around the room, walks hurriedly down the corridor past the row of candelabra and leaves the castle. The door shuts silently behind him. He walks slowly down the stairs and along a balustrade decorated with stone statues of fierce-looking dogs. He stops and looks around him. (*Beauty* 208)

The entire cinematographic sequence—the opening of the doors, the Merchant's walk down a corridor, the sight of human arms holding candelabra, the mobile marble bust, the hand that takes hold of the wine decanter, the arm of the chair carved in the form of a lion's head that begins to roar, the candelabrum that extinguishes itself, to name but a few of the objects that take on motility—is endowed with ritualistic reverberations and metaphysical magnetism. The *verism*, to use Cocteau's word, of these entities injects them with such authenticity and such psychic energy as to endow them with magical qualities. Like the sacred objects, hierophanies or fetishes, used in religious ceremonies, particularly those inviting visitations, apparitions, voices, and the like—be they at Epheses, Lourdes, Saint James of Compostela, the Mount of Olives, or in hypnotic séances—each possesses its own form, overtones, and voices. The energies emanating from these visible/invisible intensities may, depending on the depth of the believer's projection, pave the way into another plane of existence.

Endowed with new functions and prerogatives, the newly displaced objects create feelings of uneasiness and diffidence in the Merchant, lifting him out of his mundane preoccupations into a world of fantasy. "Even familiar objects," Cocteau wrote, "have something suspicious about them" (Cocteau, *Oeuvres complètes* V, 3).

After descending several more steps, the Merchant finds himself in a beautiful rose garden—perhaps more like a sanctuary. He walks toward the flowers, recalling Beauty's request. Fearful that someone might be observing him, he looks around but continues on until he unexpectedly "stumbles" on the body of a dead deer. Shocked by the sight of the animal, he perhaps wonders whether it is an omen of some kind. Spying now "a perfect rose" which "changes color as he watches it," he stoops to pluck it. So taken is he by the power of its divine radiance that he is oblivious to the huge, formidable, monstrous Beast who has just made his appearance in what may be identified ironically as a paradisaic realm. Venting his anger at the Merchant for his unthinking, even sacrilegious act of picking a rose, thereby divesting him of what he holds sacred, the Beast will force him to suffer the consequences. Nonetheless, he explains the reasons for the imposition of his harsh punishment. "My roses are the most precious things in the whole world to me" (*Beauty* 209). The picking of one results in the imposition of the death sentence. The shock effect of the Beast's pronouncement, coming immediately after the Merchant's feelings of beatitude imparted by the rose, underscores the polarities victimizing this man who lives in an undifferentiated empirical world.

The rose image has been used with felicity since ancient times in artistic and religious iconography. In the Song of Solomon, the rose conveys both spiritual and physical love:

I am the rose of Sharon, and the lily of the valley:
As the lily among thorns, so is my love, among the daughters.
As the apple tree among the trees of the wood, so is my beloved among the sons. I sat down under his shadow with great delight, and his fruit was sweet to my taste. (1:1–3)

In Christian iconography, the rose is identified with sacred blood and spiritual love, as attested to in such myths as the Holy Grail and the Crucifixion. Joseph of Aramathea had gathered blood from a wound made by the lance during Christ's Crucifixion. It was he as well, who, along with Nicodemus, "took the body of Jesus . . . wound it in linen clothes, [to] where he was crucified, [where] there was a garden; and in the garden a sepulchre, wherein was never man yet laid" (John 19:38–42). The Rosicrucians, whose influence was important in French mystical thought, placed five roses in the center of their cross, indicating the Sacred Heart, and one on either bar. In Dante's *The Divine Comedy*, the rose is associated with the Virgin Mary and with the maiden, Beatrice. As a symbol of regeneration in Apuleius's *Golden Ass*, the author is able to recover his human form after having eaten a crown of vermillion roses given to him by Isis's Great Priest.

As an expression of love and blood, the Beast's sacred rose garden was set apart, *consecrated*—that is, belonging to a deity. Because of their holiness, his roses were to be venerated and to remain untouched until his beloved—the single individual capable of affecting his transfiguration into human form—would enact the required ritual. Understandably, death awaited anyone who disturbed or mutilated the sacred roses.

THE BEAST: THE WHITE STALLION. In this same scene, Cocteau fills the visual space with the evocative image of the Beast, a metaphor for a man's nefarious instinctual behavioral patterns. Described as resembling a "were-wolf," Cocteau's protagonist is endowed with long fangs and grotesque features. His horrific exterior conforms to the stereotypic visualization of the unredeemed and uninitiated individual who allows his impulses—killer instincts—to hold sway. "His huge gnarled hands end in claws and, like the rest of him, are covered in thick matted fur" (*Beauty* 209). To combine the extremes in behavioral patterns between so-called civilized human and instinctual animal, the Beast's body is covered with a long and sumptuous bejeweled cloak and luxurious velvet breeches. His legs are hidden in elegant high leather boots. Cocteau's humanization of the Beast is so terrifying to the Merchant that he fails to make the connection between the person (civilized, thus good) and the animal (instinctual, thus evil). He sees only what he considers to be his destructive, that is, his monstrous side. Believing him to be a supernatural being—an aberration of sorts—the Merchant falls to his knees before him. Far from reassuring him, the Beast's categorical imposition of the death penalty for having attempted to desecrate a holy object triggers extreme anxiety in the miscreant.

The psychologically weakly structured Merchant claims innocence. Rather than take the blame, he confesses to having transgressed in order to fulfill his daughter's wishes. Thoughtless actions, however, in no way disculpate the Merchant in the eyes of the Beast who, on the contrary, is increasingly riled, possibly because the Merchant has used his daughter as a scapegoat. The intruder earns the Beast's further ire by addressing him as "My Lord." Such a lofty appellation, a paradigm for hypocrisy, or for pseudo-diplomatic "compliments," is summarily rejected by the Beast. Unwilling to waste any more time on the matter, he advises the Merchant to prepare himself for death, unless one of his daughters agrees to die in his place (*Beauty* 210).

Why does the Beast offer the Merchant a way out of his punishment? Maidenhood, or virginity, as identified with flowers in general and the rose in particular, is evident in such expressions as the *deflowering* of a bride. The bloodletting that releases her from her maidenhood and prepares her for motherhood is an archetypal, but also physical, experience or rite of passage, which must be lived out by each maiden.

Rather than offer himself up for death and thereby protect his daughters, the egotistic and cowardly Merchant again conveys his fear of losing his way in the forest. The Beast, hoping to find a means of releasing himself from the spell that had transformed him, placates the Merchant's terror by providing him with a white stallion called "Magnificent One." Whoever whispers, "Go where I am going, Magnificent One, go, go," into the stallion's ear will be taken directly home (*Beauty* 210).

For the Greeks, the fiery steed Pegasus was known as a powerful and gorgeously muscular winged animal. More rapid than wind, when he reached the immortals, he dwelled in the palace of Zeus, bringing him thunder and lightning. For Cocteau, this beautiful, magic, mighty, and fiery white stallion (appearing as early as 1917, in his production of *Parade,* a "ballet-réaliste," and years later in his play *Orpheus* [1926], among other works), symbolized poetic inspiration. Able to transcend three-dimensional space/time concepts, and gravity as well, The Magnificent One, like the dreamer/creator during slumber, existed in a world of becoming.

THE SACRIFICIAL VICTIM. Arriving home, the Merchant apprises his family of the Beast's demands. Even as the wrangling among the children reaches new highs, Beauty, always conscientious and altruistic, offers herself as sacrificial victim. To her father she sputters: "I'd rather be devoured by the monster than die of the heartbreak of losing you" (*Beauty* 212).

Offering herself up for sacrifice to *beastly* powers, albeit a harrowing act, would be, like the proof of a knight's physical prowess, instrumental in Beauty's transformation into a woman. Unlike her father whose psychological development had been arrested, Beauty had the courage and the intelligence to accept *terror* as a prerequisite to fulfilling her individual destiny (E. Neumann, *Amor and Psyche* 64).

Beauty's departure necessitated a cut, a separation, a distantiation from her family. Unlike her Greek sister, Psyche, who had not been exposed to the stresses and strains of economic want, nor the loss of a parent, Beauty's difficult upbringing had developed in her certain qualities, including perseverance, a sense of responsibility, and an ability to deal with people. Like Psyche, Beauty would be exposing herself to the vagaries of fortune. But she was neither blind to the possible dangers of riding through the forest under cover of darkness, nor expectant of anything from the Beast. To save her father was her only goal.

Astute as well as kind and giving, Beauty waits for her family to retire for the night. Donning her long dark cloak, she goes to the stable, mounts the white horse, and then whispers the password: "Magnificent One, go, go!" (*Beauty* 213) No sooner said than the farm gates open, and Beauty rides into the forest. She reaches the castle in no time, is led by Magnificent through the foliage which, as had been her father's experience, closes behind her.

THE CASTLE AND A WORLD OF OBJECTS. As if living a dream, Beauty enters the castle's great hall. She seems "to float past the rows of candelabra . . . up a flight of stairs . . . through a door which leads to a long gallery with billowing white curtains." Seemingly carried along by some magical force, "she comes to a door flanked on each side by human arms carrying candelabras. The arms move toward the door, casting their light onto her" (*Beauty* 215).

In that inanimate objects are humanized by Cocteau throughout the film, it comes as no surprise to hear the door speak to Beauty as it is in the process of opening onto her room—her sanctuary. She enters, amazed by its luxurious furniture and appointments, the flowers and plants set about, and the mobile marble bust that moves its head in her direction as she walks. She is particularly perplexed by the large bed and its "luxurious fur cover [being] pulled back by invisible hands" (*Beauty* 215).

Beauty faces objects endowed with the aura of ritualistic symbols and shorn of their customary functions. They acquire new and startling powers. In awe of the miraculous solemnity of these entities, she looks upon them with the same reverence as had the ancients living out their mysterious rituals at Epidaurus, Eleusis, Delphi, or in the concealed rooms within the Egyptian pyramids. Did Beauty conjure something sinister in her virtually sealed sanctuary?

Glowing at the magnificence of it all, Beauty nonetheless feels lonely. She runs impulsively to the window as if seeking freedom, then stops, aware of the futility of her action. Once reason takes hold, she sits down at her dressing table. Her attention is drawn to another miraculous object: a talking mirror. "Beauty, I am your mirror; reflect in me; I will reflect for you" (*Beauty* 215). Obedient to its commands, she gazes into the glass, which not only images her radiance and harmony of features, but, like the magic mirror of shamans, allows her to travel through space. To her distress, she sees her father lying ill in bed at home.

If the mirror, as Plato indicated, reflects the soul, its presence at this juncture would indicate Beauty's need to *collect* herself after her flight—psychologically, to experience a period of introversion that would teach her how to cope with her new and fearsome environment. But the magic mirror, by providing also the means of traveling mentally through invisible matter, helps her retain her connectedness with her family via love, not servitude; via relatedness, not enslavement. Her offer to sacrifice herself to help her father brought to the fore both her altruism and her unconscious pull for independence. What appeared in the looking glass confirmed what she had most feared—her father's illness, ergo, a further deterioration of an already chaotic family structure. The increase of indirect knowledge afforded to her by the mirror, however, serves to strengthen her determination to implement her sacrifice.

Overwhelmed by the impact of her father's suffering, Beauty rushes down the stone staircase leading into the courtyard and, as she is about to open the doors, comes face to face with the Beast. She shrieks at the monstrous apparition, and faints. Most gently, he carries her up the stairs to her room and, as he puts her on the bed, a sleight of hand occurs: the farm clothes she had been wearing are transformed into a magnificent silk-embroidered gown encrusted with sparkling jewels. Has she been transformed into a princess? Riveted by the beauty of this maiden, he is incapable of taking his eyes off her! Beauty, regaining consciousness, again cries out in terror. Sensitive to her turmoil, the Beast backs out of the room, asking her not to look into his eyes, adding that henceforth he will appear to her only at dinner, at seven o'clock in the evening.

That the Beast has told Beauty not to look into his eyes brings to mind Zeus's prohibition to Semele after having impregnated her. Zeus's understandably jealous wife Hera encouraged Semele to ask her lover to see him in his divine splendor. The greatest God of the Greek pantheon, yielding to his beloved's request, appeared to her in his roaring thunder and flaming lightning, and consumed her. Divine interdicts, such as the one imposed on Semele, are psychologically significant: they warn individuals not to attempt to face what they are emotionally unprepared for or insufficiently mature to contemplate and deal with. The libido or psychic energy generated by a powerful vision may be so intense as to lead to a breakdown of the psyche. In Beauty's case, the shock of the Beast's animal physique, including his furry exterior, snout, fangs, claws, and the like, caused her to faint, thereby blocking out all possibilities of dealing rationally with her emotions. Whether out of fear of the Beast or confidence in her own inner determination to fulfill her mission, Beauty obeyed his command to avert her eyes from his.

By asking Beauty not to gaze into the Beast's eyes, Cocteau indicates Beauty's emotional unpreparedness to take the next step in her rite of passage: to face her fear of him and of the world he represents. Her devotion to her father, and by extension to her family, to the point of willingly sacrificing her well-being, had endowed Beauty with a profound sense of mission as well. Perpetual kindness, nonetheless, while fulfilling society's highest moral values, enhances the giver's prestige in the eyes of others as well. In Beauty's case, her habitual acts of self-sacrifice gave her the security of the known, thereby protecting her until now from the terrors of the unknown— or exposure to the outside world and its exogamous spirit of contest.

Routine, however, may lead to a vegetative and thus negative existence. The struggle for independence focuses on the goals to be reached, not on the harrowing ordeals they entail.

THE AGAPE. Only during the evening *agape*, or love feast, are the two to come together. As the magic dinner ritual is about to begin on her first night in the castle, Beauty is dressed in the exquisite gown adorned with jewels that had been placed in her room. Regal in stance, Beauty sighs in despair as she senses the ominous events to come. She then closes her eyes. Is she, in so doing, attempting to shut out the outer world? Or to escape the fate of the sacrificial victim which she herself had chosen to be? Or is she beginning to become acclimatized to her new environment?

Humanized beasts, in their utmost wisdom, are perhaps deprived of the ability to rationalize in our terms, but they have other sensibilities. Beauty must have realized that since the Beast walked and talked like a man, he may have been expelled from the human species and forced to live out an ordeal of his own. Could he have felt her repugnance for him? What she failed to understand, but what readers and viewers sense, was the Beast's awareness of her fears. Rather than inflict further distress on her, he has restrained his impulses.

The Beast's ugliness may be seen from a feminine point of view as symptomatic of the role played by the male in the defloration or rape of the maiden he takes to the marriage bed. To spare the young and innocent Beauty tumult and feelings of degradation, the Beast dominates his sexual urges until she might begin to understand him better—even to love him for his sensitivity and gentleness. Placing her comfort before his own, he chooses to spare her the horror of gazing at him during dinner by standing behind her armchair, attempting all the while to reassure her, and asking only to allow him to watch her eat. Responding sraightforwardly, she tells him that as master of the castle, his choice prevails. He moves to the side of the chair to declare that she alone is mistress of his domain, adding rhetorically, "I revolt you; you must find me very ugly" (*Beauty* 216). The essence of integrity, Beauty will not lie. Yet, at present, she seems less overwhelmed by his ugliness than she had been at their first meeting. Perhaps disarmed by the Beast's comforting manner, she becomes increasingly sensitive to his dilemma, instead of focusing exclusively on her own sorrow and fear. Empathetically, she replies: "But I know you're doing your utmost to help me forget your ugliness" (*Beauty* 216). Responding in kind, he confesses that his monstrous looks compel him to live the life of a pariah. In his defense, however, he tells her that he possesses human attributes as well: kindness, gentleness, and a loving nature. No longer completely self-involved, and with an increased understanding of the *other,* Beauty answers on an empathetic/empirical level: "Many men are more monstrous than you, but they hide it well" (*Beauty* 216). The Beast's animal attributes, nonetheless, account at moments for his lack of mannered ways—or perhaps better expressed, his inadequate training in society's hypocritical verbal courtesies. Were he not what is termed *gauche,* he might not have placed such luxurious material gifts at Beauty's disposal, believing, perhaps naively, that they would impress her, thus endear him to her. By flaunting his wealth, however, he is blinded to her desire to return home. On the other hand, might not her own suffering have helped her empathize with the Beast's own agony? Not sufficiently, however, to respond favorably to what is to become his nightly query: "Beauty, will you be my wife?" (*Beauty* 217) Her negative reply elicits the Beast's farewell until the following evening.

THE BEAST'S AGONIA. Walking across the gallery of the castle that night, Beauty hears sounds resembling "the roar of wild beasts followed by the screams of an animal in pain" (*Beauty* 217). Although unaware of her presence, she sees "a look of hideous despair" imprinted on the Beast's face. Observing him more intently, she watches him staring at his "huge grotesque hands" with their sharply clawed fingers, then burying "his head in his arms" in sorrow. Shortly thereafter, he enters her room, searches for her, sits down at her dressing table and looks into the mirror (*Beauty* 217). "Where is Beauty?" he shouts, whereupon smoke billows forth from the magic object.

Seconds later, Beauty returns to her room and, allowing her own instinct to prevail, castigates the Beast for his intrusion. In keeeping with his undifferentiated animal nature, he resorts, as if automatically, to a sleight of hand, and offers her an exquisite pearl necklace to placate her. Considering it an affront that sets her on a par with her materialistic sisters, Beauty orders him to leave. The film audiences nonetheless see her contemplating her necklace.

At the conclusion of the Beast's first evening visit to Beauty, viewers sense that a common denominator has been established between the two. The evolution of their mutually deepening understanding is conveyed by Cocteau in four different stages.

STAGES OF TRANSFORMATION

The Walk. The day Beauty steps out of her room and strolls through the castle grounds marks her increased comfort in her new environment, and greater confidence in her ability to handle herself in the Beast's company. No longer tormented by fear, she has begun to look outside of herself—to examine her surroundings. Upon coming to a door, she naturally and thoughtlessly, and aggressively as well, "pushes" it open (*Beauty* 218).

To push (L. *pulsare*, to strike, to drive) something, even a door, requires physical, and sometimes even *brute* strength. That Beauty accomplished such an act—particularly in a fairy-tale context—was her way of fulfilling a rite of passage. Again she ventures forth from her circumscribed realm into another dimension of *mystery*. In that the door once opened will take her from the known to the unknown, or from the exoteric to the esoteric realm (*isôtheô*, "I make enter"), she must open it if she seeks to discover what has been hidden behind it or buried in darkness for so many years.

Once outside the castle, Beauty glimpses the Beast on his knees at the edge of the pool "lapping up water like an animal"—in his element and in harmony with his animal nature (*Beauty* 218). Having until now only seen his persona with its human element, and having accustomed herself to this image, Beauty is startled by his altered behavior, and she backs away. By having activated that side of himself with which Beauty was unfamiliar, he has become unacceptable to her. The extra libido, or psychic energy charges that this out-of-context image has stirred in her will, via projection, help her process and redefine her understanding of the Beast archetype (Franz, *Projection and Re-Collection in Jungian Psychology* 86). The shock of confrontation compelled her to close the door, to block out the scene, but her destabilized psyche has, nonetheless, undergone a marked change. Less intransigeant, her now-expanded vision of him allows her to fathom the Beast's multifaceted personality, including the reasons behind his gift of the strand of pearls, which she now places around her neck. Indeed, when next the Beast reappears in his normal guise, she conveys greater ease and conviviality in his company than heretofore. He, too, seems more comfortable in her presence. Why had she not started to dine? he asks. Surprisingly, she replies that she would prefer walking with him. This overt expression of camaraderie with one who had been at first an object of terror may not only preempt a positive marital sexual relationship at some future date, but presage as well a slow liberation on her part from her highly restricted feeling world. So taken aback is the Beast by her change of attitude toward him that he again, unthinkingly, broaches the question of marriage. With increasing self-confidence, Beauty asks that he refrain from querying her about any future marital plans, but that they remain friends—and nothing more (*Beauty* 219).

As the two walk together, Beauty asks how he spends his days, giving the impression that she is not simply indulging in small talk but is genuinely interested in his welfare. As they approach a fountain, a deer suddenly leaps through the bushes, and Beast stares "at it greedily as it runs into the woods"

(*Beauty* 219). As a metaphor for instinct and/or for the carnal sexual act, the Beast seems cognizant of having offended Beauty by his reckless show of desire. Ashamed, he asks her forgiveness. His affirmation of friendship and respect for her, evidenced now by his silence regarding marriage, increases her sense of comfort in his company—perhaps to a disarming degree!

Unable to verbalize his offensive instinctual attraction for the maiden, the Beast conveys his desires analogically, by expressing instead his great "thirst." The compassionate Beauty extends her hand, which he takes, and the two approach the fountain. It is then that she cups her hands, fills them with water, and offers him to drink. "Doesn't it revolt you to give me drink?" he asks hesitantly (*Beauty* 219). She confesses to gaining pleasure from such an act, adding that she would never want to cause him any pain.

That horror has been transformed into compassion is apparent from the hand-to-hand contact they now enjoy. Not only has she grown accustomed to his outer ugliness; she seems to have discovered within him a responsive tenderness and relatedness that she has enjoyed with no one else. Indeed, his late appearance at dinner that night gives rise to concern on her part, while he, reciprocally, conveys his thanks to Beauty for noticing his tardiness. The Beast's character undergoes a marked transformation: Beauty's exquisite inner nature having been constellated in his psyche, he no longer lusts after her beauty/body.

The Touching Game. Their relationship having grown increasingly close, Beauty feels confident enough to appeal to what may be considered the Beast's higher nature. After kneeling before him, she takes hold of his cloak and asks him permission to visit her family, promising him to return in a week's time. Taken aback, the Beast again impulsively repeats his request: "And when you return, will you be my wife?" (*Beauty* 220) His attempt to force her to agree to his wishes tortures her. Nonetheless, she understands his dilemma and knows that if she did not return, he would die of heartbreak. "I respect you too much to cause your death," she assures him (*Beauty* 220). As in the medieval image of the "Unicorn and the Maiden," the Beast lowers his head, bows before her, and affirms his subservience to Beauty, the virgin.[1] So involved is he with his own yearning for her that he fails to fathom the closeness of her ties to her family. Although her transference from primal-father to husband has begun, she is not yet sufficiently strong to begin her life as wife by breaking the emotional ties with her family.

Beauty's gentle stroking of the Beast's head now resting on her lap accentuates their closeness, and the rhythmic motion in the stroking of his head symbolizes the foreplay in the sublimated sexual act. Indeed, the more they touch, the closer they feel toward each other, and the greater grows his

courage to again pose the question (L. *quaestus)* basic to his quest. Psychologically, his progress in the individuation process will lead to his eventual
transformation from Beast to Man.

His urgent yearning to give his life an inner orientation brings to mind
the arduous journeys of pilgrims who underwent deep suffering in order to
reach their goal of casting off their egoistic preoccupations, reorienting them
toward the larger aim of realizing their own individual uniqueness. The *centering* of oneself may bring harmony to a life where chaos and one-sidedness
had once prevailed. Quests of this nature are frequently the sine qua non of
fairy tales and myths: Osiris's night sea journey, Orpheus's descent into
Hades, Sita's and Rama's search for illumination, and many others. In most
cases, the quest illuminates the protagonists' darkened inner realm, reward-
ing them with a sense of plenitude.

Soothed by Beauty's gentle strokes, the Beast asks whether she has
ever received a marriage proposal from someone else? Yes, she responds.
Who? She names Avenant. And her reason for not accepting him? She did
not want to leave her father. So emotionally mutilated is Beast by the
thought that she could love another that he runs away, deaf to her calls and
to the world at large.

Blood. That night, the Beast returns to Beauty's room. Although he is standing in the shadows, she realizes he is covered with blood. Overcome with
"shame and self-disgust" and virtually "groveling" before her, he asks her forgiveness. "For what?" she responds, annoyed. "Go clean yourself and go to
sleep" (*Beauty* 224). He leaves, but not before telling her to close her door.
"Quick . . . quick, close the door. Your look is burning me, I can't bear it"
(*Beauty* 224). Beauty, a product of traditional patriarchal programming, and
totally unaware of his uncontrollable sexual urge, observes him backing away
and closing the door behind him.

Blood, a life-giving substance, altering form and consistency through
its own energetic process, can inject health into the ill. Identified psychologically with libido, the blood circulating in the heart that warms and ex-
udes love and understanding may also generate hate and envy. At the very
mention of Avenant's name, the Beast had grown so jealous, and so envious,
that, to punish himself still further for his lustfulness, he may have attempted to live out his own passion by slashing himself—either in a symbolic
suicide, a castration, or a crucifixion. Cocteau does not disclose the origin of
the blood scene.

Catharsis. Time passes. The Beast's bloodletting acts seemingly having rid
him of his impulsive sexual urges, he returns to Beauty's room. Looking into

the mirror, he is apprised of the disastrous events that have taken place in her home: the Merchant has fallen mortally ill as a consequence of his son's rashness and the usurer's removal of the furniture from their home. Beauty again asks the Beast to send her home for a week. Before agreeing to her request and in a show of confidence, he takes her into his secret pavilion, which hides his five magic powers. Unlike Bluebeard who was driven by inner motivations, the Beast surrenders his secret powers to his beloved: his key, rose, mirror, horse, and glove. Should she be prevented from returning in a week's time, she should put the glove on her right hand and she will be carried to the destination she chose.

The Beast has evolved from the undifferentiated, self-oriented, instinctual animal he was at the outset of the drama to the generous, considerate, and psychologically aware being he now is. That for the first time he has given of himself (disclosed his innermost secrets) to another augurs well for his future development.

FROM CHAOS TO COSMOS: HOME TO CASTLE. No sooner does Beauty arrive home than she rushes to her father's side to comfort him. While he maintains he was sick with fear that the Beast would harm her, she stresses his positive qualities: "One half of him is in constant struggle with the other. I think he is more cruel to himself than he is to others" (*Beauty* 228). As the recipient of the Beast's gentleness and kindness, she has unconsciously begun distancing herself from her self-indulgent, egocentric father. How could she even bear looking at the Beast's hideousness? he questions. "Yes, at first he's a very frightening, father. But now, he sometimes makes me want to burst out laughing. But then I see his eyes, and they're so sad, I turn away so as not to weep" (*Beauty* 228).

Clearly, Beauty not only has seen into the Beast's dual nature, but considers him "a victim of some terrible affliction" (*Beauty* 229). Maintaining that "the monster is good," she would devote her days to helping him forget his ugliness and, in so doing, discover another kind of happiness (*Beauty* 229). Let us note that the word monster (M.E. and O.F. *monstrum*, portent of misfortune, unnatural event), used in this context, suggests a psychological imbalance of one or more personality functions or characteristics. A harmonious/ beautiful personality is dependent on its ability to relate, adapt, and assimilate its own contents, and thus work in concordance with both inner and outer worlds. To function in a balanced manner one must enjoy some independence of action within "the psychic hierarchy" (Jung 6, 254). If incompatibility exists between the ego and a specific complex, a breakdown of the complex may ensue. Because in the Beast's case the sexual instinct prevailed, it dominated temperance or understanding of female qualities, or anything else. His inability to differentiate or distinguish other attributes enslaved him to his sexual—perhaps even priapic—drive. What served to expand his consciousness, or split or differentiate his complex—that is, to create what Beauty called his conflict—was the introduction of her goodness into his life. Like Lucifer (L. *lux* + *ferre*, or light bringer) or Satan (H. *satan*, to persecute, to accuse, thus obstruct), Beauty kindled his dormant qualities with her warmth of personality, and illuminated them by her innate wisdom and loving kindness. Thus, she helped him to overcome his one-sidedness and evolve into a balanced being.

Revealing to her father the riches the Beast had given her in the form of diamonds and gowns, Beauty admonishes him not to disclose her secret to her sisters. If they heard of her wealth, their jealousy would reach new highs. Meanwhile, one of the sisters, having spied Beauty's golden key lying on her dressing table, snatches it. The two also peer into Beauty's magic mirror: one sister sees a hag in reflection, the other, an ape. Revolted by the images, they discard the object. Bemoaning their fate, they quarrel even more relentlessly with Ludovic and Avenant for indulging in drinking and gambling rather than earning money to support them all.

Upon sight of Beauty, Avenant begs her not to return to the Beast, despite her solemn promise to do so. Impossible, she replies. The Beast has given her his treasures, and should she not return, she would be the monster. Making a mockery of her integrity, Avenant and Ludovic decide to "slay the Beast . . . And take his treasure" (*Beauty* 234). After another fruitless attempt to convince Beauty to remain at home, Avenant speaks his love for her, envisaging their glorious future together: "[W]ith you beside me, I'd work. We'd leave the town and its taverns behind us" (*Beauty* 240). He tries to convince Beauty that the Beast has forgotten her, which so fills her with sadness that she runs out of the room sobbing.

As plans to kill the Beast are set in motion by Avenant and Ludovic, "the Magnificent One," who had been sent by the Beast to bring Beauty home, enters the yard just in time for the "boys," having been given the golden key by one of the sisters, to say: "Go where I am going, Magnificent one, go, go" (*Beauty* 243).

Alone in her room, Beauty gazes into the mirror and sees the Beast wearing "a look of intense suffering" (*Beauty* 244). In despair herself, she remembers he had given her the magic glove. Picking it up and putting it on her right hand, in *no time* she is transported to her bedroom in the castle.

DEATH. Upon her arrival, Beauty calls out frantically for "my Beast." To no avail, until she suddenly sees him lying nearly dead on the ground at the edge of the pool. Kneeling before him in what is the most moving scene in Cocteau's work, she calls to him, lifts up his head, and begs for his help.

Beauty: I'm the monster, Beast. You shall live, you shall live!
The Beast: It is too late.
Beauty: You're no coward, I know the strength of your claws. Clutch at life with them, fight! Sit up, roar, frighten death away!
The Beast: Beauty, if I were a man . . . doubtless I would . . . do as you say . . . but poor beasts who would prove their love . . . only know . . . how to lie on the ground . . . and die. (*Beauty* 245, 246)

At this moment, she not only proclaims her love for him, but makes it clear that she would willingly exchange her life for his.

Simultaneously, another scene is played out nearby. Avenant and Ludovic, having arrived at the pavilion, are bent on killing the Beast so as to acquire his posessions. To this end, the aggressor, Avenant, followed by the reticent Ludovic, climb to the roof of the pavillion, gaze through the skylight, and salivate at the sight of the jewels and treasures piled next to the statue of Diana. Beauty's brother, preaching caution and retreat, unsuccessfully attempts to dissuade his friend from any further act of desecration. Deaf to his pleas, Avenant breaks the glass of the skylight, after which the passive Ludovic helps lower his friend into the room. As punishment for such a transgression (the violation of the feminine principle as symbolized by the breaking of the glass—a metaphorical rape), the statue of Diana (the virgin—*parthenos,* archer, and huntress) comes to life and shoots an arrow between Avenant's shoulder blades, killing the criminal.

THE TRANSFIGURATION. Ludovic, staring at his dead friend in horror, bears witness to two miracles: Avenant's transfiguration, his features turning into those of the Beast, and the pile of treasures transformed into dead leaves and branches.

Concurrently, as the still-kneeling Beauty looks at the dying Beast with extreme tenderness, she cries out her despair: "Where is the Beast?" Almost immediately, "a handsome young man"—a Prince—appears before her, explaining that "the Beast is no more. It was I, Beauty. My parents wouldn't believe in fairy tales. The fairies punished them—through me. I could only be saved by a look of love" (*Beauty* 247).

Hardly able to believe the reality of such a miracle, Beauty stands transfixed, as the Prince, ironically, attempts to render the irrational credible by analogizing his transfiguration in philosophical and comprehensible but pedantic terms: "Love," he whispers to Beauty, "can make a Beast of a man. It can also make an ugly man handsome" (*Beauty* 247). Why, he queries, does she look so sad when she should be radiating joy? Because the Prince resembles her brother's friend, Avenant. Does such a resemblance displease her? he asks. Vacillating, she first answers in the affirmative, then in the negative; whereupon the Prince takes her in his arms.

Since the Prince was both the Beast and Avenant, he speaks nostalgically of his past. "The first time I carried you in my arms I was the Beast" (*Beauty* 248). At the mention of his name, audiences/readers observe the Beast's remains as a heap of burned leaves on the ground. Aware that she, too, must adapt to both spiritual and physical change, Beauty will go with her Prince to his kingdom where she will not only become its Queen, but will also be reunited with her family. "Is it far?" she asks. Taking her in his arms, they begin their flight, but not before he poses one more question: "You won't be afraid, will you? (*Beauty* 249). To which she replies, knowingly: "I don't mind being afraid . . . with you." (*Beauty* 250). The couple glance for the last time at what had once been the Beast, then begin their flight through the immensities of space—clouds and sky—injecting into the the panorama a sense of mystery, magic, and beatitude.

Cocteau's imaging of the agony implicit in the "miracle" of the transfiguration reflected the breadth and scope of the physical and emotional change undergone by Beauty, the Beast, and Avenant. The mystery of transfiguration usually refers to "the supernatural and glorified change in the appearance of Jesus on the Mountain" (*Webster's New Universal Unabridged Dictionary*). In this regard, we read in Matthew:

> And after six days, Jesus taketh Peter, James, and John his brother, and bringeth them up into an high mountain apart (17:1)
> And was transfigured before them: and his face did shine as the sun, and his raiment was white as the light (17:2)
> While he spake, behold, a bright cloud overshadowed them: and beheld a voice, which said: This is my beloved Son, in whom I am well pleased; hear ye him: out of the cloud. (17:5)
> And when the disciples heard it, they fell on their face, and were sore afraid. (17:6)
> And Jesus came and touched them, and said, Arise, and be not afraid. (17:7)

Cocteau's understanding of the transfiguration suggests, in Hegelian terminology, ability to transcend the "dialectical ambiguity," which, for some, leads to redemption, and for others, becomes a means of sublimating, or going beyond the "tragic condition" of empirical existence (Vysheslawzeff, "Two Ways of Redemption," in *The Mystic Vision* 8).

The transfiguration occurred after Beauty had experienced the love stemming from the Beast's higher or spiritual values rather than from Avenant's material and sexual desires. Her suffering at the sight of the Beast's torment released her from her painful adolescent ordeals and attachments. The Beast's sex-obsessed behavioral patterns had been tempered, enabling him to fuse esthetics (his love for Beauty) with ethics (a higher code of morality). Beauty's initial fear of defloration and viscerality yielded to a conscious and loving relationship which liberated her from bondage; it opened her up to the joys of sharing her future with her Prince. Transfigured or reborn into a single individual, her future husband became a composite of the Beast's sterling inner qualities and Avenant's handsome physique. Their sacred marriage, or *hieros gamos*—a paradigm of the treasure Avenant tried to acquire by breaking the glass of the skylight—took place during the miraculous transfiguration—when the two became one.

The sense of enchantment, magic, and illusion effected by Cocteau through his veristic use of objects (mirror, glove, key, arms, statues, etc.) and animals (the Beast, the Magnificent stallion) transformed them into talismans (*telesma*, from Greek *telein*, to initiate into the mysteries). Like consecrated objects, they provoked and evoked the miraculous finale of *Beauty and the Beast*. Or, as Cocteau so aptly wrote, "[I]sn't Beauty one of the ruses employed by nature to attract one being toward another?" (Cocteau 1957, 143).

CHAPTER

12

ANDREE CHEDID'S
THE SUSPENDED HEART
THE MYSTERY OF BEING

Andrée Chedid's fairy tale, *The Suspended Heart* (*Le Coeur suspendu,*
[1981]), incites readers to penetrate the magical lands of her multiple heritage—Egypt, Lebanon, and France, her adopted country.
Glimpsed in her verbal distillations are secreted images, mysteries, and paradigms of both the plenitude and scantiness of the human heart. Shorn of
mortal limitations, Chedid's Gods and genies stride the earth. Their sweeping metamorphoses and incandescent resurrections, incorporated as they are
in rapid verbal patternings and tonal modulations, usher the reader into
transpersonal spheres where darkness provokes the phenomenon of light.

That Chedid is the product of three civilizations, three ways of life, and
three psyches discloses not a single but a dichotomous approach to culture. It
invites as well a broadening approach to writing in general, and to the fairy-
tale genre in particular. By delineating her thoughts and feelings in giant,
frequently hieratic verbal frescoes, she heightens their dramatic fabulations;
by juxtaposing meticulously chosen symmetrical versus asymmetrical components, she transforms formless matter or infinite space into cosmic happenings that are, paradoxically, clearly defined. The choices facing Chedid's
protagonists, as they think out or order the consequences of what could be
their salubrious and/or miasmic paths, evoke not only the *chance* factor, and
the comcomitant fears it inspires, but superstitions, occult practices, and
feats of magic. By contrast, the most spiritual of ideologies and altruistic of

relationships also come to the fore. *The Suspended Heart* reveals mysteries involved in deity's immanence, through the narration of one of the most sophisticated religious rituals of ancient Egypt and of all time, that of Osiris's death and resurrection. Events, daubed by Chedid in contrasting luminosities, make inroads into the unfathomable arcana of the human psyche.

Andrée Chedid was born in Cairo in 1920. Her parents were separated when she was very young and she was sent to boarding schools in Cairo and Paris. Although she had little family life, she always maintained a warm and loving relationship with both her father and mother. She received her B.A. degree from the American University in her native city. Married at the age of twenty-one to Louis Chedid, a medical student, she spent the next three years (1942–1945) in Lebanon. The couple moved to Paris in 1946, where Louis earned his degree in medicine and later became associated with the Pasteur Institute.

Chedid's writings—novels *Sleep Unbound (Le Sommeil délivré)* (1952); *The Sixth Day (Le Sixième jour)* (1960); *The Fertile City (La Cité fertile)* (1972); *Steps in the Sand (Les Marches de sable)* (1981); poems *Caverns and Sun (Cavernes et soleil)* (1979); *Territories of Breath (Territoires du souffle)* (1999); and theater pieces *Bérénice of Egypt* (1968); *Numbers* (1968); *The Puppeteer* (1969)—mirror the land of her birth in the Middle East; yet, they all bear the veneer of Europe as well. The known and the unknown of ancient and modern civilizations fascinate Chedid. As she ushers a past into being, creatures are enticed to spin their web, to evolve, to act; and as they do so, each in his or her own way reveals a tarnished or unblemished inner world. Endowed with a sense of both proximity and distance, Chedid's characters are a composite of rootedness and rootlessness; paradigms of personal quests and of collective searches. The need to communicate not only with one's own multileveled self, but also with those organic and inorganic forces that surround and implode in each being, is crucial to their makeup. "The search for a convergence point in the depth of human beings, of a common source, a shared land" is present in all of Chedid's works. "It's probably because of this that I feel the need to express, in diverse forms, that which is elementary and fundamental in each of us, death-love-life" ("Huit questions posées à l'auteur," *A la rencontre d'Andrée Chedid* 2).

THE SUSPENDED HEART

The Suspended Heart, considered an archetypal Death and Resurrection mystery and in this case Osiris's Passion, is reminiscent of those mysteries lived out by the Mesopotamian Tammuz, the Greek Dionysus, and the Palestinian

Christ. Chedid's reenactment of this universal and eternal religious ritual was freely drawn from sections of the ancient Egyptian "Story of Two Brothers," written on papyrus c. 1300 B.C.E. and discovered only around 1850. The voices emanating from *The Suspended Heart* date back to Egypt's New Kingdom (1570–1405 B.C.E.), a period of intense turbulence for its populations, busy as they were in their attempts, and final success, in expelling the Hyksos ("Foreigners") who had dominated their land from c. 1720 to 1550 B.C.E.

Chedid's title, *The Suspended Heart*, is the key to our hermeneutic study of her fairy tale: it contains the words *suspended* (L. *suspendere*, to hang, to exclude, to privilege) and *heart* (L. *cor*), a vital organ that played such a significant role in Egyptian cosmogony. The image, featuring a heart hanging in midair, creates a sense of uncertainty, instability, and unresolvedness which serves to accentuate feelings of apprehension, anxiety, and, of course, suspense. The state of hanging in the open, that is, of unprotectedness, arouses feelings of vulnerability and insecurity, of noninvolvement either in heavenly spiritual concerns or in earthly matters. On the other hand, the momentary state of inoperativeness created by the hanging heart ushers in the allure and timelessness of measurelessness, thus enhancing the breadth and scope of the Passion to be told.

The physical heart, the body's central organ—receiver and sender of blood from the veins through the arteries by alternate dilation and contraction—is veritably at the *heart* of Chedid's story. Its rhythms and energy, as is found frequently in fairy tales, serve as barometers for measuring the protagonists' emotional or affective levels. Cosmic breath is instrumental in the tale's shifting, pendulous pulsations. Like the cardiac rhythm and its feeling components, they emphasize the manner in which dualities impact on the characters in their universal and eternal battles with the vicissitudes of life.

INVASION: CONQUEST. Chedid's fairy tale begins about four thousand years ago, as Geba, a small, peace-loving territory on the shores of the Mediterranean Sea, is suddenly invaded and conquered by the tyrant Zezi. Unsparing in his army's use of lances, spears, arrows, and hatchets, following his victory he proclaims himself sovereign of the country and announces that anyone failing to obey his orders will be put to death. Similar to other arrogant tyrants of fairy-tale manufacture, we learn that Zezi feels threatened by, and thus despises, one man, who in this case is Kheo. Kheo is adept not only in the art of magic, but in the divine art of pottery, their secrets having been handed down to him by his father. The young man's unassuming and righteous character has enhanced his prestige among his people and served to win their love. Indeed, so beloved is he that they urge him to flee. "You are our only hope, you must remain alive. We give you our soul, Kheo; enclose it in your heart and take it with you to some faraway place. As long as you keep it hidden, no harm will come to it. One day you will come back, return it, and save us!" (A. Chedid, *The Suspended Heart* 7). Kheo follows their advice and leaves Geba.

Failing to have his archenemy captured, the tyrant is now determined to exterminate his memory among the tribe. To this end, Zezi has Kheo's house with its few meager possessions—some furniture and a few scrolls of papyrus—burned down. Standing victoriously atop the charred remains, he announce to the terrified populace that anyone sheltering Kheo will be summarily put to death, but "he who returns his heart to me," will be named co-regent (*Heart* 7).

KHNUM: THE ART OF POTTERY. Kheo's father's deep involvement in the art of pottery may be directly linked to the Egyptian Myth of Creation. Not only did the ram-headed God Khnum ("molder") fashion on his potter's wheel the great cosmic egg containing the sun, but he was responsible as well for the creation of the Gods and of humankind. In that a potter mixes water with his clay, or earth mud, Khnum was understandably identified with the Nile God, Hapy. When Khnum flooded the Nile twice yearly, it was said that he brought joy, jubilation, and laughter to the people; but plunderings, assaults, and other crimes were also rampant.

> Khnum groans in weariness.
> Lo terror kills; the frightened says . . .
> Lo, —throughout the land,
> The strong man sends to everyone,
> A man strikes his maternal brother.
> What has been done. (Lichtheim, *Ancient Egyptian Literature* I, 154)

KHEO'S EXILE. Prior to Kheo's exile from Geba, he goes secretly to his family's hut outside of town to say good-bye to his mother and his nine-year-old brother, Bastos. Although his mother begs him to stay, Kheo's sense of responsibility takes priority. Having been entrusted with the soul of his compatriots, their safety becomes his guiding principle. Speaking in hushed tones, Kheo confides to his family his reasons for leaving and his future plans.

> The heart no longer belongs to me alone: it contains the hopes of our people. I must hurry and find a safe place for myself. I am leaving for a distant place. Once there, and separated from my heart, I shall not worry. I shall be able to think and gather my strength to return. (*Heart* 8)

Anxiously, Kheo's mother questions him about the fate of his body if it were deprived of its beating heart. In reassuring terms, he replies that while it would be "hidden to the eyes of others," his heart would be visible to him— "the one would be keeping guard on the welfare of the other " (*Heart* 8). But how could he possibly manage such a feat? she asks concernedly.

I shall hide it on Parasol Pine hill, near the hamlet where you were born, my mother, which you have described to me so many times. With the help of the magic formulas bequeathed to me by my father prior to his death, I shall detach my heart from my chest and fix it to the summit of the highest tree. It will remain suspended there! . . . Henceforth, no lance, no arrow, no javelin will be able to kill me. As long as the heart remains in a safe place, I shall be invulnerable. I have told this secret to no one but you and my brother. (*Heart* 8)

Bastos, still being initiated into his father's art, hugs his brother despite his clay-steeped hands and begs him to take him with him. Impossible, Kheo responds. Bastos will have to look after their mother and, besides, time is needed to further his initiation—literally, into pottery but, psychologically speaking, into manhood. Furthermore, Kheo's departure and the hoped-for success of his mission will prove to himself and his people as well, he explains, his ability to complete his *rite of passage*. His itinerary to different lands will teach him how to deal with a variety of customs and, most importantly, how to protect himself from ever-present dangers. Tearfully, Kheo says good-bye to his brother and mother, indicating that they will meet again, "unless. . . ."

Before drawing close to his brother and mother, Bastos picks up his great friend, the ageless tortoise, Shu, once his grandfather's companion, and places it most carefully in the palm of his hand. He then listens carefully to Kheo's revelations.

One day, should you put your beer pots to your lips, and see the water inside suddenly grow muddy, quiver, agitate, bubble, and overflow, you will know that I am in danger! At this very moment you must leave everything and rush to help me.

When you reach my hill, and, if, unfortunately, you find that the Parasol Pine tree has been cut down, and my body lying on the ground, immobile, and cold as ice, you will know that my heart has fallen from the tree! Believe me, Bastos, its fall will have caused [my heart] to shrink so drastically, that not one of my enemies will take note of its existence, dissimulated as it is, between all the surrounding pine needles and pebbles. Even you will not see it right away. But don't be discouraged. Even if you have to spend hours, days, seasons, and years searching for it, I implore you not to let yourself be discouraged! Tell yourself that not only is your brother's life at stake, but that of your people as well. Search, search, and keep searching, for you will find this heart in the end, even though it has shrunk to the size of a tiny seed.

Once found, you will pick it up with care and tenderness, first placing it in the palm of your hands, and then, very quickly, in a cup of fresh water. Sprinkle it [with the water] carefully with both hands. Don't let it out of your sight, speak to it; speak to it with your entire mouth. Little by little, this minuscule heart will awaken, beat, inflate, take form again. Even if I appear to you less animated than a stone, return the heart to me. Deposit it calmly on my chest; have confidence; it will assume its proper place. (*Heart* 11)

Kheo's mother gives him a brown wool coat to protect him from the cold of the lands he will traverse; then, gazing at him with an expression of joy blended with sadness, she accepts the fact that she, like all other mothers, will have to learn to allow her son to make his own way in life.

SHU'S AND BASTOS'S ROLES IN OSIRIS'S PASSION. The tortoise played an important role not only in Chedid's tale but in Egyptian cosmology as well. Its rounded shell symbolizing both the sky above and the earth beneath, the tortoise was frequently featured in the position of "raising up the sky," and was thus considered by worshippers to be a protective force—imaged, for example in Tutankhamun's ivory headrest of the Eighteenth Dynasty, c. 1350 B.C.E. (Lamy, *Egyptian Mysteries* 42). Added to its cosmic associations was its identification with wisdom, stability, and magic, curative, or mediating powers. The tortoise's longevity and the ease with which it navigates on earth and in water transformed this chthonian deity into an object for sublimation as well.

That Bastos kept Shu in the palm of his hand (L. *manus*, that which takes hold of and grasps) indicated his affinity with this reptile's instinctual patterns: its ability to retreat silently into its shell in time of danger replicated Bastos's tendency to indwell in periods of tension and call upon his unconscious—or his inner reserves—for sustenance and guidance. That he closed his hand on Shu in times of loneliness indicated his profound yearning for friendship and love. Bastos, like Shu, was not volatile: he took his time to think and meditate before he acted.

Important as well in Egyptian theology was the belief that the tortoise was an incarnation of the Benu Bird (the Greeks called it Phoenix), a supernatural flying creature born from the flames atop the sacred persea tree of Heliopolis. Indeed, the "spell for becoming the *Benu Bird*," as noted in the Book of the Dead (ch. 83), refers explicitly to the notion of Death and Resurrection in the verses in which the soul reveals itself to a worshipper as the life principle.

I flew up as the Primeval God and assumed forms—
I grew in the seed and disguised myself as the Tortoise,

I am the seed corn of every god,
I am yesterday . . .
I am Horus, the god who gives light by means of his body. . . .
(Clark, *Myth and Symbol in Ancient Egypt* 248)

In keeping with Egyptian theology as well, and somewhat reminiscent of Christianity's *homousian* theory, the dead Osiris lying in his tomb remained, paradoxically, the source and dispenser of earthly and divine power. What remained viable in the God was his *Ka*, or spiritual double: the "abstract element symbolizing an individual's tendencies," or physical, moral, and spiritual "appetites." In that the *Ka* was more or less attached to empirical existence, it could be recalled at some future date to be born again (Lamy 26). However, "to achieve beatification and to function as a 'spirit,'" the dead king, Osiris, needed a living king, in this case, his "beloved son" and heir Horus, to act as care-giver. "If the [living] king carried out the required rites for his father, the latter could then become 'a soul,' which meant that the powers of life and growth would begin again in nature" (Clark 107).

Still unknown to Bastos was the important role he would play in the great mystery that was to be the Passion of Kheo/Osiris.

Kheo's Difficult Path. Kheo's long and arduous trajectory takes him through a variety of topographies—rivers, torrents, deserts of "solitary and burning dunes," hills, commercial shipping centers, fertile orange groves, vineyards, and almond and olive plantations in areas bordering the Mediterranean. So passionate is the need of his people, so powerfully had his father indoctrinated him in the art of magic, and so accurate had been his mother's directions prior to his departure that it takes Kheo only thirty days to arrive at his destination (*Heart* 12).

How much fun he would have had, he laments, had his brother been with him. Taken aback by the frivolity of his thoughts, he realizes it is no time for fun. He is on a serious mission. Since suffering is rampant in his land, he has to put his people's welfare ahead of his own. With this in mind, he sets out to climb the mountain on which the Parasol Pine is said to be located. Although the ascent is slow and arduous, the people he meets along the way fete him, give him drink, food, and hospitality. After twenty more days of trekking, he finally reaches his mother's hamlet. At the bottom of the hill, as if dug into the rock itself, he notices a grotto. It must certainly be that of the hermit Orose, he reasons, about whom his mother had talked in such praiseworthy terms.

THE HERMIT. The archetype of the Hermit, the wise old man of fairy tales, has appeared in people's dreams, visions, meditations, and other periods of active imagination since time immemorial. Known in India as a *guru* and in myths and fairy tales as a *psychopomp*, the Hermit has acted as magician, doctor, priest, teacher, and virtually any other kind of authority or compensatory figure, whose goal is to help the naïve or the unknowing, thus furthering their spiritual or praxis-related quest (Jung 91, #398).

Given the Hermit's advanced age of one hundred and twenty-one years, Kheo is surprised to see him still alive. (In fairy tales, life endures as long as the helping individual is needed.) Recalling his mother's description of Orose, he is aware of his dependence on him. His insight, understanding, and determination have nurtured and shaped so many initiates, whose direction and inner resources had been either deficient or limited. Interestingly, however, while Kheo places his confidence in the Hermit, knowing that he will work for his welfare, he is wise enough to keep concealed the deepest of his secrets. That he reveals to the Hermit only his reasons for having exiled himself from his land, but not the mysteries revolving around his heart, indicates his already increased discernment—his first step in fulfilling his rite of passage.

The Hermit confesses with delight to having known that Kheo would visit him, but admits with humility that the exact date of his arrival had remained unknown to him. Moreover, he confesses that although Kheo's presence fills him with joy for its own sake, he also looks upon it as a kind of self-deliverance. After accomplishing the tasks required of him during his long stay on earth—the last will be to help Kheo—the Hermit will have fulfilled his destiny and may, in all good conscience, depart from the world of the living and enter the Egyptian's *Tuat* (Underworld or Otherworld).

Aware of Orose's desire to enter the Otherworld, where he will meet the family, friends, and Gods who have been awaiting him so long, Kheo listens carefully to the Hermit's sage advice. Rather than encouraging Kheo to continue to his destination, he suggests with fatherly solicitude that the lad sleep in the grotto he calls his home and leave at dawn. Not only will he enjoy a much-needed rest, but their hours together will allow the Hermit to show him the shortest way to the Parasol Pine forest located between "heaven and earth," the clearest springs of fresh water from which to drink, the most healthful herbs, seeds, and nuts to be eaten, and the birds and rabbits that will be his companions along the way (*Heart* 14).

Following Kheo's departure the next morning, the Hermit returns to his grotto, the weight of his responsibilities having been lifted. Smiling, he finds the strength and calm to continue on his journey into death.

THE ASCENSION. Kheo spends the following days ascending and descending mountains, hillocks, and rocky embankments. Gazing at the forested lands, and observing multiple dawns and dusks unfolding before him, a strange sense of inner ebullience seems to permeate his being: an increase in those good energies that egg one on to reach a goal. When he sees the great Parasol Pine forest in the distance, any semblance of languor he may have felt yields to elation. He feels as if he were gliding along, each step taking him closer to his goal. After observing the Parasol Pines as a whole forest, he narrows his search down for the one he judges would best meet his needs. Finally touching the Parasol Pine of his choice, he puts his arms around its mighty trunk, braces his chest and cheeks against its bark, and murmurs: "I place myself under your protection. With my heart, I entrust my people to you" (*Heart* 16).

The following morning, after a night of deep slumber, Kheo faces the great Parasol Pine, breathes in deeply, invokes the name of his father, and pronounces the appropriate magic formula. Moments later, his scarlet heart, without apparent trace of blood or injury, appears before him. With utmost gentleness, he takes it in his hands, places it in a cloth bag whose straps he tightens, removes his sandals, climbs the sacred tree, chooses the flower closest to its trunk, and hangs his heart on the flower's pistil. In keeping with the botanical definition of *pistil,* let us note the sexual imagery involved in Kheo's act.

> The pistil is usually called the reproductive organ of a flowering plant. . . . The pistil has a bulbous base (the ovary), containing the ovules, which develop into seeds after fertilization of eggs. A pistil is composed of one or more modified leaves (carpels), each containing one or more ovules. . . . Usually, there is above the ovary a stalk (the style) bearing on its tip the stigma, where the pollen grains land and germinate. The style is usually long and slender, which improves the chances of cross-pollination, and the stigma is often sticky or hairy to retain the pollen. (*The New Columbia Encyclopedia* 1993, 2157)

For his own protection, Kheo judges that an added precaution should be taken in hiding his heart: he chooses the pistil so that the heart's "conical shape" and coloration should blend into the tree's fruits. Although he is "pained" as a result of his dismembering act, he takes comfort in the thought that, because of his sacrifice, "the soul of his people would not be destroyed!" (*Heart* 17).

THE HEART AND THE PARASOL-PINE/DJED COLUMN. Why did the tree play such a significant role in Kheo/Osiris's Passion?[1] Associated in many religions with the Tree of Life, the Tree of Wisdom, or the world axis, in our fairy tale the tree may be identified with the Egyptians' Djed Column located in the Nile delta. (*Djed* means "stability" or "durability.") In a semiotic humanization of the tree, its outspread branches function as head and arms, and its phallic trunk as sacrum (L. *sacrum,* literally "sacred bone," so called from being used formerly in sacrifices), or seat of virility.

Osiris's Djed Column, or symbolic tree (and Kheo's by extension), was unusual in that the representation of the phallus was not in the trunk but at the top, or head, of the tree, thus implying a new understanding of a desexualized generative force. The phallus was awarded a "higher" and more sublimated status. Fertilization, then, was no longer equated with the lower extremities, but with the more abstract upper thinking regions (Neumann, *The Origins and History of Consciousness*, 230–233). That Kheo's heart was suspended on the Parasol Pine (Djed Column) suggests both an ascension of the feeling function as well as activity in the sexual domain. The implication of this transfer of values conveys greater emphasis on—and understanding of—the welfare of others, increased compassion, and increased generosity on behalf of the collective. The goal of the Djed Column ritual took the whole being into account; it included spiritual matters, but did not exclude the joys of physical love. Not one without the other.

Once deprived of his heart, Kheo feels neither extreme distress nor ecstatic joy. His well-tempered feelings, divested to a great extent of his adolescent emotional dependency on others, are drawn inward, thus better serving him to observe worldly and cosmic happenings. Greater lucidity will encourage increased mentation; greater exercise in the forest will strengthen his muscles. To this end, and in keeping with the Hermit's instructions, Kheo builds himself a hut, making a large hole in it that enables him to see and sense the presence of his suspended heart from a distance. Perception, cognition, and emotion will work as one.

BES AS KHEO'S PROTECTIVE DEITY. Kheo's protective deity, Bes, whose original Egyptian name Chedid retained, was patron of the arts and, paradoxically, of war as well. Stout, bald, earthy, and hairy, this grotesque dwarf with protruding tongue and ears and flat nose was endowed with the remarkable ability to make people laugh (Mercatante, *Who's Who in Egyptian Mythology* 23). His outlandish verbalizations, his buffoonery, his irreverent, irresponsible frolicking and general impulsiveness, have endeared this archetypal figure to young and old alike. Psychologists, nonetheless, aware of the complexities involved in the notion of humor, have associated Bes's openness and brashness with obscure, even repressed, samplings of the unconscious.

Dwarves were not unusual in ancient Egypt, as evidenced in certain extant sculptures, paradigmatically the one featuring the dwarf Seneb and his wife, dated 2475 B.C.E., which was discovered in a *mastaba* at Giza (Zabern, *Le Musée égyptien du Caire* 39). The physical deformities of dwarfs may be ascribed mainly to the Egyptian custom of intermarriage, as well as to the importation of pygmies from Africa, the latter serving in temples as performers of "the dwarf's dance in honor of the gods" (Zabern 39).

Deep-thinking and sensitive to the pain of others, Chedid's invulnerable gnomelike deity, or genie, Bes, may be identified with both "higher" transcendent reasoning powers and the trickster's "lower" telluric behavioral patterns. Associated with the world of intuition or spirit, as well as with instinct, Bes had dual powers: he had access to heavenly spheres and, as a telluric force, he penetrated earth mysteries denied the "normal" human being.

Bes's radiance and highly charged energy sequences dynamizes Kheo, musters in him the necessary strength to face the ordeals ahead, making of him, in the alchemist's term, a *filius regius* (Jung 91, #397). As Kheo's guiding or patron saint, the clairvoyant Bes, who claims to have the power to chase away demons with the tail of the animal skin he wears around his waist as a belt, is unlike other Gods, Chedid writes, because he is denied the ability to fly or to alter his appearance on demand.

After joining him who would one day become Geba's liberator, Bes realizes that in addition to the harsh topography of the earthly space Kheo now calls home, its loneliness will not be conducive to his happiness. He will, therefore, be on the alert for the right companion for Kheo.

In keeping with the chance factor that plays such an important role in fairy tales, Bes, making his way through the countryside, is suddenly entranced by a most marvelous (L. *mirabilis*, causing wonder, astonishment, supernatural, and miraculous) perfume, more exquisite than all worldly flowers combined. As if drunk with rapture, he follows the aroma, stopping in front of the heaviest, largest, and most beautiful ebony tresses he has ever seen. Sensing a presence behind this opulent hair, he looks around, and beholds an exquisite young girl. So transfixed is he by the perfection of her face that he remains, virtually, nailed to the ground. Sensitive to the dwarf's minuscule size, the young girl kneels on the ground, thereby equalizing their height, and begins to converse. The compassionate nature of her approach to Bes elicits a warm response in the deity. A diplomat in human relations, the young girl, Thabée, immediately tells him that a sculpted ivory effigy of his face adorns her box of salves, an item she uses daily for her hair. Open in his approach to her, Bes informs Thabée of his mission to guide her toward her destiny: to provide her with a companion for life. In keeping with the laws of the land, the dwarf and the beautiful girl travel to her parents' home to ask permission to fulfill her purpose in life. Not only is it immediately granted, but crowds gather about them—the beautiful maiden and the grotesque deity—to wish them well.

OPULENT AND PERFUMED HAIR. The properties and esthetics associated with women's hair had always been emphasized in ancient Egypt. Thabée's lustrously long and opulent tresses complemented her exquisite features. Identified with the earth's tresses, or grass, hair was associated in agrarian societies such as Egypt's with vegetation and nurturing forces. As a mark of a woman's beauty, prestige, and sensuality, hair (head) symbolized spiritual qualities as well. It followed that the male choosing a woman endowed with bountiful locks would be the recipient of the values and vital forces identified with them.

The styling, combing, shaping, and coloring of hair or headpieces were deemed to reflect the female's personality, whether it be her openness, availability, carnality, sensitivity, understanding, or other traits. To conserve hair in its living form or as a wig or fetish, or in other ways, indicated for some a desire to retain the memory of the individual to whom it belonged. Understandably, then, hair was highlighted in Egyptian sculptures (Nofret, wife of Prince Rahotep, Heliopolis, 2620 B.C.E.), in limestone reliefs (King Smenkhkare and his wife, Meritaten, Tel el-Amarna, 1360 B.C.E.), on canopic jars (during Akhenaton's reign, 1379–1362 B.C.E.), in sculptures of Hathor, the Cow Goddess, (Luxor, Late Period), and in tomb paintings ("Musicians and Dancers," Necropolis, Thebes, 1400 B.C.E.).

Let us also note that Thabée's hair, rendered more irresistible by its fragrance than even the sight of her bodily beauty, suggests the importance of aromatics in Egyptian mores. Indeed, so significant a role did the sense of smell play in ancient Egypt that the Sun God of Memphis, Nefertum, was created to preside over perfumes. Although Nefertum was identified with the cosmic lotus as it emerged from its watery bed at dawn and opened its buds, releasing its heavenly fragrance to an expectant and rejoicing world, he was not considered by worshippers to be the flower per se. Rather, he represented "that great god who [was] within the lotus bud of gold." What was actually rising from the opening flower was "the world soul which [was] the light, life and air of the sun" (Clark 67). Accordingly, the head of the lotus, as "the emerging soul," becomes the paradigm "for the final defeat of the powers of the Abyss" (Clark 67).

Depictions in Egyptian, as well as Babylonian, Greek, and Roman texts of beautiful divinities or supernatural beings such as Thabée, from whom the most exotic of aromas exuded, often represented idealized women. Having been brought into being to serve not their own purposes but those of their society, or of humanity in general, they had an empiric function that was cultic in emphasis. Aromatics played a significant role in invoking the presence of supernatural beings in religious rituals in ancient Egypt, as they do today for purposes of blessing in Roman Catholic, Greek, and Russian Orthodox services. At certain points in the Egyptian ceremony, statues and steles featuring specific deities were sprinkled with perfumes and/or incense.

Incense (L. *incensum*, something kindled, or set on fire) in Egyptian ceremonies was burned to enhance a mood or to pay homage to an individual or deity. In that aromas ascend in air waves to celestial spheres, rituals of this nature were and still are deemed efficacious for processes of purification. Let us make mention of the custom in ancient Egypt of laying or rubbing aromatic salves and ointments on cadavers for esthetic and/or religious reasons during embalming. Persons of the highest classes used flowers and plant extracts in the belief that their fragrances would attract their yearned-for deity. Let us again note in this connection that the longer the aroma lingered, the more powerful the memory of the individual would remain.

Not surprisingly, then, no sooner had Bes introduced Thabée to Kheo than her wonder-working aroma, as well as her exquisite beauty and altruistic character, enticed him to love!

KHEO'S THABEE. A divinity, genie, or supernatural creature frequently appears in fairy tales and myths to expedite matters. The archetypal Thabée, to be identified with the *hierodule* (a servant of a God), is just such a being. Like the temptress or sacred prostitute of patriarchal societies who figures in such epics as the Babylonian *Gilgamesh* and the Hindu *Ramayana*, the *hierodule* is usually associated with religious worship, including the performance of sexual rites (Kluger, *The Archetypal Significance of Gilgamesh* 32). The popularity of this archetypal figure throughout the centuries gives evidence of the male's self-interest and his fixated fear of women, and thus his urge to dominate them. In some cases, as we shall note, the *hierodule*, be it in harem life or elsewhere, may also be a status symbol. Thabée is called into being to play the role of a servant of a God.

Instantly mesmerized by Thabée's fragrance and beauty, Kheo takes her in his arms, then invites her into the hut of branches which he has built for himself. So swept up is he by what he senses to be Thabée's warmth and gentleness that he conveys his feelings of love to her not by sex alone, but as only he knows how: by an act of unheard-of generosity. "What I possess is yours," he tells her, "and we shall divide everything" (*Heart* 20). Their instant spiritual and sexual entente is to prelude many harmonious and delectable hours together—interspersed with cruelly sorrowful ones as well.

Even as they live out their idyll in the Parasol Pine forest, there are moments when the impressionable Thabée senses something awry in their relationship. Has their love reached an impasse, a condition of stasis? she wonders. Have the constancy and ease they have previously enjoyed with each other now diminished? Has boredom set in? Unable to pinpoint her negative feelings concerning their love, nor what she interprets to be Kheo's increasingly withdrawn and despondent moods and less than reassuring affirmation of love, she notices that he directs his gaze elsewhere even when he holds her closely and speaks words of love to her. Her heart beats loudly, but she has never heard his. In fact, it is as if his "heart were absent" (*Heart* 22).

Sensitive to Thabée's suffering, and unwilling to cause her increased anxiety, Kheo is to take another giant step toward soldering their relationship. Having already promised to share his material possessions with her, he now feels it to be the right time to reveal his secret commitment to a higher principle—his people. Pointing to the Parasol Pine, he confesses that his heart is suspended above one of the red fruits hanging from its branches (*Heart* 22). Since it has been severed from his body, its beat, concordantly, has grown fainter, albeit nonexistent. "Be patient, my love, this heart will once again live in my body. Then I will be able to love you as you wish to be loved, and as I would like to love you" (*Heart* 22).

Thus, the lovers renew their idyll, but while harmony and well-being reign in their world, upheavals of catastrophic proportions are about to explode.

YAM, ZEZI'S PROTECTIVE GOD. Chedid's Storm God, Yam, reminiscent in some respects of the Egyptian deity Onuris, now appears on the scene. The earthly representative of the warlike Sun God, Ra, Onuris was known as the hurler of thunderbolts, the provoker of high winds and other climatic disorders. As manifested in Yam, his apparently unprovoked furor is suddenly unleashed. He creates a devastating condition throughout the land—even as far away as the distant mountains of the sacred Parasol Pines.

Violent storms released into the atmosphere in fairy tales or myths are usually manifestations of an unsatisfactory inner condition within the psyche of the deity provoking them, or, by projection, the psyches of the individuals involved. By destroying the accustomed order of things, a storm roots up what binds an individual to earthly conventions. Pyschologically, it displaces the ego's patterned existence, thus awakening it from an enslaved, lethargic, or routine condition. Kheo's seeming unresponsiveness to Thabée's love represents just such an impasse.

Once Yam's rage has been spent, in keeping with a basic life principle he begins to inhale deeply, only to be suddenly overwhelmed by the most extraordinary of aromas. Like Bes, he is mesmerized by the fragrance surrounding him, and grows giddy with anticipation. Determined to discover the source of this exquisite essence, Yam peruses the entire area until, much to his delight, he comes upon the exquisite ebony-colored tresses exuding the supernal aroma. Intent upon discovering the identity of their owner, he first circles them, while musing as to how best to seize these uniquely textured aromatic locks. Serendipitously, he finds himself face to face with Thabée. Then and there, he decides to bring this exquisite creature to his protégé, the tyrant

Zezi, who is already surfeited with harem wives, but who, Yam knows, will be unable to resist this latest example of feminine pulchritude.

He sends out a great wind designed to knock down the hut that Thabée and Kheo call their home, as well as alternating gusts of hot and cold air intended to further destabilize Thabée, who is alone at the time. Kheo never hears her frantic calls for help. Nor are her attempts to flee from her persecutor by climbing up and down the surrounding slippery rocks successful. Not only is she encapsulated by the swirls of raging winds, but one sharp blast cuts off her hair close to her neck.

Delighted with the newly acquired hairpiece, Yam vanishes from the mountain of the Parasol Pines, only to reappear in Zezi's palace as the helmeted God of war. After handing the aromatic tresses to the tyrant, he describes their owner, Thabée, as one of the most radiant woman he has ever seen. With utmost diplomacy, or cunning perhaps, he informs Zezi that the stars have revealed to him that Thabée will give birth to the country's future sovereign. Zezi is entranced by the perfume exuded by the tresses and by the idea of fathering a new dynasty. Yam adds yet another boon he thinks will be pleasing to the tyrant. His knowledge of the whereabouts of Zezi's archenemy, Kheo, the lady's protector, so excites the tyrant that he makes immediate plans to have him eliminated and Thabée kidnapped.

In no time Yam, accompanied by Zezi's army, arrives at the Parasol Pine forest. Not only do they find Kheo's hut rebuilt, but the lovers asleep in it in each other's arms. Much to their surprise, they also notice that Thabée's hair has grown back and is even more opulent than before. Action is taken. The cruelties perpetrated by Zezi's soldiers's knows no bounds. Although they break into Kheo's hut and stab him multiple times, they notice that not one drop of blood is visible on his slashed and gashed body. He must be a demon, the soldiers conclude. Whereupon, they bind him to the Parasol Pine, plunge a sword through his heart, and leave him for dead. After winding a cord around Thabée's body, they transport their immobilized victim to Zezi's castle.

MATERIAL AND MEDICINAL PERSUASION. Immensely taken by Thabée's beauty and sensuality, Zezi smiles at the thought of winning her love for himself. How best to achieve his end? By overwhelming her with material possessions. Precious jewels, exquisite gowns, imported ebony furniture, to mention but a few items on his list, will surely secure her affection. Sumptuous feasts, to which palace officials and townspeople shall be invited, will give him the opportunity to show her off to the people.

Predictably, Zezi's egotism blinds him to the workings of human nature and to Thabée's qualities: her innate kindness, generosity, and compassion. Zezi, believing everyone to have been created in his own image and with his own greed, acquisitiveness, cunning, and bombast, fails to recognize the hurt, fear, and anger in the hearts of his people following the promulgation of his restrictive laws of the land. One of his edicts reads: if someone is accused of the slightest infraction, the accused individual will be beaten, decapitated, or have his hands, legs, or tongue amputated.

Upon learning from one of his lieutenants that Kheo is not only alive but invulnerable, possibly even immortal, his elation gives way to terror. However, the tyrant's sudden mood swing—indicative of his inner psychological upheavals—opens new and insidious paths destined to work in his favor. Playing on the certitude that each person suffers from at least one weakness, he will seek to draw from Thabée the secret of Kheo's vulnerable spot. He will approach her at the appropriate moment with tact and suavity—that is, with utmost hypocrisy—and then proceed to perpetrate his crime.

He chooses one of his huge sumptuous feasts as the proper time to proclaim Thabée his "Great Favorite." What he has failed to foresee, however, is her reaction to his proclamation. Traumatized by the announcement, she stands as if transfixed in the banquet hall, motionless, dead to the world. Nor do the following days give evidence of any change in her condition: she refuses all food, is unable to sleep, and remains stubbornly silent.

Angered by the thought that his plans have not come to fruition, Zezi calls Hepy, his doctor-sorcerer, for consultation. The equivalent for this learned therapist in Egyptian theology would be Khensu ("the Navigator"), an early moon deity known as healer and regenerator of life. Homer and Herodotus had proclaimed Egyptian doctors noteworthy for both their medicinal cures and their surgical feats. However, in that illness was believed to have been God-and/or demon-sent, magical arts and prayers were called into play to placate the responsible forces. Like many contemporary worshippers, the ancient Egyptians resorted to prayer, amulets, medals, signs, and rituals of all types to prevent and/or ward off disease.

To Hepy's magical pronouncements are added complex gesticulations, vocalized incantations, and exorcistic rituals designed to cast out the devils. This clever deity of medical science also uses a tried-and-true powder of his own concoction. Made from ground poppy seeds (opium), it will, needless to say, be instrumental in altering Thabée's mental state. Forced to take this narcotic, she falls into a state of deep slumber, during which, psychologically speaking, she suffers an eclipse of her ego (center of consciousness). In this virtually unconscious state, she succumbs to the will of her tormenter and unwittingly verbalizes her torments in protracted shrieks. "Don't come to rescue me, Kheo! Don't take your heart back, leave it on the tree where it belongs. Otherwise, they will run their daggers through it and kill you!" (*Heart* 32). Suddenly, as if awakened from a trance, she runs to the terrace of the palace. Her disoriented movements and wild eyes are fearsome to behold. "Don't come near me, my love!" she shouts. "Protect the Great Pine! Watch your tree day and night. If our enemies destroy the house in which your heart resides, you will die. Remain forever dead!" (*Heart* 32).

Delighted by the disclosure of the information he sought, Zezi orders his military to take but a single hatchet and destroy the Parasol Pine—adding that his soldiers need not bother with the man.

BEER AND THE MIRACLE OF THE WATERS. Five years have elapsed since Kheo's abandonment of his young brother Bastos, his mother, his home, and his country. Bastos, inspired by the memory of his father, and an assiduous student of the sacred art of pottery, has deepened his knowledge of his *métier* and in the process has acquired a sterling reputation. That his mother is in charge of maintaining the kiln's even heat insures the fine workmanship and the splendid colorations of the objects during the firing process. The multishaped vases, plates, bowls, jars, and pitchers displayed in the workshop not only are a feast for the eyes, but afford observers an exceptional visceral experience.

Given that bowls, jars, or other concave or oval-shaped ware are objects that contain, they have always symbolized the feminine: the uterus, for example, which nourishes and protects the fetus until its organs are sufficiently developed to take on an independent existence of its own. An unborn or nonverbalized thought, act, or mystical vision, prior to coming to term in the uterus, may be analogized to an incompleted initiatory process. In Bastos's case, he is not yet equipped to proceed.

"Let us drink to Kheo's return," the mother suggests to Bastos, uncorking one of the hermetically sealed jars. Pouring some beer into a bowl, she offers this savory concoction to her son. No sooner has she done so, however, than "the liquid turned muddy, agitated, bubbling over" so powerfully that, like the twice-yearly flooded waters of the Nile, the beer streams down the sides of its container.

Beer was a popular drink in ancient Egypt, which had taken on sacrality and was considered just as hallowed as holy water is for Roman Catholics. Beer came to be identified with regeneration, infinite potential, and transcendent powers. In a Pyramid Text (829/d) the Sun God, Ra, had ordered beer to be poured onto the fields to save humanity from destruction by the Lion Goddess Sekhmet. "The fields were flooded to a depth of three palms with the liquid, through the power of this great God" (Clark 183). The sacred beer which Bastos's mother has poured into the bowl has been produced from a mixture of barley and water, the latter drawn from the Nile; its miracle of boiling and bubbling warns Bastos of evils to come. "My brother is in danger! I am leaving!" he shouts, hurling the bowl to smash it. Within minutes he dons the traveler's garb kept in readiness for such an eventuality, fills his sack with food, and, never separating himself from his protective power, carefully places his turtle, Shu, into the sack. After kissing his mother good-bye, he takes hold of his walking stick and goes out in search of his brother.

ON THE TRACK OF KHEO. Every step of his journey takes him into what seems to be a return to some remote past time: to deserts, over seas, into lean and stark landscapes that his mother had described to him during his childhood and adolescence. Climbing what seem endless hills, valleys, and knolls bursting with bushes and trees of all sizes, some with branches heavy with almonds, figs, and olives, he passes the Hermit's grotto. Noticing to his dismay that it is empty, he wonders whether it could be a premonition of another kind of emptiness. Bastos grows increasingly apprehensive. Stepping up his pace, he climbs higher and higher until he finally reaches the Parasol Pines.

Moments later, a ghastly sight becomes visible to him. The Parasol Pine is lying on its side, an enormous gash running through its length. A few steps away lies Kheo's still-warm cadaver. Sobbing, Bastos runs toward it, kneels before it, and caresses his brother's stiff hands and leaden face. Suddenly he noted a change in Kheo's expression; a "prodigious smile" written across his brother's lips brings to mind the words he spoke to him prior to his exile. "My heart will have shrunk to such an extent that not one of my enemies will have noticed it. But it is here! Look for it. Do not be discouraged" (*Heart* 37).

Remembering his brother's words, Bastos meticulously organizes his search for Kheo's heart. He scientifically plans forays up and down the hills and mountainsides of the Parasol Pine forest, examining each of the trunks, branches, leaves, pine needles, and flowers of the surrounding trees. Days and seasons pass. Bastos despairs at times. But he musters his will, dominates his feelings of failure, and learns to subsist and sustain himself, inured by his sense of commitment. At times, he seems buoyed up at the sound of his brother's voice emerging as if from the depths of his being. "You hold my fate and that of an entire people in your hands. Remain hopeful, Bastos, you'll finish by finding what you seek!" (*Heart* 37). The presence of Shu, his constant companion, provides him with additional comfort and increased will to pursue his great task.

BES VISITS ZEZI. Meanwhile Bes, Kheo's protective genie, arrives at Zezi's palace and becomes aware of Thabée's psychological breakdown. He decides to enter into the tyrant's good graces by playing the buffoon and making him laugh. Once relaxed, Zezi will surely reveal his secret machinations. Accordingly, Bes creates an outlandish clown costume, including an array of motley-colored plumes (a metaphor for his high energy), a tambourine, and other accouterments designed to provoke banter and lightheartedness. His antics provoke such delight that he and Zezi soon become inseparable. The tyrant goes so far as to confide to him that he was the one responsible for Thabée's breakdown and for having the Parasol Pine cut down, thus causing Kheo's death. "I have nothing more to fear," he boasts with satisfaction (*Heart* 40).

THE RESURRECTION. The passing days and seasons sees Bastos still searching for his brother's vital organ, until one day, glancing at a pile of twigs, he thinks he sees a rose-colored seed in the form of a heart. He approaches it and intuits that it is Kheo's. With trembling hands, he picks it up cautiously and tenderly and, in keeping with his brother's recommendations, places it in the clay cup which he fills with the lustral waters flowing down from the rocks. Sprinkling it ever so patiently, and observing it continuously for the slightest change in shape or texture, or possible movement, he intones:

Little heart	Come, little heart	But your glimmer
Your hour has come	This is our hour	And our ardor
To return to us	You are growing	Have made you leaven
Stronger and fuller	You are enlarging	Tomorrow's flower.

You have been hurt	You have been hurt!	
Hurt hurt and hurt!	Hurt hurt and hurt! (*Heart* 40)	

The seed grows, takes on color, enlarges, and finally becomes a heart again, beating in its normally measured rhythms. Carrying the precious cup in his hands, Bastos manages to climb the sharp rocks leading to Kheo's lifeless body and to dispose the heart in its rightful place. Suddenly, and without warning, the miracle occurred: his brother opens his eyes—as if he were just emerging from a deep sleep: "You came, Bastos." Whereupon the two brothers hugged each other lovingly!

How may one interpret the mystery of Kheo's Resurrection? A tree—Osiris's Djed Column, or the Tree of Knowledge, or the Tree of Life—symbolizes growth and proliferation, generative factors in the creative process.[2] As a hierophany, its branches reach toward the heavens; its roots burrow deep into the earth; and its trunk may be related to empirical matters. The three together endow the growing entity with cosmicity, becoming a paradigm of humanity's eternal quest for the miracle of truth. In keeping with numerical symbolism, the three in the hierophantic tree become one, indicating not merely human tripartism (body, spirit, soul), but the continuity and cohesiveness of nature's and humankind's design and purpose. The tree, then, may be said to merge the lower phallic aspects of being (as evidenced in the trunk of the Parasol Pine), with its higher branches, metaphors for the Egyptians' cosmic soul, or heart-soul complex *(ba)*,[3] thereby replicating humankind's *ka* (an individual's spiritual double or vital energy) (Lamy 25). Kheo's Resurrection, or "tree birth," as analogized with Osiris's, symbolizes a human apotheosis—or ascension into a new spiritual orientation.

In keeping with the Egyptians' theological understanding of Resurrection, Osiris, unlike Kheo in Chedid's fairy tale, did not emerge from his tomb as a physical man.

> It was [Osiris's] soul that was set free, to ascend as a star in the life-forces of the ensuing year. . . . The god was more than his myth, he was the spirit of life itself, manifest in the sprouting of vegetation and in the seed of animals and men. But the greatest religious achievement of the Egyptians was to take this general fertility god and make him into the saviour of the dead; or, more exactly, the saviour from death. It was in the soul of Osiris that the Egyptians believed they would live on. The rising of the Osiris soul was therefore the sentimental core of life, the central fact in the structure of the universe. To signify this tremendous thing they used a fetish from their half-forgotten past, a strange wooden object called the *Djed* or "Stability" Column. (Clark 235)

As Kheo pointed out to his brother prior to his exile, if the great Parasol Pine (Djed Column) were found lying on the ground, it would represent the physically dead or unconscious Kheo (Osiris); raised, however, it stood for the "higher" or "head" phallus, the resurrected Lord, the "everlasting begetter." For the Egyptians, death had divested Osiris of his telluric identification, but it transformed him into a Uranian or sky deity: "I set up a ladder to the Heaven among the gods," he said, "and I am a divine being among them" (Neumann 231–233).

The harvest ceremonies revolving around the Djed Column in Egypt focused on the "stable" and/or "durable" Osiris and his death and dismemberment drama. They proclaimed the retention of his "vital essence" in the livingness of the last sheaf: that is, the active spirit of every entity. In order for Osiris to remain alive and dominate the harvest rituals, the Djed Column had to be fixed and upright. The raising of the column at the outset of ceremony was followed by the attachment of a loincloth around its middle and feathers on its top, indicating the presence of a "living God." In later centuries a pair of human eyes were painted on the pillar, analogizing even more conclusively the God and the Column. In time the Djed Column, or Parasol Pine in Chedid's tale, came to symbolize a cosmic pillar supporting the sky, assuring thereby that everything was kept in its proper place (Clark 236).

KHEO'S RETURN. Soon after Kheo's Resurrection, the two brothers set out for home. So stirred is the mother at the sight of her sons, whose profiles recall her beloved husband's, that she prostrates herself and kisses the earth with gratitude.

Time has also effected salutary inroads in the collective domain as well. Rebellion against Zezi is in the air! In town, the people, looking at Zezi with distrust and even animosity, are already gathered in support of the brothers. Yam, who earlier stirred up the elements for Zezi's gratification, now has a change of heart; he conveyes his outrage at this paradigm of tyranny by inhaling Zezi, then carrying him through the air to ever higher spheres beyond the clouds, where he places him, forever far from humans, "in the regions of eternal wandering" (*Heart* 44).

Nor is the miraculous Bes to be outdone, for it was he who concocted a secret mixture of powders that served to awaken Thabée from her stupor and restore her responsiveness. Upon sight of each other, she and Kheo reenter their world of love and well-being!

Chedid's childhood days and her early memories, particularly those associated with Egypt, played an important role in *The Suspended Heart*. The emotional colorations and images that mark her fairy tale bear the impress of a dry, ever-parched land. Sun-drenched tones range from deep ocher to sandy browns; blanketed expanses of seemingly endless skies are daubed in incandescent blues and blazing colors of the sun's rays; and constantly changing perspective serves to heighten the isometry of the sequences. Juxtaposed for their dramatic, psychological, and mystical effects are meditations on the sinuous and easy-flowing but sometimes turbid waters of the Nile, and the brilliant or, at times, dimmer tones of the fertile green valleys and hills of the Parasol Pines. "It [writing] is less a matter of a nostalgic return to the past," Chedid remarked in an interview, "or of a concerted search for memories, than it is a need to experience the permanent presence of an inner sentiment—pulsations, movements, chants, misery, and joy, sun and serenity, which are inherent in the Middle East. I seem to feel all these emotions pulsating within" (Knapp, *Andrée Chedid* 58).

Preoccupied with questions that have faced humankind since the beginning of time, Chedid, like Aeschylus, Sophocles, Euripides, and Virgil, chose to draw upon one of the great myths of the past to reveal to her readers, in fairy tale form, the giant maw facing every mortal during his or her earthly trajectory. In *The Suspended Heart*, the vehicle chosen to share with the world her own preoccupations, Chedid reaffirms the need for humans and their religious pronouncements and prognostications to be humble and peace-loving.

Although Kheo is resurrected in the flesh such a rebirth is to be considered by mature readers of *The Suspended Heart* as a metaphor for spiritual, ideational, and/or psychological renewal. Most children will, however, understand realistically the fabulations related in Chedid's charming fairy tale. A third possibility is offered to young and old: to consider Kheo's Resurrection as the bestowal of a special gift to each human being, the tale allowing a reworking of their lives by expansion of consciousness, renewal of cognition, and increased awareness through greater understanding of "the other." It offers everyone a second chance, so to speak, to recycle their lives, to opt for new directions, fresh orientations, and uncharted horizons.

For Chedid, as for the ancient Egyptians, Osiris's Resurrection, theologically speaking, was not to be taken literally, as previously indicated. His was not a resurrection in the flesh. Nor was it an earthly one. Rather, his reappearance in the minds of the populace is to be understood as a paradigm of a cyclical recurrence: that of the ever-present archetype of the "helpless" victim who, although suffering the pain and anguish of all mortals, represents as well, but paradoxically, the great fertility deity of nature's earthly and cosmic growth. Kheo was reunited in flesh and blood with Thabée in Chedid's fairy tale. Let us note that the ancient Osiris was resurrected by his wife, Isis, as soul. Both women, as archetypes of the Eternal Feminine become, each in her own way, instrumental in perpetuating future earthly life.

Whatever the conclusion—and conclusions are at best only temporary—Chedid indicates one great caveat to her readers: finite mortals, no matter their gender, provenance, or status, must approach death and resurrection as finite human beings—thus with humility. Unlike many hubristic so-called seers who consider themselves arbiters of humanity's destiny, we should never consider ourselves on a par with infinite immortals.

Just as Osiris lived on in his mystery for nearly three thousand years, infusing a sense of beatitude in the minds and psyches of his people, so Chedid's resurrection of him in *The Suspended Heart* underscores the human drama facing each individual during the course of his or her life. Like giant frescoes replete with mysterious and arcane forces, Chedid's dialogue is crisp and stark. Readers are not spared the violence, shock, and hurt underlying human activities. The raw emotional response of her beings frequently reveals willful disorders and malaises in the human condition. Never, however, does she offer blind hope as a palliative. What emerges, instead, is the need of frequent—always modest—reassessments and appraisals of the individual's earthly lot, his or her strengths and weaknesses, achievements and failures, loves and hates. Change and chance being constants of empirical existence, so too is the ever-elusive and altering world of the potter's universal mold.

CONCLUSION

We have come a long way in our journey through French fairy tales. Our probing of a variety of psychological types, from medieval to modern times, in addition to our excursuses into religious beliefs, customs, and philosophical and artistic processes, have unveiled many fairy-tale figures in modern dress. Because fairy tales link readers and/or listeners to a past, they reinvigorate the "vestigial memory of one's own childhood," thereby resurrecting certain seemingly forgotten or repressed incidents, relationships, thoughts, beliefs, feelings, and sensations, as well as generating archetypal images that belong to the whole human race (Jung 91, #273). Countless creative beings throughout the ages have transformed their visionings into innovative artistic, literary, musical, and scientific forms and masterpieces.

To consider the fairy-tale genre only as entertainment and educational fare for the young is to deprive it of what has come to be understood as its rich and textured imagistic, rhythmic, and melodious patternings. Why, we may ask, do certain fairy tales speak in some mysterious way to specific readers and/or listeners but not to others? Why, when deeply involved in the characters and/or in the plot lines of a narrative, do some readers or listeners hear their own inner voice sing out the ventures/adventures? Then, suddenly and inexplicably, every object seems to tingle with life! Trees, flowers, mountains, water beds, buildings, and beings of all sorts burst into activity. Why is it as well that certain protagonists or incidents in a fairy tale may generate dreams in sleepers, whether they are old and/or young? Have not people since ancient times believed steadfastly in the reality of their fantasies? In the truth of their visionary experiences? In their imagined spatial trajectories? In the descent of Gods, Goddesses, and other supernatural beings onto earth and their ascension back into heavenly spheres? Why do religious creeds and cults based on human inner experience take hold of believers so powerfully as to compel them to convert others to their way of thinking through persuasion or threat of death? How do phantasms and imagination come into being? As Jung wrote:

> Imagination is the reproductive or creative activity of the mind in general. It is not a special faculty, since it can come into play in all the basic

forms of psychic activity, whether thinking, feeling, sensation, or intuition. Fantasy as imaginative activity is, in my view, simply the direct expression of psychic life, of psychic energy which cannot appear in consciousness except in the form of images or contents, just as physical energy cannot manifest itself except as a definite physical state stimulating the sense organs in physical ways. For as every physical state, from the energic standpoint, is a dynamic system, so from the same standpoint a psychic content is a dynamic system manifesting itself in consciousness. We could therefore say that fantasy in the sense of a fantasm is a definite sum of libido that cannot appear in consciousness in any other way than in the form of an image. A fantasm is an idée force. Fantasy as imaginative activity is identical with the flow of psychic energy. (Jung 6, # 722)

The inner workings of the fairy tales discussed in this volume—beginning with *Mélusine* and concluding with *The Suspended Heart*—reveal a psychological "system of functioning in the present whose purpose is to compensate or correct, in a meaningful manner, the inevitable one-sidedness of consciousness" (Jung 9₁, #276). We may aver that fairy tales delve not only into the past but, based on the depth of their projections onto the protagonists and the events depicted, may reveal potential as well. People may come to realize, via the link to the past of the fairy tale, that they are no longer alone to joy or to suffering, but are part of a living process—of cultures that have, by dint of the creative imaginations of individuals, passed through many forms and existences. Early oral traditions of fairy-tale telling, for example, were transformed into a literary genre for grown-ups, as we know, which, by the end of the seventeenth century in France, was thought to be useful for a child's development as well. Not only could fairy tales help the young get along with others, but by introducing them to fearsome images and circumstances at an early age, they could provide strength in later years in dealing with adversity and stress. Dreams and fantasies as recounted in fairy tales are effective in triggering the imagination of child and adult alike. In how many cases have utopian societies and dulcet heavenly spheres, or their opposites, wars and cruelties, been fashioned from humankind's fantasies?

The connections made by readers or listeners with their former experiences may serve to breathe new life into the symbology of the fairy tale and provoke increasing awareness of their own situations. Each step forward in the analytical process may help those clinging to worn and hackneyed attitudes to begin detaching themselves from conditions of overdependency on systems or people. To succeed in freeing one's thoughts from enslavement to ready-made or robotic answers is to allow them to ponder infinite and unknowable questions.

In fairy tales recorded by Jean d'Arras, Perrault, Mme d'Aulnoy, Diderot, Rousseau, Nodier, Gautier, Ségur, Sand, Maeterlinck, Cocteau, or Chedid, readers are confronted with incompatible personalities, age differences, power struggles, sex, hurt, violence, love, collisions of obligations, estrangement, personality dissociations and disorders, memory losses, joys, and fears. With the introduction of the world of animals in fairy tales, readers are provided with different forms of knowledge and a variety of new and possible options for resolving the problematic situations confronting them.

I have used a Jungian route in my attempt to surface certain possible truths in specific French fairy tales, but the real work is left to readers and/or listeners who, by availing themselves of the written document, will—perhaps unbeknown to them—ferret out elements to which they have reacted powerfully. The questioning of affects aroused by certain characters in the texts may trigger unsuspected reactions and riches in the readers' or listeners' psyches, which in turn invite them to pursue an exciting inner adventure of their own.

Increasing awareness, however, paves the way for a desublimation process, each new development leading to a change of attitude and/or focus. A leap forward may be envisaged as the death of some aspect of a quiescent past, but ironically, it may also be considered a renewal of heretofore repressed and unlived parts of one's psyche. What had unwittingly suffered psychological mutilation in some distant past may be resurrected in a new and, perhaps, more effective form with an increase in consciousness, encouraging the individual to participate more actively in her or his life experience. The fairy tale's ensuing chain of events decoded by the analyst, reader or listener, like a variety of melodies, rhythms, and feeling relationships or lack of these, engage the individual to follow new motifs rather than allow her or himself to be swallowed up, and thus momentarily destroyed, by old visionings.

Since we began this volume with Yvette Guilbert's gift of Perrault's Fairy Tales to me, I should like to conclude it with his addenda to the narrative "The Fairies:"

> While Diamonds and Money
> May dominate many a mind
> Gentle words, nonetheless,
> Are of greater power, and of superior worth. (*Contes* 275)

NOTES

CHAPTER 1. MÉLUSINE

1. The menstruating woman in most primitive societies was considered a pariah. Parsis and Hindus (according to the laws of Manu) for example, forbade menstruating women to approach a cooking or heating fire, for fear of polluting it. Interestingly, thereby, is the Hindus' highly prized custom of covering the statue of their Mother Goddess during her menstrual periods, then displaying her bloodstained clothes. The only way men had of protecting themselves, it was believed, was to segregate women during certain days of the month. On the other hand, there were occasions when women used menstruation as a means of ridding themselves at least temporarily of an unwanted husband (Harding, *Woman's Mysteries*, 61).

2. Mani, a third-century philosopher, attempting to reconcile ancient Zoroastrian beliefs with Christianity, declared the world to be a battleground between two forces—Good and Evil. Implicit to his credo was the rejection of the Christian beliefs in God as the Creator, in the Incarnation, and in the resurrection of the body.

3. Gautier de Coincy (1223) wrote of a monk who "was dying of a putrid disease of the mouth." After reminding the Madonna/Wisdom of his years of service to her, she appears at his bedside, "drew forth her breast that was so sweet, so soft, so beautiful, and placed it in his mouth, [and] gently touched him all about and sprinkled him with her sweet milk" (Warner, 198).

4. According to the Ophites's description of Irenaeus, the "prurient" or lower Sophia (Sophia-Prunikos), "the transmundane Mother," sent the serpent "to seduce Adam and Eve into breaking" God's command" against "the world and its God" (Jonas, 93). In keeping with Valentinian speculations, Sophia objectified her pain and anguish, reflected on her fate, and moved by "grief, fear, bewilderment and shock, repentance," realized that it was her "ignorance concerning the Father which produced Anguish and Terror" (Ibid., 183). While Christos saved her by freeing her of her passions, "things external were founded," and thus did "the Savior 'potentially' bring" on the subsequent demiurgical creation" (Ibid., 189). In "The Secret Book According to John," although alluded to as "wisdom," and "afterthought,"Sophia becomes "Faith Wisdom" (Pistis Sophia). (*The Gnostic Scriptures*, Translated by Bentley Layton, 25, 66, 103, 278).

5. Although personified in the Judeo-Chistian Bible, Sophia is referred to only as Wisdom and not given a personal name. The Trappist monk, Thomas Merton writes: "Hagia [Greek, Wisdom] Sophia is God Himself. God is not only Father but a Mother. He is both at the same time, and it is the 'feminine aspect' or Feminine principle in the divinity that is the Hagia Sophia. . . . For the masculine and feminine relationship is basic in all reality—simply because all reality mirrors the reality of God" (Monica Furlong, *Merton: A Biography.* Quoted by M. Woodman, *Addiction to Perfection,* 76).

6. Mélusine may be compared to the legendary Tyrian princess Dido, founder and future queen of Carthage (between 824 and 813 B.C.E.). Determined and desperate women, both were endowed with enormous will power, courage, engineering and organizational abilities, and knowledge of city planning. Their industry and enthusiasm inpired constructive activity on the part of others (Knapp, *Women in Myth,* 121). Let us not omit the twelfth-century Aliénor of Aquitaine in our list of remarkable women. The builder of fortresses, abbeys, and churches in the Poitou area, she was instrumental in the development of the port city of La Rochelle and of helping to evolve the notion of liege knight in the new relationship between male and female in the "amour courtois" (Jean Markale, *Mélusine,* 43).

7. Rashi's grandson, Jacob Ben Meir Tam (b. 1100), grammarian, poet, and Talmudist, who was born in Ramerupt on the Seine, was tortured and almost killed in 1147 by crusaders as vengeance for the crucifixion of Jesus.

8. Contradictions also arose between the Christian notion of God and that of Egyptians, Sumerians, and other ancient Moon-goddess worshipers. Christianity had excluded evil from the Godhead. Jews accepted the notion of God being both good and evil: "I form the light, and create darkness: I make peace, and create evil: I the Lord do all these things" (Isaiah: 45:7). God's darker side was personified in such figures as Lucifer, Satan, and countless demonic figures.

9. St. Augustine wrote: "In a dream I saw Perpetua, transformed into a man, wrestle with an Egyptian. Who can doubt that this masculine figure was her soul, not her actual body, which had remained completely feminine and which lay there, unconscious, while her soul was wrestling in the form of a masculine body" (*De Anima,* IV, l8,26. Quoted from M. L. von Franz, *Projection,* 138).

CHAPTER 2. CHARLES PERRAULT'S MULTI-VEINED DONKEY
SKIN, SLEEPING BEAUTY, AND BLUEBEARD

1. In contemporary times the term surrogate mother may be applied to a woman who is willing to be inseminated with the sperm of a specific man and carry the fetus to term for the husband and the infertile or dead wife.

2. Let us note in this connection that in ancient societies, and even today, fertilizer represents biological power, a vital force needed to grow food and make medicines. In the practice of coprophagia, the qualities of the one who defecated are assumed by the worshipper.

3. "One might say that every culture sign is eucharistic in some sense and to some extent; or, to pursue this vein of thought one step further, one might say that all cookery involves a theological, ideological, political, and economic operation by the means of which a nonsignified edible foodstuff is transformed into a sign/body that is eaten. In their own inimitable way, Perrault's fairy tales never stop telling a single story, and this story is the tale of the dialectical relations between a series of oppositions: the edible and the eaten, a thing and a body, what is shown and its sign, need and desire. While in the *Logic of Port-Royal*, the Catholic Church's universal and ceaselessly repeated miracle of eucharistic transubstantiation is presented as though the circumstances of its production were as natural and reasonable as those pertaining to any utterance governed by the rules of common sense and ordinary communication, in the tales of Mother Goose, this miracle is retold. In the retelling, however, the miracle becomes wholly marvelous, involving marvelous beings and actions, figures and processes, social ranks and kingdoms" (L.Marin, *Food for Thought*, 121).

4. According to legend, Eaque, the son of Zeus and Egina, ruled the Myrmidons (Gk. *murmékès*, "ant"). Hera, exasperated by her husband's infidelities, transformed the population into ants. After Eaque prayed to his father, the island was repopulated with warriors led by the king's son, Peleus, who emigrated to Thessaly, and whose son was Achilles.

CHAPTER 4. DENIS DIDEROT'S *THE WHITE BIRD*

1. "Woman's lot in the eighteeenth century was unenviable. A woman had no status of her own according to Salic laws and was offred little protection in the courts. *Contrats de mariage* provided scant protection as Diderot discovered when drawing up one for his beloved daughter Angélique. A widow often had to request a *lettre de cachet* to secure minimal inheritance rights and a modest *rente*. In law a woman was treated as a chattel and was powerless against masculine tyranny in the home" (Niklaus, "Diderot and Women," in *Women and Society in Eighteenth-Century France* 69).

CHAPTER 5. WAS JEAN-JACQUES ROUSSEAU'S *THE FANTASTIC QUEEN* MERELY A TONGUE-IN-CHEEK FAIRY TALE?

1. "I sometimes saw the little games young women play when feigning to want to breast feed their children. One knows just how to get out of fulfillling such a whim: by cleverly calling upon husbands, doctors, and especially mothers to intervene" (OC. *Emile* IV, 257).

2. What were the qualities with which Rousseau endowed Sophie, the ideal wife of his student, Emile? Inferior to the male in every way, the woman/wife was obliged to obey her husband's commands and fulfill his desires, even as she assumed her rightful place in the household. Most notably, a woman was created with the purpose of pleasing a man, and because of this natural order of things, she had to allow

herself to be subjugated by him. Sophie's restricted education, necessarily was different from that of her future husband, Emile. She was taught to be amiable, modest, simple, tender, vigilant, laborious, and follow the rules of decorum. Her education pertained to household matters and the rearing of children. Having been engaged since childhood to learn to please men, to be useful to them, and to be caring and loving to her husband, her imagination would be limited, her fantasies curtailed, protecting her heart from dangers (OC. *Emile* IV, 693ff).

CHAPTER 6. CHARLES NODIER'S *THE CRUMB FAIRY*

1. Gustave Le Rouge in his *La Mandragore Magique* wrote that according to Laurens Catelan (1568–1647), this root was "virile sperm." Shakespeare speaks of this plant in *Antony and Cleopatra*: "Give me to drink mandragora." The shrieking of the plant when it is touched is alluded to in *Romeo and Juliet*: "And shrieks like mandrake torn out of the earth, that living mortals, hearing them, run mad." Machiavelli's *The Mandragora* tells of the plant's erotic powers that aroused men to sexual delights.

2. The three forces in the universe (God, nature, man) are in alchemical tradition manifested in three chemicals (sulfur, salt, mercury). Similarly, man is divided into spirit, body, and soul. Michel's relationships could have consisted of a triumvirate as well, each an analogy of the other, had the third force been acceptable to him.

CHAPTER 10. MAURICE MAETERLINCK'S
PELLÉAS AND MÉLISANDE

1. Lugné-Poë claimed that he added the name Poë to Aurélien Lugné at the outset of his career because of his distant family relationship to the American poet. In reality, it was out of respect and admiration for the writer—and his translator, the poet Charles Baudelaire—who had introduced him to a world of mystery and the occult.

2. The *feeling* function has been defined by M. L. von Franz as follows: "Feeling, which evaluates what has been perceived, in the sense of pleasant-unpleasant, to be admitted—to be rejected, better—worse" (Franz, *Projection and Re-Collection in Jungian Psychology* 46).

3. The poet Henri de Régnier, a friend of Maeterlinck, spoke of the play to the then unknown and impoverished composer Claude Debussy. Maeterlinck gave Debussy permission to compose an operatic score for it. In August 1893 Debussy set to work on what would become his greatest opera—adding to Maeterlinck's fame the world over.

CHAPTER 11. JEAN COCTAU'S *BEAUTY AND THE BEAST*

1. Christ has been identified with the Unicorn in this image.

Chapter 12. Andrée Chedid's *The Suspended Heart*

1. Parallels have been made between the raising of the *Djed Column* on which Osiris's body rested, the chaining of Prometheus to a pillar in the Caucasus, and Christ's crucifixion on the wooden cross (E. Neumann, *The Origins and History of Consciousness* 250).

2. Within Kheo's being, accordingly, there existed not only Osiris's vital essence, as exemplified by the Djed Column, but that of the God Ptah, associated frequently with Osiris. In Memphis theology, Ptah created the universe with his heart, prior to creating it with the Word. Protector of artisans and artists, Ptah himself had been a worker in metals and had via his heart and tongue, not only endowed the Gods with power, but had brought forth cities, nomes, and shrines.

3. "The *ba* incarnates itself; it defines the character and affinities of the individual, each according to its nature" (Lamy 25).

REFERENCES

Albistur, Maité, and Daniel Armogathe. 1979. *Histoire du féminisme français*. 2 vols. Paris: Des Femmes.

Audiat, Pierre. 1939. *Paris-Soir* (May 4).

Aulnoy, Mme d'. 1997. *Contes des fées*. Introduction par Jacques Barchilon. Texte établi et annoté par Philippe Hourcade. Paris: Société des Textes Français Modernes, I & II.

Augustine, Saint. 1948. *Basic writings of Saint Augustine*. New York: Random House.

Aziza, Claude, and Claude Olivieri. 1978. *Dictionnaire des symboles et des termes littéraires*. Paris: Nathan.

Bachelard, Gaston. 1942. *L'eau et les rêves*. Paris: José Corti.

Barchilon, Jacques. 1975. *Le Conte merveilleux français de 1690 à 1790*. Paris: Champion.

———, and Edgar Flinders. 1981. *Charles Perrault*. Boston: Twayne Publishers.

Baring, Anne, and Jules Cashford. 1993. *The myth of the goddess*. London: Penguin Books.

Beaussant, Claudine. 1988. *La Cometesse de Ségur ou l'enfance de l'art*. Paris: Laffont.

Béguin, Albert. 1967. *L'âme romantique et le rêve*. Paris: José Corti.

Bergerat, Emile. 1879. *Théophile Gautier*. Paris: Charpentier.

Berlioz, Jacques, ed. 2000. *Le Pays cathare. Les régions médievales et leurs expressions méridionales*. Paris: Seuil.

Berthier, Philippe. 1983. *Colloque de Cerisy*. Paris: Sedes.

Berthier, Philippe. 1983. Corambé: Interprétation d'un mythe. In *Colloque de Cerisy*, ed. Simone Vierne. Paris: Sedes, 7–20.

Bettelheim, Bruno. 1976. *Psychanalyse des contes de fées*. Traduction de Théo Carlier. Paris: Robert Laffont.

Birch, Una. 1903. *The disciples at Saïs and other fragments*. London: Methuen.

Bleton, Pierre. 1963. "Une sociologue: La Comtesse de Ségur." *Temps modernes* 18: 1246–1271.

Bluche, François. 1988. *Le Petit monde de la Comtesse de Ségur*. Paris: Hachette.

Bodde, Derk. 1981. *Essays on Chinese Civilization*. Edited and introduced by Charles Le Blanc and Dorothy Borei. Princeton: Princeton University Press.

Boehme, Jakob. 1973. *Confessions*. Paris: Fayard.

Boschot, Adolphe. 1933. *Théophile Gautier*. Paris: Desclée de Brouwer et co.

Braun, Allen R. 1999. Rem sleep. *New York Times* (Nov. 2), F.1.

Briggs, K. M. 1969. *The fairies in English tradition and literature*. Chicago: The University of Chicago Press.

Brix, Michel. 1996. *Gautier, "Arriela Marcella" et le monde gréco-romain. Vingt études pour Maurice Delcroix*. Amsterdam: Rodopi.

Brown, Penny. 1994. "La Femme enseignante": Mme de Genlis and the moral and didactic tale in France." *Bulletin of the John Rylands University-Library of Manchester* 76, no. 3: 23–42.

Brun, Jean. 1966. *Empédocle*. Paris: Seghers.

———. 1969. *Héraclite*. Paris: Seghers.

Butler, Judith. 1990. *Gender trouble: Feminism and the subversion of identity. Thinking gender*. New York: Routledge.

Campbell, Joseph. 1956. *The Hero with a thousand faces*. New York: Meridian.

———. 1944. Folklorist commentary. In *Grimm's fairy tales*. New York: Pantheon.

Campbell, Robert J. 1989. *Psychiatric Dictionary*. New York: Oxford University Press.

Cannon, Beekman C., Alvin H. Johnson, and William G. Waite. 1972. *The art of music*. New York: Thomas Y. Crowell Co.

Caradec, François. 1977. *Histoire de la littérature enfantine en France*. Paris: Albin Michel.

Castarède, Marie-France. 1997. Opéra et feminin. In *Voix et création au XXème siècle*. Paris: Honoré Champion, 27–36.

Castex, Pierrre-Georges. 1951.*Le Conte fantastique en France de Nodier à Maupassant*. Paris: José Corti.

Castillejo, Irene Claremont de. 1973. *Knowing Woman*. New York: G.P. Putnam's Sons.

Chedid, Andrée. 1981. Huit questions posées à l'auteur. In *A la rencontre d'Andrée Chedid*. Paris: Flammarion.

———. 1981. *Le Coeur suspendu*. Paris: Casterman.

———. 1991. *Sud Voix multiples*. N.p.

Chipp, Herschel B. 1968. *Theories of modern art*. From Paul Gauguin's Notes synthétiques, in *Vers et Prose*. Berkeley: University of California Press.

Clark, Rundle R.T. 1978. *Myth and symbol in ancient Egypt*. London: Thames and Hudson, Ltd.

Clier-Colombani, Françoise. 1991. *La Fée Mélusine au Moyen Age*. Préface de Jacques Le Goff. Paris: Le Léopard d'Or.

Cocteau, Jean. 1946-1951. *Oeuvres complètes*. Genève: Marguerat.

———. 1946. *La Belle et la bête. Journal d'un film*. Paris: Janin.

———. 1951. VI. *Portraits-souvenir*. In *Oeuvres complètes*.

———. 1951. X. "Essay on Indirect Criticism." In *Oeuvres complètes*.

———. 1957. *La difficulté d'être*. Paris: 10/18.

———. 1970. *La Belle et la bête*.Texte inédit par Robert M. Hammond. New York: New York University Press.

———. 1972. *Three screen plays. L'éternel retour. Orphée. La Belle et la bête*. Translated by Carol Martin-Sperry. New York: Grossman Publishers.

——. 1972. *Beauty and the Beast. Diary of a film by Jean Cocteau.* Translated by Ronald Duncan. New York: Dover Publications.

Coudrette. 1993. *Le Roman de Mélusine.* Texte présenté, traduit, et commenté par Laurence Harf-Lancner. Paris: Flammarion.

Cowan, Lyn. 1982. *Masochism. A Jungian view.* Dallas: Spring Publications.

Cox, David. 1968. *Modern psychology.* New York: Barnes & Noble, Inc.

Crawford, Virginia. 1899. *Studies in foreign literature.* Boston: L.C. Page & Company.

Creech, James. 1986. *Diderot threshholds of representation.* Columbus: Ohio State University Press.

Crichfield, Grant. 1983. The Alchemical *Magnum Opus* in Nodier's *La Fée aux miettes. Nineteenth-Century French Studies* 11: 231–245.

——. 1988-1989. "Nodier's numbers: Multiplicity, acceleration, unity in *La Fée aux miettes. Nineteenth-Century French Studies* 1 and 2: 161–169.

——. 1990. "Fantasmagoria and optics in Théophile Gautier's *Arria Marcella.* In *Seventh international conference on the fantastic in the arts.* New York: Greenwood Press.

Datlof, Natalie, Jeanne Fuchs, and David A. Powell. 1991. *The world of George Sand.* New York: Greenwood Press.

d'Aulnoy, Marie-Catherine. 1997. *Les Contes des Fées.* I. Introduction by Jacques Barchilon. Texte établi et annoté par Philippe Hourcade. Paris: Société des Textes Français Modernes.

Davis, E. Hadland. 1989. *Myths and legends of Japan.* Singapore: Graham Brash Ltd.

De Graff, Amy V. 1984. *The tower and the well. A psychological interpretation of the fairy tales of Madame d'Aulnoy.* Birmingham, Ala.: Summa Publications, Inc.

Delaporte, P. Victor. 1891 and 1968. *Du Merveilleux dans la littérature française sous le règne de Louis XIV.* First edition, Paris: Retaux-Bray; Second edition, Geneva: Slatkine Reprints.

Delarue, Paul. 1964-1985. *Le conte populaire français.* Paris: Maisonneuve et Larose.

Deulin, Charles. 1878, 1969. *Les Contes de Ma Mère l"Oye avant Perrault.* Paris: Dentu; Geneva: Slatkine Reprints.

Diamond, Marie J. 1991. *Elle et lui:* Literary idealization and the censorship of female sexuality. In *The World of George Sand.* New York: Greenwood Press, 163-171.

Diderot, Denis. 1951. *Oeuvres.* Préfaces, notes, bibliography by André Billy. Paris: Gallimard.

——. 1979. *Oeuvres. Les Bijoux indiscrets.* III. Edition critique présentée et annotée par Jean Macary, Aram Vartanian, Jean-Louis Leutrat. Paris: Hermann.

Diesbach, Ghislain de. 1999. *La Comtesse de Ségur.* Paris: Perrin.

Di Scanno, Teresa. 1975. *Les Contes de fées à l'époque classique (1680–1715).* Naples: Liguori.

Dontenville, Henri. 1973. *Mythologie française.* Paris: Payot.

Doray, Marie-France. 1990. *La Comtesse de Ségur: une étrange paroissienne.* Paris: Rivages.

Dormoy-Savage, Nadine. 1983, Identité et mimétisme dans quelques romans de George Sand. In *Colloque de Cerisy. George Sand,* ed. Simone Vierne. Paris: Sedes, 158-169.

Duby, Georges. 1983. *The age of the cathedrals: Art and society, 980–1420*. Translated by Eleanor Levieux and Barbara Thompson. Chicago: University of Chicago Press.

———. 1981. *Le chevalier, la femme et le prêtre, le mariage dans la France féodale*. Paris: Hachette.

———. 1996. *L'Europe des cathédrales 1140–1280*. Geneva: Skira.

Dumas, Alexandre. 1868. *Le Fils naturel*. Paris: Levy.

Durand, Gilbert. 1969. *Les Structures anthropologiques de l'imagination*. Paris: Bordas.

Edinger, Edward. 1968. *An outline of analytical psychology*. *Quadrant* 1.

———. 1972. *Ego and archetype*. New York: G. P. Putnam's Sons.

———. 1978. *Melville's Moby-Dick. A Jungian commentary*. New York: New Directions.

———. 1985. *Anatomy of the psyche. Alchemical symbolism in psychotherapy*. La Salle, Ill.: Open Court.

Eigeldinger, Marc. 1978. *Jean-Jacques Rousseau. Univers mythique et cohérence*. Neuchâtel, Suisse: Editions de la Baconnière.

———. 1991. *Le Soleil de la poésie. Gautier, Baudelaire, Rimbaud*. Neuchâtel, Suisse: Editions de la Baconnière.

Eilberg-Schwartz, Howard, and Wendy Donoger. 1995. *The denial of women's identity in myth, religion, and culture*. Berkeley: University of California Press.

Eliade, Mircea. 1958. *Patterns in comparative religion*. Translated by Rosemary Sheed. New York: New American Library.

———. 1963. *Aspects du mythe*. Paris: Gallimard.

———. 1971. *The forge and the crucible*. Translated by Stephen Corrin. New York: Harper & Row Publishers.

———. 1972: *Ego and archetype*. New York: G.P. Putnam's Sons.

———. 1974. *The myth of the eternal return*. Princeton: Princeton University Press.

Ellenberger, Henri F. 1970. *The discovery of the unconscious*. New York: Basic Books.

Elliott, Robert C. 1966. *The power of satire*. Princeton: Princeton University Press.

Ellis, Peter Berresford. 1991. *A dictionary of Irish mythology*. Oxford: Oxford University Press.

Ergal, Yves-Michel, and Marie-José Strich. 1990. *La Comtesse de Ségur*. Paris: Perrin.

Farrell, Michèle L. 1989. Celebration and repression of feminine desire in Mme d'Aulnoy's fairy tale: La Chatte blanche. *L'Esprit Créateur* (Fall): 52–64.

Fellows, Otis E., and Norman L. Torrey. 1942. *The age of enlightenment*. New York: Appleton-Century-Crofts, Inc.

Fierz-David, Linda. 1950. *The dream of Poliphilo*. New York: Pantheon.

Filstrup, Jane Merrill. 1977. Individuation in "La Chatte Blanche." In *Children's literature annual of the MLA*, 72–92.

Flahaut, François. 1972. *L'extrême existence*. Paris: François Maspéro.

———. 1988. *L'Interprétation des contes*. Paris: Denoel.

Flandrin, Jean-Louis. 1976. *Familles: parenté, maison, sexualité dans l'ancienne société*. Paris: Hachette.

Foster, Brian. 1950. *Les fées dans la littérature française du Moyen Age*. Paris: Université de la Sorbonne.

Foucault, Michel. 1961. *Histoire de la folie*. Paris: Plon.

Fourrier, Anthime. 1960. *Le courant réaliste dans le roman courtois en France au Moyen Age*. Paris: Nizet.

Fowler, J. E. Diderot's Family Romance: *Les Bijoux indiscrets Reappraised*. *Romanic Review* 88: 89–102.

Franz, Marie-Louise von. 1970. *Interpretation of fairy tales*. New York: Spring.

———. 1970. *A psychological interpretation of The Golden Ass of Apuleius*. New York: Spring.

———. 1971. *Jung's Typology*. *Spring* 24.

———. 1972. *Creation myths*. Zurich: Spring.

———. 1972. *The feminine in fairy tales*. New York: Spring.

———. 1974. *Shadow and evil in fairy tales*. Zurich: Spring.

———. 1974. *Number and time*. Translated by Andrea Dykes. Evanston: Nothwestern University Press.

———. 1977. *Individuation in fairy tales*. Zurich: Spring Publications.

———. 1978. *Time*. London: Thames and Hudson.

———. 1986. *On dreams and death*. Boston: Shambhala.

———. 1988. *Projection and re-collection in Jungian psychology*. London: Open Court.

Freeman, Henry G., ed. 1998. *Relire Théophile Gautier*. Amsterdam: Rodopi.

Furbank, P.N. 1992. *Diderot. A critical biography*. New York: Alfred A. Knopf.

Galef, David. 1984. "A sense of magic: Reality and illusion in Cocteau's *Beauty and the Beast*. *Literary Film Quarterly* 12, no. 2: 96–106.

Gautier, Théophile. 1856. *Pochades et paradoxes*. V. Paris: Hachette.

———. 1955. *Le Roman de la momie*. Texte établi par Adolphe Boscot. Paris: Classiques Garnier.

———. 1962. *Contes fantastiques*. Paris: José Corti.

Gilson, René. 1969. *Cocteau: An investigation into his films and philosophy*. Translated by Ciba Vaughan. New York: Crown Publishers.

Giraudoux, Jean. 1939. *Ondine*. Paris: La Petite Illustration.

———. 1958. *Ondine*. Translated by Maurice Valency. New York: Hill and Wang.

Gnostic Scriptures (The). 1987. Translated and annotated by Bentley Layton. New York: Doubleday and Co.

Goebbels Diaries: 1941–1943, The. 1948. New York: Doubleday & Co.

Goethe, Johann Wofgang von. 1950. *Faust*. Translated by George M. Priest. New York: Alfred A. Knopf.

Goldberg, Rita. 1984. *Sex and enlightenment*. Cambridge: Cambridge University Press.

Grant, Richard B. 1975. *Théophile Gautier*. Boston: Twayne Publishers.

Grontkowski, Christine, and Evelyn Fox Keller. 1983. The Mind's Eye. In *Discovering reality: Feminist perspectives on epistemology, metaphysics, methodology, and philosophical science*, ed. Merril Hintikka and Sandra Harding. Dordrecht: D. Reidel.

Hains, Maryellen. 1989. Beauty and the Beast: 20th century romance? *Marvels and Tales* 1 (May): 75–83.

Hall, W. D. 1960. *Maurice Maeterlinck: A study of his life and thought*. Oxford: Clarendon Press.

Hannah, Barbara. 1981. *Active imagination*. Santa Monica: Sigo Press.

Hannon, Patricia. 1991. Out of the kingdom: Madame d'Aulnoy's *Finette Cendron*. In *Actes de Las Vegas. Papers on French seventeenth century literature*, ed. Marie-France Hilgar. Paris: Biblio 17-60, 201-208.

Harding, Esther. 1965. *The parental image*. New York: G.P. Putnam's Sons.

———. 1971. *Woman's mysteries*. New York: G.P. Putnam's Sons.

———. 1973. *Psychic energy*. Princeton: Princeton University Press.

———. 1975. *The way of all women*. New York: Harper & Row Publishers.

Harf-Lancner, Laurence. 1984. *Les Fées au Moyen Age*. Genève: Slatkine.

Hart, George. 1990. *Egyptian myths*. Austin: British Museum Publications.

Hazard, Paul. 1932. *Les Livres, les enfants et les hommes*. Paris: Flammarion.

Henry, Freeman G., ed. 1998. *Relire Théophile Gautier. Le plaisir du texte*. Amsterdam, Holland: Rodopi.

Herzog, Edgar. 1967. *Psyche and death*. New York: G. P. Putnam's.

Hesiod. 1999. *Theogony. Works and days*. Oxford: Oxford University Press.

Hilgar, Marie-France, ed. 1991. *Actes de Las Vegas. Papers on French seventeenth century literature*. Paris: Biblio, 17-60.

Hirsch, Michèle. 1983. Lire un conte merveilleux: *Le Château de Pictordu*. Edited by Simone Vierne. Paris: Sedes, 115-123.

Hodson, W.L. 1984. The presence of Maeterlinck in Proust's style and thought." In *Essays in French literature*. Nedlands, Western Australia: University of Western Australia Press, 38-61.

Hofer, Hermann. 1980. La Pensée mystique et religieuse de Charles Nodier. In *Romantisme et religion*. Actes publiés par Michel Baude et Marc-Mathieu Munch. Paris: Presses universitaires de France.

Holland, Claude. 1991. Mademoiselle Merquem: De-mythifying woman by rejecting the law of the father." In *The World of George Sand*. New York: Greenwood Press, 173-180.

Homer. 1965. *The odyssey*. Translated by S. H. Butcher and Andrew Lang. New York: Airmont Publishing Company, Inc.

Huizinga, Johan. 1955. *Homo ludens*. Boston: Beacon.

Humphrey, George René. 1969. *L'Esthétique de la poésie de Gérard de Nerval*. Paris: Nizet.

Jacobi, Yolande. 1959. *Complex archetype symbol in the psychology of C. G. Jung*. Translated by Ralph Manheim. Princeton: Princeton University Press.

Jonas, Hans. 1967. *The Gnostic religion*. Boston: Beacon Press.

Juden, Brian. 1971. *Traditions Orphiques et tendances mystiques dans le romantisme français, 1800-55*. Paris: Editions Klincksieck.

Jung, C. G. 1953. *Collected works*. Vol. 7. Translated by R. F. C. Hull. New York: Pantheon Books.

———. 1956. *Collected works*. Vol. 5. Translated by R. F. C. Hull. New York: Pantheon Books.

———. 1959. *Collected works*. Vol. 91. Translated by R. F. C. Hull. New York: Pantheon Books.

———. 1960. *Collected works*. Vol. 3. Translated by R. F. C. Hull. New York: Pantheon Books.

——. 1960. A letter on parapsychology and synchronicity. *Spring*: 205–207.

——. 1963. *Collected works*. Vol. 11. Translated by R. F.C. Hull. New York: Pantheon Books.

——. 1963. *Collected works*. Vol. 14. Translated by R. F. C. Hull. New York: Pantheon Books.

——. 1964. *Collected works*. Vol. 10. Translated by R. F.C. Hull. New York: Pantheon Books.

——. 1967. *Collected works*. Vol. 13. Translated by R. F. C. Hull. New York: Pantheon Books.

——. 1968. *Collected works*. Vol. 92. Translated by R. F. C. Hull. Princeton: Princeton University Press.

——. 1969. *Collected works*. Vol. 8. Translated by R. F. C. Hull. Princeton: Princeton University Press.

——. 1976. *The visions seminar*. 2 Vols. Zurich: Spring Publications.

——. 1984. *Seminar on dream analysis*. Edited by William McGuire. Princeton: Princeton University Press.

——. 1990. *Collected works*. Vol. 6. Translated by H. G. Baynes, revised by R. F. C. Hull. Princeton: Princeton University Press.

Jung, Emma. 1972. *Animus and anima*. Zurich: Spring Publications.

Kearney, Hugh. 1971. *Science and Change 1500–1700*. New York: McGraw Hill Book Company.

Kemp, Robert. 1939. *Le Temps* (May 5).

Kempf, Roger. 1984. *Diderot et le roman*. Paris: Seuil.

Klapisch-Zuberm, Christiane, ed. 1992. *A history of women in the West, II. Silence of the middle ages*. Cambridge: Harvard University Press.

Kluger, Paul. 1978. Image and sound: An archetypal approach to language. *Spring*: 136–151.

Kluger, Rivkah Scharf. 1963. Dream and reality. *Spring*: 54–81.

——. 1967. *Satan in the Old Testament*. Evanston: Northwestern University Press.

——. 1991. *The archetypal significance of Gilgamesh*. Einsiedeln, Switzerland: Daimon Verlag.

Knapp, Bettina L. 1974. *Céline: Man of hate*. Birmingham, Ala: University of Alabama Press.

——. 1975. *Maurice Maeterlinck*. Boston: Twayne Publishers.

——. 1976. *French novelists speak out*. Troy, N.Y.: The Whitston Press.

——. 1980. *Gérard de Nerval: The mystic's dilemma*. Birmingham, Ala.: University of Alabama Press.

——. 1980. *Theater and alchemy*. Preface by Mircea Eliade. Detroit: Wayne State University Press.

——. 1984. *Andrée Chedid*. Amsterdam: Rodopi.

——. 1989. *Jean Cocteau*. New York: Twayne Publishers.

——. 1997. *Women in myth*. Albany: State University of New York Press.

——. 1998. *Women, myth, and the feminine principle*. Albany: State University of New York Press.

Krappe, Alexander H. 1964. *The science of folklore*. New York: Norton & Co. Inc.

Kravitz, Nathaniel. 1972. *3,000 years of Hebrew literature*. Chicago: The Swallow Press.

Lambert, Marie-Sophie. 1985. La Fée aux miettes: une autre dimension. In Michel Malicet, *Hommage à Jacques Petit*. Paris: Centre de Recherches, 713–739.

Lamy, Lucie. 1981. *Egyptian mysteries*. London: Thames and Hudson.

Lannes, Roger. 1947. *Jean Cocteau*. Paris: Seghers.

Laruccia, Victor. 1975. Little Red Riding Hood's metacommentary: Paradoxical injunction. Semiotics and Behavior. *Modern Language Notes* 90: 517–534.

Lastringer, Valêrie Crétaux. 1992. Mutisme, maturité et maternité: Sophie de Ségur et ses mères. In *Romance languages annual*. West Lafayette: Purdue University monographs in Romance Languages, 97–102.

Latham, Robert A., and Robert A. Collins, eds. 1995. *Modes of the fantastic*. New York: Greenwood Press.

Lecercle, Jean-Louis. 1969. *Rousseau et l'art du roman*. Paris: Armand Colin.

Le Goff, Jacques, 1980. *Time, work, and culture in the middle ages*. Translated by Arthur Goldhammer. Chicago: The University of Chicago Press.

Lemaitre, Georges. 1971. *Jean Giraudoux*. New York: Frederick Ungar Pub. Co.

Le Riche, Mathilde. 1980. L'Importance de la nourriture dans l'oeuvre de la Comtesse de Ségur née Rostopchine. *Revue littéraire mensuelle*: 192–203.

Le Roman de Mélusine ou l'Histoire des Lusignan. 1979. Mis en français moderne par Michèle Perret. Préface de Jacques Le Goff. Paris: Stock.

Le Rouge, Gustave. 1966. *La Mandragore magique*. Paris: Belfond.

Lévy, Eliphas. 1971. *Key to mysteries*. New York: Samuel Weiser.

Lewis, Philip. 1996. *Seeing through the Mother Goose tales*. Stanford: Stanford University Press.

Lichtheim, Miriam. 1975/1976. *Ancient Egyptian Literature*. 2 Vols. Berkeley: University of California Press.

Lubin, Georges. 1983. George Sand et Renan. In *Colloque de Cerisy. George Sand*, ed. Simone Vierne. Paris: Sedes, 85–93.

Luton, Lisette. 1999. *La Comtesse de Ségur. A Marquise de Sade?* New York: Peter Lang.

Maeterlinck, Maurice. 1925. *Pelléas et Mélisande*. New York: Henry Holt & Co.

———. 1948. *Bulles Bleues*. Monaco: Editions du Rocher.

Maines, Rachel P. 1999 *The technology of orgasm*. Baltimore: The Johns Hopkins University Press.

Malarte-Feldman, Claire-Lise. 1995. La Comtesse de Ségur, a witness of her time. *Children's Literature Association Quarterly* 20, no. 3: 134–139.

Malicet, Michel. 1985. *Hommages à Jacques Petit*. Vol. 41. Centre de recherches Jacques Petit. Paris: Annales littéraire de l'université de Besançon.

Marchant, Jean. 1927. *La Légende de Mélusine. Jean d'Arras*. Paris: Boivin.

Marin, Catherine. 1987–1996. Féerie ou Sorcellerie? Les contes de fées de Mme d'Aulnoy. In *Merveilles et contes*. Boulder, Colo.: 45–58.

———. 1998. "Plaisir et violence dans les contes de fées de Madame d'Aulnoy." In *Violence et fiction jusqu'à la Révolution*. Tübingen, Germany: Gunter Narr, 263–272.

Marin, Louis. 1971. Essai d'analyse structurale d'un conte de Perrault: *Les Fées*. *Etudes sémiotiques logiques*. Paris: Klincksieck.

——. 1978. *Le Récit est un piège critique*. Paris: Minuit.

——. 1997. *Food for thought*. Translation with an afterword by Mette Hjort. Baltimore: The Johns Hopkins University Press.

Markale, Jean. 1980. *Contes populaires de toute la France*. I. Paris: Stock.

——. 1983. *Mélusine*. Paris: Editions Retz.

Martin-Civat, Pierre. 1969. *La Mélusine, ses origines et son nom*. Poitiers: Oudin.

Mathé, Sylvie. 1980. La Poupée perdue: Ordre et désordre dans *Les petites filles modèles* de la Comtesse de Ségur. In *Theory and practice of feminist literary criticisms*, ed. Gabriela Mora and Karen S. Hooft. Ypsilanti: 117–130.

Maury, Alfred. 1974 (1896). *Croyances et légendes du Moyen Age*. Genève: Slatkine Reprints.

McGlathery, James M. 1991. *Fairy tale romance. The Grimms, Basile, and Perrault*. Urbana and Chicago: University of Illinois Press.

Mellor, Alec. 1971. *Dictionnaire de la Franc-Maçonnerie et des Francs-Maçons*. Paris: Pierre Belfond.

Mélusine, The Tale of. 1969. Translated from the French before 1500. Introduction, notes, and glossorial index by Rev. Walter W. Skeat. New York: Greenwood Press.

Mercatante, Anthony S. 1978. *Who's who in Egyptian mythology*. New York: Clarkson N. Potter, Inc.

Micklem, Niel. 1974. On hysteria: The mythical syndrome. New York: Spring Publications. (147–165).

Morgenstern, Mira. 1996. *Rousseau and the politics of ambiguity*. University Park: Pennsylvania State University Press.

Mortier, Roland. 1981. *Le Soleil et la nuit*. Bruxelles: Editions de l'université de Bruxelles.

Mourey, Lilyane. 1978. *Introduction aux contes de Grimm et de Perrault*. Paris: Lettres modernes.

Murray, Timothy C. 1976. A Marvelous Guide to Anamorphosis: *Cendrillon ou la petite pantoufle de verre*." *Modern Language Notes* 91: 127–195.

Mylne, Vivienne. 1965. *The eighteenth-century French novel*. Manchester: Manchester University Press.

Najinski, Isabelle. 1991. *Consuelo* and *La Comtesse de Rudolstadt*: From Gothic Novel to Novel of Initiation. In *The World of George Sand*, ed. Natalie Datlof, Jeanne Fuchs, and David A. Powell. New York: Greenwood Press, 107–117.

Neumann, Erich. 1954. *The origins and history of consciousness*. Translated by R. F. C. Hull. New York: Pantheon Books.

——. 1959. *Art and the creative unconscious*. New York: Pantheon Books.

——. 1963. *The great mother*. Translated by Ralph Manheim. New York: Random House.

——. 1971. *Amor and Psyche*. Translated by Ralph Manheim. Princeton: Princeton University Press.

Niklaus, Robert. 1979. Diderot and women. In *Women and society in eighteenth-century France*, ed. Eva Jacobs, W. H. Barber, Jean H. Block, F. W Leakey, Eileen Le Breton. London: Athlone Press, 69–82.

Nodier, Charles. 1968. De quelques phénomènes du sommeil. In *Oeuvres*.V. Geneva: Slatkine Reprints.

——. 1961. *Contes*. Edition de P.-G. Castex. Paris: Garnier Frères.

Nodot, Paul-François. 1698,1876. *Histoire de Mélusine. Tirée des chroniques de Poitou, et qui sert d'origine à l'ancienne Maison de Lusignan.* Niort: Favre. Paris: Champion.

O'Brien, Dennis. 1980. George Sand and Feminism. *The George Sand Papers*. Conference Proceedings at Hofstra. New York: AMS Press, Inc., 76–91.

O'Flaherty, W. D., ed. 1978. *Hindu myths*. Ontario: Penguin Books.

Onori, Lorenza Mochi, and Rossella Vodret. 1998. *Capolavori della Galleria Nationale d'Arte Antica Palazzo Barberini.* Rome: Edizioni de Luca.

Opie, Iona and Peter. 1974. *The classic fairy tale*. London: Oxford University Press.

Orr, Linda. 1976. *Jules Michelet, Nature, History, and Language*. Ithaca: Cornell University Press.

Pagels, Elaine. 1989. *Adam, Eve, and the serpent*. New York: Random House.

Paris, Jean. 1965. *L'Espace et le Regard*. Paris: Seuil.

Perrault, Charles. 1989. *Contes*. Textes établis par Marc Soriano. Paris: Flammarion.

Plato, The Works of. n.d. Translated by B. Jowett. New York: Tudor Publishing Company.

Plessner, Helmuth. 1957. On the Relationship of Time and Death. *Eranos Yearbooks*. III. New York: Pantheon Books, 233–263.

Pongracz, M., and J. Santner. 1965. *Les Rêves à travers les ages*. Paris: Buchet/Chastel.

Postic, Marcel. 1970. *Maeterlinck et le Symbolisme*. Paris: Nizet.

Powell, David A. 1990. *George Sand*. Boston: Twayne Publishers.

Poulet, Georges. 1949. *Etudes sur le temps humain I*. Paris: Plon.

——. 1961. *Les Métamorphoses du cercle*. Paris: Plon.

Propp, Vladimir. 1970. *Morphologie du conte*. Paris: Seuil.

Proust, Marcel. 1954. *Contre Sainte-Beuve*. Paris: Gallimard.

Ramond, Michèle. 1984. "Le déficit, L'excès et L'oubli." In *Le Personnage en question*. Toulouse: Université de Toulouse-Le Mirail, 142–151.

Raphael, Alice. 1965. *Goethe and the philosopher's stone*. New York: Garrett Publications.

Raynal, Maurice. 1949. *History of modern painting from Baudelaire to Bonnard*. Geneva: Skira.

Réa, Annabelle. 1979. Maternity and marriage: Sand's use of fairy tale and myth. *Studies in the Literary Imagination of George Sand* XII, no. 2: 37–45.

Reik, Theodore. 1957. *Of love and lust*. New York: Farrar, Straus and Cuddahy.

Rewald, John. 1961. *The history of impressionism*. New York: The Museum of Modern Art.

Rice de Fosse. 1996. Nodier's post-revolutionary poetics of terror: *Thérèse Aubert*. *Nineteenth-Century French Studies* 24 (Spring/Summer): 287–295.

Robert, Raymonde. 1982. *Le Conte de fées littéraire en France*. Nancy: Presses universitaires de Nancy.

Rogers, Brian. 1985. *Charles Nodier et la tentation de la folie*. Geneva: Slatkine.

Rogers, Nancy. 1979. "Psychosexual identity and the erotic imagination in the early
novels of George Sand." In *Studies in the Literary Imagination. George Sand*.
Atlanta: Georgia State University, 10–35.

Rouger, Gilbert. 1967–1972. *Contes de Perrault*. Paris: Garnier.

Rousseau, Jean-Jacques. 1964–1969. *Oeuvres complètes*. 3 Vols. Edited by Bernard
Gagnebin et Marcel Raymond. Paris: Gallimard.

———. 1964. *Confessions*. Paris: Garnier Frères.

Sand, George. 1970–1971. *Oeuvres autobiographiques*. 2 Vols. Textes édités par
Georges Lubin. Paris: Pléiade, Gallimard.

———. 1982. *Contes d'une grand-mère*. Texte établi, présenté et annoté par Philippe
Berthier. Dessins originaux par Roland Figuière. Meylan: Les Editions de
l'Aurore.

———. 1990. *George Sand Correspondance*. Texte édité par Georges Lubin. XXIV. Paris:
Classiques Garnier.

Sartori, Eva Martin, and Dorothy Wynne Zimmerman, eds. 1991. *French women writers* . New York: Greenwood Press.

Sartori, Eva Martin, ed. 1999. *The feminist encyclopedia of French literature*. Westport:
Greenwood Press.

Sautman, Francesca Canadé. 1995. *La Religion du quotidien*. Firenze: Leo S. Olschki.

Scanno, Teresa di. 1975. *Les contes de fées à l'époque classique (1680–1815)*. Napoli:
Liguori.

Schapira, M. C. 1984. *Le Regard de Narcisse*. Lyon: Presses universitaires de Lyon.

Scholem, Gershom G. 1965. *Major trends in Jewish mysticism*. New York: Schocken
Books.

Schuré, Edouard. 1961. *The great initiates*. New York: St. George Books.

Sébillot, Paul. 1983. *La Terre et le monde souterrain*. Paris: Editions Imago.

Ségur, Sophie de. 1930. *Nouveaux contes de fées*. Paris: Nelson.

Seifert, Lewis C. 1996. *Fairy tales, sexuality, and gender in France 1690–1715*. Cambridge: Cambridge University Press.

———. 1991. Marie-Catherine Le Jumel de Barneville, Comtesse d'Aulnoy,
1650/51–1705. In *French women writers. A bibliographical source book*. New
York: Greenwood Press, 11–20.

———. 1991."Tales of difference: Infantilization and the recuperation of class and gender in 17th-century *Contes de fées*." In *Actes de Las Vegas*, ed. Marie-France
Hilgar. *Papers on French seventeenth century literature*. Paris: Biblio 17-60,
179–193.

Seyffert, Oskar. 1964. *Dictionary of classical antiquities*. Revised by Henry Nettleship
and J. E. Sandys. New York: Meridian Books.

Sharp, Daryl. 1987. *Personality types*. Toronto: Inner City Books.

Shirer, Willliam L. 1941. *Berlin Diary*. New York: Alfred A. Knopf.

———. 1969. *The collapse of the Third Republic*. New York: Simon and Schuster.

Sidky, H. 1997. *Witchcraft, lycanthropy, drugs, and disease*. New York: Peter Lang.

Simpson, William Kelly, ed. 1993. *The literature of ancient Egypt*. New Haven: Yale University Press.

Singley, Carol J., and Susan E. Sweeney. 1991. *Anxious power. Reading, writing, and ambivalence in narrative by women*. Albany: State University of New York Press.

Soriano, Marc. 1968. *Les Contes de Perrault, Culture savante et traditions populaires*. Paris: Gallimard.

Spiegelman, Marvin J. 1976. Psychology and the Occult. *Spring*: 104–156.

Starobinski, Jean. 1971, *Jean-Jacques Rousseau. La transparence et l'obstacle*. Paris: Gallimard.

———. 1984. "Le pied de la favorite: Diderot et les perceptions mêlées. *Esprit Créateur* 24, no. 2: 62–72.

———. 1994. *L'invention de la liberté 1700–1789*. Geneva: Skira.

Storer, Mary Elisabeth. 1928. *La Mode des contes de fées (1685–1700)*. Paris: Champion.

Taggart, James. 1990. *Enchanted maidens*. Princeton: Princeton University Press.

Tatar, Maria. 1987. *The hard facts of Grimm's Fairy Tales*. Princeton: Princeton University Press.

———. 1992. *Off with their heads*. Princeton: Princeton University Press.

Taylor, Una. 1914. *Maurice Maeterlinck*. London: Martin Secker.

Tennant, P. E. 1975. *Théophile Gautier*. London: The Athlone Press.

The New Larousse Encyclopedia of Mythology. 1973. New York: The Hamlyn Publishing Group.

Thomas, Edward. 1974. *Maurice Maeterlinck*, New York: Haskell House Publishers, Ltd.

Thompson, Stith. 1946. *The folktale*. New York: Holt.

Trouille, Marie. Sexual/textual politics in the enlightenment: Diderot and d'Epinay. *Romanic Review* 85: 191–210.

Undank, Jack, and Herbert Josephs. 1984. *Diderot and digression*. Lexington, Ky.: French Forum.

Underhill, Evelyn. 1916. *John Ruysbroeck*. London: J.M. Fent.

Vareille, Jean-Claude. 1983. Fantasmes de la fiction. Fantasmes de l'écriture. In *Colloque de Cerisy*, ed. Simone Vierne. Paris: Sedes, 125–136.

Upanishads, The. 1983. Translations from the Sanskrit with an Introduction by Juan A Mascaro. New York: Penguin Books.

Upanishads, The. 1987. Translated for the Modern Reader by Eknath Easwaran. Blue Mountain Center of Meditation. Nilgiri Press.

Velay-Vallentin, Catherine. 1992. *L'histoire des contes*. Paris: Fayard.

Viatte, Auguste. 1969. *Les Sources occultes du romantisme*. I and 2. Paris: Champion.

Vidal-Naquet, P. 1981. Recipes for Greek adolescence. In *Myth, religion, and society*, ed. R. L. Gordon. Cambridge: Cambridge University Press.

Vinson, Marie-Christine. 1987. *L'Education des petites filles chez la Comtesse de Ségur*. Lyon: Presses universitaires.

Vysheslawzeff, Boris. 1968. Two ways of redemption: Redemption as a solution of the tragic contradiction. In *The Mystic Vision*. Princeton: Princeton University Press.

Warner, Marina. 1976. *Alone of all her sex*. New York: Alfred A. Knopf.

Welch, Marcelle Maistre. 1987. Le Devenir de la jeune fille dans les contes de fées de Madame d'Aulnoy. *Cahiers du dix-septième siècle* 1, no. 1 (Spring): 53–62.

——. 1989. "Rébellion et Résignation dans les contes de fées de Mme d'Aulnoy et Mme de Murat. *Cahiers du dix-septième siècle* 3, no. 2 (Fall): 131–142.

——. 1993. La Satire du rococo dans les contes de fées de Madame d'Aulnoy. *Revue Romane* 28, no. 1: 75–85.

White, T. H. 1960. *A book of beasts*. Translation from a Latin Bestiary of the Twelfth Century. New York: G.P. Putnam's Sons.

Whyte, Peter. 1996. *Théophile Gautier, conteur fantastique et merveilleux*. Durham, England: University of Durham.

Wilkins, W. J. 1981, *Hindu mythology*. Bombay: Rupa & Co.

Wilson, Arthur M. 1957. *Diderot, the testing years*. New York: Oxford University Press.

Wilson, Katharina M., and Frank J. Warnke. 1989. *Women writers of the seventeenth century*. Athens: The University of Georgia Press.

Wilson, Thomas. 1899 (1971). *Bluebeard*. New York: Benjamin Bloom, Inc.

Woodman, Marion. 1980. *Addiction to perfection*. Toronto: Inner City Books.

Yearsley, Macleod. 1924. *The folklore of fairy-tale*. London: Watts Co.

Zabern, Philipp, von. 1987. *Le Musée égyptien du Caire*. Mayence: Verlag von Zabern.

Ziegler, Alfred, J. 1976. Rousseauian optimism, natural distress, and dream research. *Spring*: 54–65.

Zipes, Jack. 1979. *Breaking the magic spell, radical theories of folk and fairy tales*. Austin: University of Texas Press.

——, ed. 1986. *Fairy tales and society: Illusion, allusion, and paradigm*. Philadelphia: University of Pennsylvania Press.

——, ed. 1989. *Beauties, beasts, and enchantments in classic French fairy tales*. New York: New American Library.

——. 1994. *Fairy tales as myth*. Lexington: University Press of Kentucky.

INDEX

398.2
Kna

Knapp, Bettina
  Liebowitz,
  1926-

French fairy tales.

DATE			